SCHWEITZER

D1175434

INDIA
AT THE
GLOBAL
HIGH TABLE

GEOPOLITICS IN THE 21ST CENTURY

For a quarter century since the fall of the Berlin Wall, the world has enjoyed an era of deepening global interdependence, characterized by the absence of the threat of great power war, spreading democracy, and declining levels of conflict and poverty. Now, much of that is at risk as the regional order in the Middle East unravels, the security architecture in Europe is again under threat, and great power tensions loom in Asia.

The Geopolitics in the 21st Century series, published under the auspices of the Order from Chaos project at Brookings, will analyze the major dynamics at play and offer ideas and strategies to guide critical countries and key leaders on how they should act to preserve and renovate the established international order to secure peace and prosperity for another generation.

INDIA

AT THE

GLOBAL
HIGH TABLE

THE QUEST FOR
REGIONAL PRIMACY
AND STRATEGIC AUTONOMY

TERESITA C. SCHAFFER AND
HOWARD B. SCHAFFER

Brookings Institution Press
Washington, D.C.

The Brookings Institution is a private nonprofit organization devoted to research, education, and publication on important issues of domestic and foreign policy. Its principal purpose is to bring the highest quality independent research and analysis to bear on current and emerging policy problems. Interpretations or conclusions in Brookings publications should be understood to be solely those of the authors.

Library of Congress Cataloging-in-Publication data

Names: Schaffer, Teresita C., author. | Schaffer, Howard B., author.
Title: India at the global high table : the quest for regional primacy
    and strategic autonomy / Teresita C. Schaffer and Howard B.
    Schaffer.
Description: Washington, D.C. : Brookings Institution Press, 2016.
    | Description based on print version record and CIP data
    provided by publisher; resource not viewed.
Identifiers: LCCN 2016000604 (print) | LCCN 2015040688
    (ebook) | ISBN 9780815728221 (epub) | ISBN 9780815728238
    (pdf) | ISBN 9780815728214 (hardback) | ISBN 9780815728214
    (pbk.) | ISBN 9780815728221(epub)
Subjects: LCSH: India—Foreign relations—21st century. | BISAC:
    POLITICAL SCIENCE / International Relations / Diplomacy. |
    BUSINESS & ECONOMICS / International / Economics.
Classification: LCC DS449 (print) | LCC DS449 .S35 2016 (ebook) |
    DDC 327.54—dc23
LC record available at http://lccn.loc.gov/2016000604

9 8 7 6 5 4 3 2 1

Typeset in Sabon and Scala Sans

Composition by Westchester Publishing Services

Contents

Preface   ix

1 India's Pre-Independence Legacy   1

2 Foreign Policy: The Cold War Years   14

3 Foreign Policy: The Post–Cold War World   43

4 Indian Strategic Visions   60

5 Foreign Policy Institutions   82

6 Negotiating for India   107

7 Negotiating Security Issues   127

8 Negotiating Nuclear Cooperation   150

9 Negotiating Economics   182

10 Multilateral Negotiations   213

11 Negotiating with Pakistan and China   248

12 Negotiating with Smaller South Asian Neighbors   271

13 India in a Changing World   293

Notes   311

Index   353

Preface

AS WE COMPLETE this work, India's foreign policy has undergone changes that neither of us could have imagined when we first became professionally involved with India as U.S. Foreign Service officers assigned to the American Embassy in New Delhi. U.S.-India relations—our bread and butter during both of our long diplomatic careers—went from being thin and often disagreeable to acquiring major importance and warmth for both sides. In the twenty-first century, India has leaped from the sluggish economics of the "Hindu rate of growth," derided by cynics, to become a world growth leader. This has helped to make India a well-qualified contestant for a place at the global high table we allude to in this book's title.

The story of this transformation was what first inspired us to write about Indian leaders' vision of the country's global role. When we sat down to sort out our thoughts and commit them to paper, however, we were as struck by the continuity in India's approach as by the change. Accordingly, the story we have told is built around a series of themes that have driven Indian foreign policy, inspired its global vision, and shaped its negotiating style at least since India gained independence in 1947. The two most prominent themes are India's determination to retain primacy in its immediate region and its conviction that India must chart its own global course—nonalignment or, in current parlance, strategic autonomy. More recently, Indian foreign policymakers have added a third theme: India's economic power and the need to tap its potential to the fullest as it pursues its foreign policy goals. A fourth driving force, more philosophical but fundamental to the negotiating style with which India pursues these goals, is the exceptionalism born of India's pride in its ancient civilization. We have developed these themes through three different perspectives: the record of India's foreign policy, the global visions that compete for the ear of policymakers, and India's practice in negotiating, primarily with the United States but also with its neighbors and in multilateral forums.

This book was a labor of love, and we owe a deep debt of gratitude to the many people who have helped us bring it to birth. The Brookings Institution gave one of us a professional home and the book project a secure mooring while we worked. Strobe Talbott, Martin Indyk, and Bruce Jones provided support and encouragement. Steve Cohen, with whom our friendship goes back to our earliest days in India, and Tanvi Madan provided valuable insights on the draft in preparation. Shruti Jagirdar provided unique research help. Colleagues at McLarty Associates, especially Nelson Cunningham and Rick Rossow, filled out our understanding of U.S.-India business relations. Polly Nayak once again offered her wise counsel and was the first person to read and critique the whole draft. Our access to the Lauinger Library at Georgetown University, where one of us teaches, was an invaluable asset. Bill Finan, Janet Walker, and their team at the Brookings Institution Press guided us through the editorial process. Angela Piliouras's and Karen Brogno's editing insights helped us sharpen up the text.

Support for this book was generously provided by the Smith Richardson Foundation. Brookings recognizes that the value it provides is in its absolute commitment to quality, independence, and impact. Activities supported by its donors reflect this commitment.

In over a half century of involvement with India, we have learned from more friends and professional colleagues in India and elsewhere than we could possibly name. We are confident that they know who they are, and we are grateful to all of them. Any errors we have made are, of course, our responsibility.

Most of all, we want to thank our sons, Michael and Christopher, who as children shared our life in India and elsewhere on the subcontinent, and their wives, Keltie and Juliana. They have all put up with our preoccupation with both the book and India. We dedicate this book to Mike's daughters, Eleanor and Eva, and Chris's sons, Nicholas, Thomas, and Anthony. We hope that some day they will have the opportunity to visit our old Indian stamping grounds and share our enthusiasm.

INDIA

AT THE

GLOBAL
HIGH TABLE

CHAPTER ONE

India's Pre-Independence Legacy

ON THE EVE OF India's independence, Jawaharlal Nehru spoke to India's Constituent Assembly in words that convey the excitement and the promise of the moment. "Long years ago," he said, "we made a tryst with destiny, and now the time comes when we shall redeem our pledge, not wholly or in full measure, but very substantially. At the stroke of the midnight hour, when the world sleeps, India will awake to life and freedom."

The end of that speech was not as deeply etched in the collective mind as the opening paragraph, but it set the stage for the global role an independent India wanted to play. In closing his stirring remarks, Nehru formally asked a pledge of each member of the Constituent Assembly: "At this solemn moment when the people of India, through suffering and sacrifice, have secured freedom, I . . . dedicate myself in all humility to the service of India and her people to the end that this ancient land *attain her rightful place in the world* and make her full and willing contribution to the promotion of world peace and the welfare of mankind" (emphasis added).[1] Nehru's promise that India would be a global actor, advancing world peace and human welfare, was built into the fabric of independent India along with the monumental challenge of providing for India's own people. Despite the major challenges in India, its neighborhood, and the world, and despite dramatic changes in India's international role, these goals still shape the way India sees itself in the world and conceives of its role.

In the six and a half decades since India's dramatic rebirth as an independent country, it has sought a role worthy of its ancient heritage and of the promise of its independence struggle. It was undertaking an epic task internally: bringing democratic governance and prosperity to the largest population of poor and illiterate people in the world. On the global scene, India's uniqueness, the majesty of its culture and history, and the soaring hopes as India "awoke to life and freedom," all informed India's vision of its place in the world and the policies designed to make that vision a reality.

A decade and more into the twenty-first century, India is a regional power with a global footprint and one of the world's big growth stories. This book explores the dynamics of this role through three lenses: first, the key policies that have shaped Indian foreign policy since independence, and how they are formed; second, the visions of India's global role that have inspired its policy elites; and third, the way the Indian government negotiates in its effort to fulfill its goals.

From the earliest days, two principal themes shaped Indian foreign policy: the drive to maintain Indian primacy in South Asia and Nehru's signature concept of nonalignment. These themes have remained remarkably persistent, although the tactics for maintaining primacy and the interpretation of nonalignment (and its intellectual descendant, strategic autonomy) have evolved. Since 1990 the drive to make India's economy a real source of power has become a core foreign policy objective. The national leaders and senior officials who shape Indian policy have an expansive vision of India's role in the world, one that regards India first and foremost as the heir to a great civilization. The details of the vision have evolved over time and vary from one leader or thinker to another, but the centerpiece has always been the idea of a unique and exceptional India. This vision is expressed in the ethos of its foreign policy and democratic institutions.

India pursues its foreign policy goals and global vision through diplomacy. This book argues that the core goals of its foreign policy and the exceptionalism and prickly sovereignty of its global vision are reflected in the blend of high-mindedness and toughness with which India conducts its international diplomatic negotiations. These basic characteristics run through negotiations on security and economic issues and in both bilateral and multilateral settings; they appear both in negotiations that reach a solution—most notably the U.S.-India negotiations on the 2008 nuclear agreement—and in those that do not, such as some features of U.S.-India defense sales.

These basic concepts will continue to evolve, reflecting India's experience and changes in its own and global power patterns. But they are likely to remain central to India's foreign policy and negotiating practice.

THE INHERITANCE FROM ANCIENT INDIA

The starting point for our examination of India's foreign policy and global vision goes back well before Indian independence, to its ancient civilization and the historical memory of successful empires. This is the standard by which the leaders of today's India evaluate their country's global role. It is also, to an important degree, the standard by which Indians judge the way other countries deal with them. Lalit Mansingh, who served as India's foreign secretary from 1999–2001 and then as its ambassador to Washington, wrote that "Washington's problems with India for [its] first fifty years arose out of its inability to comprehend that India's cultural and national sensitivities outweighed its desire to conclude favorable 'deals' with the United States."[2]

India's early leaders felt keenly the responsibility and excitement of bringing back the grandeur of ancient India to independent political life. Nehru saw India's civilization as a source of strength and vitality, one which the "monstrous" rule of Britain had almost repressed. He contrasted India, with her age-old roots, with the United States, "a new people, uninhibited and without the burdens and complexes of old races."[3] Nehru himself, who had his higher education in Britain and was among the most anglicized of the leaders of the independence struggle, had in important ways lost touch with the older sources of his own culture. His cousin B. K. Nehru, who served as ambassador to the United States, described him as an "Englishman."[4] The future prime minister spent his prison years in the 1940s immersing himself in Indian history and tradition. His *Discovery of India*, written during those years, was his effort at integrating ancient India with the modern world in which he was to lead the country.

Whatever its value as a guide to ancient history and scriptures, *Discovery of India* tells us a great deal about how these cultural elements were perceived by Nehru and arguably others who shaped India's early policies. He recounts with evident wonder the sheer age of Indian culture, starting with the Indus Valley civilization in Mohenjo Daro some 5,000 years earlier. "It is odd," he comments, "to think of India with her caste system and exclusiveness having this astonishing inclusive capacity to absorb foreign races and cultures." He stresses the distinctively Indian character of the philosophy and civilization from the Indus Valley civilization till the time of his writing.[5] Where others have been fascinated by India's regional identities, Nehru comes down resoundingly on the side of the unity of India, and this emphasis was reflected in his insistence on giving independent India a strong central government.[6] Nehru reflects on the meaning of "Hindu culture" and "Indian culture," but in the end, although he is careful to say they are not synonymous, the two bleed into one another. In later years, the relationship between these two became more contentious, and the reference to "Hindu culture" would be associated primarily with the Hindu nationalist movement.

Nehru sees the Hindu faith as revealed in the Vedas and especially the Upanishads as "vague, amorphous and many-sided, all things to all men," whose "essential spirit seems to be to live and let live." He finds the more dogmatic character of Christianity and Islam wanting in comparison. These observations suggest that he saw in India's ancient scriptures, at least in a general sense, the spiritual foundation for the ideals underpinning India's international relations.[7]

India's heroic literature is another rich source of traditions that shape its leaders, language, and the society. The best-known examples are the *Mahabharata* and the *Ramayana*, India's epic accounts of civil war, love, duty, loyalty, and betrayal. These stories have counterparts in many civilizations. They live on in stories passed on by grandparents to young children, in popular culture, television programs, school plays, turns of phrase, and illustrations adorning three-wheel rickshaws in Indian cities. Their heroic figures still serve as icons today: Ram, who left his wife Sita in his brother's safekeeping to go off to find a deer she found entrancing; Lakshman, the brother, who drew a line around Sita's dwelling to keep her inside a protective boundary (the term *Lakshman rekha*, in widespread use, is the Indian equivalent of "red line"); Sita, the icon of feminine loyalty and purity—though Ram in the end rejected her because she had been out of his sight for too long; Vikramaditya, whom Nehru cites as the "beau ideal" of a prince; the Gauravas and Pandavas, the warring clans in the *Mahabharata*; the prince who demonstrated the proper concentration when, in an archers' contest to bring down a bird, he told his mentor that he could see nothing but the pupil of the bird's eye. The stories themselves do not carry over into foreign policy. However, the virtues they exalt—notably concentration, determination, and loyalty to the group—are highly respected by those who make foreign policy.

ANCIENT EMPIRES—AND TWO STRATEGIC ICONS

The history of India's empires has left a powerful imprint on the way its contemporary leaders think of their country. Most of the earliest dynasties controlled only part of the territory of contemporary India, and for hundreds of years there were multiple, often warring kingdoms within its current space. The Maurya dynasty, starting in the fourth century BCE, is sometimes seen as the first herald of modern India. The emperor Ashoka, in the third century BCE, ruled the largest Indian empire in ancient times, including most of present-day India as well as part of Pakistan and Afghanistan.

These imperial governments furnish two competing strands in the intellectual inheritance of India's diplomacy and foreign policy. Kautilya, also known as Chanakya, served as adviser to the emperor Chandragupta Maurya in the fourth century BCE, about the time Alexander the Great invaded what is now Afghanistan and Pakistan. His treatise on statecraft, *Arthashastra*, is often compared to Machiavelli and Clausewitz. Its goal was to expand the power of the prince. Kautilya looked on everything as an act of war. Peace, international agreements, and what we today would call the "international system" are to be respected only when it suits the ruler. Diplomats are "potential spies with diplomatic immunity." Kautilya believed in the importance of geography, including the observation that a neighbor's neighbor or an enemy's enemy should be an important friend (in modern India, the obvious example is Afghanistan). He distinguished between two types of enemies: weak kings "fit to be exterminated," and strong ones, who must be weakened before a ruler acts on his enmity to them. Kautilya wrote of three types of warfare: open war; concealed or guerrilla war; and "silent war," meaning hidden hostilities, such as intelligence and psychological operations, carried out in a time of ostensible peace. He urged his ruler to sow dissension even in times of peace. In writing of the three types of conquerors—"righteous" ones demanding only submission, "greedy" ones demanding land and goods, and "demoniacal" ones demanding everything including "sons, wives, and life"—Kautilya counseled some measure of restraint, believing that an army that had some hope was less likely to resist to the death.[8]

The competing model from ancient times is the emperor Ashoka, who ruled about a century before Kautilya's emperor Chandragupta Maurya. Ashoka's reign was largely peaceful. He is most vividly remembered today for engravings on pillars and rocks around India that expounded the moral code he wished his subjects to follow, including filial duty, reverence for living things, and respect for teachers. His passionate embrace of Buddhism, recorded in the longest of his edicts, the Rock Edict, was said to have followed his remorse over the death and destruction caused by his one war of aggression. That same engraved message also includes his call to tolerance of heterodox beliefs, especially unusual for that period.[9]

India's foreign policy has drawn on both the Kautilyan and the Ashokan heritage. Foreign policy hawks have long admired Kautilya's toughness. His approach to power, as we will see, strongly influences the global vision popular on the Indian right. The government of Narendra Modi that took office in May 2014 has embraced some features of Kautilya's vision and is, like him, completely unapologetic about pursuing India's interests. Even under nationalist governments, however, Indian policy has generally not embraced Kautilya's single-minded pursuit of power, much less the ruthlessness he advocates.

Kautilya is admired by most of the Indian foreign policy establishment. Nehru writes admiringly of his intellectual contribution, noting that despite being "proud and revengeful," Kautilya recognized that restraint sometimes brings greater rewards than ruthlessness.[10] Some of his dicta form part of contemporary India's diplomatic toolkit. In particular, Kautilya described asking for negotiations as a tactic of the weak. Indian diplomats are still extremely reluctant to be the petitioners, or *demandeurs*, in any diplomatic encounter. One student of India's negotiating style, Raymond Cohen, comments that "with an acute sense of natural pride, India developed a unique formula for saving face: it would accept needed assistance, but would not say please or thank you."[11]

Where the Ashokan heritage shines most brightly today is in the way India's foreign policy is framed and articulated. India's signature concept of nonalignment, which we will examine more closely in the next chapters both for its impact on foreign policy and for its influence on the prevailing visions of India's global role, had an unquestioned practical dimension, but it is articulated in a framework of moral superiority and expressed in a language of soaring idealism. Indian policy speeches and interventions at multilateral meetings generally start by claiming the moral high ground. This is very much in the tradition of Ashoka, but also of Mahatma Gandhi. Even Modi has his Ashokan moments. His sole foreign policy speech during the 2014 election campaign and his maiden speech to the United Nations General Assembly as India's prime minister in September 2014 were built around the theme of "Vasudhaivam kutumbakam," or "all the world is a family."[12] The Kautilyan emphasis on winning every encounter and the Ashokan appeal to harmony do not always coexist comfortably.

MUSLIM RULE: THE MUGHALS

Starting in the twelfth century, a succession of Muslim rulers and dynasties entered India from the northwest. Some established themselves as primarily Indian rulers; others remained closer to their Central Asian roots. Muslims had been present in India since shortly after the time of the Prophet, but this influx of successful warriors helped create the conflicted position that the Muslim community still occupies in India. On the one hand, Muslims ruled at least part of India for the better part of 800 years; on the other, especially at times of tension with Pakistan, one still hears Indians talk about "invading Muslims."

The Mughals swept south from Kabul in the sixteenth century and eventually made Delhi their imperial capital. The first six Mughal emperors differed widely in skill and in their approach to governing. However, at least in some degree, they all incorporated existing society with its institutions and its local and communal leaders into their own governing structures. Most of those who administered the Mughal Empire, in other words, were Indians, not migrants from Central Asia. Both the emperors and some of the Hindu personalities from this era are immortalized in the names of streets in the central part of New Delhi. The most iconic Indian monuments also date from the Mughal period: the Red Fort in Delhi, where Indian prime ministers have delivered some of their most important national speeches, for example, and the Taj Mahal, tomb of the emperor Shahjahan. The pre-Mughal Muslim rulers too left behind monuments that shape both the city of Delhi and Indian political culture. The tombs of the Lodhi kings, who ruled Delhi from 1451 to 1526, are the centerpiece of one of Delhi's loveliest and best-known parks.

The last of the Mughals was Bahadur Shah, whom the British deposed after a mutiny in 1857 led them to assume direct rule of much of India. By that time, the dynasty had lost most of its vitality. However, the notion of foreigners from across the sea ending what had once been a glorious and successful empire contributed to a yearning to restore the glory and success of an earlier time, and to intense wariness of foreign interference.

THE LEGACY OF THE RAJ

With independence, India broke loose from the subjugation of the British Raj, but it also embraced many of the governing structures the British had created in their 200 years of rule. The viceroys who represented the crown in India provided strong central leadership. Nehru's idea of the appropriate government for his nation was likewise built on strong national authority. Early on, he and his Indian National Congress vividly demonstrated this view by rejecting the idea of a confederal India as had been recommended by the British to reassure the subcontinent's Muslims. Similarly, India's pressure on recalcitrant princes to accede to independent India rather than pursue the independence Britain was offering them as at least a theoretical possibility illustrated the importance India's new leaders, like the British authorities, gave to a strong center.[13]

India still retains important elements of the system used by the British Raj to safeguard the security of the subcontinent. The "outer line" used by the British to define their outer defense perimeter became the international border, at least in India's definition; the "inner line" that formed the perimeter of the area where the Raj's writ was fully respected has remained an important administrative boundary; and the space between the two lines continues to be governed by special arrangements between the central authority and the local residents, many of them ethnically distinct from those of the Indian heartland.[14]

The Raj legacy also extends to India's internal governing arrangements, including many of the administrative pillars that India maintains to this day. India's civil and foreign services are direct descendants of Raj-era governing bodies, which included Indian officials, many of them by the time of independence in quite responsible positions. A handful of these officials were given diplomatic assignments before independence. The Indian army and its Pakistani counterpart were direct descendants of the British Indian army. Separating the army into two forces that were almost immediately hostile was one of the traumas of the 1947 partition of the subcontinent. In India, though not in Pakistan, the tradition of the military being subordinate to civil authority also carried over into independence. The complex interaction in today's India between national administrative structures and their counterparts in the individual states has its roots in the pattern established during the last decade of the Raj, when a robust federal political structure was created.

Even during the days of colonial rule, Indians enjoyed a measure of self-rule. Local bodies and, after 1937, provincial assemblies were elected based on a limited franchise. Indian officials elected under this system moved smoothly into the political system of independent India. The Indian National Congress, the most important body spearheading the independence movement and the party that held power without interruption in New Delhi for India's first thirty years of independence, was founded in 1885—ironically, by an Englishman. Independence of course brought momentous changes to India's governing apparatus, notably universal suffrage, the end of separate electorates for different communities, Indian rather than British leadership in the administrative institutions, and the abolition of the institutions that governed the princely states, whose integration into the Indian union was one of the first and most important accomplishments of the Indian state. But the structures and institutions of independent India were built on a large measure of continuity.

In foreign policy, establishing an independent role for India was a mission close to the founders' hearts that involved both continuity and sharp changes from the pre-1947 pattern. India's strategic and security outlook was built on the imperial legacy. The British Indian Empire had been a hub of power throughout the region, extending from Britain's protectorates in the Persian Gulf to its colonies in Southeast Asia. It was only natural to assume that independent India would inherit much of this role, despite the loss of key strategic territories that became part of Pakistan. The Indian security forces continued to give priority, as the British Indian army had done, to land warfare and the security of land borders to India's north. With the establishment of Pakistan and the hostile relationship between the two neighbors, India had an immediate ground security threat, adding to its focus on land forces. The maritime perspective associated with Britain has only become a major part of Indian security thinking since about 1990. India continued to seek primacy in its relationships with the other neighbors, both those that had been ruled from Britain (such as Sri Lanka, which became independent six months after India) and those that remained formally independent but in which Britain had a major security interest (notably Nepal). It kept the basic structure of its relations to the north. In the case of Bhutan, India's 1949 treaty committed Bhutan to "be guided by India in its external relations," using language that was drawn directly from a 1910 treaty between Bhutan and the British Raj. The requirement for Indian "guidance" was only revised in 2007.[15]

Another element of continuity came from India's pre-independence involvement in international organizations. India joined the League of

Nations when that organization was founded after the First World War. Until 1928, India's principal representative was British. After that, Indians led the delegation. They enjoyed some measure of independent action, though they exercised it selectively, primarily on social, economic, and technical matters. India was also a member of the International Labor Organization (ILO), and in 1932 an Indian was elected to chair that organization's governing body.

Membership in these organizations provided Indian diplomats with experience negotiating international conventions, such as the Geneva Opium Convention. They also provided occasional opportunities for India to take an independent stand on foreign policy. India's representative at the League of Nations, for example, spoke out against race-based laws in areas under a League mandate, a position that would have strong echoes in its later foreign policy. India also used its ILO platform to push back against Britain's mercantilist, imperial economic policies and its record in labor legislation.[16]

When Nehru's "stroke of the midnight hour" rang out, India had the administrative structures that would continue to provide the sinews of independent government and the foundations for strong democratic institutions. Its unique civilization had shaped society for 5,000 years. It had a strong historical memory of successful government by Indian emperors and a more recent experience of colonial subjugation: one imperial legacy of pride, one of humiliation. India, albeit under the British Raj, had been the undisputed great power in South Asia and the Indian Ocean. From the first days, India sought a role on a global scale, even as it sought to govern, feed, and employ its enormous poor population.

A ROAD MAP

The coming chapters explore how India has integrated this heritage into its foreign policy, its global vision, and its negotiating style. We start with a brief snapshot of India's foreign policy, looked at through the guiding principles that have been most important to successive Indian governments. In the early years (chapter 2), Nehru dominated foreign policy, and his vision of India's role set the tone. This account focuses on the two core ideas at the center of his policy: first, Nehru's concept of nonalignment and the related perception of India as the global moral voice, the peacemaker, the broker that could bring the world's Cold War competitors together; and second, India's determination to retain preeminence in its immediate neighborhood. Both remain constants in India's policy and vision, though they were interpreted differently by Nehru's successors and especially by his daughter, Indira Gandhi. As we have seen, both of these core ideas had important elements of continuity with the past. Some elements of the Nehruvian vision had their roots in the country's distant history; others, notably India's view of its strategic space, continued the strategic priorities of the British Raj.

After the end of the Cold War, India's foreign policy options expanded, the pattern of its global relationships changed, and its economic growth surged (chapter 3). From this time onward, building on India's economic success and using it as an element in Indian power became a third central element in the vision that drove policy. India's determination to march to its own drummer was always implicit in the idea of nonalignment. After the Cold War, it was often articulated as "strategic autonomy."

After examining India's policies, we explore the visions that compete for the allegiance of India's contemporary policymakers (chapter 4). There has always been a feisty internal debate among competing perspectives on India's international role. In today's debate, one can distinguish three broad categories that prioritize respectively the heritage of nonalignment, the greater importance of economics in India's post–Cold War policy, and security issues. Aspects of all three leave their imprint on foreign policy.

Winding up the first section of the book, we look briefly at the institutions, officials, and politicians who make and implement Indian policies (chapter 5). Many of them live at the junction between India's traditions and a globalizing world. They represent a noisy democracy, in which parliament is supreme and government ministers can be called to account before it at any time. They belong to strong professional civil and diplomatic services, trained to prepare meticulously for their task. They work within a strong institutional and legal structure and cannot easily change established service practices and prerogatives. Politicians and officials often seem to inhabit different worlds, and they certainly face different rewards and dangers in their respective professional lives. Their different operating styles have largely remained in place for almost seven decades.

Against this background, India's negotiators and policy managers set out to secure India's specific national interests and pursue its larger ideals, trying to craft an international role consistent with their perception of

India as a great and ancient civilization. The second half of the book is devoted to India's negotiating style, one of the primary vehicles for achieving India's goals. Chapter 6 summarizes the broad features that characterize India's negotiating practices: a detailed mastery of the negotiating brief and the historical record, a steely determination not to be taken advantage of, an overwhelming concern with protecting India's sovereignty, an aversion to anything that smacks of putting India in a dependent position, and above all, a conviction that India is unique and can therefore insist on unique solutions. In the words of Jairam Ramesh, former minister in a Congress government and veteran of the Copenhagen environmental negotiations, "India is not an easy country to negotiate with. We are moralistic, we are argumentative, we are regressive."[17]

India's vision and these negotiating habits manifest themselves differently in different areas. Because the United States now has a central place in Indian foreign policy, this book looks primarily at India's negotiations with Washington (chapters 7 to 9), with additional perspectives on multilateral negotiations (chapter 10) and on India's negotiations with its neighbors (chapters 11 and 12). In negotiations on security issues and in the broad management of India's foreign relations, the Ministry of External Affairs and the diplomatic service play the primary role. On economic and technical issues, the economic ministries, staffed by officers of the Indian Administrative Service (IAS), are more likely to be in the driver's seat. Defense issues are primarily handled by civilian IAS officers in the Ministry of Defense, with the uniformed military usually playing a secondary role. Multilateral issues are often the responsibility of the Ministry of External Affairs, though other economic or technical ministries may have the lead on specific negotiations (the Ministry of Commerce, for instance, on trade issues). Each of these institutions has its own way of dealing with foreigners and with its Indian colleagues or competitors. Multilateral issues have long been the thorniest area for U.S.-India interaction, whoever the main players on the Indian side may be.

Finally, chapter 13 looks ahead at how changing global trends may affect the principal drivers of India's policy and its negotiating style. Many of the characteristics described here have served prime ministers as different as Jawaharlal Nehru, Indira Gandhi, Manmohan Singh, and Narendra Modi, and are likely to remain enduring features of India's approach to the world. India will remain committed to regional primacy and will continue to try to mobilize its growing economy as an instrument of power.

India's commitment to strategic autonomy too is almost certain to endure in some form. The big question is how the interpretation of that concept will be molded by changing power relationships in the world and in India's neighborhood. Dramatic changes in India's security environment led to reinterpretation of nonalignment in Nehru's day. Half a century later, China's increasingly assertive presence close to India might also lead India to reexamine whether the aloofness it cultivated for many years is still the best way to maximize its national security.

CHAPTER TWO

Foreign Policy: The Cold War Years

INDIA'S APPROACH TO foreign policy in its first half-century of independence was dominated by two themes. The first was nonalignment, the signature concept that India contributed to a world dominated by Cold War rivalries. This was the most important ingredient in India's global vision and drove many other aspects of the country's policy. The second theme was India's determination to maintain primacy in the South Asian neighborhood and to secure its land and sea frontiers. In a geographic setting transformed by the partition of the subcontinent, this was a post-independence version of the high policy priority the Raj had long given the defense of India's northern and northwestern borders.[1] This second theme gave Indian foreign policy a harder, more "realistic" quality that some critics found conflicted with the "idealistic" approach that non-alignment seemed to imply. Both were essential to Nehru's vision for India in the world, and both, as modified through the years, remain critical elements of the visions that compete to shape India's foreign policy today.

Our snapshot of India's foreign policy divides this period into two parts. The first, from independence until the early 1960s, was dominated by Nehru. As prime minister and minister of external affairs during the first seventeen years of India's independence, he framed and carried out his country's approach to the world, in all but his last couple of years in power with the broad approval of the Indian political class. The concepts he developed guided Indian foreign policy well beyond his lifetime, if often in a form that differed from his original blueprint.

The second period, ushered in by the war with China and Nehru's death, lasted until the end of the Cold War. These years saw a shift toward a more formalized concept of nonalignment, foreshadowed by the establishment in 1961 of the Non-Aligned Movement (NAM) over Nehru's initial objection but with his eventual concurrence. Over time, leaders of countries that joined the NAM came to focus much more on global economic issues than Nehru had in his day, and the movement was increasingly marked by sharp divisions within its swelling membership. The post-Nehru period was also marked by tougher, less subtle efforts on New Delhi's part to ensure Indian regional predominance.

THE EARLY YEARS: HEYDAY OF NEHRUVIAN NONALIGNMENT

In its early years of independence, India played a far more prominent role on the global stage than its economic strength and military power seemed to warrant. Politically secure at home, where his foreign policy positions were hailed by his colleagues in the Indian National Congress and aroused only limited opposition outside it, Prime Minister Nehru became one of the best-known and most respected figures in the postwar world. Even his most trenchant critics acknowledged his major role on the international stage.

Under Nehru's leadership, Indian diplomats and military officers played key roles in dealing with critical problems in Korea, Indochina, the Congo, and elsewhere. India readily sounded forth on a host of international issues, many of them only distantly related to its immediate interests. It paid special attention to Asian and, later, African disputes involving racism and colonialism. It was listened to with attentive interest, if not always with approbation, by the two contending Cold War power blocs as well as its fellow third-world nations. India's active, well-publicized international role was applauded at home and earned useful dividends there for Nehru and the Congress Party. This widespread approval largely removed foreign policy from the national political agenda at a time when India was struggling with many challenging and divisive domestic problems.

India's advocacy of nonalignment was the key element in this singular achievement. Together with its major subthemes of opposition to racism and colonialism, nonalignment provided Nehru a distinct foreign policy platform that attracted other emerging Asian and African countries. Without this signature concept, the prime minister and his colleagues would have drawn much less attention on the international stage. Nor could India have punched above its diplomatic weight the way it did during his years in power.

Nehru's approach to nonalignment emphasized preserving India's freedom of action. As he succinctly put it in a speech at Columbia University during his 1949 American visit: "[India] has tried to combine idealism with national interest. The main objectives of [its] policy are: the pursuit of peace, not through alignment with any major power or group of powers, but through an independent approach to each controversial or disputed issue; the liberation of subject peoples; the maintenance of freedom both national and individual; the elimination of racial discrimination; and the elimination of want, disease, and ignorance which affect the greater part of the world's population."[2]

Although he did not say so at Columbia or elsewhere, nonalignment made good strategic sense. India was by far the most powerful nation in its South Asian neighborhood and would benefit if the other countries there did not ally with strong outside powers. And as would become apparent in the late 1950s, a nonaligned India could also profit from access to economic assistance from both rival power blocs.

Nehru rejected the definition of nonalignment as "equidistance" between the two power blocs, a common misunderstanding among its critics. In March 1949 he declared: "obviously [nonalignment] does not mean that we should not be closer in our relations with some countries than with others. At the present moment we have far closer relations with some countries of the Western world than with others [outside it]."[3] He stressed the important distinction between active, involved nonalignment, as India pursued it, and passive Swiss-model neutralism.

As time went on, nonalignment increasingly acquired a more ambitious definition. Both Nehru and his confidant and later defense minister V. K. Krishna Menon rejected the idea of an Indian-led "third force" rivaling the two hardening Cold War blocs. Menon held that a "third bloc means superior economic power," which the nonaligned nations could not muster.[4] Nehru, for his part, also claimed he was not seeking Indian leadership. But he used nonalignment to enhance India's international influence as the self-appointed spokesman for countries comprising a "zone of peace" that would stand aloof from both the U.S.-led Western alliance system and the Soviet-dominated communist bloc. In a 1949 speech, he tried to draw a contrast between these two roles: "Some people talk rather loosely and . . . rather foolishly of India becoming the leader of this or the leader of that or the leader of Asia. It is a bad approach, this business of leadership. But," he added, "a certain responsibility is cast on India . . . for taking the initiative sometimes and helping others to cooperate."[5]

Nonalignment also came to be described in moral terms. Both this moral dimension and what Nehru saw as nonalignment's uniquely Indian and Asian character were underscored in the *Panchsheel*, the Five Principles of Peaceful Coexistence, derived from teachings of the Buddha, that had been launched from ancient India. The *Panchsheel*, which stressed noninterference, nonaggression, and equality, were formally incorporated into a 1954 agreement between India and China. The pact reflected what his biographer S. Gopal has written was Nehru's fond hope "that friendship with the new China would not only maintain peace in Asia but start a new phase in world affairs, with Asia giving the lead to a more humane as well as a more sophisticated diplomacy."[6] The concept of a resurgent China joining India in throwing off its colonial bonds figured importantly in his approach to Asia.

The determination to foster international peace and a conviction that nonalignment was the best way to promote it was a major driving force in Nehru's policy. In his view, peace was indispensable for India to achieve the economic progress it desperately needed to sustain its efforts at nation-building. As he told another biographer, the Canadian academic Michael Brecher, "if there is a war, big or small, it comes in the way of that [economic growth] which is for us the primary factor."[7] He held that "nonalignment . . . was not just a matter of ideology. If the whole world were divided up between the two big blocs the inevitable result would be war."[8]

Nehru enjoyed the personal prominence India's influential role on the world stage gave him. In his unpublished writings he was less coy about his quest to establish that role. As early as 1946, he stated in an internal memo that "our natural position in world assemblies is going to inevitably be one of the leadership of all the smaller countries of Asia." He wrote in the same period of India's hope to be a peacemaker between the United States and the Soviet Union.[9] And he also stressed what he held was the uniquely Indian quality of India's nonaligned voice. Speaking to a joint session of the U.S. Congress in 1949, he declared: "India . . . may perhaps appear somewhat alien to you. . . . India's voice is somewhat different; it is the voice of an ancient civilization, distinctive, vital. . . ."[10]

Nehru and Menon both spoke with evident satisfaction of India's angering the world's leading powers by its independent stance. The prime minister was convinced that his government's determination to avoid foreign entanglements would eventually earn India their grudging respect. This respect came slowly. It was only after Premier Joseph Stalin's death in 1953 that the Soviets moved away from their disdain for India and other newly independent, nonaligned third-world countries and designed political and economic assistance policies to woo them. In the West, influential figures faulted India for what they alleged was its hypocrisy in calling on other nations to meet standards of international behavior that in their view New Delhi regularly flouted. Some critics, most famously U.S. Secretary of State John Foster Dulles, condemned nonalignment as immoral. Others found it fraudulent. In their opinion, India tilted too far toward the communist bloc to be considered genuinely nonaligned. It was only during President Dwight Eisenhower's second term (1957–61) that Washington fully accepted nonalignment. The Nehru government, for its part, dismissed these sometimes-contradictory allegations or attributed them to Western critics confusing nonalignment with equidistance or neutralism.

CHINA: CHALLENGE TO SECURITY AND TO NONALIGNMENT

The rise of Communist China would over time pose serious challenges to the security of India and to Nehruvian nonalignment. Although the Chinese communists, then still close to Moscow, could hardly be regarded as nonaligned and had not been fighting directly against Western colonial rule, Nehru warmly welcomed their 1949 victory in the long Chinese civil war. India was among the first countries to recognize Mao Zedong's new government. Nehru spoke enthusiastically of China's having been reborn and, as we have seen, he hoped that this rebirth would be part of an Asian resurgence that could have a positive transforming impact on world politics.

The victorious communists were initially hostile to the Nehru government despite its professions of friendship, early recognition of their regime, and strong support for the People's Republic in its bid for the seat on the UN Security Council still held by the defeated nationalists. Replying to a congratulatory message from the Communist Party of India, Mao Zedong wrote: "India certainly will not long remain under the yoke of imperialism and its collaborators. Like free China, a free India will one day emerge in the Socialist and People's Democratic family."[11]

Nehru worried that China's newly established communist government, in its quest for national unification, would invade Tibet, a vast area bordering India that had operated virtually as an independent state under a long succession of weak central Chinese regimes. Independent India, like the Raj, had recognized Chinese suzerainty over Tibet and had inherited from the British certain special rights there.[12] Beijing summarily rejected the prime minister's effort to persuade it not to invade, telling him that Tibet was Chinese territory that China had a sacred duty to liberate.

Despite the Chinese invasion and criticism from within the Indian National Congress that he had taken too weak a position, Nehru persisted in his effort to cultivate better ties with Beijing. But at the same time he took the precaution of strengthening India's position in the three Himalayan buffer states—Nepal, Bhutan, and Sikkim—that lay between Tibet and India. As the Chinese moved into Tibet, New Delhi negotiated new treaties with these three small monarchies that reflected and expanded the special positions the Raj had enjoyed there. Nehru publicly stated that Nepal's northern border was India's strategic frontier.

THE KOREAN WAR: INDIA ON THE GLOBAL STAGE

The victory of the communists in China's civil war set the stage for the Korean War, an event that would offer Indian foreign policy unusual opportunities, challenges, and international exposure. Triggered by North Korea's invasion of the South in June 1950, the war eventually led India to adopt a more anti-Western form of nonalignment. The Nehru government had initially supported U.S.-led initiatives at the United Nations to condemn North Korean aggression and force Pyongyang to withdraw its troops from South Korean territory. But it soon backed away from this position. India's initial focus on collective security efforts to deal with aggression was overshadowed by a broader concern that American military measures against Communist China following the North Korean invasion could reignite the Chinese civil war and threaten world peace.[13]

In a message to Soviet Premier Joseph Stalin and U.S. Secretary of State Dean Acheson, Nehru linked the admission of Communist China to the United Nations to a Korean settlement. This initiative won support from Moscow and Beijing, but was strongly opposed by Washington and its allies. Indian relations with Washington were soon further rattled when the United States ignored a warning from the Indian ambassador to Beijing that China would enter the war if UN forces moved north of the 38th parallel that divided North and South Korea. (That Ambassador K. M. Panikkar was right only made matters worse.)

The Korean War escalated to a large-scale conflict between the Chinese People's Liberation Army (PLA) and American-led UN forces before eventually settling into a military stalemate. India withdrew from any significant diplomatic role to end the fighting. However, it did win considerable international recognition—both praise and criticism—for the operation of a specially assigned Indian military force that dealt with the difficult task of supervising the disposition of prisoners at the end of the conflict. This assignment, carried out under very trying circumstances, foreshadowed India's prominent role in international peacekeeping operations that still continues.

During Nehru's time the Indian military won plaudits for its role in UN peacekeeping in places as distant from India, and from one another, as Gaza and the Congo. India also chaired the three-nation International Control Commission in war-torn Indochina, where it earned good marks in its role as the "neutral" member of the group.[14] Indians relished these military and diplomatic opportunities. They demonstrated India's attachment to peace, won it international publicity, and led other countries to take it seriously as a player on the world stage.

FOCUS ON ANTICOLONIALISM

Nehru had taken the lead long before independence in persuading his Indian National Congress colleagues to adopt resolutions encouraging anticolonial movements elsewhere in Asia. As independence neared he stoutly opposed the efforts of European powers to reestablish their prewar colonies in Southeast Asia following Japan's surrender. As leader of the interim government in March 1947, he supported the convening of a conference of delegates from twenty-eight Asian countries to discuss their common problems and their prospects for freedom.[15] In early 1948 and by then prime minister, Nehru sponsored a meeting of Asian leaders in New Delhi to rally opposition to Dutch efforts to restore their control over Indonesia.

Nehru took a particular interest in Indochina. He denounced efforts by the French to place local leaders loyal to them in positions of authority in the Indo-Chinese states and criticized the United States for supporting those regimes. He worried about a confrontation in the region between the communist bloc and the West, and characteristically sought to play a peacemaking role. As he wrote to the Indian chief ministers: "between these rival giants and their loud trumpeting, there is the small and perhaps feeble voice of India."[16]

India won support for its proposals to bring about peace in Indochina at a meeting of Asian prime ministers in Sri Lanka in 1954. Although it was excluded from a more broadly attended conference on Korea and Indochina held soon afterward in Geneva, Krishna Menon's strenuous behind-the-scenes efforts led delegates there to accept India's proposals for the withdrawal of all foreign troops from Laos and Cambodia, an accomplishment that enhanced the country's standing as a major diplomatic player.

INDIA, PAKISTAN, AND KASHMIR: NEHRU AS REALIST

The perceptibly pro-communist tilt that Indian foreign policy had taken during the Korean War became even more pronounced when in early 1954 Pakistan joined the U.S.-led Western alliance system and became, as it proudly proclaimed, "America's most allied ally in Asia."

Nehru sought unsuccessfully to head off this alliance, which clashed with both major themes in India's approach to foreign policy: nonalignment and a determination to maintain Indian primacy and security in South Asia. He recognized that Pakistan would not accept India's regional preeminence. But it could only actively challenge India if it was bolstered militarily by outside powers.

As reports of the forthcoming pact began to circulate, Nehru wrote to Pakistan Prime Minister Mohammed Ali Bogra: "If such an alliance takes place, Pakistan definitely enters into the region of the cold war. . . . It must be a matter of grave consequence to us . . . if vast armies are built up in Pakistan with the aid of American money."[17] He told the chief ministers of the Indian states that "a military pact between Pakistan and the U.S. changes the whole balance in this part of the world and affects India more especially. The U.S. must realize that the reaction in India will be that this arming of Pakistan is largely against India or might be used against India, whether the U.S. wants that or not. . . ."[18] Nehru scornfully rejected President Eisenhower's offer of a similar U.S. security relationship with New Delhi and dismissed Eisenhower's pledge that the arms Washington supplied to the Pakistanis would not be used against India.[19]

This anger with Washington's South Asia policy followed years of increasing Indian dismay with the U.S. stand on the bitter dispute between India and Pakistan over the political future of the former princely state of Kashmir. The dispute had led to a fifteen-month war between the two countries soon after partition. Nehru's government probably devoted more diplomatic energy at the United Nations and elsewhere to advocating its position on Kashmir than it spent on any other foreign policy issue. India resisted international efforts to resolve the conflict through a plebiscite as provided by UN resolutions and argued that the United States and its Western allies who supported such a plebiscite were biased in favor of Pakistan. Moscow, which had increasingly moved toward accepting the Indian position, fully and dramatically endorsed it when Soviet leaders Nikita Khrushchev and Nikolai Bulganin visited Kashmir in 1955.

The downward trajectory of U.S.-India relations and the Indian drift toward stronger relations with the communist bloc within the framework of nonalignment slowed and then stopped toward the end of 1956. As has happened at other points in the development of Indian policy toward the United States in Nehru's time and afterward, the change in New Delhi's viewpoint seems to have been influenced by a concern on its part that it had drifted too far from its nonaligned moorings and needed to bring its signature contribution to the conduct of foreign affairs into better balance.[20]

India's improved ties with Washington did not allay its concern about the threat posed to its security and regional primacy by a hostile and revanchist U.S.-armed Pakistan. The establishment of Pakistan as a homeland for the Muslims of South Asia was a major challenge to India's strategic situation. The Raj's territories had stretched to the distant, forbidding mountains of the Hindu Kush on imperial India's frontier with Afghanistan; independent India faced Pakistani forces that were deployed only a few hundred miles from New Delhi across the flat plains of the Punjab.

Nehru took a tough line toward Pakistan. Like other Congress leaders, he had acquiesced with regret in the British decision to divide the Raj. Once it had been carried out, he hoped that when the turmoil that accompanied partition was over the two states might reunite by the free will of their peoples. He had a contemptuous attitude toward the generals, bureaucrats, and civilian politicians who led successive Pakistan governments. Aside from Kashmir, the two countries also persistently squabbled over the division of the waters of the Indus River system that flowed into Pakistan from the mountains of upper riparian India. This crucial issue was eventually resolved by a 1960 treaty negotiated between the two sides with the help of the World Bank. The bank, along with other international donors including the United States, financed the massive construction of canals and dams the settlement called for. The Indus Waters Treaty, an "all win" arrangement that has survived a succession of wars and other India-Pakistan crises, was a rare example of Nehru's willingness to allow outsiders to play a major role in resolving an important India-Pakistan issue.[21]

But while he generally adopted tough positions on India-Pakistan disputes, Nehru did not want to provoke a war or allow the Pakistanis to provoke India into starting one. He was prepared to use India's superior military strength to coerce Pakistan into adopting more forthcoming policies, as he did in 1950 when communal rioting in Pakistani East Bengal and adjacent Indian West Bengal led to the widespread slaughter of members of the minority communities in both provinces and the flight of survivors to safety across the international border. As the crisis heightened, Nehru resisted calls by many of his colleagues for a more aggressive Indian strategy. One of his main concerns was the fear that a war could lead to even greater assaults against Muslims in India and Hindus in Pakistan. This concern about a bloody communal backlash would continue to influence Nehru's policy toward Pakistan on Kashmir and other issues.

India's dealings with its smaller South Asian neighbors were generally friendlier. Problems arose, but Nehru's government was generally prepared to allow these countries to toe their own domestic political and economic policy lines provided they did not threaten India's security interests or challenge its regional hegemony by drawing outside powers into South Asia in ways New Delhi found objectionable.

BANDUNG: ANTICIPATING THE NEW NONALIGNMENT

Nehru's efforts to encourage newly emerging countries to play a constructive role as a group in promoting world peace and combating colonialism, neocolonialism, and racism reached their high point with the convening of a broadly based Afro-Asian conference in Bandung, Indonesia, in 1955. While initially skeptical, Prime Minister Nehru played a major role in organizing the gathering and creating a broad consensus among the twenty-nine participating countries. In his view, Bandung's main purpose was to reassert the significance of Asia and Africa in the world; he thought it important that the conference succeed.

Marred by strong policy differences among the nonaligned, pro-Western, and communist states that participated, the Bandung Conference failed to create an Afro-Asian bloc that would be a credible player on the international stage. But it is credited with setting the stage for the establishment of the NAM five years later. This movement's membership was by definition not the same as the Afro-Asian gathering. But it, too, was conceived as a forum at which countries not seated at the high table of international power could make their voices heard.

Nehru developed close ties with leaders who like himself were widely recognized as the most active and important in promoting nonalignment.[22] But he initially resisted the idea of a conference of nonaligned countries when it was proposed by presidents Josip Broz Tito of Yugoslavia and Gamal Abdel Nasser of Egypt in 1961. He wrote: "Nonalignment did not mean standing aloof only from the Soviet Union or the Western Powers; *it means nonalignment with other countries as well. To be tied up with a group of countries except in terms of broad policies was to limit one's freedom of decision and action.*" (Emphasis added.)[23] Despite these misgivings, Nehru decided that India had to be represented at the conference, which brought together leaders from twenty-five countries in Belgrade in September 1961.[24]

At this first nonaligned summit session, the only one Nehru would live to attend, the prime minister once again gave top priority to the immediate danger of nuclear war, an issue that had increasingly come to trouble him. The Soviets had resumed nuclear testing when he was on his way to Belgrade and the crisis over the status of Berlin was worsening. Nehru argued forcefully that the age of classic colonialism and racism was essentially over and he tried, with some success, to steer the conference into taking a more cautious, more neutral position between the two power blocs.[25]

The final Belgrade communiqué reflected Nehru's concerns by stating that "war has never threatened mankind with greater consequence than today."[26] Imperialism was weakening and "colonial empires and other forms of foreign oppression of people in Asia, Africa, and Latin America are gradually disappearing from the stage of history." But the communiqué also included other, more provocative points such as the concept of an ongoing conflict between "the old established and the new emerging nationalist forces" and the demand that urgent measures be taken to lessen economic inequality between the developed and the developing world.[27] These concepts and other "North-South" issues would play an important role in the NAM after Nehru's death three years later.[28]

Unlike Bandung, Belgrade led to the creation of a formal movement despite Nehru's initial skepticism. India became a major player in the NAM, especially during the prime ministerships of Nehru's daughter Indira Gandhi (1966–77, 1980–84). The goals, values, and tactics that India pursued there would in many cases have been unfamiliar and probably not altogether congenial to Nehru. But they too reflected the basic concepts of Indian foreign policy, if in a much altered way.

DEFEAT BY CHINA: SECURITY PUSHES NONALIGNMENT ASIDE

Relations between India and China reached a high point in the mid-1950s, when the two countries signed the Panchsheel Agreement and Nehru and Zhou Enlai cooperated amiably at Bandung. But these promising ties, captured by the phrase "Hindi Chini Bhai-Bhai" (India and China are brothers), gave way in the last half of the decade to an increasingly confrontational relationship that culminated in China's swift and stunning victory over outmatched Indian forces in the Himalayas in late 1962.

This disastrous conflict and the events leading to it severely undermined Nehru's position at home and abroad and prompted widespread public and parliamentary challenges to his long-undisputed role as the architect of Indian foreign policy, which no doubt contributed to his physical decline and death two years later. The unexpected rout of the Indian Army forced him to abandon, if only temporarily, India's commitment to nonalignment and to seek military support from the Cold War power blocs whose policies he had so often criticized.

The principal cause of the war was the competing Indian and Chinese claim to sizable areas along the Indo-Tibetan frontier in both Ladakh in the western Himalayas and the North East Frontier Agency (NEFA, now Arunachal Pradesh) in the eastern sector of the mountain range.[29] This border dispute was closely linked to the expansion of Chinese control over Tibet. In 1954, India reluctantly acknowledged China's full sovereignty there and gave up the special privileges it had inherited from the Raj. The Chinese, for their part, undertook to respect Tibet's autonomy and political system. This 1954 agreement, better known for its promulgation of the *Panchsheel* as principles for international behavior, contributed importantly to the general improvement in Sino-Indian ties over the next few years. We look more closely at Sino-Indian border negotiations in chapter 11.

The easier relations ended in 1959, when the Tibetans revolted against Chinese rule. Their young spiritual leader, the Dalai Lama, soon fled with thousands of his followers to India, where they sought political asylum. Facing strong anti-Chinese sentiment at home, Nehru let them come in.

India played an activist role in the rebellion—as the Chinese charged and the Indians untruthfully denied. Ashley Tellis has called this intervention, carried out in collaboration with the CIA, the most prominent example of Indian support to rebel activists in low-intensity conflicts vis-à-vis China.[30] Meanwhile, India assured the Chinese that it would not permit the Dalai Lama to carry on political activities on Indian soil. (Defining the Dalai Lama's "political activities" remains a sore point in Sino-Indian relations.) These Tibetan developments inevitably heightened Sino-Indian tensions already strained by the border dispute.

After Zhou and Nehru failed to resolve the issue at a summit meeting in New Delhi in April 1960, India intensified its aggressive military "forward policy" designed to strengthen its presence in contested areas. This set the stage for large-scale Chinese attacks that overwhelmed Indian troops in the eastern sector and forced them back in the west.

Badly shaken, and facing a revolt within the Indian National Congress, Nehru desperately looked to foreign governments for military equipment and logistical support. The United States, Britain, and other Western countries quickly agreed and rushed assistance to India. To the prime minister's relief, Washington did not seek to make this assistance conditional on New Delhi's acceptance of a military alliance, which he recognized would have meant the end of India's nonaligned foreign policy.

But as Indian troops in the eastern sector broke again in disarray, triggering widespread panic in New Delhi, Nehru frantically sought a military arrangement with Washington that, if implemented, would by any reasonable definition have ended Indian nonalignment. In a plea to President Kennedy, he called for massive U.S. air support including two dozen squadrons of fighter aircraft, two squadrons of B-47 bombers, and U.S. pilots to fly the bombers until Indian pilots could be trained.[31] Reacting to this bombshell, Secretary of State Dean Rusk declared: "As we read this message it amounts to a request for an active and practically speaking unlimited military partnership between the United States and India to take on [the] invasion [of] India."[32]

Gopal is correct in concluding that "if India was to be defended by massive American aid, nonalignment, if it survived, would require a fresh definition."[33] Even before he sent Kennedy his request for air support,

Nehru, by Gopal's account, "had accepted that military assistance from the United States introduced an element of confusion into India's policy of nonalignment, although he contended that the essence of that policy was the refusal to join any military bloc, and this India had not done."[34]

Kennedy was still considering the prime minister's request when the Chinese abruptly announced a unilateral cease-fire followed by withdrawal of their forces from the territory the PLA had seized in the east and much of their gains in the west. Military assistance from the United States continued after the fighting stopped, but it was more limited in scope than Nehru had asked and hoped for. The aid ended in 1965, when the second India-Pakistan War led Washington to cut off arms supplies to both countries.

Not surprisingly, Nehru was concerned about the impact the border war and its repercussions would have on India's important ties with Moscow. During the fighting, the Soviets took a pro-Chinese position. They stalled on an earlier agreement to supply MiG-21 fighter aircraft to the Indian Air Force and urged New Delhi to accept the proposal Beijing had put forward to stop the fighting.[35]

The Soviets began to adjust their position toward a more neutral posture while the war was still going on. Then, after the cease-fire, they adopted a pro-India stance. (Beijing's very critical reaction to Moscow's decision to remove its missiles from Cuba is believed to have influenced this volte-face.) This more sympathetic Soviet posture, which included the delayed arrival of the MiG-21s in India, led some Indians to rationalize that nonalignment had been transformed into a kind of "double alignment," to the country's benefit.[36]

Most nonaligned countries maintained neutral positions and did not rally to India's side as the Indians had expected. Ironically, the Afro-Asian countries that did back India were mostly pro-West in their foreign policy orientation. None offered India military support. After the war ended, a group of six nonaligned Afro-Asian leaders met in Colombo, Sri Lanka, and developed proposals to bring about fresh Sino-Indian talks. To India's disappointment, the leaders failed to condemn China's attack. Although the Indians were reluctant to agree to hold talks while the Chinese still occupied Indian-claimed territory, New Delhi was eventually able to interpret the Colombo group's proposals in a way that allowed it to accept them. The Chinese, for their part, refused to do so. This may have eased India's sense of isolation, though not its dismay in finding that when the chips were down it could not count on its fellow nonaligned countries for meaningful support.

The war was a national humiliation for India and for some years sharply reduced the regard other countries had for it as a player on the international stage. The battlefield defeat led India to place less emphasis than it had over the years on international peacekeeping efforts, the struggle against colonialism and racism, the fostering of nonalignment and Afro-Asian solidarity, and other matters that did not directly relate to its own interests, particularly an acute concern for its own security. These interests were now more narrowly defined. With some Western assistance, and to Pakistan's dismay, India embarked on a major expansion and modernization of its armed forces and undertook a sizable program to produce its own military supplies. Not surprisingly, it adopted a strongly anti-Chinese posture in international forums and no longer urged member countries of the United Nations to award the Chinese seat to the People's Republic.

India continued to profess fealty to nonalignment. But it redefined the concept in a way that allowed it to accept grant aid for military equipment from both sides in the Cold War. India only drew the line, as Nehru had said, at formally allying itself with one or the other of these blocs.

This determination on the Indians' part to avoid entangling foreign alliances was never tested. Neither of the blocs was interested in having India as a formal ally. The United States and other Western powers welcomed a degree of military cooperation but stopped well short of undertaking to come to India's rescue if the Chinese again attacked,[37] let alone offering New Delhi any kind of treaty relationship. As President Eisenhower had told his colleagues, Washington could not financially afford to have as large a country as India as an ally.[38]

Some Americans foolishly hoped that India's enmity toward China would lead it to join the West's efforts to counter what they considered Beijing's aggressive designs in Southeast Asia. They soon found that the Indians were not interested. New Delhi had enough on its plate in the Himalayas and, as would soon become evident, in Kashmir. The Indians probably concluded too that involvement in anticommunist efforts in Southeast Asia would risk impairing their improved relationship with the Soviet Union and place them in the unwelcome position of backing regimes they considered neo-colonial creations.

KASHMIR NEGOTIATIONS: THE LAST EFFORT
AT INTERNATIONAL MEDIATION

President Kennedy's conclusion that the Sino-Indian War offered "what may be a onetime opportunity"[39] for a reconciliation between India and Pakistan—including a settlement of their dispute over Kashmir—introduced a further challenge for Indian policymakers at a time when they were reeling from the traumatic impact of their Himalayan defeat. In Kennedy's view, such an historic development could lead the two countries to devote their military resources to providing security for the whole subcontinent against the communist threat rather than using them against one another. His administration reckoned that with both India and Pakistan now dependent on the United States for military and economic assistance, such an initiative would have a good chance of winning acceptance.

The Indians had always resisted international efforts to resolve the Kashmir issue. Under ordinary circumstances they would have spurned this latest instance of unwelcome foreign intervention to bring about a settlement that would almost certainly involve significant concessions on their part. But in the immediate aftermath of their defeat by the Chinese they were not in a position to resist U.S. (and U.K.) insistence that they enter into negotiations with the Pakistanis.

With American and British diplomats hovering in the background, India and Pakistan engaged in six rounds of fruitless negotiations. Both sides stoutly resisted American and British pressure to come to an agreement and at no time were they close to reaching one. When the Americans offered their own formula for a settlement—the partition of the Kashmir Valley—it was summarily rejected by both countries.[40]

India's determination to hold its ground and not make meaningful concessions was strengthened by the improvement in its political and security situation during the six months of negotiations. The Indians became less fearful of another Chinese attack. Their confidence in Soviet support grew. The trauma of the war receded. And U.S. pressure on the Indians to make progress relaxed: although Kennedy had personally told the Indian ambassador that "the question of Kashmir is inescapably linked to what we can do to assist India militarily," military aid continued to flow despite the Indians' recalcitrance at the negotiating table.[41]

This unwelcome American effort to resolve the Kashmir issue at a time when India was militarily weak and dependent was an important factor in the gradual falling away of the goodwill Indians felt toward the United States after it had come to their rescue. As their self-confidence and self-esteem returned, they became increasingly uncomfortable with what was for them the unfamiliar and unwanted position of being dependent on another power. Fifteen years of practicing and preaching nonalignment had a profound impact. The gratitude Indians had felt for U.S. support at a time of grave crisis gave way to resentment over perceived American interference and high-handedness. The era of good feeling between Washington and New Delhi, with all the implications this had for Indian allegiance to nonalignment, turned out to be remarkably short-lived.[42]

This development, combined with the improvement of Indo-Soviet ties, put Indian relations with Washington and Moscow into better balance. In a sense, as some Indians claimed, the new equation was indeed a restoration of nonalignment, if in an altered definition.

Nehru never recovered either physically or politically from the impact of India's defeat. His foreign and domestic policies came under unprecedented criticism. In the first phase of the conflict he was forced to drop Krishna Menon from the cabinet. The Indian National Congress that he led felt beleaguered as its candidates lost badly in by-elections to outspoken critics of the prime minister. Seriously debilitated in January 1964 by a stroke, Nehru's last foreign policy initiative was to release the long-imprisoned, separatist-minded Kashmiri leader Sheikh Abdullah and send him to Pakistan to talk to President Ayub Khan. Ayub agreed to meet with Nehru in New Delhi. Before he could do so, the prime minister died in May 1964 at the age of seventy-four.

THE END OF THE NEHRU ERA

Lal Bahadur Shastri, a veteran Congress Party politician who had been close to Nehru, was chosen by party leaders known as the "syndicate" to succeed him. Shastri had no foreign policy experience and when elected had never traveled outside India. He quite sensibly appointed one of his senior party colleagues to be minister of external affairs. Short, unassuming, and unworldly, the new prime minister seemed to many at home and abroad a weak reed who would prove unable to give India the firm leadership it needed at a critical time. They were wrong.

Shastri's first major foreign policy act was to lead India's delegation to the second NAM summit, held in Cairo in October 1964. At this session, the new prime minister reiterated India's allegiance to nonalignment in Nehruvian words and cadences. He told his fellow leaders, who represented forty-seven countries, "what unites us . . . is not any pact, not any alliance, not even a common allegiance to any particular dogma or doctrine. By being nonaligned we have asserted and proclaimed the right to think for ourselves. Our voice is not an echo."[43] He listed nuclear disarmament, peaceful settlement of border disputes, freedom from racial discrimination, and full support for the United Nations as India's major goals. The conference's final communiqué largely reflected these objectives. Shastri's stress on nuclear disarmament led to a call in the communiqué for the dispatch of a NAM delegation to Beijing to ask the Chinese to desist from developing nuclear weapons, as they were reportedly doing. (Ignoring the NAM, the Chinese exploded their first nuclear bomb a few days later.)

At Cairo, Shastri also asserted that the widely voiced NAM call for self-determination did not extend to areas and regions within a sovereign and independent country. This obvious reference to Kashmir came at a time when the situation in the disputed state had become tense and the alienation of many of its people from India more evident.

THE 1965 WAR WITH PAKISTAN

Following the breakdown of India-Pakistan talks sponsored by the United States and United Kingdom on the future of Kashmir, President Ayub Khan adopted a "leaning on India" policy. The Pakistanis were concerned that as India rearmed following its war with China, and as the disparity in the military strength between the two countries widened, prospects for a Kashmir settlement favorable to them would diminish. Those who favored armed action against India also cited its many economic and political problems, including Shastri's inexperience and alleged weakness. The Pakistan army's success in battling Indian forces along the border in the disputed Rann (marsh) of Kutch added to the Pakistanis' self-confidence.

Triggered by Pakistan's effort to ignite a rising in Indian-administered Kashmir, the second India-Pakistan War broke out in September. Although it ended in a stalemate, India as the status quo power "won by not losing." Pakistan was unable to wrest Kashmir from Indian control, which had been its purpose in starting the war. An armistice arranged by the United Nations was followed by a peace agreement worked out under Soviet auspices at Tashkent in Soviet Central Asia (now the capital of independent Uzbekistan).

The brief conflict had an important impact on India's view of itself and its approach to foreign policy. Indian self-confidence, badly damaged in the Sino-Indian War, was greatly strengthened. The war heightened Indians' belief in the importance of military power. And New Delhi's attitude toward the United States and the Soviet Union, and hence the way it practiced nonalignment, significantly changed.

Indians contrasted the policies the two superpowers had adopted during the war, to Washington's disadvantage. The United States had cut off military and economic assistance to both India and Pakistan, a move Indians bitterly resented (though the action was more damaging to the Pakistanis than it was to them). Fed up with the two South Asian antagonists' policies, and increasingly convinced that neither country would help advance U.S. foreign policy interests increasingly dominated by Southeast Asian concerns, President Lyndon Johnson had ruled out any significant American role in helping end the war.

By contrast, the Soviet prime minister had himself traveled to Tashkent where he camped for days before successfully working out an agreement ending the war on terms considerably more favorable to India than to Pakistan. The Indian Ministry of External Affairs declared: "The Soviet Union's contribution to the triumph of peace at Tashkent and her understanding of the many steps that India has taken in implementation of the [Tashkent] Declaration has been deeply appreciated in this country."[44] Though other important factors were also involved, these Indian perceptions later contributed to a return in 1966 to the pro-Soviet tilt within the framework of nonalignment that had characterized Indian foreign policy in the 1950s.

INDIRA GANDHI

Long a heart patient, Lal Bahadur Shastri died just hours after he signed the Tashkent Declaration. He had been prime minister for only nineteen months. The same syndicate of party leaders who had chosen him selected Nehru's daughter Indira Gandhi as his successor, confident that she would be guided by their counsel (as they had mistakenly thought Shastri would be). To their surprise and distress, she soon outmaneuvered them and became as dominant a government and party leader as her father had been in his heyday.

Aside from a stint as minister of information and broadcasting in Shastri's short-lived government, Mrs. Gandhi had not held public office before becoming prime minister. But she was the longtime confidant and traveling companion of her father and served briefly as the president of the Indian National Congress. Thus she came to the prime ministership well acquainted with Indian foreign policy and domestic issues.

Unlike her father Mrs. Gandhi chose not to serve concurrently as minister of external affairs, assigning the portfolio as Shastri had to one of her senior colleagues. (She later held it herself for two short periods.) She was rarely involved as intimately as he had been in the detailed management of foreign policy. But after a brief teething period she came to be universally recognized as the architect of the main features of India's approach to the world. The policies her government pursued during her two terms in office (1966–77 and 1980–84) bore her imprint and reflected her concept of her country's place on the international stage.

Mrs. Gandhi's determined quest for power was the principal driver in her approach to foreign affairs, as it was in her handling of domestic matters. Mrs. Gandhi was more aggressive than her two predecessors in seeking to ensure India's predominant power in South Asia and to protect its land and sea frontiers. She tilted Nehru's balance between idealistic nonalignment and regional preeminence strongly in the latter direction. But far from shying away from the principle of nonalignment, she embraced it and became one of the most influential and outspoken leaders of the NAM. In 1983, the year before she died, she arranged to have a NAM summit meeting held in New Delhi under her chairmanship. She used the NAM to win support for major, often radical global economic policy reform. But she also saw the organization as an instrument for projecting India's power and influence in the third world and beyond.

As Nehru had, Mrs. Gandhi viewed nonalignment as a way of preserving India's freedom of action. Like him, she rejected the definition of nonalignment as equidistance between the two power blocs. India could favor one or the other on different issues provided it maintained its independence. Her one major violation of nonalignment—as reasonably defined—was her signing a 1971 peace and friendship pact with the Soviet Union when she feared that the United States, China, and Pakistan were ganging up against India on the eve of the third India-Pakistan War. She reportedly had serious reservations about doing so because of its impact on India's nonaligned status, and she resisted other Soviet efforts to draw India into its orbit.[45] When Prime Minister Leonid Brezhnev visited India and tried to persuade Mrs. Gandhi to advocate his plan to "safeguard security in Asia through collective effort," she let him know that she was not interested. And at the 1983 Non-Aligned Movement Summit in New Delhi, she pointedly rejected Fidel Castro's concept that the Soviet Union was a "natural ally" of the NAM.

Nonetheless, critics in the West and elsewhere were correct in charging that Mrs. Gandhi's foreign policy generally tilted to the East. Not without reason, she became convinced that the Soviet Union was more sympathetic to India's approach to foreign policy and the objectives that policy was designed to pursue than the United States and its Western allies were. There were periods of good if not close relations between New Delhi and Washington during her years as prime minister. But over time she came to harbor a considerable mistrust for American motives and intentions and to resent the way Washington dealt with issues important to India.

As we have seen, an important element in India's concept of nonalignment was a determination to stand on its own and avoid being placed in a position of relying on other powers for its security and well-being. But India could not realistically achieve complete strategic autonomy. It depended on foreign sources for military hardware, which it sought to procure on concessional terms. Since the late 1950s it had been the beneficiary of sizable economic aid from both East and West. But it sought to avoid asking for assistance and resisted efforts by foreign donors to lay down either political or economic policy conditions for providing aid. Its watchword was "aid with no strings attached." Mrs. Gandhi shared this long-standing position.

DEALING WITH WASHINGTON

As we will consider at greater length in chapter 9, economic issues loomed large in U.S.-India relations in the mid-1960s. President Johnson's tough "short tether" and "ship to mouth" approach to the supply of grain during multiyear famines succeeded in forcing India to reform its economic policies but left a residue of bitterness. The negotiations on these issues, described in greater detail in chapter 9, were among the most difficult the United States and India ever engaged in.

The reforms caused a severe political backlash in India. In dealing with it, Mrs. Gandhi returned to the underlying principles of Indian foreign policy. She had been prepared to sacrifice a large measure of India's freedom of action in economic policy. She had also been willing to curb her government's criticism of U.S. policy in Southeast Asia at a time when most concerned Indians considered this policy an unacceptable example of the neocolonialism her father had condemned. The lessons she drew from the adverse reaction to these initiatives would be important as she determined the future directions of Indian foreign policy. In doing so, she would demonstrate firmness of strategic purpose coupled with considerable tactical flexibility.

GEOPOLITICS IN 1971 AND THE BREAKUP OF PAKISTAN: THE TRIUMPH OF REALISM

The pro-Soviet tilt in India's foreign policy became most pronounced during the crisis sparked by the efforts of Pakistan's martial law regime to suppress the 1971 uprising in the country's eastern wing, now independent Bangladesh. The strong support the Nixon administration gave Pakistan in that struggle, and India's concern that Nixon's opening to China, facilitated by the Pakistanis, could create an unholy Washington-Beijing-Islamabad alliance gravely threatening to India's interests, led Mrs. Gandhi to accept the Soviet offer of a treaty of peace and friendship that went well beyond her earlier warm ties with Moscow. The role of the treaty in igniting the India-Pakistan War of December 1971 is much disputed, but there can be no question that it represented an extraordinary development in Indian foreign policy. The momentous events of 1971 heightened Mrs. Gandhi's longtime concerns about U.S. goals and intentions and sent U.S.-India relations to an all-time low. Relations remained poor throughout the six remaining years of Mrs. Gandhi's first term.

But if 1971 was a low point in India's efforts to avoid dependence on either of the power blocs, the year was a huge milestone in India's path to regional predominance. In the wake of India's military intervention, Pakistan suffered a humiliating defeat and could no longer realistically contest India's preeminent position. While the Pakistanis avoided formally renouncing their demand for Kashmir, they agreed to deal with the issue peacefully and bilaterally, a formula that effectively removed the disputed area from the India-Pakistan (and world) agenda for eighteen years.

Mrs. Gandhi exercised India's unchallenged hegemony elsewhere in the region. As historian Surjit Mansingh found, her self-image was that of a benevolent, democratic, non-imperialist leader.[46] The small neighboring countries, to the contrary, often found her government overbearing and its style in political and economic negotiations heavy-handed.

In her day, as now, New Delhi's relations with some of these neighbors were influenced by ethnic ties. Despite such occasional domestic pressures, Mrs. Gandhi was generally prepared to allow neighboring South Asian countries to pursue their own political and economic agendas, provided their dealings with important outside powers did not challenge Indian interests as she defined them. India's 1974 annexation of the small Himalayan principality of Sikkim, which was prompted by concerns about the political reliability and ambitions for international recognition of the ruler of a strategically placed state bordering China, demonstrates the prime minister's willingness to take drastic steps when she believed them necessary.[47]

Like other Indian leaders before and since, Mrs. Gandhi was highly sensitive to the involvement of any major foreign power in South Asia, except on India's own terms. This applied most evidently to the United States, especially but not exclusively for its relationship with Pakistan. But as the Sikkim crisis indicated, India also worried seriously about possible Chinese inroads in the Himalayan monarchies. In Mrs. Gandhi's view, these countries lay within India's defensive perimeter. As we will see, geography and India's drive for regional preeminence have had a powerful influence on the way it dealt with these smaller countries, both during Mrs. Gandhi's time and beyond.

THE CHANGING NON-ALIGNED MOVEMENT

Under Indira Gandhi's leadership India continued the active role in the NAM that it had pursued from the organization's establishment in 1961. The prime minister played a major part in four NAM summits. She took the burgeoning organization seriously but realistically recognized its weaknesses as well as its strengths. She wanted India to take a lead in NAM activities, but never allowed its agenda to become the driving force in her foreign policy.

During Mrs. Gandhi's years India continued to maintain the generally moderate position in the NAM it had pursued during the Nehru and Shastri governments. It followed similarly restrained approaches in the third-world international organizations closely associated with the NAM—the Group of 77 and the United Nations Commission for Trade and Development (UNCTAD). The three bodies had largely overlapping memberships and goals, and they set up parallel action groups that facilitated their cooperation.

Like other countries in the NAM, India paid more attention at its sessions to economic issues during Mrs. Gandhi's time than it had earlier. The focus in Nehru's and Shastri's years had been much more on the struggle against colonialism and neocolonialism and the peril of great-power nuclear confrontation. These issues, especially anticolonialism, remained important for the nonaligned countries. For years, no NAM summit document would have been complete without condemnation of South Africa's apartheid policy, the Portuguese colonial presence in Africa, and America's armed intervention in Southeast Asia. Complaints about Moscow's hegemony in Eastern Europe and Central Asia were not part of this litany.

But increasingly the NAM spotlight fell on resolutions calling for reforms in the world economic system that its members hoped would radically change and strengthen the position of developing countries in a "New International Economic Order" (NIEO). The NAM called for a North-South dialogue that would focus on these economic demands and reverse what its leaders claimed was the increasing prosperity of the first world at the expense of the impoverished third world.

At many NAM sessions, India took positions that put it at odds with more radical members. These opponents varied over time: Indonesia before Sukarno's overthrow in 1965; then Algeria; and during Mrs. Gandhi's last years in office, Fidel Castro's Cuba. In the NAM and its associated institutions, Indian delegates argued for calls for debt relief and access to the markets of developed countries. But they thought these richer countries would take such demands more seriously and act on them if they were seen to be moderate and workable.

On the political front, Mrs. Gandhi consistently opposed the long-standing demand made by Cuba and like-minded pro-Moscow countries to align the movement more closely with the Soviet Union. She held to the traditional NAM stance of keeping distance from both Eastern and Western camps—though not necessarily equidistance—and as noted rejected Castro's thesis that the communist countries were the "natural allies" of the nonaligned. The acceptance of this Indian position by a large majority of the NAM countries was a noteworthy triumph for the prime minister.

THE NUCLEAR QUESTION

The Chinese nuclear weapons test of September 1964—just two years after the Sino-Indian War—had led many in the Indian National Congress and elsewhere to demand that India also join the exclusive nuclear weapons club. Prime Minister Shastri and other senior party leaders resisted this demand and reaffirmed India's long-standing policy opposing the acquisition of a nuclear weapons capability. Although the initial clamor soon died down, continuing Chinese testing periodically provoked further calls from nuclear bomb proponents.

These tests also prompted India to explore the possibility of a United Nations guarantee against a Chinese nuclear threat as an alternative to India producing its own weapons. In New Delhi's view, such a guarantee backed by both superpowers would meet the nonaligned criteria that governed Indian foreign policy. But nothing came of this approach. Some Indians thought that expecting Washington and Moscow to come to India's rescue in the event of a Chinese nuclear threat was unrealistic. In the period of greater self-confidence that followed the 1965 war with Pakistan, Indians became even more reluctant to put their national security in the hands of others. In any event, neither the United States nor the Soviet Union proved interested.

India also rejected U.S. and Soviet-led efforts to persuade it to adhere as a non-nuclear weapons state to the Nonproliferation Treaty (NPT) negotiated in the late 1960s. In May 1974, India conducted what it called a "peaceful nuclear explosion" in the Rajasthan desert. The blast was welcomed by the Indian public, but international reaction was largely negative. In the United States the test led to the adoption of legislation on nuclear fuel supply to foreign countries that severely complicated bilateral relations. Nor was India afforded the status of a nuclear weapons state under the NPT. To the surprise of many observers, it did not stage another nuclear test for twenty-four years. (For further discussion of the issue, see chapter 8.)

Somewhat surprisingly, the prime minister's imposition of an emergency in 1975 and the suspension of political and civil liberties that continued for seventeen months afterward had no discernible impact either on India's own foreign policy or on Washington's policy toward India. As Dennis Kux accurately wrote: "Secretary [of State Henry] Kissinger believed that the United States should not base its external relations on whether or not it liked the domestic political character of foreign governments. He also did not want to provide Mrs. Gandhi ammunition to have gratuitous U.S. criticism serve as an impulse for an even greater strengthening of Indo-Soviet relations."[48] Other democracies adopted similar positions. Moscow, for its part, applauded Mrs. Gandhi's action and stepped up its support for the prime minister. The pro-Soviet lobby in India dutifully echoed this praise with great enthusiasm.

Mrs. Gandhi was less grateful for the applause than the Soviets might have hoped. Although as we have seen, her policies often tilted toward Moscow, like other Indian political leaders and officials before and since, she seems to have recognized that it was not in India's interest to identify too closely with one side or the other in the Cold War competition. If she had strained the bounds of nonalignment when she signed the friendship treaty with the Soviet Union in 1971, it was only under very trying and unusual circumstances.

Mrs. Gandhi unexpectedly lifted the emergency in March 1977, released political prisoners, restored civil liberties, and called parliamentary elections. These actions resulted in the stunning defeat of her Congress Party and the coming to power of a coalition of her opponents led by Morarji Desai.

Desai's new Janata Party government pledged to pursue a foreign policy of "genuine nonalignment" in contrast to the generally pro-Soviet line Mrs. Gandhi had followed. The new prime minister was well disposed to the United States, which had been careful to remain in touch with him when he was in the political wilderness.

The new Indian government took office only a few weeks after President Jimmy Carter had entered the White House promising to shift U.S foreign policy from its longtime Cold War focus to one that rested to a greater extent on democratic values, human rights, and recognition of the importance of the third world. The Carter administration sought to cultivate regional influential countries as a means of devolving to them some of the international burden the United States shouldered. It made it clear that India was in this group of influentials; Pakistan was conspicuously excluded.

Many in both countries anticipated that with such like-minded new governments installed in Washington and New Delhi, Indian nonalignment would for the first time take on a pro-U.S. slant.[49] These expectations were strengthened by Carter's visit to India, the first by an incumbent American president since Eisenhower two decades earlier, and the stirring declaration issued at that time affirming the two countries' concern for human rights, development, and democracy.

The expectations were never fulfilled. Legislation the United States enacted following the 1974 Indian nuclear test led to a legal and political dispute over prior American commitments to supply nuclear fuel that came to overshadow more promising features in bilateral ties. The more benign relationship between Washington and Moscow that had provided a promising background for Carter's new foreign policy withered as the Soviets adopted aggressive policies in Angola and the Horn of Africa and strongly backed the communist regime that took power in a military coup in Afghanistan. The Janata government, like its predecessors, saw value in good relations with both Cold War contenders and was unwilling to endanger New Delhi's important political, economic, and security ties with the Soviet Union. And, in any event, the unwieldy Janata coalition was increasingly distracted from foreign policy by internecine fighting and collapsed in late 1979 after only two-and-a-half years in office.[50]

THE SOVIET INTERVENTION IN AFGHANISTAN

Indira Gandhi's Indian National Congress won the election that followed. But before she returned to the prime ministership, an event occurred that had profound consequences both for India's nonalignment policy and its quest for security and regional hegemony, still the two driving forces in New Delhi's approach to the world. This was the Soviet invasion of Afghanistan on Christmas Day 1979.

Mrs. Gandhi initially adopted a position markedly sympathetic to the Soviets. She accepted at face value Moscow's assurances that its troops had gone into Afghanistan at the request of the authorities in Kabul and its pledge to withdraw when the Afghans asked it to do so. Although she later modified this position somewhat, India's line throughout the long Soviet occupation differed sharply from the stand taken by both the Western countries and most of India's fellow third-world nations. These countries had condemned the invasion and called for the immediate withdrawal of Soviet troops from Afghan soil. New Delhi stopped well short of this demand, privately telling Moscow it was disturbed by the presence of Soviet troops in Afghanistan and would prefer that they withdraw. It called for a consensus among neighboring regional states, including Pakistan, to prevent the Afghan crisis from spreading. It argued that this could create a suitable environment in which Soviet withdrawal could take place.[51]

To India's distress, the Soviet invasion also led to the resurrection of U.S. security ties with Pakistan. In Washington's view, the arrival of the Red Army on Pakistan's border with Afghanistan had converted it from a nuclear delinquent that violated U.S. nonproliferation legislation to a "frontline state" in the Cold War. The revived relationship did not fully bloom until President Ronald Reagan took office in January 1981. But well before then, the Indians became distressed by the prospect of U.S. military equipment and political support for the Pakistanis. Indeed, from the American viewpoint, India seemed more troubled by the renewed Washington-Islamabad link than by the incursion of Soviet forces into South Asia that had prompted it. Although the Indians argued that security assistance to Pakistan could provoke Soviet retaliation, their real concern was that it could alter the balance of power in South Asia to India's disadvantage (though Indians generally recognized that in the wake of the 1971 Bangladesh War, Pakistan was no longer a serious military threat).[52]

The Indians eventually recognized that the Reagan administration would not be moved by their protests. They also seem to have concluded, as has so often been the case in Indian relations with the Cold War superpowers, that they should not unduly impair their ties with Washington in Moscow's favor. The two governments in effect agreed to disagree on Afghanistan and arms to Pakistan, and the issues largely faded from their dialogue.

Mrs. Gandhi demonstrated this interest in repairing relations with the United States by accepting President Reagan's 1982 invitation to visit Washington (which she pointedly did before traveling to Moscow a few months later). During the visit the two sides were able to formulate an agreement on the vexing issue of fuel supplies for the U.S.-built nuclear reactor at Tarapur. By then one of the world's most senior national leaders, the prime minister was well received and made a very positive impression. This favorable reset in bilateral ties lasted throughout the balance of Mrs. Gandhi's second term, which ended tragically with her assassination in September 1984.

RAJIV GANDHI

Mrs. Gandhi was succeeded by her son Rajiv, who had entered politics only a few years earlier. He accepted the conventional premises of Indian foreign policy: he saw the Soviet Union as India's chief foreign partner but also wanted a good relationship with the United States that would lead to better balance in India's nonaligned foreign policy. He focused importantly on fostering greater cooperation with the United States in helping India develop its defense production capability, though Washington's concerns for the security of the sophisticated equipment that New Delhi sought limited progress in this area. This U.S. resistance to technological transfers was important in eventually cooling the Rajiv Gandhi government's enthusiasm for improved ties with Washington.

Closer to home, Rajiv adopted an assertive attitude in promoting India's regional primacy based on its growing military power. We examine his intervention in Sri Lanka in chapter 12. He also sent Indian forces to the Indian Ocean republic of the Maldives off India's southwest coast to successfully foil a coup there. These actions reflected India's heightened interest in flexing its enhanced military muscle in South Asia and exerting greater and more evident hegemony there than ever before.

The Indian National Congress, beset by scandal, was defeated in the 1989 parliamentary election and Rajiv lost his prime ministership. His exit from office coincided with the end of the Cold War, which as we have seen had been a key factor in shaping the contours of foreign policy during India's first five decades of independence. His successors would have to deal with a new and unfamiliar international equation that brought major challenges and opportunities to Indian foreign policymakers.

CHAPTER THREE

Foreign Policy:
The Post–Cold War World

IN THE LATE 1980S and early 1990s, three major and seemingly uncon-nected developments challenged the earlier Nehruvian verities of Indian foreign policy, ushering in enormous changes both in the ways the coun-try dealt with the outside world and in its thinking about India's role on that new and unfamiliar stage. These events were the end of the Cold War and the breakup of the Soviet Union; the reform of India's economic policies, which made it a much more involved player on the world's trad-ing and investment stage as well as a more prosperous one; and the ad-vent of government by coalition that replaced the long-standing practice of rule by a single party, usually the Indian National Congress.

In the ensuing quarter century these and other important develop-ments undercut old orthodoxies and stimulated approaches to the world that could not have been imagined in the earlier years of Indian indepen-dence. But despite these altered circumstances, India's long-term foreign policy imperatives, most notably its dedication to nonalignment—increasingly termed "strategic autonomy" in the post–Cold War world—and its quest for regional predominance and the security of its land and sea frontiers, continued to play key roles. Added to them was a third major driver of Indian foreign policy: strengthening the Indian economy and treating that strength as a source of Indian power.

THE END OF THE COLD WAR AND THE BREAKUP
OF THE SOVIET UNION

India warmly welcomed the winding down of the Cold War in the late 1980s and early 1990s. Its foreign policy had been designed to mitigate the impact of the Cold War by promoting nonalignment and participating with other nonaligned states in efforts to lessen the threat of a nuclear confrontation between the two rival power blocs. It had tried to keep the Cold War away from South Asia and had angrily resented the recruitment of Pakistan into the Western alliance system.

Admittedly, the Cold War had brought India some advantages. It could not have exerted the influence it did on the international stage had the Cold War not provided it an opportunity to preach its nonaligned gospel. The Cold War had also allowed India to tap both power blocs for economic assistance. But the Nehru government and its successors had been sincere in their efforts to lessen Cold War tensions and eventually end what they saw as a dangerous East-West confrontation that could threaten India's interests.

This basic Indian unhappiness with the Cold War was evident in the warm reception the Rajiv Gandhi government gave to Soviet President Mikhail Gorbachev's promotion of détente with the United States. India was pleased by Gorbachev's acknowledgment that his new approach to foreign policy relied for its philosophical underpinnings on the ideals of nonalignment.[1] It was also satisfied with his decision to withdraw Soviet troops from Afghanistan, which ended a situation that had set India at odds with the West and much of the third world.

In contrast to the welcome they gave to Gorbachev's foreign policy initiatives, many Indians reacted with dismay to the unexpected collapse of the Soviet Union at the end of 1991. The USSR had long been India's most important international partner. It provided a great-power counterweight to American and Chinese policies, which New Delhi often found inimical to its aspirations to play the role of South Asia's "security manager." Moscow had been prepared to exercise its UN Security Council veto power to defeat any resolution on the Kashmir issue that India found unacceptable. Except for a short period during the 1962 Sino-Indian War, Moscow had supported the Indians on foreign policy issues important to New Delhi. Unlike the United States, the Soviet Union was considered a friend that could be counted on.

Moscow also offered India an attractive export market for products it would have had difficulty selling elsewhere. The long-standing rupee-ruble barter arrangement that facilitated these exports, which the Indians exchanged for goods the Soviets made available to them at bargain-basement prices, did not survive the USSR's fall. Nor could India any longer obtain Soviet military equipment on attractively discounted terms. From the time of the MiG aircraft purchases in the early 1960s, the Soviet Union had been India's principal foreign source of sophisticated aircraft and other major military hardware. Post-Soviet Russia continues to play an important role as an arms supplier, but India no longer gets the bargain prices Moscow had offered in Soviet times.

PROBLEMS AND PROSPECTS IN A UNIPOLAR WORLD

India now faced a unipolar world in which the United States was the sole remaining superpower. This new, unprecedented situation displeased many Indian policymakers and pundits whose suspicions of Washington's motives and intentions had long been part of their DNA. But although old-thinkers in the Ministry of External Affairs and elsewhere remained dubious about the United States, successive governments in the 1990s concluded that it was in India's interest to strengthen its ties with Washington.

This was not easy to do. As we have seen, the bilateral relationship had always been a thin one; efforts to give it greater substance had made only limited progress. The Indians, with their tradition of nonalignment and strategic autonomy, could not be expected to adapt easily to the dynamics of a relationship with a newly triumphant superpower. Nor was it likely that Washington could develop strong ties with New Delhi without seeking, consciously or not, to dominate that relationship, as it often did in its dealings with allied or friendly powers. Any seemingly "unequal" relationship would inevitably disturb the Indians, who were sensitive to such treatment and quick to perceive it.

THE COMING OF ECONOMIC REFORMS

The radical transformation of India's economic system undertaken by the Congress Party government led by Prime Minister Narasimha Rao provided the enhanced economic substance to U.S.-India ties on which a more productive relationship could be built. Rao's reforms also set the stage for closer political and economic relations with countries in Northeast and Southeast Asia that Indian policymakers had ignored or snubbed.

India's long-standing, government-dominated economic system that had given priority to the public sector and insulated the country from world market forces faced a major crisis when Rao and Manmohan Singh, the apolitical professional economist he appointed finance minister, took office in 1991. Foreign exchange reserves had fallen to barely two months' import needs. Rao and Singh boldly adopted initiatives designed to restructure the country's economic policy framework and release energies that would move India into the global investing and trading system it had long spurned.

These reforms, which led to a spectacular rise in India's foreign trade/GDP ratio, were stoutly opposed by interests that had profited from the old system, and they took some time to bear fruit. Rao and Singh persisted despite this domestic opposition and an unpromising international economic situation. The subsequent expansion of the Indian economy, long derided for its low "Hindu rate of growth," to near double-digit growth rates stem from these radical reforms of the early 1990s.

The revamping of India's economic system had a major impact on its foreign policy. New business lobbies in India and abroad called for strengthened political and security ties between New Delhi and its trading and investment partners. India's economic growth led it to develop new political interest in countries that had the raw materials and markets it needed.

India's political ties with Southeast and Northeast Asia were major beneficiaries of these economic reforms. Aside from the roles early Indian governments had played in international efforts to deal with East-West confrontations in Korea and Indochina, these areas had figured surprisingly little in New Delhi's policies despite the impressive economic progress they came to achieve. The nonaligned India of the Cold War era had viewed with some disdain what it considered the unacceptable dependence of Japan, South Korea, and some of the Southeast Asian countries on U.S. political and security support.

To develop stronger ties, Rao announced in 1992 a new "Look East" policy that led India to build much closer relations over time with the Association of Southeast Asian Nations (ASEAN) and its member states as well as with Japan and South Korea. This policy built on Indian economic growth, but it also involved expanding Indian political and security relationships in East Asia and, arguably, balancing Chinese dominance in the region. India eventually became an ASEAN summit-level partner and reached agreements with ASEAN on amity and cooperation in

Southeast Asia, comprehensive economic cooperation, combating terrorism, and free trade. India also signed free trade agreements with South Korea and Japan and its fleet has conducted joint exercises with the Japanese, Australian, and U.S. navies.

Prime Minister Narendra Modi picked up and intensified this priority. It is noteworthy that his first trip outside South Asia after taking office in 2014 was to Japan. His visits to Korea and Australia, and his joint statement with President Barack Obama on the common U.S. and Indian strategic interests in Asia, have showcased a balancing policy that India is conducting simultaneously with its efforts to expand its already substantial economic ties with China.

The strengthening of India's economy made available greater resources for its armed forces and for higher-profile diplomatic activities that eventually included economic assistance to developing countries. Its more powerful military gave India greater confidence in confronting any potential Chinese threat and in dealing with problems with Pakistan. Joint military exercises between the Indian armed services and their foreign counterparts added a significant dimension to India's relations with the United States and countries in East and Southeast Asia.

India's greater wealth and international economic connections also provided grist for the mills of those who called for it to play a larger role in the world, as befitted a country with these enhanced assets. As we observed in chapter 2, during the Cold War India often could punch above its weight in the international arena. It had derived its influence from its ideas and the diplomatic skill it mustered in propagating them. The reforms of the 1990s and beyond gave India the heft and credentials to claim more realistically and with better prospects of international acceptance the seat at the global high table to which it had long aspired.

COALITION GOVERNMENTS

During Jawaharlal Nehru's seventeen years as prime minister the Indian National Congress under his leadership enjoyed overwhelming parliamentary majorities. India's first-past-the-post election system resulted in most of the leftist, rightist, and state- and caste-based opposition parties winning only a handful of seats. They often were, in effect, little more than splinter groups. The Congress Party also commanded substantial parliamentary majorities during most of Indira Gandhi's sixteen years as prime minister.

This single-party dominance gave way in the late 1980s. Beginning then and for the next quarter century, India was almost always ruled by coalition governments in which a single party played a dominant role but depended on others to keep it in office. It was not until the Bharatiya Janata Party's sweep of the 2014 parliamentary election that long-term single-party rule was restored.[2]

Coalition governments posed problems for foreign policymaking. The most obvious need was winning the support of smaller parties for government-proposed policies they found distasteful for ideological or parochial reasons. The refusal of the Left Front parties in parliament to back Prime Minister Manmohan Singh's efforts to negotiate a civil nuclear agreement with the United States in 2007–08 was a prime example of the difficulty ideological interests can pose. A revolt by a Tamil Nadu-based party against Singh for his sponsoring what they considered an unacceptably weak policy toward Sri Lanka demonstrated how a regional party can cause trouble. We will look at both these confrontations in chapter 5.

The management of unstable coalition governments could also be a serious distraction from post–Cold War foreign policymaking. Prime ministers at times found themselves so preoccupied with balancing the political interests of their supporters that they had little time to devote to international issues, let alone devising new ways to resolve them. This was especially true when these coalition governments did not themselves enjoy parliamentary majorities and depended on the votes of other parties that agreed to extend support to the government but declined to participate in it. Prime ministers who lacked broad support were vulnerable to challenges from within their own party ranks, which sometimes inhibited them from adopting foreign policies that they feared could provide ammunition to rivals looking to undercut and replace them. And the short tenures of some post-1990 governments left little time for ministers responsible for foreign and security policymaking to master their briefs and bring the bureaucracy to accept changes in existing policies.

REVAMPING NONALIGNMENT

The end of the Cold War forced a reexamination and redefinition of the working of Indian nonalignment, though the politicians who led the country in the 1990s rarely discussed these changes in public forums.

Indian post–Cold War nonalignment retained its central Nehruvian precepts, and the country's new leaders continued to pursue independent foreign policies determined by India's own ideals and interests. But many of the principles, policies, and perspectives that had guided Indian foreign policy under the broad banner of nonalignment had become less meaningful or even irrelevant with the end of the Cold War. The most obvious example was New Delhi's relations with Moscow. The Russian Federation that had replaced the Soviet Union was not in a position to provide the level of political, economic, and security support India had grown accustomed to over the Cold War years. In the mid-1990s some Indian strategists and politicians promoted the idea of a Russian-Chinese-Indian bloc to balance the United States. But nothing significant came of this until the establishment of the BRICS group many years later.[3]

Other changes were important if not as dramatic as the disappearance of the Soviet connection. With the end of the rule of European powers in Africa and the impending demise of South Africa's apartheid regime, colonialism had become a dead letter, at least in any form India was prepared to criticize. The old gospel of solidarity among former colonial nations had become less salient as their internecine rivalries intensified and the shared memory of their struggles for independence faded. India continued to participate with apparent enthusiasm in the Non-Aligned Movement (NAM) and associated organizations that sought to rectify the North-South economic imbalance. But New Delhi seemed increasingly to recognize that its role as shop steward for the South in that struggle was only marginally advancing its own economic and political interests. The movement remained a vehicle for mobilizing developing countries' support, but it was no longer the major feature of Indian foreign policy it had been in the post-Nehru, Cold War years.

Embracing the market economy at a time when the capitalist countries had just won the Cold War, India now looked to the more prosperous of these developing nations—and the triumphant West—for trade and investment prospects. Its interest in the poor countries of what had been the third world diminished. This outlook would change later as India's rapidly growing economy competed for raw materials and markets in African and other developing countries. As we have seen, this new focus and the enhanced role that economics consequently came to play in Indian diplomacy was important in leading it to pay increasing attention to the rapidly growing market-economy countries in East and Southeast Asia regardless of their political coloration.

RELATIONS WITH THE UNITED STATES

New Delhi's dealings with Washington were a crucial element in its efforts to maintain strategic autonomy and the security of its land and maritime boundaries. Substantial growth in bilateral trade and investment helped create a better climate for friendlier U.S.-India ties, though American firms continued to encounter frustrating political and bureaucratic difficulties despite India's economic reforms. There was also a surge in U.S.-India military-to-military relations. A pro-India lobby developed in the U.S. Congress, where members' criticism of India gradually gave way to expressions of support. The growing involvement of the Indian diaspora in American political life intensified this positive change in attitudes on Capitol Hill and elsewhere. The withdrawal of Soviet troops from Afghanistan in 1988 and the termination in 1990 of Washington's economic and military assistance to Islamabad because of its continuing nuclear weapons program lessened Indians' concern over what they had long considered the pro-Pakistan bias in U.S. dealings with South Asia.

But it was by no means all smooth sailing. During the first post–Cold War decade, progress at the government-to-government level was difficult to achieve. There was widespread skepticism in the U.S. bureaucracy about the usefulness of pushing for change in dealing with India, and U.S. State Department officials and others who favored positive policy initiatives found themselves hamstrung by the resistance of other bureaucrats, both civilian and military, to moving forward. Some American officials found it difficult to deal with their Indian counterparts and remained largely unconvinced that it was worth making the effort to understand India's often unfamiliar ways.

And on the Indian side, negative "old think" toward the United States persisted and often made progress in important areas difficult to achieve. The Indians did not sacrifice their own important interests in devising their policy toward the United States. Their suspicion and resentment of the United States lessened but did not disappear. They rarely looked to Washington for guidance, let alone leadership, in international affairs and pursued policies the United States sometimes found unhelpful or worse. India's refusal to join the U.S.-led coalition to liberate Kuwait from Iraq in 1990–91 was one of many instances of its continuing insistence on an independent foreign policy that was not necessarily to America's liking.[4] And no less than before, New Delhi resented U.S.

advice on what it considered internal issues, particularly Washington's public criticism of India's human rights record in suppressing a major insurgency in Kashmir and its questioning of the disputed state's accession to the Indian Union. Senior U.S. officials' reluctance to afford India the importance and sympathetic care it believed it deserved did not help.

But it was differences over India's nuclear policy more than any other issue that impeded the development of closer and more confident bilateral relations. For much of the 1990s, this issue was the top item on Washington's India agenda. To American dismay, New Delhi remained determined to maintain the capacity to produce nuclear weapons. It refused to put all its nuclear facilities under the "full scope" international safeguards Washington called for. Instead, it pursued a policy of "nuclear ambiguity," neither forswearing nuclear weapons nor testing them.[5] Determined to maintain its strategic autonomy, India continued to refuse to sign the Nuclear Non-Proliferation Treaty (NPT) as a non-nuclear weapons state. Post–Cold War governments insisted, as earlier ones had, that the NPT was an unequal and discriminatory pact unfairly favoring the "nuclear club" comprising the five countries that had tested nuclear weapons before the treaty was signed in 1968.

U.S.-India differences over nuclear issues heightened in 1995 when New Delhi, reversing its earlier position, declared that it would not ratify the recently negotiated Comprehensive Test Ban Treaty (CTBT). India had long supported the idea of a treaty banning nuclear tests: it considered such a pact an important step toward global nuclear disarmament, a major foreign policy goal to which it devoted considerable diplomatic energy, expertise, and negotiating skill. But it became convinced that the main purpose of the treaty's sponsors now was to maintain their own nuclear weapons monopoly, not to promote disarmament. India's decision—one of the clearest examples in the 1990s of its resistance to measures that it believed would compromise its strategic autonomy—made other advances toward U.S.-India reconciliation seem somewhat tentative. We will look at the CTBT negotiations in chapter 10.

In May 1998 the newly elected BJP-led coalition government headed by Prime Minister Atal Bihari Vajpayee conducted a series of nuclear weapons tests in the Rajasthan desert.[6] Washington was caught by surprise.[7] A few weeks later the Pakistanis followed suit, despite strenuous U.S. efforts to persuade them not to.

When the foreign ministers of the five permanent UN Security Council members met soon afterward, the United States played a leading role in drafting a tough communiqué, unanimously accepted by the UN Security Council's other permanent members, calling on India and Pakistan to shut down their nuclear weapons programs and ratify the CTBT. To India's further chagrin, the communiqué also "actively encouraged" New Delhi and Islamabad to find through direct dialogue "mutually acceptable solutions" to the "root causes" of their tensions, "including Kashmir."[8] The UN Security Council adopted a similar, somewhat harsher resolution a couple of days later.[9] Tough sanctions and other economically painful measures were slapped on India and Pakistan by the United States, other governments, and multilateral development banks.

The nuclear tests threatened to undo the modest gains that India and the United States had made over the previous decade in bolstering their bilateral ties. Resentful and convinced that they had been deliberately misled about the tests,[10] U.S. policymakers were not mollified by Vajpayee's claim in a letter to President Clinton that India's decision to test was forced on it by threats from both nuclear-armed China and from Pakistan, which, the prime minister charged, Beijing had materially helped become a nuclear weapons state.[11] Nor were they satisfied by his announcement of a unilateral moratorium on further tests. U.S.-India ties seemed to be slipping to new depths.

But in one of the most unexpected turns in the roller-coaster history of these bilateral ties, relations instead began to improve. Within a year they were arguably the soundest they had ever been. This sudden change was sparked by both countries' recognition of a mutual interest in turning things around and their willingness to reach out to one another to do so. The Indians took the initiative, passing word soon after the tests that they were prepared to send to Washington veteran BJP leader Jaswant Singh, Vajpayee's senior adviser on defense and foreign affairs, to discuss their possible adherence to the CTBT and other nuclear issues.[12] The Americans responded favorably. According to Deputy Secretary of State Strobe Talbott, whom Clinton chose to lead the U.S. team in a long series of confidential bilateral discussions, the president "had been frustrated at not having made much of a dent in U.S.-India relations during his first six years in office. With only two years to go in his presidency, the nuclear tests gave him a powerful incentive to make up for lost time."[13]

Vajpayee himself weighed in helpfully when he declared in a remarkable speech that September in New York City that "we in India believe that Indo-U.S. relations, *restructured on an equal footing* [emphasis added], constitute the key element in the structure of tomorrow's democratized world order." Expressing his belief that the two countries shared a convergence and commonality of interests, the prime minister famously declared: "India and the United States are natural allies in the quest for a better future for the world in the twenty-first century."[14]

Some commentators in both countries such as former U.S. ambassador to India Frank Wisner and senior Indian analyst C. Raja Mohan have argued that the tests might have paradoxically made it easier to revitalize the U.S.-India relationship by giving the Indians greater self-confidence and moving the bilateral agenda away from its primary focus on nuclear issues. As Strobe Talbott wrote, paraphrasing Wisner, "Perhaps [the Indian tests] had 'unshackled the diplomacy' in the sense that neither the United States nor India could hide any longer behind the ambiguity of past Indian policy; they would now have to deal with the issues—and with each other—head on."[15] Writing five years after the tests, Mohan found that "instead of letting nuclear differences define the relationship [India and the United States] have chosen to put in place a broader engagement that will help manage the nuclear divergence in a mature manner."[16]

In the Talbott-Singh talks, the U.S. negotiators focused on persuading the Indians to ratify the CTBT. Talbott eventually concluded that the lifting of the U.S. sanctions as a trade-off for Indian acceptance of the CTBT offered the most hopeful formula for a breakthrough. His efforts were undercut by Senate Republicans, who eventually brought about the rejection of the treaty in a 51–48 vote in October 1999.[17] Talbott's long efforts to persuade the Indians to sign on petered out three months later. But India subsequently maintained the unilateral moratorium on testing that it pledged at the time of its tests. Nor has Pakistan conducted further tests.

Although the two sides did not make any significant progress on the immediate issues they tackled, the Talbott-Singh talks were a singularly important contribution to the unexpected warming of bilateral relations in the final years of the Clinton administration and the Bush administration that followed. The most candid and extensive discussions ever held between senior American and Indian officials, they offered the two countries an unprecedented opportunity to understand one another's thinking and to establish an easy, informal relationship at a time when both sought the opening that had so long eluded them. The two teams' ability to appreciate where the other side was coming from had rarely been found in earlier encounters during the often difficult relationship between Washington and New Delhi. As Singh wrote, "At least [the two countries] were meeting and talking, which in itself was more progress than we had ever achieved before."[18]

U.S.-India relations were bolstered further by the position the Clinton administration took when in the winter of 1999 Pakistani troops surreptitiously crossed the Line of Control in Kashmir and occupied territory on the Indian side of the line in the disputed state's remote, mountainous Kargil district. Washington's insistence that the Pakistanis withdraw came as a pleasant surprise to New Delhi. Most Indians had for years been convinced that in India-Pakistan disputes, especially those involving Kashmir, the United States would tilt toward Pakistan. Washington's support for India in the Kargil crisis—highlighted by President Clinton telling the self-invited Pakistani Prime Minister Nawaz Sharif at a tense White House meeting that he could expect no American support or sympathy if he did not pull his forces back at once—contributed importantly to the heightening of Indian trust in the United States.[19]

Kargil also set the stage for President Clinton's long-delayed official visit to India in March 2000. All such visits are routinely billed as successes, but Clinton's was a genuine triumph that reflected and enhanced the improvement in the U.S.-India relationship that Washington's handling of the crisis had generated. The president's five-day stay contrasted sharply with his subsequent five-hour stop in Pakistan, by then under army rule following a coup that overthrew Sharif. Much to India's pleasure, Clinton used that brief occasion to reiterate that there was no military solution to the Kashmir issue.[20]

We end our discussion of U.S.-India relations in this chapter with this watershed presidential visit, which seemed at least to the more optimistic to put the two countries on a fast track toward firmer, broader, and more sustainable bilateral ties. We will carry the story forward in the chapters ahead that deal with India's global visions and its negotiating style.

In those chapters, we will find that as in the past, U.S.-India relations have had their ups and downs. High points in the new partnership included the launching of a security relationship and the landmark agreement on civil nuclear cooperation reached in 2008. We examine the lengthy negotiations for this agreement in detail in chapter 8. Some stubborn trade disagreements and the badly mismanaged arrest of an Indian diplomat in New York in 2013 were among the low points. But in contrast to the early years of Indian foreign policy, strong ties with the United States were widely regarded as critical for India's future, though the two countries' relationship still carried some of the baggage of suspicion engendered in those Cold War times.

INDIA AND ITS BIG NEIGHBORS

In the post–Cold War years India's foreign policymakers continued to give the same high priority as they had earlier to protecting the security of land and sea frontiers and maintaining the country's preeminent position in South Asia. New Delhi's concerns remained focused on China and Pakistan: both are considered hostile countries that collude with one another in ways that threaten important Indian interests. India has come to consider rapidly rising China a challenge not only in the Himalayas but also in the Indian Ocean. Its concerns about an unfriendly extra-regional "foreign hand" in the smaller South Asian countries have increasingly come to focus on Beijing rather than on Washington. New Delhi's South Asia diplomacy has been complicated by state governments and other political forces in Tamil Nadu and West Bengal that have their own parochial ideas of how India should fashion its Sri Lanka and Bangladesh policies. The discussion here recounts the main developments in India's relations with its larger neighbors, Pakistan and China; we take a closer look at India's negotiating style with these countries in chapter 11.

Pakistan

The long period of relative stability in India-Pakistan relations ushered in by the 1972 Simla Agreement ended in 1989, when the Kashmir Valley's predominantly Muslim population began a mass uprising against Indian rule. The Pakistanis were not significantly involved in fomenting this outbreak, but they could not long resist the temptation to fish in troubled waters. India-Pakistan ties quickly frayed. Successive governments in New Delhi have dealt harshly with the agitation in Kashmir and Pakistan's role in it. They have continued to insist that any settlement preserve India's control over the Valley, the territorial crux of the dispute. Pakistan, for its part, has persisted in supporting the insurgency while claiming it is not involved. In violation of the Simla Agreement it has also raised the issue in international forums, with little impact.

By now recognized as one of the world's most intractable international affairs problems, this unresolved Kashmir dispute continues to make difficult any substantial, sustained progress in India-Pakistan relations. Efforts by the two sides to settle it, or at least to reduce its impact on overall India-Pakistan ties, occasionally seem to be making progress, only to be upset by provocative actions, usually taken by Pakistan, the party in the dispute that wishes to overturn the status quo. As we have seen, Pakistani efforts to seize the strategic Kargil district of Kashmir in 1999 led to months of fighting between the two armies. Some called it the fourth India-Pakistan War.

The attacks on the Indian Parliament in 2001 and on Mumbai in 2008, both almost certainly engineered by the Pakistan's Inter-Services Intelligence (ISI) or rogue elements associated with it, twice brought the two countries perilously close to hostilities. Each time there was widespread demand within India for retaliatory action, including calls for armed attacks against Pakistani targets. In both instances, the governments in power—Vajpayee's BJP-led coalition in 2001 and Manmohan Singh's Congress-led one in 2008—resisted, though Vajpayee mobilized large forces along the Line of Control in Kashmir and on the international border in a year-long exercise in coercive diplomacy that he eventually ended following international crisis-management efforts led by the United States.

India also remains concerned about Pakistani collaboration with the Chinese. Beijing's assistance to Pakistan's nuclear and missile programs has long been an issue. The Indians also worry about China's help in developing Pakistan's defense production; its role in the construction and operation of the strategically located port of Gwadar on Pakistan's western Arabian Sea coast, which some Indian analysts fear could be converted into a Chinese naval base; the road and rail transport links ("the economic corridor") it has pledged to build and finance to connect Gwadar with western China through Pakistan-administered Kashmir; and the joint exercises, intelligence sharing, and professional training arrangements it has with the Pakistan military. We discuss the India-China-Pakistan triangle and other aspects of the India-China relationship further in chapter 11.

While the post–Cold War events we have outlined have kept the perceived security threat from Pakistan high on India's foreign policy agenda, the nature of Indian concerns has gradually shifted. New Delhi had earlier worried most about a Pakistani armed attack into Indian-held territory, as happened in 1965 and 1999. Its main fear now is that elements based in Pakistan will undertake disruptive terrorist operations similar to the attack on Mumbai and that the Pakistanis will try to subvert disaffected Muslims not only in Kashmir but elsewhere in India as well.

The Indians were more relaxed about the restoration of the close security relationship between the United States and Pakistan following the 9/11/2001 attacks on the U.S. mainland than they had been when the two countries established military ties in the 1950s and 1980s. New Delhi's protests that the Pakistanis would use their newly acquired American arms against India were more muted than they had been during those earlier periods of close U.S.-Pakistani security cooperation. This reflected both the improvement in U.S.-India relations that had occurred in the years leading up to 9/11 and India's growing self-confidence. For its part, Washington appreciated the Vajpayee government's prompt offer to help in Afghanistan, where India was already providing covert assistance to rebel forces opposed to the Taliban government, but turned down the offer largely because Pakistan was better situated geographically to serve as a base for operations.

China

Post–Cold War India and China have become major trading partners, collaborate as members of BRICS, find common cause on such global issues as climate change, and exchange much ballyhooed visits by their high-level civil and military leaders.[21] Yet concern about Beijing's challenge to its security and regional preeminence remains highly important in the way New Delhi shapes its foreign and security policies. This apprehension has been heightened by the stunning progress a rising and increasingly assertive China has made toward internationally accepted great power status.[22]

Despite repeated negotiating sessions, India and China continue to claim substantial areas held by the other in the Himalayas. Neither seems to be ready to decide on a settlement that would inevitably involve giving up some of their claims. An analysis of the protracted border negotiations and what they reveal about how India and China deal with one another appears in chapter 11. However, since 1993, the two countries have largely insulated the rest of their expanding relationship from the intractable border issue.

The support Beijing has provided Pakistan and other neighbors of India demonstrates its interest in developing a strategic hedge against New Delhi, with Islamabad playing a central role in this project. But at the same time, broader strategic considerations limit the length to which the Chinese are prepared to go in supporting Pakistan. It does not want to drive India closer to the United States or cause it to band together with ASEAN countries in opposing Chinese ambitions in Southeast Asia. The "all-weather highway" that Beijing and Islamabad publicly call their relationship is no longer an accurate description, if it ever was (China does not support Pakistan's position on Kashmir, nor did it come to Pakistan's assistance during the Kargil fighting in 1999).[23] But China is becoming increasingly concerned about the restiveness of its Muslim population in Xinjiang. This issue has come to play an important part in its relations with Pakistan and Afghanistan, where some of these Muslim rebels have now based themselves.

Chinese post–Cold War efforts to develop closer economic and political ties with India's smaller neighbors have most notably included the construction of a harbor at Hambantota in the southern part of Sri Lanka. This is considered by some Indian analysts to be part of a "string of pearls," potential Chinese bases in the Indian Ocean that could lead to the encircling of India. The defeat in early 2015 of the pro-Chinese Rajapakse government—widely hailed by the Indians—was a setback to Chinese ambitions in the island. The Chinese have become more active in Nepal and Bhutan as well as in Bangladesh. New Delhi, for its part, seems to have concluded that it can no longer hope to exclude Chinese influence from these small states and that its interests are better served by outdoing Beijing in its neighborhood relations, especially in promoting regional economic development under its own leadership.

India's concern about growing Chinese assertiveness in the South China Sea (and potentially elsewhere in Southeast Asia) reflects its expanding economic and political interests in the area, originally set forth in the 1990s in its Look East policy. In 2014 Prime Minister Narendra Modi began to refer to this policy as "Act East," to give the concept a more dynamic quality. New Delhi is committed to freedom of navigation in the South China Sea, as elsewhere, and has made its presence felt with an expanded navy. India is not a direct party to the territorial disputes between China and some of the riparian states, but it has been involved in exploratory energy projects off the coast of Vietnam. It calls for a negotiated settlement of the maritime boundary problems.

The competition between India and China for natural resources has played out in places as remote from one another as Myanmar, Afghanistan, the South China Sea, and the African continent. This competition has been an important element in leading India to pay greater attention to economic diplomacy, which we will consider at greater length later.

An earlier concern, Sino-American cooperation on policy toward South Asia, viewed by Indians as an unacceptable exercise in great-power hegemony, has abated as Washington's relations with India have improved.[24] India now shares with the United States an interest in avoiding the creation of an Asian political, military, and economic architecture in which one power—China—dominates. But neither New Delhi nor Washington wants to involve India in an American-led, anti-Chinese coalition to prevent this from happening. India would reconsider its policy only in the event of egregious Chinese military moves against it.

HOW DOES INDIA SEE THE WORLD?

We will now shift our focus and examine India's competing global visions, foreign policy institutions, and negotiating style. The intellectual backdrop for its global visions owes much to India's foreign policy experience before 1990; the geopolitical background, and in particular the changed relationship with the United States, derives more from the experience of the post–Cold War period as reviewed in this chapter.

CHAPTER FOUR

Indian Strategic Visions

A VISION OF INDIA'S unique greatness runs through the history of its foreign policy. It is rooted in pride in India's civilization: not many countries refer to themselves as "civilizational states." It also reflects India's early experience of ruling an empire and the ethos of its independence movement. There has always been a debate about what India's international persona should be and how it should balance idealism and realism. Thinking on these themes has become increasingly complicated as the Cold War faded into history.

India's vision of its international role starts with a few concepts that are widely, almost universally shared. Most of them relate to the character of India itself. We start by describing this common core, in which one can recognize many of the themes that Nehru underlined as the heart of India's approach to the world.

Beyond this core lies the foreign policy debate. Any brief categorization of something this sophisticated and complex will be guilty of oversimplifying, but to provide a rough map of this intellectual landscape, we next look at three broad and sometimes overlapping tendencies that account for much of India's foreign policy thinking. The *Nonalignment Firsters* see India as the center of the developing world and regard its voice on behalf of the world's poor as a key instrument for exercising India's influence in the world. Of the contemporary visions, this is the one closest to the post-independence Nehruvian model. For the *Broad Power Realists*, India's relations with the major powers and its growing economy are the critical assets that can enhance India's role in global affairs. The third vision, that of the *Hard Power Hawks*, regards military strength as India's principal instrument of power, and approaches great power relationships with considerable skepticism. In sketching out each of these schools of thought, we focus especially on how they address four elements of their international vision: the international character of India; its key relationships both with world powers and within the region; military power; and the economy as a factor in India's international role.[1]

Finally, we examine how government policy draws on these three schools of thought. All three have left their imprint on policy, with the relative balance among them shifting over time. All three continue to coexist as powerful sources of Indian foreign policy.

THE COMMON CORE

The most widely shared elements of a distinctive Indian view of its position in the world are centered on an idealistic and proud vision of what kind of country India is and wants to be. At the heart of this concept is India's extraordinary civilization, with some 5,000 years of history in setting the rhythms of India's social life and with its own legacy of imperial glory. Amitava Tripathy put this idea well in a 2011 article in the *Indian Foreign Affairs Journal*: "India . . . is on the verge of reviving its golden age. Mistakes made in the past led to our fall from glory and eventual enslavement. We need to exercise eternal vigilance to ensure that the gains of the recent decades are not frittered away but consolidated and built upon."[2]

Despite India's enormous social, linguistic, and geographic diversity, and despite the importance of family, caste, and other smaller categories in individual Indians' social identity, Indian civilization is seen as one overarching cultural space. Ambassador K. S. Bajpai captured both these characteristics well: "India is perhaps the first major instance of a multicultural or civilizational state, almost a multilateral state. . . . Still, the concept of India has been a cementing force throughout history."[3] Indians recognize only a handful of other "civilizational states" in the world, China being the most prominent example.

Many point to India's contemporary success in science, space exploration, and information technology as manifestations of the genius of Indian civilization. Different foreign policy schools may emphasize different aspects of India's history and heritage. There are also significant differences in the heroes and archetypes that different foreign policy tendencies emphasize. But there is deep consensus about the unique global importance and value of India's civilization, and about the respect that is due India as a result.

A logical extension of this exceptionalism is a widely shared commitment to "strategic autonomy," the conviction that India cannot allow its foreign policy to be dictated or constrained by outsiders. We have already seen how India's founders described nonalignment as an outgrowth of India's independence movement.[4] A study, fittingly named "Nonalignment 2.0," explicitly labels it as the precursor of the strategic autonomy concept: "Strategic autonomy has been the defining value and continuous goal of India's international policy ever since the inception of the Republic. Defined initially in the terminology of Nonalignment, that value we believe continues to remain at the core of India's global engagements even today."[5] Indian government and nonofficial commentators speak readily of India's dependence on foreign suppliers of energy, such as Iran, but it is hard to find an Indian commentator who will publicly acknowledge that in an interdependent world, every country is in some degree constrained by others.

By the same logic, India's reluctance to join international norm-setting organizations has broad resonance. India has been called a "sovereignty hawk" and has shied away from international engagements, like the "responsibility to protect," that could involve intervention in response to humanitarian crises.[6] Joint action on security issues with other countries, especially major powers, are warily examined through the filter of protecting India's strategic autonomy. This is especially the case for relations with Washington, which is sometimes looked on as if the United States were India's former colonial ruler. India is sometimes reluctant to make choices, since doing so may involve future constraints on foreign policy.

Indians oppose joining alliances. When India's prime minister, Atal Bihari Vajpayee, referred to the United States and India as "natural allies," the statement raised eyebrows—but he clearly did not mean "allies" in the way that term is used in the United States, referring either to treaty allies or to countries that normally move together on the international scene. The milder term "partners" is less neuralgic in India, but still raises hackles in parts of the foreign policy elite. Lalit Mansingh, who served as foreign secretary, high commissioner to the United Kingdom and ambassador to the United States, noted in a 2012 presentation that India had "twenty or so" strategic partnerships drawn from India's "old friends" (Russia, Germany, France, Britain, Australia, Japan, Brazil, South Africa), "old adversaries" (including the United States), and others. These are nonexclusive relationships, and the degree of strategic cooperation involved varies tremendously.[7]

By the same token, press commentators covering international issues express bitter complaints about "pressure" any time a major power advocates that India adopt particular policies. One vivid example was U.S. diplomacy in Iran in 2011. In one set of messages revealed by WikiLeaks, U.S. diplomats reported to Washington on their efforts— ultimately successful—to persuade the government of India to side with the United States at the International Atomic Agency in a vote on Iran's nuclear program. The advocacy reported in these cables was the kind of thing diplomats from all countries are expected to do. When the cables were leaked, India's well-known TV commentator Karan Thapar expressed outrage over "arm-twisting."[8] India's own diplomats, of course, understand that they and their foreign counterparts all do advocacy, but this great sensitivity to perceived "arm-twisting" is part of the political environment in which they work.

There is a wide consensus that Indian foreign policy depends on the country's domestic success. This is true in most countries, but it is an important baseline for India's international vision. India's democratic system is the touchstone. All shades of political opinion and Indian officials across the board acknowledge the supremacy of parliament and, more generally, the Indian voter in setting the nation's foreign policy course. Democracy, however, is not looked on as an export product. India considers its own successful domestic institutions a strong building block in making friends with other democracies. However, there is no appetite on the Indian scene for pushing reluctant countries to democratize.

Nehru and India's early leaders stressed that the ultimate objective of India's policies—international as well as domestic—was to support the dominant goal of bringing India out of poverty.[9] Leaders since then, most recently and forcefully Narendra Modi, have made the same point. India's ambitions for a better world order do not imply any diminution of its focus on its domestic requirements.

Other aspects of the common core of India's international vision address more specifically how India operates in the world. There is a strong agreement that the subcontinent is a single strategic space.[10] There is also consensus that India has, and must retain, primacy within the South

Asian region. Different foreign policy philosophies may disagree on how best to sustain or assert this primacy. With India's greater economic success and increasing engagement with the Middle East and East Asia, there is an emerging consensus that India's security space includes the entire region from the Persian Gulf through Southeast Asia. The relative importance of these more distant areas is debated, as we will see. Concern about the security implications of a rising China is widely shared, though there is disagreement on how best to handle this issue. But no one seriously disputes the notion that India must not just be preeminent in South Asia but also must be seen in this light by countries in the region and elsewhere.

Finally, the shared core of India's international vision casts India as a long-term leader in a world order that is both more favorable to India and better attuned to the world's poor countries. Most Indians who think and write about international affairs hope for a multipolar world, with India as one of the poles. The manifestations of developing country solidarity that played such a big role in India's foreign policy through the years, notably the Non-Aligned Movement (NAM) and the Group of 77 (G-77), still have strong resonance as steps toward this ambitious vision. India's role in BRICS—a more recent group that also includes Brazil, Russia, China and South Africa—similarly has broad acceptance. It is valued as an international club that does not rest on Cold War relationships. Perhaps the most visible symbol of the status India should enjoy in this brighter future is a permanent seat on the UN Security Council. President Obama's public support for this goal during his 2010 visit to India made a tremendous hit across the Indian political spectrum.[11] We will examine in chapter 10 how India has tried to achieve this goal. Again, commentators may differ on which of these long-term goals and which aspects of India's international recognition ought to have top priority. We will explore these differences in looking at the three broad schools of foreign policy thinking. But the overall vision of India as a leader in a world whose basic architecture better suits India's needs is shared across the political landscape.

Paradoxically, this expansive vision coexists with an outlook that is fundamentally inward-looking. India's near-continental size and internal diversity contribute to this perspective, as does the legacy of two centuries of colonial rule in which India's own leaders played little international role. So too does the primacy accorded to moving India out of poverty, though not everyone sees this as a goal that requires trade-offs with an active foreign policy. One retired Indian ambassador told a

Washington audience that there was "angst" in India over whether it was ready to play a global role, adding that it would probably have to do so, ready or not.[12]

The result of these two paradoxical tendencies is considerable ambivalence about how deeply India should involve itself in global governance and how far it should go in developing international partnerships. India's appetite for making changes in international institutions is not always matched by a willingness to devote resources and personnel to the effort. There is considerable ambivalence about the appropriate role of the United Nations. On the one hand, there is near-consensus that proposals for Indian military engagement in international efforts beyond its immediate neighborhood should require a United Nations mandate. On the other hand, India has a well-developed and widely shared allergy to any United Nations role in South Asian disputes, or indeed to other international mediation efforts in its home region, most notably in Kashmir.[13] Similarly, India is very cautious about any new rule-setting bodies or mechanisms on the international scene.

THREE COMPETING VISIONS

Building on a large measure of consensus about what kind of civilization India has and what kind of country it is, one can distinguish three principal schools of thought. They differ in how they interpret India's civilizational legacy in today's global environment; in their assessment of India's relations with the world's larger powers and its own regional neighbors; in the role they assign to military power in India's international role; and in the nature and importance of India's economy in its global role. Each of the sketches here inevitably oversimplifies a complex set of views on Indian foreign policy. In practice, there are areas of overlap among the three tendencies. Many, perhaps most, serious discussions of India's foreign policy may fit broadly into one school of thought while drawing some elements from others. None of them fully describes Indian government policy; however, official policy draws on all three. These tendencies nonetheless provide a useful guide to the different visions that inspire Indians interested in foreign policy.

Nonalignment Firsters

Of the three competing visions, the group we are calling "Nonalignment Firsters" is well represented in the Congress Party and on India's political left, in important parts of the active and retired Indian foreign policy bureaucracy, and among media commentators on foreign affairs. In discussing India's character as a state and as an international actor, those in this school of thought often stress the most inclusive aspects of its ancient historical and cultural heritage, notably India's tradition of assimilating the many peoples of the subcontinent and its role as the birthplace of religions. They almost invariably place themselves in the tradition of the leaders of India's independence movement, especially Nehru. The impact of this vision on Indian policy was strongest during the years before 1990. Among recent prime ministers, Inder Kumar Gujral was the one who most often articulated this view.[14]

What really stands out, however, is how strongly this group embraces the Nehruvian notion that India would seek a different kind of power, one that comes from its moral voice espousing the international ideals of ending colonialism and seeking world peace. Nehru spoke with evident pride of the fact that India's moral voice irritated other countries, notably in the West. Gujral makes the same comment; so does retired diplomat Rajiv Sikri.[15]

The "Nonalignment 2.0" study has a discussion of the character of India that captures the heart of the vision of this group. It starts with the observation that India's success "will leave an extraordinary footprint on the world, and define future possibilities for human kind." Explaining the thought further, it goes on, "The fundamental source of India's power in the world is going to be the power of its example." Near the end, the study relates the independence struggle to an Indian mission to reshape the world: "[India's nationalist movement] was unique in its intellectual ambition. All of India's great leaders—Gandhi, Tagore, Nehru, Ambedkar—had one aspiration: that India should be a site for an alternative universality. India's legitimacy today will come from its ability to stand for the highest human and universal values."[16] A number of the arguments in the study fall outside the "nonalignment first" template, and not all these leaders are equally revered within the Nonalignment First school, but this articulation of the character of India is squarely within it.

The idea that nonalignment was not simply a refusal to join either of the two Cold War blocs is especially important to this group. Sikri argues that nonalignment was always supposed to be about "having an independent foreign policy." Gujral described the NAM not as a "camp of the neutrals" but as the "expression of the camaraderie that naturally existed between the victims of the colonizers who were politically and economically enslaved."[17]

The moral position that defined India's highest foreign policy aspirations led naturally to its quest for a "bridging" position between contending parties in the world. During the 1950s and 1960s, India frequently sought out mediating assignments. More recent examples are infrequent. One was the unsuccessful visit to Baghdad by Gujral, who was then India's foreign minister, as the first Gulf War loomed in 1990. The vision of India as bridge, or peacemaker, remains important for the Nonalignment Firsters. Sunil Khilnani extends it beyond dispute resolution into a role for India in bridging the gap between the world's powerful and powerless countries, using its power of persuasion to compensate for its relative weakness in the more usual economic and military currency and power.[18]

For the Nonalignment Firsters, India's key relationships are in the neighborhood. Sikri's book on Indian foreign policy devotes fully half of its region- or country-specific content—the first half—to India's South Asian neighbors. Within this school of thought, there is some divergence of opinion on how to deal with India's smaller neighbors. Some espouse a version of the "Gujral Doctrine," which offered these neighbors non-reciprocal benefits. Others, including Sikri, take a harder line, insisting on some degree of foreign policy conformity in exchange for close relations.[19] But all build India's foreign policy on a neighborhood base.

Iran has a special importance for this group "Civilizational ties" between Iran and India going back many centuries give it historical and evocative importance. Its poisonous relations with the United States and the long-standing U.S. effort to line up global support against Iran's nuclear program make it a symbol of India's foreign policy independence and hence important to the character of India as this group understands it.[20]

China is both a neighbor and a global power. Nonalignment Firsters are certainly conscious of the security challenges China presents for India, but they are solicitous of Sino-Indian relations and reluctant to take steps that might antagonize Beijing. They remain suspicious of the United States, despite the massive changes in relations between Washington and Delhi. They remain very warmly disposed to Russia, which they still regard as a critical relationship both because of the large Indo-Russian military supply relationship and because they see Russia as an important balancing factor in a world where the United States and China have disproportionate power.[21]

India's standing as a leader of developing countries looms especially large in this vision. While most Indians continue to regard the concept of nonalignment as a permanent feature of their foreign policy, this group extends that same loyalty to the NAM and to other international groups whose core membership includes developing countries with India featured in a leading position. BRICS has pride of place. The membership of Russia and China makes this a grouping with the potential for global action and an obvious balancer to Washington; both features are especially attractive to this group.

The Nonalignment Firsters are perhaps the most multilaterally oriented of India's foreign policy thinkers. They look on leadership in multilateral institutions, notably a permanent seat on the UN Security Council, as a key indicator of the status India should have. They also share the general conviction that India should not have to compromise to attain the great-power recognition it deserves. Part of their philosophy is rejection of a world order they consider Western-devised and Western-dominated.[22]

Nonalignment Firsters, like virtually all Indians, strongly defend their country's decision to test a nuclear weapon and object to the two-tier regime established by the Non-Proliferation Treaty. They also support military modernization, seeing it, like the nuclear program, as an extension of the country's independence. However, they do not regard India's military strength as the most important tool in its quest for power, and their discussion of India's foreign policy goals is almost always couched in terms of political instruments—building a consensus for world peace, for example—rather than in military terms. Mani Shankar Aiyar told a Washington conference that it was India's voice that would matter internationally, not any thoughts of becoming a military great power, which he characterized as a domestic "nightmare."[23]

Similarly, this group is well aware of India's tremendous economic progress in the last two decades. In their vision, this is an advantage, but is not a driver of India's future policy. Nonalignment Firsters put greater weight on solidarity with other developing countries on economic issues and in economic institutions. They are skeptical about open trade in general and about market-based solutions to resource supply. They do not want to buy into "Western solutions" to Indian or global problems.[24]

Underneath this awareness of India's economic success is a sense of economic vulnerability that appears somewhat greater than one finds in the other schools of thought and coincides with a greater concern that

India's engagement with the world economy may come at a cost to the economic advancement of its poor. The result is a vision that is much more cautious than the others when it comes to India's economic opportunities.

Broad Power Realists

A second vision of India's role in the world is a product of the transformation of India and of the world that followed the Cold War. It has profoundly influenced Indian government policy in the post–Cold War years, as we will see. Both India's transformed relationship with the United States and its economic outreach to Africa, Latin America, and the economically successful countries of East and Southeast Asia are concrete manifestations of this vision. It has numerous adherents among senior and retired public officials and considerable resonance among business leaders interested in foreign affairs. The most prominent writings that express this perspective come from C. Raja Mohan's work on India's post–Cold War foreign policy, vision, and strategic outlook and from two studies on the longer-term strategic outlook, whose authors include an economist, a retired admiral, and a retired ambassador.[25]

The thinking of the Broad Power Realists was shaped by the disappearance of the two Cold War blocs, the reduction in Russia's international role, the equally dramatic warming of U.S.-India relations, and India's own economic surge in the two decades that followed its initial economic reforms. Broad Power Realists share the perspective that India's foreign policy is an extension of its independence and must be based on maximizing India's options and its ability to operate independently. Only a handful of writings question the primacy given to strategic autonomy, often by arguing that India can best maximize its options in the long run by picking strong strategic relationships in the short term.[26]

Broad Power Realists believe India can and should aspire to global power, as defined by conventional economic, political, and military metrics. Rajiv and Santosh Kumar argue that India has a window of opportunity in which the risk of war is low and must use it to build up its strength. They discuss at some length how India measures up according to the kind of metrics favored by China.[27] Mohan, writing of the transformation in thinking wrought by the end of the Cold War, says that India has come to see itself as an "emerging great power." His assessment that India "no longer want[s] to remain in the Third World" would be sharply disputed by the Nonalignment Firsters, who find the third world a ready platform on which to exercise leadership.[28] Articulating global morality is attractive, but the Broad Power Realists do not see in it a path to a larger global role. For them, the route to greater Indian power passes through economic growth, international political engagement, and a credible military, including a nuclear weapons capability. They are not arguing for a "different kind" of power; Mohan writes of the "de-ideologization" of foreign policy.[29] Historical examples provide inspiration, including India's more successful emperors and also, paradoxically, those who shaped the strategic priorities of the British Indian Empire—priorities that have lived on in independent India.

Political analyst Radha Kumar articulates a global vision of India's strategic role: "India's rise in the first decade of this century was based on a strategic vision of India's role as a stabilizer in its neighborhood, a balancer in Asia, a reformer of global trade and monetary policies, and an actor in global peace and security."[30] Broad Power Realists generally share this vision, but look on India's ties with the big powers as its most important relationships. Great-power relations occupy four and a half of the ten chapters of Mohan's classic work on India's post–Cold War foreign policy, *Crossing the Rubicon*.

First comes the United States. The Broad Power Realists came into prominence with the end of the Cold War and the dramatic improvements in New Delhi's ties with Washington that followed. Its adherents see U.S.-India ties as the entry point for the things that will bring India the status it deserves in the changed geopolitical environment, starting with U.S. recognition of its major power status and including a larger role in global trade and investment. Rajiv and Santosh Kumar specifically cite India's strong relationship with the United States as one of its assets in developing its strength.[31]

China generally comes next. This group exhibits relatively little of the third world solidarity toward Beijing that is common among the Nonalignment Firsters; instead, Broad Power Realists are acutely conscious of the strategic challenge India faces from China. However, they also see China as a vital economic partner for India and as the country most likely to build up its global role should the United States falter. China enjoys the global power and status India would like to have. Significantly, Mohan's chapter on China in *Crossing the Rubicon* is titled "Emulating China," and he argues that India needs to try to match China's performance during the early years of its rise, in economic growth and in prudent international behavior.[32] Many foreign affairs analysts, business people, and economists echo this sense that India needs to emulate the things that have led to China's success.[33]

Russia, the great power with which India has the closest historical ties, ranks well below the United States and China. It is a major military supplier to India. It provides an international counterweight to Washington and Beijing, which Indians of all persuasions like to have available. But this group invests fewer hopes than the Nonalignment Firsters in the old ties with Russia.

Broad Power Realists share the widespread ambition for a multipolar world, with India as one of the poles. Their focus on great-power relationships is directly related to this perspective: India will need to work with today's great powers as it develops the ability to join their ranks. Mohan argues that India needs to be at least as committed to a multipolar Asia, and that the logic of Asian security relationships may in fact require India to build closer ties—he even uses the phrase "an alliance-like relationship"—with the United States. In this respect, he departs from the Broad Power Realist template or, more precisely, exposes one of its apparent internal contradictions.[34]

India's immediate South Asian neighbors are also important, but in the Broad Power Realists' perspective they do not determine India's strategic place in the world. Mohan refers to "containing Pakistan," a problem in which India's ties with the United States and China figure prominently. He also writes about reintegrating the subcontinent, primarily by reducing economic barriers within the region. Rajiv and Santosh Kumar assert that "war [with Pakistan] is not an option"—a judgment that the hawks dispute, as we will see. Menon and Rajiv Kumar stress the need for strategic patience with Pakistan.[35]

The Broad Power Realists' vision gives more space to countries beyond these two key categories than either of the competing views. Southeast Asia and the Persian Gulf have strategic weight by virtue of geography, but for Broad Power Realists, their economic ties with India are equally important. And this vision sees a vigorous Indian private business sector extending India's presence in Latin America and Africa, buttressed in the latter case by an active Indian aid program.

This group's view of India's multilateral associations is more utilitarian and less messianic than the Nonalignment Firsters. Broad Power Realists see enhanced standing in multilateral organizations as a second-order objective, which will fall into India's lap when its overall power relationships are better aligned. Radha Kumar's paper on multilateralism supports this perspective.[36] Rajiv and Santosh Kumar go so far as to argue that India should stop pursuing a permanent Security Council seat, which will come India's way when its power has strengthened.[37] India's standing as a dialogue partner to the Association of Southeast Asian Nations (ASEAN) and its membership in the East Asian Summit are seen as vehicles for pursuing its interests in East Asia. BRICS is valuable in part because it features two great powers as members, China and Russia. The large third-world organizations, like the NAM, sustain India's ability to nurture its ties with developing countries as a group, but the vocation of leader of the world's poor has less resonance for Broad Power Realists. Their vision prefers to cast India as one of the world's success stories.

Broad Power Realists are in tune with the generally skeptical Indian consensus about global governance. They are, interestingly, ambivalent about India taking on an acknowledged leadership role, at least in the short term. They recognize that leadership requires resources, and some would prefer to postpone the day when India will need to meet this cost.[38]

For Broad Power Realists, India's nuclear test was the entry ticket to the ranks of future great powers, and military modernization is a given. But what is distinctive about their vision is how heavily it depends on India's economic performance. The surge in economic growth that followed the economic reforms of 1990 demonstrated that India could and should look on its economy as a strategic asset and indeed as a prerequisite for developing other kinds of power. Both the study by Rajiv and Santosh Kumar and the assessment by Admiral Raja Menon and Rajiv Kumar see a more prosperous India as a critical strategic change. Sanjaya Baru, an economic journalist who worked as press adviser to Manmohan Singh, has written at length on this theme, analyzing the sources of economic growth, the linkages between economic success and a country's ability to build up its industry, its military strength, and even its diplomacy, and the particular importance of India's economic performance to the relationships it needs to build up in Asia.[39] He cites admiringly China's formula for assessing comprehensive national power. Neither he nor others in this school of thought have attempted to apply this same type of detailed mathematical calculation to India, although Menon and Kumar clearly have that sort of analysis in mind and they and Baru accept the logic behind it. They consider India's productive capacity the key to other forms of power.[40] They extend this logic to the international domain, and it reinforces the judgment prevalent in this group that India's key relationships are those that will also help India build its economy.

Hard Power Hawks

The third foreign policy vision differs starkly from the first two in its tone and emphasis on military strength. Hard Power Hawks are found primarily among security scholars at think tanks and among retired military and intelligence officers. Politically, their natural home is in the Bharatiya Janata Party (BJP). In office, however, BJP leaders have espoused more nuanced policies than the theoreticians advocate. Atal Bihari Vajpayee, the first BJP prime minister, had a much softer touch in relations with his neighbors than the Hard Power Hawk writings would suggest. His decision to test a nuclear weapon in 1998, however, came from this group's playbook. Narendra Modi, universally regarded as a hawk, has made important modifications in what this group's theoreticians have been propounding.

The Hard Power Hawks draw on different historical antecedents from the other two approaches described so far. Nonalignment Firsters and Broad Power Realists invoke the memory of Gandhi and Nehru, with different points of emphasis. Hard Power Hawks are more likely to invoke Sardar Vallabhbhai Patel, known to the independence generation as the "iron man" who organized the integration of over 500 princely states into India with a mixture of guile, toughness, and occasional use of military force.[41]

Hard Power Hawks are in the greatest hurry to achieve their vision of a powerful India and are the most unsparing in their judgment of India's present condition. India's foreign policy and national security officials of all stripes tend to be admirers of Kautilya, the "Indian Machiavelli." The Hard Power Hawks go further and specifically admire Kautilya's ruthlessness. Theirs is a Hobbesian view of the world.[42] They favor using power to accumulate more power and believe that this end justifies hard-edged means. They have an uncompromising view of the demands of strategic autonomy and a largely military definition of what autonomy means. The theoreticians are more willing to contemplate the use of military force than those of other foreign policy schools. They are even less interested in spreading democracy abroad than the other schools of thought. Bharat Karnad told a Washington audience that such policies had "lost Myanmar" for India.[43] Unlike the previous two groups, hawks were enthusiastic proponents of a nuclear weapons program long before India conducted its first overtly military test.

Hard Power Hawks have a utilitarian and mistrustful view of India's relations with other countries. The great powers, starting with the United States and China, are the most important ties India has. They can influence India's strategic environment and hence its future. This group regards both with great suspicion—China because it is India's principal strategic rival; the United States because it is powerful and there is no guarantee that its power will be deployed to India's advantage. These are recurring themes in Brahma Chellaney's writings. He writes disparagingly of the unfulfilled promises of the nuclear deal with the United States, for example: "Gone is the pretense of Washington extending India 'full' nuclear cooperation or granting it 'the same benefits and advantages as other leading countries with advanced nuclear technology, such as the U.S.,' as the 2005 deal stated."[44] He writes with foreboding about China's determination to dominate the Indian Ocean.[45]

Insofar as the hawks admire other countries' leaders, they tend to favor leaders with a hard-headed approach like their own—Republicans rather than Democrats in U.S. politics, for example.[46] Russia is less important to them. Hard Power Hawks were the first to argue that India should develop strategic ties with Japan and Israel, based on what they perceive to be those countries' similar interests in Asian security. But, true to their Kautilyan heritage, they regard no external relationship as sacred. India should cultivate those that can be useful, but should have no illusions that other countries will act to defend India's interests.

Hard Power Hawks take a tough position toward India's South Asian neighbors, especially Pakistan. In a memorable blog, the late B. Raman, longtime senior intelligence official and hawkish commentator on strategic issues, wrote of Pakistan: "A divided Pakistan, a bleeding Pakistan, a Pakistan ever on the verge of collapse without actually collapsing—that should be our objective till it stops using terrorism against India."[47] Brinksmanship is characteristic of the writings of this group, which frequently offer quite creative ways of squeezing Pakistan just short of the point of collapse. Hard Power Hawks' confidence that India can and should emerge as a major military power is matched by their certainty that they can judge precisely how far to push without triggering a nuclear response. Bharat Karnad's *India's Nuclear Policy* argues that Pakistan would not be able to escalate to nuclear war because of a "disparity in the ability to bear pain" between India and Pakistan—in other words, because a nuclear attack by Pakistan would be suicidal.[48] Hard Power Hawks do not consider Pakistan a strategic threat: rather, it is a smaller neighbor that India should feel free to push around in pursuit of its own interests and especially in pursuit of regional primacy.

This group has relatively little interest in more symbolic indicators of India's global standing. A seat on the UN Security Council, an enhanced quota in the International Monetary Fund—these and similar accomplishments are ego trips, but for Hard Power Hawks they have little real value in enhancing India's power. On the other hand, this group is quite prepared to use the tools of symbolism and protocol to make a statement about India's importance. Karnad, for example, blasted the leader of the BJP, for "pleading" with the United States to grant a visa to the party's standard-bearer, Gujarat Chief Minister Narendra Modi, whose visa was publicly revoked following the killing of Muslims in his state. Karnad argued that Modi, if elected prime minister, should refuse to visit the United States except for the required annual appearance at the United Nations.[49] Modi, once in office, did not follow this script.

Hard Power Hawks are certainly conscious of the impact of India's economic performance on its power profile, but for the theoreticians of this view, the driver that really matters is military strength married to a diplomacy that shows it off to best advantage. They argue that a strong military is the only language China respects.[50] They favor large military budgets and are bitterly critical of the gap between plans and performance in India's military acquisitions and planning. They advocate an unconstrained nuclear program whose size should reflect the capabilities of India's strategic adversaries, notably China. Basing military posture on more elusive judgments of intentions is, in their view, a recipe for keeping India down.

WHAT VISION GUIDES THE GOVERNMENT'S POLICIES?

Once in office, India's leaders have adapted their views to the current needs of national policy. During the first four decades of independence, India's foreign policy followed the broad patterns that Nehru developed and was most heavily influenced by the vision we refer to here as Nonalignment First. Policy speeches and other major statements fit squarely within that tradition. The Nonalignment First view of India's character also found expression in the way India articulated its policies. This was the period when India actively sought out a role in addressing such conflicts as the Korean prisoner exchange and the operation of Laotian neutrality. The relationships that were most important to India were centered on its home region, the developing world, and the Soviet Union. India saw itself as a country whose moral voice was its steadiest instrument of power and regarded its economy as a weakness, not an asset.

During this time, India's actions often, as we have seen, had a decidedly realist character. This occurred most frequently when India's primacy in its immediate region was at stake. Examples include a military intervention to bring about the independence of Bangladesh in 1971 and the dispatch of the Indian Peace Keeping Force to Sri Lanka in 1987. On those occasions, India acted in defense of its security and well within the realist policies Nehru used in the neighborhood. Similarly, India pulled its moral punches when it decided not to criticize Soviet policy in Hungary (1956) or Afghanistan (1979) and when it avoided faulting other developing countries involved in international controversies. These policies rarely became the subject of the soaring oratory about creating a new form of power or a better world, for which India was famous. Policy in practice may have been realist, but the power of the pen stayed within the idealistic tradition of the Nonalignment Firsters.

The Indian National Congress was in power for almost this entire period. This vision fits naturally into the Congress Party perspective. The memory of Gandhi and Nehru, whose voices echo through India's foreign as well as domestic policy during these years, is central to the Congress tradition.

AS NOTED PREVIOUSLY, the "Broad Power Realist" vision grew out of the changes in the world and in India that took place with the end of the Cold War. It is not surprising that the dominant vision behind India's foreign policy from the 1990s until the 2014 election moved much closer to this perspective. India's circumstances had changed and there was much more rapid economic growth in those years. India's politics had also changed. Coalition governments became the norm. Some of the governments of this period were headed by Congress, others by their major domestic opponents, the BJP, and more rarely by a "third front." These party differences had less impact on foreign policy than one might have expected.

The area where the vision changed least after the Cold War was the reigning view of the character of India. It is hard to overstate the impact on Indian foreign policymakers of Nehru the man and his articulation of what India is and what kind of world it seeks. Those who served in government in his day still treat Nehru's stewardship of India's foreign affairs with reverence. The Indian Foreign Service remains proud of its Nehruvian heritage. Nonalignment is part of this inheritance, especially in its emerging reinterpretation as synonymous with strategic autonomy. Both Indian and foreign observers have noted that India's is primarily an oral culture. Policy as declared or formally articulated is only part of the real policy that one can observe in practice. But the declaratory part of India's policy toolkit has remained largely Nehruvian, even during times when the BJP or a third force ran the government. In one symbol of the BJP's adoption of a tradition long considered foreign to this Hindu nationalist party, during a visit to Washington in September 2000, Prime Minister Atal Bihari Vajpayee dedicated a statue of Mahatma Gandhi that had been erected in front of the Indian embassy.

When it comes to thinking about which international relationships matter most for India, however, the foreign policy vision for the first twenty-five years after the Cold War was in line with that of the Broad Power Realists. The change in relations with the United States after the Cold War was put in place by governments from both major political parties. The diminished importance of Russia was the product of global events far beyond India's control. China's standing as India's major strategic challenge, born in the 1962 war, was intensified by China's post–Cold War emergence as a major power. India began to seek actively a permanent seat on the UN Security Council during these years, but this effort did not produce a major mobilization of India's leadership.

After the Cold War, India's national security managers came to see India not just as a country leveraging its eloquence and moral high ground in the international arena, but as a country with a legitimate claim on more conventional forms of power. They became less eager to volunteer to mediate the world's conflicts, however. Post–Cold War policymakers were more wary of throwing Indian resources at a problem that is not inherently India's. They remained as quick as ever to discourage others from mediating in India's neighborhood.

Another major change in the Indian government's post–Cold War foreign policy vision came from the dramatic increase in India's economic growth since 1990 and the correspondingly greater role of economic issues in India's expectations for its own future. Here, too, Indian government policy has largely followed the vision of the Broad Power Realists. This was apparent even before Manmohan Singh, with a doctorate in economics and a background as an economic technocrat, became prime minister in 2004. But Singh's speech to a meeting of Indian ambassadors in November 2013 took this economic emphasis one step further than his predecessors. Of the basic principles he enunciated—"Manmohan's own *Panchsheel*" or "five principles," in the words of one commentator—four addressed India's economic ambitions for itself and the world.[51] In practice, the Indian government walks a fine line regarding its ambition to use economic success as a springboard for greater global influence. Its long-term vision is of an economically rising India, making global policy on equal terms with the world's most prosperous countries and participating through its world-class industries and companies in the success of the global economy. India is ready to join the ranks of aid donors in pursuit of this vision. But in the short term, the government wants to make sure India takes full advantage of whatever benefits its developing country status might afford in navigating global trade rules, and it is determined to avoid externally imposed global norms that might be economically costly, such as carbon emissions constraints.

In the military arena, too, the vision that underpinned government policy during the twenty-five years after the Cold War appears to be close to that of the Broad Power Realists, pursuing a serious upgrade in India's military capacity but not expecting military strength to be India's primary pathway to greater power. India's explicitly weapons-related nuclear tests in 1998 were carried out by a BJP government, but support for the decision to go nuclear spanned the political spectrum. India's nuclear vision embraces some Nehruvian elements: the government, for example, continues to support the nuclear disarmament proposal Rajiv Gandhi put forward in 1988. But the government's declaratory policies on India's strategic autonomy, as manifested during the long negotiations with the United States on the civil nuclear agreement, took the uncompromising stance that is more typically associated with the Hard Power Hawks. In fact, India has shown considerable restraint in responding to military provocations, avoiding the kind of brinksmanship that Hard Power Hawks have written about but rarely had the opportunity to consider in practice.

IN THE FIRST two decades following the end of the Cold War, when governments of different political parties have succeeded one another, they have followed broadly similar policies and a common vision to a remarkable degree. In describing their policy differences with their Congress Party counterparts, BJP personalities have focused chiefly on relations with Pakistan and other immediate neighbors, where the BJP tended to take a more assertive line. But they acknowledged that these differences were clearer when the BJP was out of power, since, as one senior party leader put it, "oppositions oppose reflexively."[52] BJP statements and writings also put greater weight on India's cultural identity, including a culturally determined definition of who really deserves to be called Indian.[53]

The election in May 2014 of the BJP's Narendra Modi as prime minister, with a decisive single-party majority in the lower house of parliament (in contrast to the governments that had ruled for over two decades), may turn out to be the beginning of a new period in India's global vision. Modi has long been considered the leading hawk among India's politicians. His only major foreign policy campaign speech, in October 2013, stressed three themes. The first was cultural nationalism of a sort more prevalent on the Hard Power right than elsewhere. His reference to the world as one family—*Vasudhaivam kutumbakam*—we wrote about in chapter 1. He has continued, in office, to find Sanskrit and Hindi aphorisms for many of his major campaigns, thus linking all his policy actions— foreign and domestic—back to the country's cultural ideals. The second major theme in his speech was the balance between *shakti* and *shanti* (power and peace). He cited the first BJP prime minister, Atal Bihari Vajpayee, as his role model and praised both Vajpayee's decision to test a nuclear weapon and his efforts to avoid war with Pakistan. Hard Power Hawks would recognize and admire the toughness; the praise for flexibility and peace deviated from their standard script.

The third theme sets Modi apart from the Hard Power Hawk theoreticians: the centrality of economics for India's strategy and power. Modi certainly has not downplayed the importance of a strong military. Both before and since his election he has attached great importance to streamlining and reequipping the Indian armed forces. But economic strength is the critical ingredient, the factor that will enable India both to escape poverty and to play the role it deserves in the world.

In his first year as prime minister, Modi pursued a foreign policy blitz. In his energetic outreach to India's South Asian neighbors, he has, as expected, stressed India's primacy in the region. His policies have relied on Indian power, but in dealing with the smaller neighbors other than Pakistan, he has made greater use of economic incentives than his reputation, or the standard Hard Power Hawk script, would have suggested. He has also reached out to the global powers, including specifically China, Japan, the United States, and Russia. The emphasis has been on economic projects more than on abstract policies: building up India's own manu-facturing capacity, bringing in capital for both manufacturing and infrastructure, recruiting partners for his "smart cities" scheme. He has had three summit-level meetings with President Obama, including invit-ing the president to be guest of honor at India's Republic Day. Obama extended a hand early to Modi; Modi has evidently decided to work with the United States in pursuit of his goals, in spite of the nine-year U.S. visa denial he suffered.

Multilateral goals have been less important. The nastiest dispute be-tween India and the United States during Modi's initial six months was triggered by India's decision to back away from an agreement the previ-ous government had reached in the World Trade Organization (the episode is discussed in chapter 10). This suggests that in Modi's vision, strategic autonomy and willingness to break crockery in defense of Indian interests has greater weight than a harmonious rise or the man-agement of multilateral institutions. It is too early to pass definitive judgment, but at this writing, Modi appears to have shifted the center of gravity in the Hard Power Hawk vision.

DO THESE VISIONS HAVE STAYING POWER?

India's foreign policy establishment consists overwhelmingly of people over the age of sixty—the age at which officials must retire from govern-ment service. Conversations with two groups of younger foreign policy scholars suggest that the way these younger observers think about India's role in the world is not dramatically different from their parents' genera-tion. The younger scholars seemed to lean toward the Broad Power Re-alist perspective. They were generally cautious, acutely aware of India's strategic challenge from China, focused on the importance of East Asia, and convinced that the economy would have the primary impact on India's rise. In one arresting comment, a young academic speculated that India's foreign policy was likely to draw closer to the policy of the British imperial authorities, reflecting geographic more than philosophical imperatives.[54]

The Indian government does not have an official strategy. The culture of the Indian Foreign Service (like many of its counterparts, including the U.S. Foreign Service) is passed on through mentorship, and those les-sons may endure for several professional generations. This accounts both for the extraordinary staying power of the giants who created inde-pendent India's foreign policy and for the salience now enjoyed by some ideas that would have been unimaginable to India's founders.[55]

The policymakers most admired within the Indian foreign policy establishment are all Kautilyan rather than Ashokan in style: they are disciples of the iconic realist in India's ancient history, rather than followers of the emperor best known for his tolerance. J. N. Dixit's book *Makers of India's Foreign Policy* illustrates this point. Dixit was a legend in his own time: he was foreign secretary, high commissioner in Sri Lanka at the time of India's decision to send troops to try to enforce a cease-fire in the civil war there; he was also high commissioner in Pakistan and later became national security adviser to the prime minister. Nearly all the foreign secretaries, foreign ministers, and prime ministers he profiles in his book were prepared to play Kautilya-style hardball—as indeed he himself was.[56]

In all the visions described here, India presents itself as a revisionist power. Despite a number of unsettled border problems, this does not mean that India primarily seeks territorial changes. Rather, India seeks to revise a world order that gives primacy in its international institutions to a handful of powers, most of them European or American, and it aims to take its place among those who are acknowledged to run the world. Even the Hard Power Hawks, who present the most assertive face to the world, seek expanded military strength and power projection capacity primarily for "active defense" purposes. They seek not to conquer new territory but to prevent others from limiting India's strategic autonomy or encroaching on its regional primacy.

CHAPTER FIVE

Foreign Policy Institutions

THE IMPOSING RED SANDSTONE government buildings built by the British Raj at the heart of imperial New Delhi were intended as symbols of a strong and enduring state. Independent India makes good use of these still magnificent structures. It is there that the major institutions at the heart of the Indian foreign policymaking process are lodged: the Prime Minister's Office, the External Affairs and Defense ministries, and the two houses of parliament. In this chapter we look at the roles these key organizations and others within the government and outside it play as they seek to devise India's approach to the world almost a century after those impressive buildings were erected.[1]

The most prominent and most identifiable of the government institutions involved in foreign policymaking is the Ministry of External Affairs (MEA). Although MEA faces increasing competition from other ministries such as Defense and Commerce, it is the lead organization in most important international negotiations other than those involving trade and military procurement and would ordinarily be represented in these negotiations as well. MEA and the professional diplomats of the Indian Foreign Service (IFS) who staff it at home and abroad are responsible for formulating, implementing, and interpreting policy under the general supervision of the prime minister. They prepare the initial draft of most major policy documents and are responsible for India's day-to-day relations with foreign governments both in New Delhi and abroad. With the possible exception of the foreign intelligence organization—the Research and Analysis Wing (R&AW)—the IFS is India's only government body whose officials spend their entire careers dealing with international matters.

In India's Cabinet system, all policy papers requiring Cabinet approval are prepared as "Cabinet Notes." Those Notes on matters involving foreign policy must incorporate MEA's views. Many foreign policy decisions are now taken through an inter-ministerial process in which all affected ministries weigh in. This too ensures that MEA has a voice in such decisions even when the immediate issue under consideration lies within the ambit of another ministry.

The minister who heads MEA is customarily a senior political figure, one of four recognized as key members of the prime minister's cabinet.[2] During the first seventeen years of Indian independence, Prime Minister Jawaharlal Nehru himself served as minister of external affairs. His successors have ordinarily given long-term responsibility for the direction of MEA to one of their senior cabinet colleagues.[3] Over the years, these ministers have varied markedly in skill and relevance. Their importance depends on the prime minister's confidence in their foreign policymaking skills and, often even more, their political power and loyalty. But some politicians who have packed a powerful wallop as state chief ministers and in other important government or political party positions could not master the external affairs portfolio and played no more than a decorative role in MEA's South Block headquarters.

Prime ministers themselves become involved in major foreign policy matters, both directly and through the operation of the Prime Minister's Office (PMO).[4] Other than the PM himself, the key foreign affairs player in this increasingly powerful organization is the National Security Adviser (NSA). The NSA's immediate access to the prime minister affords him influence that other parts of the government recognize, envy, and accept. But other senior officials in the PMO can also become significantly involved in foreign policy formulation depending on the prime minister's assessment of their usefulness.

Aside from the Defense and Commerce ministries, the Department of Atomic Energy (DAE) and the Ministry of Food and Agriculture also play significant roles in foreign policy. They can be important in international negotiations on issues relevant to their responsibilities. DAE officials were deeply involved in the negotiations leading to and implementing the 2008 U.S.-India Civil Nuclear Agreement, to cite one well-publicized example. More recently, other ministries such as Environment, Space, Health, and Human Resource Development have begun to take part in

India's growing foreign assistance programs. Other than ministerial-level positions, most substantive slots in these organizations are staffed by officers of the elite Indian Administrative Service (IAS). In the Ministry of Defense, the uniformed Indian military have some limited role in policymaking but are overshadowed by civilian IAS bureaucrats.

The bicameral parliament's meaningful interventions in foreign affairs are episodic, and those of its members who are not government ministers have a more limited role in influencing policy than U.S. legislators do. But India's parliament has the ultimate power to vote governments out of office, and on at least one occasion in recent years it came close to doing so over a controversial foreign policy issue. Although the Indian constitution assigns responsibility for the conduct of foreign affairs to the central government, state governments and legislatures play roles—or try to—on international issues they consider relevant to the voters of their states. Their interventions are often supported by members of parliament (MPs) from these states.

The media, academic think tanks, and the business community also energetically seek to influence India's ongoing national debate on the direction its foreign policy should take. Their influence has varied over time and depends crucially on their relationship with the national government of the day. Think tanks—many of them significantly staffed by retired foreign and security policy practitioners—have become increasingly numerous, prominent, and outspoken in recent years.

THE INDIAN FOREIGN SERVICE

The prestigious IFS has long ranked high among the professional diplomatic organizations of nations with major foreign policy interests. A small, tightly knit, rank-conscious group, it staffs all policymaking positions in MEA except those held by elected officials: the minister and one or two subcabinet-level junior ministers. IFS officers head all but a handful of Indian diplomatic posts abroad. Aside from a few slots occupied by politically appointed chiefs of mission and representatives of economic ministries and intelligence agencies, all civilian officer-level jobs in these posts are IFS preserves.[5]

The IFS traces its history to the imperial-era Foreign and Political Department, a powerful organization comprising outstanding civilian and military officers that handled the Raj's relations both with neighboring countries and with the many indirectly ruled princely states within India itself. Most of the civilians in the Foreign and Political Department were members of the elite Indian Civil Service (ICS), a prestigious organization that staffed almost all of the Raj's major executive positions and was the forerunner of independent India's much larger IAS. In the decades leading to independence, Indians played an increasingly prominent role in both the Foreign and Political Department and the ICS, though top positions remained the preserve of British officials.

Unlike some of his colleagues in the freedom movement, Prime Minister Nehru considered Indian ICS officers who had served in the Foreign and Political Department and elsewhere in the Raj's senior bureaucratic ranks a valuable asset for independent India, despite their work for the British. The experience and skill of these early recruits gave Indian diplomacy an important head start that most countries emerging from colonial rule could only envy.

Nehru himself always took a special interest in the IFS, and in his combined role of prime minister and minister of external affairs involved himself deeply in its operations. A legendary figure in his own time, Nehru interviewed IFS candidates and spoke at the induction ceremonies of the successful ones. Retired IFS officers still speak with reverence about the sense the prime minister gave them of being direct participants with him in creating India's foreign policy. This early role gave the IFS an elite, privileged position that seemed (not least to its own members) to place it on a more exalted plane than other government services.

The IFS successors to these early diplomats are recruited by a highly selective process.[6] Candidates for the Foreign Service and several domestic central services, including most importantly the prestigious IAS, take a combined examination administered by the Union Public Service Commission. The examination is designed to minimize the possibility of favoritism. Only in a final brief oral examination session do examiners become aware of the identity of the candidates they are judging. This arrangement has helped ensure that the ranks of new entrants are less dominated by recruits from certain parts of the country or certain castes than might otherwise be the case (and that serving officers do not simply replicate themselves as Indian society changes).

Only a miniscule proportion of the many candidates who take the annual examination are appointed. These winners indicate which service they wish to join. Top scorers get their first choice. Until recently the IFS had the pick of the litter and could fill its small quota from successful candidates who chose the Foreign Service over other options. But this has changed, and some candidates who made the IFS their second choice have been selected in recent years. The seemingly diminished stature of the IFS may stem from the greater opportunities in private enterprise, whereas in the years before India's economic boom more candidates would have looked to diplomacy as their preferred career. Some cynical critics charge that the greater opportunities for personal financial gain (i.e., graft) in other ministries have made the IFS less attractive.

The number recruited annually for the Foreign Service is in any event very small. Until recently it has been below twenty. The Indian government's decision in 2008 to expand the service has led to an increase in recruitment, but even so, only thirty-five new officers were reportedly chosen in 2013.[7] These figures reflect the traditionally small size of the IFS. In early 2014, it numbered only around 900, of whom some two-thirds were assigned to the more than 180 posts India maintains abroad. The expansion of the service now under way is planned to be completed in 2018 and, by design, will raise the number of IFS officers to around 1,300.[8] But even if the IFS eventually attains its target, this number is unlikely to satisfy India's need for diplomats as the country seeks to expand its foreign affairs reach to reflect its status as an emerging global power with growing interest in a widening range of diplomatic activities and parts of the world largely ignored earlier.

Comparing India with its partner countries in BRICS, IFS officers complain that they have to do the same work as four of their Brazilian or seven of their Chinese counterparts. The senior leadership of the IFS and at least some politicians recognize the need for a substantially expanded service beyond the numbers provided for in the 2008–18 expansion plan, which in any event cannot be achieved with current recruitment levels. But, as in other countries, greater funding for Indian diplomatic activity faces competing demands at a time of budgetary stringency.[9]

Not all IFS officers favor a major expansion. Some of their resistance seems to stem from concern that such growth would end the comfortable arrangement in which all IFS officers can expect to become ambassadors, many of them multiple times. Many familiar with the IFS system would agree with retired Indian ambassador Kishan Rana's comment that "the only obstacle to promotion is outstanding incompetence."[10]

These opportunities contrast with the "up or out" policy the United States uses. In the American Foreign Service only a very small percentage of entry-level officers eventually get to head their own embassies. The much brighter prospects in the IFS for eventual ambassadorial appointment, following virtually automatic promotions on the way there, no doubt contribute to the service's tiny resignation rate. IFS officers only recalled about two of their colleagues resigning from the service in the last twenty-odd years.[11] The number of resignations by U.S. Foreign Service officers is proportionately far greater.

In such a thinly staffed service, IFS officers must take on heavy responsibilities when they are still fairly junior and often receive only limited guidance from their busy superiors as they make their way up the career ladder. This practice can make for a more nimble operation, but it also means that the officers, especially those assigned to headquarters, have little time to fully familiarize themselves with complicated subjects not at the top of their priority list or to interact with others doing related work within the government and in the academic, media, and think-tank worlds outside South Block. On the plus side, limited guidance from superiors and less competition from other offices can provide a greater sense of personal and professional satisfaction. Among other attractions, it means that the problem of obtaining the clearance of offices around the ministry—that bane of diplomats posted to headquarters in many other countries' foreign services, not least America's—is less onerous, time-consuming, and frustrating.

IFS officers become remarkably familiar with the career standing and personal histories of their colleagues in their small service. An Indian diplomat can always tell you in which annual "batch" a colleague was recruited and probably also what his or her present job is. When there was a change in foreign secretaries early in 2015, official handouts stated that S. Jaishankar (1977 batch) had replaced Sujata Singh (1976 batch). It is a cozy arrangement, and like similar setups in other organizations, it combines a measure of collegial loyalty and high esprit de corps with sometimes-nasty personal and professional rivalry and backbiting.

Competition among top-ranking IFS officers is particularly keen for the job of foreign secretary, the senior-most position to which they can aspire. The foreign secretary is responsible for the overall management of the IFS and its personnel. He or she[12] also customarily supervises relations with countries most important for India—including the United States, China, and Pakistan—and accompanies the prime minister on official visits abroad. Rivalry for other top jobs at home and abroad—and the bureaucratic angling that accompanies it—is similarly keen, but probably no more so than in other major foreign services. With few exceptions, retired IFS officers seem to look back at their diplomatic careers with considerable satisfaction.

IFS officers are well trained. Immediately after they join the service, they are sent to a special facility in the Himalayan foothills for a three-month "foundation course" that they take along with newly recruited officers of the IAS and other senior domestic government organizations. They then study for a year at the Foreign Service Institute in New Delhi. This course includes both class work and travel within India and to neighboring countries. Training in major foreign languages is given at the new recruit's first post abroad following graduation from the institute. Probably the most valuable of the language training courses is the two-year one in Chinese that selected IFS officers take in Beijing. This course and the assignments that follow have helped produce one of international diplomacy's most effective cadres of China specialists, a number of whom have risen to top rank in the service.[13]

The IFS is an integrated organization and its officers are expected to handle a variety of traditional diplomatic responsibilities such as political and economic reporting and analysis, commercial operations, and consular functions. Expertise in China is one of only two specialized "tracks" in the IFS. The other is disarmament, an issue in which India has always taken a major interest.

Most officers move among many posts in different regions, though capability in a language such as Russian or Arabic may lead to more frequent postings to countries where these skills are useful. But the IFS has never developed a cadre of officers who can plausibly claim special expertise in interpreting the complicated ways of the United States. Under MEA's normal assignment rules, officers may have a combined total of no more than two postings at India's embassy in Washington and its five consulates general elsewhere in the country.[14] This absence of officers who have had deep and lengthy experience at American posts apparently has not troubled the IFS leadership. As one former Indian ambassador to the United States put it to us, "New Delhi believes that anyone who knows English can understand America."[15] Despite this official position, a few senior officers including Foreign Secretary S. Jaishankar, a recent ambassador to the United States, have developed American expertise by serving in jobs in South Block that deal with the United States in addition to their Washington assignments.

The structure of the ministry has shifted to reflect the increasing prominence of multilateral diplomacy. There are now seven multilateral divisions, up from three about ten years ago. In the same time frame, the number of divisions focusing on economic issues has expanded from one to five, including three devoted to the Development Partnership Administration, India's foreign aid program, and one to energy security. During the same period, only two new geographic divisions have been created. As we will see in greater detail in chapter 10, the IFS has long prized multilateral assignments, especially those involving negotiations.[16]

Unlike their American counterparts, IFS officers are not divided into specialized career paths such as political, economic/commercial, and public diplomacy work. The ministry has sought authorization to expand its economic staff, but significant increases in the size of the IFS have been difficult to implement because of regulations that basically freeze the size of one government service in relation to the others. In the course of their careers, IFS officers will typically be given a variety of assignments, sometimes including postings to other government departments with foreign policy interests. These assignments are not sought after and are sometimes stoutly resisted or even refused. There is also a new and growing flow into MEA as IAS officers and other specialists in such fields as commercial work, disarmament, and management of India's foreign assistance program are seconded to jobs in the ministry's headquarters and posts abroad. (They do not become IFS officers.) MEA has also begun to take in a few military officers, also on secondment.

Reflecting the increasing importance of state governments in seeking foreign funding and expertise for industrial development, which the Modi government strongly supports, MEA has begun opening branch secretariats in state capitals. There is also a proposal to send IFS officers on secondment to state governments. How well IFS officers will react to such out-of-Delhi assignments remains to be seen.

Among the skills that outside observers and other countries' diplomatic practitioners single out the most in discussing the conduct of Indian diplomacy is the formidable talent IFS officers bring to the negotiating table. They are highly regarded for their tireless and ingenious effort to develop their briefs, their mastery of relevant precedents, their sophisticated knowledge of the English language, and their success in understanding their opponents' strengths and weaknesses. But they also have the reputation of saying "no" more often than their negotiating partners appreciate and can be sticklers in the drafting process. The high importance that they attach to rank and other aspects of diplomatic protocol can annoy their foreign interlocutors—and other Indians, too. We will have more to say about India's approach to negotiations in subsequent chapters.

THE NATIONAL SECURITY ADVISER

Reporting directly to the very top as a member of the Prime Minister's Office, the NSA is a key figure in India's national security management structure. This structure has for years been the target of strong criticism and calls for reform by commentators of various professional backgrounds and political persuasions who argue that it has become moribund. These critics call attention to how badly the different parts of the structure function and how ineffectively they interplay with one another.[17] But there seems general agreement that the NSA position or something like it is required. Unless, as seems very unlikely, a prime minister comes to power who wants to eliminate or radically change the role of the NSA, the adviser will continue to be a key player in Indian foreign policy.

The NSA's responsibilities and physical proximity to the prime minister in the South Block secretariat cement his[18] leading role in formulating Indian foreign and security policy, ensuring that it is properly implemented, and coordinating the policy input of the main bodies in the National Security Council (NSC) structure. Since the position was established in 1998, the NSA job has been held by outstanding senior officials well recognized by political leaders, other top administrators, and the informed public for their impressive careers and bureaucratic knowledge and skill. Three of the five incumbents have been retired IFS officers; two of them were former foreign secretaries.[19] The other two, including Modi's NSA Ajit Doval, came to the position from intelligence/police backgrounds.

Some national security advisers have overshadowed incumbent foreign secretaries and even foreign ministers. They are awarded the rank of minister of state, a prestigious subcabinet position senior to the foreign secretary. Although all of them came to the NSA office with career backgrounds in the nonpartisan bureaucracy, their time as the prime minister's closest adviser on foreign and security affairs has given them something of a partisan political coloration if not a party affiliation.[20]

The NSA's role in India is roughly analogous to that of his U.S. counterpart, though his staff, numbering only fifty-six people in 2014, is very much smaller.[21] He coordinates the functioning of a complicated bureaucratic structure.

The top tier of this structure is the NSC, a body of senior cabinet ministers concerned with security issues that the prime minister chairs. Subordinate bodies in the NSC structure comprise the Strategic Policy Group (SPG), the National Security Advisory Board, and the Joint Intelligence Committee. The SPG's members include the chiefs of the three military services and the secretaries of ministries, departments, and intelligence services that have an interest in national security. It considers strategic and military issues and helps the NSC devise strategic doctrines and development plans. The National Security Advisory Board is made up of eminent people from outside the government, often retired senior officials, with expertise in security matters broadly defined. NSAB undertakes long-term analyses and provides policy recommendations on specific issues as requested by the NSC. The Joint Intelligence Committee, which prepares long- and short-term intelligence estimates and perspectives, comprises senior representatives of intelligence agencies and the Defense, Home, and External Affairs ministries. The NSA's secretariat is staffed by officers drawn from the IFS and other civil and military government organizations.

The national security adviser and his office spend much of their time dealing with major foreign policy issues involving countries most crucial for India, such as China, the United States, and Pakistan. When the prime minister goes abroad, the NSA often advances his trip and will ordinarily accompany him. Such travel, and the proximity to the PM it has afforded, further enhance the NSA's influence—provided, of course, that his activities are successful. Shivshankar Menon's high standing as NSA suffered, for example, when Prime Minister Singh's 2011 visit to Bangladesh did not meet expectations. The NSA also travels on his own to conduct discussions and negotiations, often with heads of governments. These trips can receive considerable press play.

At home, Menon, who rose directly from foreign secretary to national security adviser in 2010, was said to have played an important role in the assignments of IFS officers to major ambassadorial positions and key jobs in South Block, an extension of the role he had played as foreign secretary. Ajit Doval, who does not share Menon's Foreign Service background, has pursued different priorities that reflect his experience in intelligence and police operations. But like his predecessors he will focus on those issues the prime minister wishes him to.

Menon offered his views on the evolution of the NSA operation and its future at a meeting at the Brookings Institution in Washington a few months after he left office. "Each NSA," he said in answer to a question we put to him, "has done the job his own way and I'm not sure that we've quite accumulated enough experience to actually say it's been institutionalized." The NSA function was needed, he contended, "to coordinate, consolidate, and bring together what otherwise falls through the cracks between ministries or involves several ministries. . . . World national security issues have become so complex and multifaceted that you need a function like that."

In Menon's view, "the job will stay, it will grow a little, it will define itself over time. . . . It's going to change as government in India itself evolves. . . . So far, it's been the individuals who define the job, but pretty soon . . . the job will start defining the individuals."[22]

THE INDIAN ADMINISTRATIVE SERVICE

Established when India was on the brink of independence, the IAS is the direct heir of the imperial Indian Civil Service (ICS). It provides, as the ICS did under very different circumstances, the "steel frame" of the Government of India. Its officers dominate the Indian civil administration. It is considerably larger than the ICS was in its heyday, but it still numbers only some 4,800 officers, roughly one for every 250,000 Indians.[23]

Competition to enter the prestigious IAS has always been fierce, though with the expansion of well-paying opportunities in the private sector some of those who might have earlier sought entry now look elsewhere. Even so, in a country where nepotism pervades competition for positions in private enterprise, government service is still seen as one of the few channels that offer upward mobility on the basis of merit. Almost 400,000 candidates sought to join in 2012–13.[24] After an extraordinarily rigorous screening process, only about 150 were eventually taken.[25] Once accepted, the fortunate few enjoy tenure; the vast majority of them remain in the service until they retire.

IAS officers are carefully trained. As noted, they share with new IFS recruits an initial three-month course at the National Academy of Administration in the Himalayan foothills, sometimes establishing long and professionally useful friendships with them. After one year at the academy, where they study public administration, law, economics, history, geography, and one Indian language other than their mother tongue, they are sent for a year's on-the-job training to the states to which they have been assigned. They remain in these state "cadres" for the rest of their careers. About half of the new entrants are assigned to the cadres of states other than their own. This is seen as a way to encourage a national spirit and to limit the personal complications that serving in their home areas could raise. In the course of their careers they develop a powerful esprit de corps.

IAS officers usually spend their first four or five years as civil administrators with relatively heavy responsibilities in outlying areas before they move to jobs in the capitals of their cadre states. From there they can apply for deputation to the central Indian government. Assignment to New Delhi is much sought after. It is a required step to advance to top IAS echelons, and aspiring officers recognize that it is there that power and the use of it to shape major policy is concentrated. Only naturally, there is a high degree of competition for "empanelment"—promotion to the senior IAS rank of joint secretary, normally after eighteen years of service.

Rotation at both the state and national levels and between them is frequent. Tours of duty can vary from as little as one year on the job to three or four. Ambitious IAS officers seek positions in the more important and influential ministries. In New Delhi, these positions include some that play foreign policymaking roles, such as in defense, finance, and commerce. As noted, in recent years a few IAS officers have been seconded to MEA.[26] Although many IAS officers attain some degree of specialization—and officers who have done so appear to advance more quickly than others—most remain generalists, moving every few years from one ministry to another that deals with a very different set of issues.[27] So a senior official who until recently dealt with food and agriculture may find himself playing a key role in determining what fighter planes the Indian Air Force should acquire.

Officers at the very top of the IAS pyramid may preside over a succession of important ministries, with the title of secretary to government. An outstanding recent example is Naresh Chandra, an IAS officer of the Rajasthan cadre who served in the central government as secretary of water resources, defense, and home, as well as in the very senior position of cabinet secretary. He also served as chief secretary of Rajasthan. After retiring from the IAS, he was made governor of the state of Gujarat. (The governor is an appointed official, with a limited role roughly analogous at the state level to that of the president of India at the center.) Such an appointment is an honor sometimes bestowed on highly successful officials when they leave the service at the mandatory retirement age, presently set at sixty years.[28]

IAS officers have a reputation for being hidebound in carefully observing rules, regulations, and precedents. They tend to be risk-averse and comfortable with established policies and procedures. This rule-bound approach has probably been reinforced by their concern that an apparent false move on their part could lead to accusations of corruption that might damage their careers. It may also be heightened by their frequent initial unfamiliarity with their briefs as they move from one ministry to another.

This seeming inflexibility often makes IAS officers difficult to deal with across the negotiating table. "Getting to yes" with them can be a difficult chore. The star performers, not surprisingly, have learned how to use the rules to advance their goals, or else to work around them. But despite these shortcomings and the angst they may create for India's negotiating partners, the IAS can rightly be called one of the world's premier civil services.

THE DEFENSE ESTABLISHMENT

India possesses one of the world's largest and strongest military forces. Its regular army comprises 1.15 million active-duty troops plus 960,000 in reserve. Paramilitary forces deployed on its borders and against insurgents elsewhere in the country make up another 1.4 million men.[29] Its growing navy has been transformed in recent years from a largely coastal defense force into a blue-ocean fleet. Its air force has grown from a tactical force to one with transoceanic reach. This military might is commanded by well-trained professional officers, some of whom have proved their mettle on battlefields in Kashmir and elsewhere. The best of them can aspire to the top positions in their services: army, navy, or air force chief of staff. The most senior of these three service chiefs becomes Chairman of the Chiefs of Staff Committee for a three-year term,[30] but he is only first among equals. There is no single chief of defense staff position similar to those in the United States and many other countries.

Professionally competent as they may be, the impressive array of generals, admirals, and air marshals and their uniformed subordinates who make up the officer corps of the Indian armed forces play only a limited role in crafting India's security policies or influencing its approach to the world. Under the political direction of the defense minister (the Hindi term "Raksha Mantri" is commonly used), high-ranking career IAS civil servants are responsible for devising and implementing these security policies, especially for dealing with the defense budget and procurement decisions. The uniformed military report to the defense minister through them. The three service chiefs have seats on the high-level Strategic Policy Group, an important component of India's national security framework. But their access to the prime minister and the defense minister is constrained, as Ashley Tellis of the Carnegie Endowment has aptly put it, "by mores and institutional traditions that are not revealed in any organizational chart."[31] The armed services uniformed brass can make suggestions on policy and budgets, but the final call rests with the civilian bureaucrats in the Ministry of Defense (MOD) and the political leaders who rely on them.[32]

A great deal has been written about why the armed services in India have historically been so subservient to civilians in the making of security and, by extension, foreign policy. Many analysts argue that it is partly the legacy of Prime Minister Nehru's mistrust of the military. In their view he regarded senior Indian military officers as an all too powerful—and possibly dangerous—legacy of the Raj who did not readily fit into his vision of independent democratic India. The concerns he and other political leaders had about the loyalty of the military to civilian authority were no doubt heightened by coups staged by armed forces in other third-world countries, especially in Pakistan and elsewhere in India's neighborhood. These military takeovers played an important part in persuading the prime minister and other Indian politicians to keep control of security policy almost entirely in civilian hands.[33] Frustrated uniformed officers and other critics cite public and parliamentary indifference to military affairs—except at times of crisis—as another reason why these old ways have for so long gone unchanged.

As in other ministries, the civilian professionals who staff the MOD are mostly drawn from the Indian Administrative Service. A very few IFS officers are assigned to MOD from time to time. Some foreign counterparts find them a refreshing change from their less flexible IAS colleagues.[34] But as one knowledgeable critic charged, "Apart from a very small number of mid-ranking officers who work together on a limited number of issues, the two anchor tenants of South Block, the ministries of defense and external affairs, might well be on two different planets."[35] (MEA itself has very few officers who have any significant experience in military affairs. Political-military matters are not a recognized area of specialization in the ministry, nor does it have a division that deals specifically with such issues.)

India's approach to national security management has been severely criticized by outside defense affairs specialists and by many within the military itself. Even some members of parliament have joined the cry. The most pressing demand has been for the creation of a chief of defense staff position whose incumbent would head an integrated defense staff and provide single-point military advice to the defense minister.[36] Others include calls for the integration of uniformed military officers into the MOD decisionmaking process, the development of greater expertise in security affairs among IAS officers assigned to MOD, more integrated gathering of military intelligence, and heightened coordination among the three military services.

For decades Indian governments of various political persuasions have appointed high-level committees to develop recommendations for military reform.[37] The bureaucracy has successfully led the resistance to many of the reforms that critics in the uniformed military and elsewhere consider necessary to improve the way security policy is made and implemented. This bureaucratic resistance has been abetted by civilian political leaders, who worry about military aggrandizement at their expense, and, on the important issue of the creation of a single chief of defense staff, by the navy and air force, which reckon that the chief would be drawn from the army, the largest and most important service. During its first year in office, Prime Minister Modi's government gave no indication that it intends to give the issue a high priority on its crowded reform agenda.

PARLIAMENT

Aside from the prime minister, the minister of external affairs, junior MEA ministers, and a few senior figures on the opposition benches, individual members of the bicameral Indian parliament play a much less prominent role in shaping the direction and the details of foreign policymaking than do their American counterparts on Capitol Hill. This reflects both the limited interest Indian MPs ordinarily have in foreign affairs and the way India's Westminster-like parliament operates. But unlike the U.S. Congress, parliament—specifically the Lok Sabha, the directly elected and more powerful lower house—can bring down a government. This happens when a sufficient number of the government's supporters defect to deprive it of its majority, usually demonstrated by a confidence vote on the house floor.

This problem was a remote danger in the years when a single party had a majority in the Lok Sabha, as was customary before the late 1980s. With the May 2014 landslide victory of the Bharatiya Janata Party (BJP) led by Narendra Modi, that is again the case. But in the intervening quarter century India was almost always ruled either by coalitions comprising often disparate political parties or by vulnerable governments that did not enjoy a parliamentary majority and depended on the support "from the outside" of (somewhat) like-minded parties that chose not to become members of the government. Both coalitions and minority governments have been vulnerable to such defections, including those prompted by differences on foreign policy.

The interest of Indian parliamentarians in foreign affairs has heightened over the years. Like others in the Indian political class, members of parliament have generally become more outward looking. More have traveled abroad and have had more meaningful contacts with the world outside India than did their mid-to-late twentieth-century predecessors. They and the many parties they represent hold a variety of views on foreign policy issues. Some MPs are attracted to major global issues and develop strong views on the way India should deal with them. The concerns of others can be highly parochial.

But even with these changes in parliamentarians' perspectives and experience, their interests and those of their constituents remain focused on more local and immediate concerns. Only rarely do foreign affairs significantly compete with these other matters for members' attention. For governments in power between the late 1980s and 2014, the most challenging of these occasions involved serious foreign policy differences among their disparate supporters. Government mishandling of major foreign policy issues, particularly those that affect Indian national security, can also arouse parliamentarians. And matters important for individual states will prompt interest among representatives from those areas. Typically, such issues involve India's relations with foreign countries adjacent to those states. At such times, state politics can take on national significance.

But the foreign policy role that individual Indian members of parliament can play on these and other less pressing occasions is normally limited. Many of the features that offer U.S. senators and representatives powerful voices in influencing the way American administrations deal with foreign affairs are not present in the Indian parliamentary system or else operate there only in an attenuated way.

The role of the Parliamentary Standing Committee on External Affairs is one example of this limited mandate. Like twenty-three other standing committees, each dealing with specific ministries and comprising members of both houses, its powers are basically advisory. It comments on the proposed budget of MEA, and these comments are taken into account when the draft budget is considered by the full parliament. It examines and reports on bills pertaining to MEA and can act as a sounding board when the government is considering new approaches. It considers and can comment on the annual report the ministry prepares. It drafts reports on long-term policy documents presented to it. The standing committee can also originate studies of its own on foreign affairs–related matters and can invite outside authorities on these issues to meet with it as it does so. These reports and studies are publicized and can have an impact on political and public opinion, especially if they deal with sensitive or controversial issues.[38]

But in contrast to the U.S. Senate Foreign Relations Committee and the House Foreign Affairs Committee, the Indian Parliamentary Standing Committee on External Affairs does not initiate legislation. It does not conduct open sessions, potentially so important in molding public opinion. Its members usually do not serve long enough on the committee to develop foreign policy expertise, and neither they nor the committee itself have significant staffs. In a system where senior MEA officials and ambassadors do not require parliamentary confirmation, it has no opportunity to exert power by aggressively questioning appointees and, if it so decides, denying them positions.[39]

The committee meets with visiting parliamentary delegations from other countries and played host to the congressional delegation that accompanied President Bill Clinton during his dramatic visit to New Delhi in 2000. One former chairman of the committee, Krishna Bose, tried to expand its role by calling committee meetings with groups of diplomats. MEA was uncomfortable with the idea of a large group meeting with the committee, so Mrs. Bose retitled her proposed meeting with African ambassadors an "informal" meeting, and it went forward, followed by other similar ones. But she candidly acknowledged that her committee, despite her efforts, had nothing like the role of the Senate Foreign Affairs Committee, which she had taken as her model.[40]

Ordinary members ("backbenchers") have a greater opportunity to make their views known on the floor of parliament through formal questioning and other forms of debate and discussion. It is on the floor that government ministers, themselves MPs, enunciate policies and defend them against criticism voiced, often loudly, by members of the opposition and an occasional dissenter on the government side. This questioning is the primary method of enforcing the government's accountability to parliament.

At a fixed time and day of each week, ministers—sitting as tradition calls for in the front ("Treasury") benches—address a barrage of questions that have been submitted in writing by ordinary members, usually those in opposition parties.[41] The government takes this "Question Hour" seriously. MEA officials spend long hours drafting careful responses to the questions and preparing the minister to deal with provocative supplementary issues the MPs may raise. Ministers try to be as unresponsive in their replies as they think they can get away with. Ordinary members use the supplementary questions to wheedle more information out of them.

Consideration of the MEA annual budget provides another occasion for parliamentary floor discussion. The government may also take the initiative in raising important foreign policy issues. "Suo motu" statements volunteered by the prime minister are one of the most formal ways of putting Indian policy on the record. Opposition parties and ordinary members can use a variety of procedural devices to try to initiate exchanges on the floor that they hope will bring about policy changes or, more realistically, embarrass the government. The main opposition parties often designate certain MPs to act as their foreign policy spokespersons in these exchanges.

Parliamentary confrontations, some of them well covered in the media, can help focus broader public interest on the government's more controversial foreign policy positions. And they can make the government uncomfortable. But a government will not feel threatened by parliamentary challenges unless they reflect differences that could lead to sizable defections among its supporters in the Lok Sabha and force the government out of office. This occurs principally under coalition or minority governments.

THIS ALMOST HAPPENED in 2008, when the four anti-U.S. Left Front parties threatened to withdraw their support from Prime Minister Manmohan Singh's Indian National Congress–led coalition government following his announcement that he would negotiate a civil nuclear agreement with Washington. The story of the nuclear negotiations appears in detail in chapter 8, but this episode illustrates how a foreign policy negotiation can lead to high-stakes parliamentary politics.

The Left Front parties' declaration in August 2007 that the nuclear agreement was "unacceptable" was followed by an impasse of close to a year. Singh named a group of six ministers, headed by Congress elder statesman and external affairs minister Pranab Mukherjee, to meet with the left parties. After several rounds, the two sides had succeeded only in agreeing on some procedural issues. In July 2008, Singh declared that he would move forward with the deal. This led the four Left Front parties and a major opposition grouping headed by the BJP to demand a vote of no-confidence. The government narrowly survived this challenge amid angry charges that it had tried to buy the votes of the MPs, complete with bags full of banknotes being publicly opened in parliament.[42] Had the government lost, the president of India would have had to decide whether to hold fresh elections or entrust formation of a new government to the BJP, which had cynically opposed the nuclear deal with that objective in mind.

The U.S.-India Civil Nuclear Agreement was eventually signed in October 2008. But as discussed in greater detail in chapter 8, the Left Front's threat to bring down the government had cost a full year in the efforts of the two countries to close the deal.

STATE GOVERNMENTS, PARTIES, AND POLITICS

State-level politics played a role in the parliamentary battle over the nuclear deal in 2007–08 as state-based parties looked for the best deal for themselves in their negotiations with the two rival blocs. The most graphic evidence of this was the maneuvering of the government and the opposition to win the support of two parties based in the large state of Uttar Pradesh. Neither of these parties particularly cared about the pros and cons of the proposed nuclear deal. They were primarily interested in what political loaves and fishes the contenders at the national level would offer them for their support.

Politicians in several states have a special interest in relations with particular countries, but those that have had the strongest impact on India's foreign policy concerned Tamil Nadu's interest in Sri Lanka and West Bengal's in Bangladesh. A confrontation in 2013 between the Singh government and political leaders in the southern state of Tamil

Nadu shows how a controversy over a foreign policy issue important to voters in a single state can affect national politics and impact New Delhi's foreign policymaking process. This issue was the Manmohan Singh government's handling of relations with Sri Lanka.

New Delhi's policy toward Sri Lanka has long been politically important to the people of Tamil Nadu and politicians seeking their votes. Both India's major Tamil parties—the DMK and the AIADMK—exist only in that state. They took different positions on the Sri Lankan Tamils' bid for independence during the island's twenty-five year civil war, but both strongly supported Sri Lankan Tamils' efforts to hold the Colombo government accountable for human rights violations over the years. India's relations with Sri Lanka remained an important issue for these parties even after the civil war ended in 2009 with the defeat of the insurgent Liberation Tigers of Tamil Eelam (LTTE).

The spark that ignited a dangerous controversy and seemed to threaten the stability of the Singh government was consideration by the United Nations Human Rights Commission (UNHRC) of a resolution pressing for accountability for the alleged slaughter of thousands of Tamil civilians by the victorious Sri Lankan army in the final weeks of the war. Both rival Tamil Nadu parties tried to outdo the other in demonstrating their support for their Sri Lankan ethnic cousins. The DMK, a member of Singh's governing coalition, took its campaign to New Delhi, persuading leading national party figures to make public statements condemning Sri Lanka's anti-Tamil "atrocities" and talking the PM into canceling an upcoming India–Sri Lanka defense dialogue. DMK-led organizations reportedly lobbied foreign embassies in New Delhi to toughen the UNHRC resolution. Citing the inadequacy of the resolution, the DMK then withdrew from the ruling coalition. The party held sixteen Lok Sabha seats and its defection put the government's existence in technical danger, though DMK leaders hinted that they would not bring it down and did not do so. Not to be outdone, the AIADMK chief minister of Tamil Nadu's state government, whose party sat with the opposition in parliament, banned Sri Lankan cricket players from participating in an upcoming match in the state.

The resulting uproar had an impact. In a highly unusual diplomatic action, India summoned home its representative to the UNHRC, then sent him back to Geneva with instructions—almost certainly from the top—to try to toughen the resolution. This last-minute effort failed. India then voted *for* the resolution, radically departing from its normal opposition to country-specific UNHRC measures. It is unlikely that it would have done so had the Tamil Nadu state parties not weighed in. The DMK then reentered Manmohan Singh's coalition government, ending the crisis.

We will examine in chapter 12 the impact of West Bengal state interests on Indian policy toward Bangladesh, its eastern neighbor with which it has strong ethnic and cultural ties and shares a long, only recently settled border. In other border states the impact of India's relations with neighboring foreign countries on local politics (and vice versa) is much less significant. An exception, of course, is the state of Jammu and Kashmir. State politics there are entangled with the broader issue of conflicting Indian and Pakistani positions on the future of the disputed territory.

MEDIA, THINK TANKS, AND THE BUSINESS COMMUNITY

India's lively and well-informed print and electronic media pay considerable attention to foreign policy issues—some of broad national interest, others of only parochial concern—and seek to influence the way the government deals with them. Commentators and columnists include retired diplomats and other specialists who can speak with some authority and personal experience on international affairs. The electronic media, which have vastly expanded in recent years, give a prominent place to thoughtful and not-so-thoughtful commentary on foreign policy, most notably on talk shows. Media coverage can be incisive—or sensational. The journalistic dictum that "if it bleeds, it leads" certainly applies to the Indian media scene. India's foreign policy officials often try hard to keep sensitive issues they are working on beyond the reach of the press, not always with complete success.

Many of India's foreign affairs commentators are also affiliated with the country's ballooning think-tank community, and a few have come to be looked on as serious strategic thinkers. Concentrated in New Delhi and a few other major cities, India's international affairs and national security think tanks conduct seminars, publish journals, and hold meetings open to the public. They provide a convenient and attractive platform for retired practitioners who have had distinguished careers in military, diplomatic, and other government operations to enlighten their successors, fellow specialists, and the interested public. In a way they are megaphones for "formers" generally older than the Indian government's retirement age. A few offer attractive internships or junior staff positions to young Indians and foreigners considering careers in diplomacy and national security affairs.

Think tanks have become a source of talented expertise for prestigious government-appointed commissions dealing with the conduct and management of foreign and security affairs. But unlike their American counterparts, with rare exceptions these bodies do not provide a place where onetime government officers can productively keep an oar in affairs while they wait for a change in administrations and a return to regular government service. If they do resume bureaucratic roles, it is ordinarily as members of special commissions and boards.

Probably the best example of the multiple roles a retired official can play in the think-tank and advisory commission worlds was K. Subrahmanyam, widely regarded before his death in 2011 as India's top strategic thinker. After retiring from the IAS, where he focused on security affairs, Subrahmanyam was twice director of the highly regarded Institute for Defence Studies and Analyses (IDSA), chaired the important Kargil Review Commission, and was the first convener of India's National Security Advisory Board. He is widely credited with shaping the prevailing Indian understanding of nuclear strategy, both during his IAS years and especially afterward.

IDSA is India's best-known national security think tank. It is funded entirely by the MOD. It advertises itself as a nonpartisan, autonomous body dedicated to publishing studies on all aspects of defense and security. The diverse contents of its monthly journal and the monographs, briefs, and books it publishes support this claim. IDSA also provides annual training programs to Indian military and civilian officers. Lectures by experts from inside and outside IDSA form the core of these programs.

Some other think tanks focus on military issues. The United Services Institution, founded over a century ago, is oriented toward all the military services. Those focusing on a particular service include the Centre for Land Warfare Studies (CLAWS), the Centre for Air Power Studies, and the National Maritime Foundation, all of which have a heavy concentration of retired senior military officers in their governing bodies.

Under the "international affairs" heading are think tanks with a broader focus, many of which receive limited (if any) government funding. There are many such organizations; the examples given here will provide a sense of the different styles of think tanks that compete for the attention of the public and of policymakers. Although the work of these organizations often overlaps, each has found a niche and won a following. Two are chiefly funded by major Indian corporations. Gateway House, in Mumbai, has loosely modeled itself on the Council on Foreign Relations in the United States. It offers membership to Indian corporations (starting with its founder, Mahindra and Mahindra, but also including several other blue-chip firms) and to Indian individuals knowledgeable about foreign affairs. Its staff and regular contributors run heavily to former officials, but also include a number of academics. Gateway House has a long list of experts and occasional contributors from India and abroad. Some of its most interesting work, as one might expect, is on international economic affairs. The Observer Research Foundation, in Delhi, was founded in 1991 with assistance from Reliance, a major conglomerate. It continues to receive institutional support from Reliance, but also has project support from a few dozen donors, including the Government of India. Its trustees have a strong business flavor and its broad research agenda is especially strong on energy, cybersecurity, and regional issues.

Outside the business-funded category, the Institute for Peace and Conflict Studies (IPCS) has received substantial funding from international foundations and has also received project funding from MEA. It was founded by P. R. Chari, another iconic figure in the think-tank world and veteran of the IAS, with two stints in senior jobs in the MOD. Unlike Subrahmanyam, Chari, who died in 2015, took a less hawkish position, pushing for global nuclear disarmament. IPCS takes a special interest in nuclear, terrorism, and disarmament issues; India's relations with neighboring South Asian countries and China; and Kashmir. Its leaders include mainly retired military and civilian officials, but in recent years its founders have turned over charge to a younger academic. Some think tanks have a reputation for tilting toward a particular philosophical orientation. The Vivekananda International Foundation, for example, is considered close to the BJP. As with think tanks in other countries, this type of philosophical affinity can be overdrawn or may influence only a small portion of the analyses the organization puts out.

Some of the think tanks that cover international affairs have a direct relationship with the government. The Center for Policy Research, one of the oldest of the group, is one of twenty-seven national social science research institutes recognized by the Indian Council of Social Science Research, a government advisory body. Another interesting example is the Research and Information System for Developing Countries (RIS), an autonomous think tank under the MEA. RIS conducts training and offers research and expertise on economic and development policy in the context of India's Development Partnership program, which provides economic assistance to other countries. RIS staffing and leadership follow a model that is somewhat similar to India's economic think tanks, relying both on academic economists and on people with experience in India's senior officialdom. Both RIS and the economic think tanks offer expertise or research capacity not easily available in the thinly staffed government institutions that need it—comparative studies on different approaches to economic assistance programs, for example, or detailed studies on the impact on India of different potential paths to trade liberalization, as was done in recent years by the Indian Centre for Research on International Economic Relations (ICRIER), a private organization staffed by an impressive group of professional economists.

The business community has a number of ways of involving itself in policy deliberations, both directly and through professional associations such as the Federation of Indian Chambers of Commerce and Industry (FICCI) and the Confederation of Indian Industry (CII). These associations will be discussed in chapter 9. In a society as diverse as India's, with as many avenues for contact with senior officials and for sharing different policy perspectives, a description like this can only scratch the surface.

The important question is how much policy influence these nonofficial institutions and spokespeople have on India's policy. Think tanks and business organizations supplement research available in government; they provide a vehicle for putting new ideas in circulation; they offer a platform for putting the spotlight on the ideas of government leaders who give speeches there—but also on the ideas of those opposed to government policy. They also participate in international conferences, getting together and occasionally publishing studies with counterparts from other countries. These are the people who most frequently participate in international "Track Two" nonofficial dialogues.

When all is said and done, however, the Indian government is generally reluctant to build its policy on ideas imported from outside organizations. So the influence of think tanks, insofar as it is a factor, is more likely to reflect the contribution of particular experts who, over a long career, have earned the respect of senior officials in the government and who often are former colleagues as well.

The role of think tanks as incubators of talent for the government and its advisory bodies, such as the National Security Advisory Board, is probably their most important form of policy influence. Modi's National

Security Adviser, Ajit Doval, had been at the Vivekananda Foundation after retiring from the Indian Police Service. The National Security Advisory Board continues to be staffed by some of the most distinguished veterans of India's government services. Of its seventeen members in early 2015, twelve had served in senior government positions, including three former ambassadors, three flag rank military officers, and three with police or intelligence backgrounds. Those without government service included journalists, business figures, and academics. Nine, including the chair (a former foreign secretary), had one or more think-tank affiliations.[43] This board's best-known contribution was the Draft Nuclear Doctrine released in 2001. As with all advisory boards, the policy impact will vary from one government to the next, but membership on the board is an important credential for those not on active government service.

CHAPTER SIX

Negotiating for India

ONE OF THE LEGENDARY FIGURES of the Indian Foreign Service, Jagat Mehta, chronicled his experience as a young diplomat in a book he chose to call *Negotiating for India.*[1] The seven case studies he picked out, spanning two decades, tell a fascinating story about the shaping of India's ties, primarily with its neighbors. It is an account that the author clearly saw as unique to India, rather than as a more general work on diplomatic tradecraft. Mehta carried the uniqueness and dignity of India in his negotiator's briefcase. He served with distinction as foreign secretary in the 1970s. In the early years, he was negotiating for Nehru, in a very personal sense.

Each country and indeed each negotiation has its own unique characteristics. These reflect the interests of those doing the negotiating, their institutions, the personalities of the negotiators, the nationality of their opposite numbers, and the underlying historical circumstances. At the same time, there are patterns that recur regularly in the negotiating behavior of a particular country and form something one can call a national negotiating style. This is not a straitjacket or a universally observed set of norms; rather, it is a set of practices that will be observed more often than not, in more or less recognizable form, when officials of one country are dealing with foreigners.

Negotiation is not policy. If policy deals with a country's goals and purposes, diplomacy is about how it pursues these objectives, and negotiation encompasses one of the key tools of diplomacy. This study defines negotiating very broadly. It is not just what happens when officials from two or more sides are gathered around a table, working out a carefully crafted text. It also includes the way a country handles relationships it considers important, the way informal agreements are arrived at, the relative weight of informal and formal agreements, the challenge of implementing agreements, and in general, the skills and practices that are used to manage differences across national and cultural boundaries.

India's negotiators are talented, but few in number. As we have seen, the principal institutions that conduct negotiations—primarily the Ministry of External Affairs (MEA) and the Prime Minister's Office; for economic issues, the Ministries of Commerce and Finance; and for military matters, the Ministry of Defense—are thinly staffed, and decisions are made and implemented close to the top. Decisions on which issues get priority attention thus become extraordinarily important. The key issues are handled with extremely detailed staff work. Issues further down the list of priorities are likely to suffer delays, the product of a system that rewards caution and "non-mistakes" more than efficiency or risk-taking. Indian officials' negotiating style draws heavily on three elements discussed in the previous chapters: the legacy of India's ancient civilization; the competing visions of its place in the world; and its institutions. It also draws on Indian traditions of social organization and strategic thinking.

This chapter sketches out the principal features of an Indian negotiating style. It looks first at elements that reflect the character of India, the dignity of the state, and the moral dimension of negotiating. Next, we examine the features that derive from India's social context. Then we reflect on how ideas of time, communication, and some of the philosophical concepts that are especially highly valued in India shape this pattern. We close with a description of a kind of "perfect storm" in U.S.-India relations, and the ways in which it can complicate the range of negotiations they are involved in. Subsequent chapters will go beyond this outline, looking at the more specific experience of negotiations on different topics, with different institutions or personalities in the lead.

REPRESENTING A UNIQUE CIVILIZATION
AND A STRONG STATE

India's negotiators do not just represent a nation that has made its mark on the world in spite of the challenges of diversity and poverty. They are also the standard-bearers of a great civilization that shapes their national identity. This is a source of pride, but also a responsibility. This heritage is a wellspring of spiritual and intellectual power, which India's leaders and negotiators have traditionally seen as a way of compensating for the country's material weakness. The ideals that shaped India's early foreign policy, nonalignment and the mission of global peacemaking, discussed at some length in earlier chapters, were similarly seen as an extension of the spiritual power of Indian civilization.[2] Negotiators do not expect foreigners to understand Indian civilization, but they do expect foreign officials to show respect for it.

The power and luster of India's civilization is in tension with the meagerness of its resources, including those available to the officials doing the negotiating. India's "hard power" resources are rarely displayed as an adjunct to India's negotiations outside its own region (though India has sometimes been less shy about using coercive power in dealings with its South Asian neighbors). One result is an official culture that prizes frugality. In many other countries at India's income level, senior officials are driven around in sleek Mercedes-Benz sedans. In India, until well after 2000, the locally made Hindustan Ambassador—a version of a 1950s vintage Morris Oxford—was used for most official vehicles. The fact that it was locally made added local pride to virtuous frugality. In time India's official motor pool modernized—but luxury vehicles are restricted to the top of the official pyramid.[3]

Another manifestation of this spirit is in the penchant for jerry-rigged solutions to engineering and, by extension, regulatory or bureaucratic problems. The Hindi term for this is *jugaad*, which translates roughly as a quick workaround—in American slang, "putting things together with chewing gum and pieces of string." Books on business practices often refer to this as a habit that outsiders need to adjust to.[4]

India's negotiators also represent a state that has tremendous power over the way things work. A traditional expression that predates Indian independence is that the government is "mother and father"—*maa-baap*—and is the ultimate provider of much that is essential to life, including food distribution in times of trouble.[5] Veterans of the Indian Civil Service from the days of the British Raj talk about their formative experiences directing famine relief in Bihar, or dealing with breakdowns of law and order in remote parts of the country. The Food Security Act passed in 2013 is its most recent formal manifestation in independent India. The dignity of the state is prized in most societies, but it is a point of particular sensitivity in India, reflecting both the vital power that the state has taken on and its standing as the embodiment of Indian civilization.

The Indian state is widely known for its strong institutional identity and inflexible bureaucracy. This reflects both the legacy of the administrative structure the British left behind and the founding fathers' determination to maintain a strong central government to hold together an exceptionally diverse nation. Negotiators are part of this larger structure and bound by the Indian government's sometimes cumbersome coordination process. A decision that has gone through the full government process becomes very difficult to change. Negotiators who wish to persuade the Indian government to change its policy or practices need to engage early and often. Americans, coming from a more freewheeling bureaucratic culture, look for ways to do an "end run" around an institution or official they see as an obstacle. The Indian system is resistant to such frontal attacks. Jumping over the regular process in an effort to overturn a decision, especially one already blessed at the top, probably would be a tough sell in any country. In India, it can be seen as an affront to the entire politico-social structure of the government. When a foreigner does it, the enterprise takes on overtones of interference in India's internal affairs. Resistance can be fierce. Finding allies who can work within the system, and engaging them before a decision is carved in stone, may be more successful.

A point of particular pride is India's democratic government. Unlike the United States, Indian policy does not generally seek to spread democracy beyond its borders, except for rather limited forms of technical cooperation on such matters as election procedures at the request of other countries. But public and parliamentary opinion looms large for public officials negotiating controversial issues. The fact that so much of India's negotiating business is carried out by its career government services, by officials whose professional lives take place entirely outside the realm of elective politics, probably intensifies their concern about deviating from the public opinion mainstream on matters that attract broad interest.

NEGOTIATING TOOLS

Negotiation starts with a government decision. As discussed in chapter 5, India has a well-defined process for making decisions. But side by side with the formal process, the oral tradition of communication is exceptionally strong in India. Major policies, and especially adjustments in important policies, may not be written down. India's foreign policy changed after the end of the Cold War in very important ways, but one searches in vain for a comprehensive official statement describing the change. More narrowly drawn statements address specific aspects of the change—the deepening relationship with Washington, for example, or the increasing prominence of economic affairs in Indian foreign policy, or the creation of an institution within MEA to manage India's emerging foreign aid portfolio. But articulating big policy shifts is often done primarily by academics, former officials, and journalists. Conversely, broad policy statements on such subjects as economic reform may not translate into concrete actions.

The oral tradition carries over into the government's internal processes. Close observers maintain that deliberations that go to the Indian cabinet do not necessarily have the kind of formal paper trail that is commonplace in the U.S. government, recording the clearances of all the concerned officials and naming a deciding official. On particularly sensitive issues, where only a small circle is in the know, key information may never get written down, in an effort to maintain secrecy.

The normal administrative procedures of the Indian government, by contrast, are heavy with papers and files. One U.S. diplomat who served several tours of duty in New Delhi recalled the first time he was instructed to raise an issue formally with MEA. He had gone through his instruction cable carefully. When he arrived, the Indian official who received him had on his desk ten years' worth of files on the same issue and wanted to know precisely why the United States wanted to change the words in which its demarche was couched, and when that policy change had been instituted. In this case—and in many others—the Indian government had more detailed files and retrieved them more readily than the U.S. government. They may be used for defending an important negotiating position or for scoring points, but there is a heavy burden on those who negotiate with Indian officials to master the details. These files are generally not declassified and made available to the public, however.

The heart of the formal negotiating process is often on paper. Senior Indian foreign policy officials are skilled and sophisticated at drafting in English. Their ability to deal with precision, ambiguity, and contradiction, sometimes in the same document, can be a recipe for success, as in the U.S.-India civil nuclear agreement, where this kind of drafting finesse provided a route around some extraordinarily tricky issues of language and status. Indian officials review negotiating drafts with an eagle eye; their opposite numbers need to do the same. The same drafting skill that solves problems can also be used to slow down a process or outmaneuver a foreign negotiator.

Some observers argue that India prefers to reach agreement in principle before tackling the details, a characteristic that is also attributed to China.[6] A closer look at the record of negotiations examined in the coming chapters suggests that this is not necessarily the case. In the negotiations with Washington on the U.S.-India civil nuclear agreement, some of the thorniest issues were agreed in principle before the details were negotiated, though the complex network of agreements involved were still extraordinarily difficult to put in final. An early result of the India-China border talks that started in 2003 was an agreement on "Political Parameters and Guiding Principles for the Settlement of the India-China Boundary Question." This agreement took two years to negotiate; ten years later, the discussions on what the principles mean were still a long way from completion.[7]

There are numerous examples, however, where despite what at least one side thought was agreement in principle, the details never were worked out. The security undertakings that normally accompany U.S. defense sales are a case in point. And at the multilateral level, when the World Trade Organization was first created, there was no agreement in principle on whether India would join. The government's initial disinclination to join was overridden only late in the process. All the examples cited here are discussed in greater detail in chapters 7 through 11. One problem that they point out is that it is not always clear how binding an "agreement in principle" really is.

When drafting, India's negotiators are careful to choose their language with a view toward showcasing the dignity of the Indian state. Referring to "assistance" to India raises hackles; "sharing best practices" works better. In recent years, India has begun providing economic help to other countries, but is careful to call itself a "development partner" rather than a "donor." This is not just out of concern for the sensibilities of the recipient country: the term is intended to distinguish India's operating practices from Western donors. The office in MEA that oversees India's economic assistance programs is called the Development Partnership Administration.

In other cases, Indian officials avoid words that to other observers seem obvious, because they might set an undesirable precedent. Jagat Mehta recalled a 1960 one-on-one meeting between Nehru and Zhou Enlai about the India-China border. Zhou had put forward six points that he hoped would be endorsed by both sides. Nehru, according to the note taker's record, had raised no objection. Mehta, however, was concerned that the first of the points—"there exists a dispute with regard to the boundary between the two sides"—might appear to legitimize China's position on the border and felt that "claim" would be the better and safer word to use. After a hasty consultation with the foreign secretary, Mehta was dispatched to raise his concerns with Nehru himself. The prime minister initially dismissed Mehta's objections, but eventually agreed and refused to endorse the six points.[8] Interestingly, to this day the Government of India will not use the word "dispute" with respect to the Kashmir issue, for essentially the same reason.

Negotiations for the U.S.-India civil nuclear agreement illustrated one of the problems this careful draftsmanship is intended to address. The negotiators spent many hours trying to avoid verbal land mines on issues like India's insistence on being treated as an equal of the treaty-recognized nuclear weapons states, without having the United States violate its treaty obligations. The text of the agreement had to be acceptable to four different audiences: the two governments, the U.S. Congress and public, and the Indian Parliament and public. This required both careful research and considerable conceptual and verbal creativity.

INDIAN NEGOTIATORS DO NOT like being the ones to make requests—being the *demandeur*, in diplomatic parlance. This reflects not just their determination to protect the dignity of the Indian state; it also fits in with the unwritten rules of negotiating in the bazaar, where the party that first proposes a price is at a disadvantage. India's reputation for being diffident about formally requesting assistance dates back to the earliest days of independence. Chester Bowles, who served his first term as ambassador to New Delhi in the early 1950s, recalled that on his way to Nehru's office to offer the prime minister a $54 million aid package, one of the earliest U.S. aid programs in India, "an uncomfortable thought occurred to me. I had heard that the Indians were very proud and sensitive and unwilling to ask for foreign aid. What if they refused even to accept our offer of assistance?" Actually, India had made a request for American provision of food grains at concessional prices a few years earlier, when Nehru, visiting Washington in 1949, had mentioned the matter. But he did so not as an agenda item at a formal negotiating session but in passing, in the course of casual discussions with President Truman and Secretary of State Acheson.[9]

There are countless more recent examples. K. Shankar Bajpai, who was ambassador to the United States when Prime Minister Rajiv Gandhi visited the United States in 1985, recalled the challenge of arranging for the prime minister to address a joint session of the U.S. Congress. The normal practice was for the visitor's ambassador to make the request of the Speaker of the House of Representatives. Bajpai, who felt India should not have to make the request, eventually found another way to get the issue before the Speaker.

Another Indian ambassador, Naresh Chandra, recalled how he managed his contacts with the U.S. government at the time of India's nuclear tests in 1998. He passed word to his U.S. interlocutors that he would be available if they wished to see him—but deliberately never requested a meeting. He managed the arrangements for a meeting between Indian Minister of External Affairs Jaswant Singh and the U.S. official Singh knew best, Deputy Secretary of State Strobe Talbott, so that it took place when Talbott was acting secretary of state, to avoid an asymmetry of rank in a meeting that was certain to be difficult. In yet another case, India's health officials were interested in getting India named as a "priority country" for President George W. Bush's HIV/AIDS initiative, a designation that would have brought in substantial additional resources for India's AIDS budget. But the Indian government was not willing to ask; ultimately Vietnam was designated instead.[10]

Unwillingness to be the *demandeur* is not an absolute. India certainly made clear that U.S. nuclear policy toward India was a major stumbling block in the way of improving relations, and that New Delhi was looking for Washington to propose a solution. Similarly, India has not hesitated to demand an improvement in the way the U.S. visa system treats Indian technology workers. And once the nuclear negotiations were under way, Indian negotiators proposed many of the winning solutions to negotiating problems. But by that time the negotiation was very much a joint enterprise, so the question of who requested what was easily buried in the larger negotiating record.

Closely related to this reluctance to ask is India's strong preference for being the author of ideas that eventually get embedded in bilateral or multilateral agreements. This characteristic can lead to distaste for ideas developed elsewhere. Who is seen to hold the pen can be important.

AMERICAN OFFICIALS REGULATE THEIR WORK, and their pursuit of larger goals, by the calendar and the clock. Both domestically and internationally, they often use timelines to drive toward a decision. Deadline-related arguments are considered particularly strong. The implicit assumption is that others will find the time-driven procedural schedule equally compelling. Some of these deadlines reflect inflexibilities in the U.S. system, such as congressional timetables; others involve travel schedules; others may be internally generated.

Indian officials, like many others, are often unmoved by approaching deadlines and indeed question whether they are really binding or just a negotiating ploy. One can speculate about the reasons for this thinking. Some will remember previous cases where deadlines turned out not to be binding; many may consider that India's negotiating partners need to show India proper respect by letting India take the time it needs to handle a negotiation in its own way. And, especially in negotiations that are difficult and have long-term consequences, Indian officials have a powerful sense of their country's past and are likely to take a long view of history. As they see it, no country's standing or power—or weakness—can be considered permanent. If India cannot achieve its goals in a particular negotiation, another opportunity, perhaps a better one, is likely to come along in the next turn of the historical wheel. India's classical and sacred writings rely heavily on cycles—the inexorable cycle of death and rebirth, larger cycles that drive millennia of history—so this approach fits comfortably into the cultural environment.[11]

INDIAN DIPLOMACY THRIVES on glittering occasions. Indian officials and leaders like summits, especially with major powers. When India is host to an important event, it pulls out all the stops. Delhi is an alluring backdrop. The sandstone buildings that Edwin Lutyens designed as the seat of the British Indian Empire have become the visually spectacular home of the Indian Republic, with guards and other staff in uniforms that showcase both the glamour and the power of the independent Indian state. The big prize is an invitation to be the Chief Guest at India's Republic Day parade with its display of contemporary and traditional pageantry. Prime Minister Modi's invitation to President Obama to attend Republic Day in that capacity, the first U.S. president to be so honored, had huge symbolic importance.

India's sense of its own uniqueness extends into the substance of negotiations. Exceptionalism is a mind-set common to Indians and Americans, and both express it in part by adopting governmental processes and procedures from which they try not to deviate—templates for treaties, for example, or special requirements for actions that in many other governments are within the discretion of government officials. Indian officials are generally not impressed by the argument that "everyone does it this way," which frequently comes up in bilateral defense relations. They are adept at finding and examining previous agreements with third countries to find favorable precedents they would like to incorporate into agreements with India. They regard unwillingness by other countries, especially the United States, to replicate a favorable precedent or offer India a unique, custom-made arrangement as evidence that India is not being taken with the right degree of seriousness.

But exceptionalism does not necessarily mean that India insists on a formal leadership position. Especially in the years since 2000, when India's economic success raised its global profile, Indian officials have become more conscious that the perks of leadership bring responsibilities and costs. Especially among Indians outside of government, there is increasing consciousness that India needs to be selective about which of these costs it takes on.

INDIA HAD A REPUTATION, especially in its early decades, for conducting its diplomacy from a stance of moral superiority. The moral high ground is desirable terrain when one wants to put one's interlocutors at a disadvantage. It fits in well with the ethos of representing an ancient civilization, one that is built around the concept of a cosmic order in which everything has its place.[12] It also accords well with the ideals of building peace and opposing injustice that were such an important feature of the Nehruvian foreign policy.

Insofar as negotiation implies give-and-take, India's preference for working from a moral stand can complicate the process. Framing issues in moral terms and zero-sum negotiations are particularly characteristic of India's multilateral negotiations. Staking out a moral position moves much of the discussion onto a plane that is considered non-negotiable. Compromise tends to be equated with weakness. Indian negotiators frequently stake out a maximalist position to start with. They may then find it peculiarly difficult to deal with half-measures or even to shift the negotiating terrain back to a discussion of interests. This can be intensified by the politics of high-profile multilateral negotiations. The impact on negotiations in the World Trade Organization is discussed in chapter 10.

One aspect of the moral dimension is the question of "fairness." Indian negotiators and their counterparts sometimes have different concepts of what fairness requires. A classic example comes from global environmental negotiations, where Indian negotiators cite the pollution accumulated by developed countries over a couple of centuries of industrialization, whereas U.S. negotiators focus more on the increasing emission of greenhouse gases by China and India as they expand their economies.

THE SOCIAL CONTEXT: GROUPS AND RANK

Indian society is in important ways made up of groups, not just of individuals. Traditionally, caste was the starting point for determining the station in life of a group and the individuals within it. Independent India outlawed many manifestations of the caste system, especially those that imposed severe restrictions on lower caste groups and those regarded as outside and below the system itself, although these limitations can still be found, especially in village life.

What drives people's loyalty and sense of identity is less the large caste categories than local subcastes, many of them associated with an occupation.[13] In traditional society, these tighter groups determined whom one would marry or with whom one might share food. These groups have long been the lifeblood of Indian politics—groups that are specific to a particular state or locality, and with whom a politician or the local branch of a party forms a working alliance. State- and town-level political reporting, which revolves around who is successfully courting these groups, can be almost incomprehensible to those not aware of the details of different local and subcaste groups.

India's economic expansion and urbanization since 1980 have brought with them considerable social mobility, weakening the presumption that social groups continue down the generations. Affirmative action programs that set aside up to 47 percent of public sector jobs for different groups of disadvantaged or "backward" castes have reinforced this process. More diverse university admissions and economic opportunities in the services economy have led to both greater social interaction and more intermarriage. Interestingly, social mobility often applies to whole groups, rather than just the most enterprising individuals within them. A group whose members have prospered may seek recognition in a higher niche than the one it had occupied earlier.[14]

Many of India's leaders, and most of its civil servants and diplomats, do not order their lives along caste lines—though for some, devotions and ceremonies of their family's caste, subcaste, or regional or religious background remain important in their lives. Many marry outside the social group they were born into. These non-arranged marriages are commonly referred to as "love matches." Foreign Service officers marrying people from the opposite end of India whom they met as students at Delhi's Jawaharlal Nehru University or in training at Dehra Dun are almost a cliché.

But group loyalty is still tremendously important. For these sophisticated and sometimes globe-trotting city dwellers, professional associations have a strong emotional hold on their loyalties. Officers in the Indian Administrative Service (IAS) and Indian Foreign Service usually remain close to their "batch-mates," those who were part of the same orientation class on entering the service. And of course the government services themselves are a powerful loyalty group. One very senior retired IAS officer shared with the authors his bitter criticism of the way the bureaucracy had stood by without stopping the communal riots that convulsed the state of Gujarat in 2002: "My tribe let me down. I mean the IAS."

This web of collective loyalties does not prevent creative thinking or heterodox views on the part of Indian officials. But it does mean that in a negotiating setting, the social pressure to go along with the arrangement that reinforces the standing of one's professional "tribe" is unusually strong.

Foreigners stand outside this social system. The same could be said for any national society, but in the case of India, traditional social organization originated in religious scripture, sanctified through millennia of tradition, so it is imbued with some of the uniqueness of India. This makes it harder to define the social rules that should govern interactions between Indian and foreign officials.

Traditional Indian society is hierarchical. Government officials' status and jobs lie outside caste and other categories of traditional society. In government services, the traditional order of Indian society has to compete with the services' internal hierarchy and also with the egalitarian drive that is part of Indian democracy and part of the service itself. A high-caste Brahmin may find himself working for a boss from a family at the bottom of the caste pyramid. Access to public service, as we have seen, is through a rigorous exam. Anyone can take the exam, and members of government services take pride in the fact that neither those who administer the written exam nor those who evaluate the oral are given any information about the social or family background of a particular candidate.

Entrance examination scores determine the successful candidate's seniority and create a pecking order that will follow a person through his or her professional life. Seniority has a powerful impact on social relationships. The main institutions of government service, and the policy officials who head them, are treated by the system, in the words of one observer, as "omniscient patricians."[15] In meetings with foreign officials, junior officers are often reluctant to speak up in the presence of their seniors. Sometimes it is the little touches that remind a visitor of the hierarchy at work. A visitor to the office of a joint secretary in MEA—roughly the equivalent of an assistant secretary in the U.S. system—will normally be offered tea or coffee with a cookie. In the foreign secretary's office, the standard offering will also include warm cashew nuts and sometimes small tea sandwiches. Reading hierarchy through the tea leaves (or coffee grounds) also happens elsewhere, of course. The U.S. government, for example, will not pay for tea or coffee, though the top few officials in a department are an exception. The authors recall that deputy assistant secretaries in the bureau where they both served agreed to chip in to buy a coffeemaker and a supply of tea bags and coffee, so as to avoid the embarrassment of receiving the ever-hospitable South Asian diplomats without any refreshments.

PROTOCOL

When Raja Mohan compared India's style to a porcupine, he was thinking in part about protocol—where the dignity of the Indian state meets hierarchy.[16] In dealing with the United States and other major powers, Indian officials are acutely conscious of the asymmetry of national power and look for ways to compensate. The level at which India's officials are received is accorded great importance, and Indian officials bridle at foreigners' expectations of asymmetric access to the top levels of their government. This is a particular problem in dealing with the United States, which rations its leaders' time more tightly than many other countries but insists on top-level access when its senior officials travel abroad. Below the cabinet level, Indian and U.S. officials have a different understanding of how ranks in their two systems relate to one another. Assistant secretaries in the U.S. State Department generally have broader territorial responsibilities than the Indian joint secretaries in

MEA, who consider themselves their protocol equivalents. The result is that, especially in meetings involving MEA, determining which visiting official should meet with whom can take as much time as their actual consultations.

The problem of asymmetric access is exacerbated by Americans' preferred operating style, which is markedly less formal than is common among senior Indian officials. In the Indian diplomatic service, where there is a large gap in seniority, the junior official will call the senior one "Sir" or "Ma'am." This practice often carries over, albeit without as precise a calculation of seniority, in dealings with foreigners.

Protocol and reciprocity are sometimes used for point-scoring purposes. The U.S. system for granting approval, or *"agrément,"* for new ambassadors is notoriously inefficient and was particularly sluggish before the appointment of Nirupama Rao to be Indian ambassador in Washington. The next U.S. ambassador proposed for Delhi, Nancy Powell, had to wait precisely the same number of days for her *agrément* to come through.

Asymmetry is not always a problem for India's negotiators. They are quite prepared to use it to India's advantage when dealing with less powerful countries in the neighborhood. This contributes to India's reputation for high-handedness among its neighbors in South Asia. Few serving Indian officials acknowledge this perception.

PERSONAL TIES

A testy relationship can sink a promising negotiation; a good personal relationship opens up possibilities, though it certainly does not ensure success. The difficult history of U.S.-India trade negotiations, discussed in greater depth in chapters 9 and 10, illustrates both the need and the limitations of the personal dimension. Multilateral trade remains one of the most difficult areas for U.S.-India negotiations, and a personal relationship does not necessarily translate into an official or political one.

Many Indian officials put a lot of effort into maintaining relationships they consider desirable. "Old India hands" often report that they have been greeted like long-lost friends by counterparts they had known, either in Delhi or in an overseas post, twenty or thirty years earlier. Indian officials are generous with hospitality. Especially where this personal relationship does not exist, however, Indian officials can take a hard-nosed view of where foreigners fit in. The classic example was Richard Nixon, who visited India when he was seemingly in the political wilderness between leaving the vice presidency and being elected president. The Indian government treated him as a nobody and has-been. Unfortunately for U.S.-India relations, Pakistan, which he also visited, treated him as a VIP, and Nixon never forgot the contrast.

Slights are not easily forgotten. Personal slights may be interpreted as offenses against India. This problem has roots in Indian officials' strong sense of embodying the state and Indian civilization. At some level, it also has cultural and philosophical dimension. In cultures that grew out of Christianity, forgiveness is a religious obligation and one of the highest forms of virtue. In cultures that came from Hindu and Buddhist traditions, the basic principle is not sin and forgiveness, but the inexorable cycle of rebirth. A person reaps the consequences of virtue or vice in the next life; the forgiveness of others, or one's own willingness to forgive, does not drive the cycle of reincarnations.

The most difficult problems have to do with slights at the national level, however, and they more typically reflect a more prosaic cause. As noted earlier, the Indian system has a much better collective memory than many other countries, notably including the United States. The United States has been hampered for nearly four decades by its reputation for unreliability as a military supplier. This view results from the U.S. decisions to cut off military supply to India (as well as Pakistan) during the 1965 war and to cancel civil nuclear fuel supply contracts for the power plant at Tarapur. The challenge in this case has been to make legal and policy changes since the 1970s credible to India. As we will see, this problem has been a major theme in U.S.-India security negotiations.

Indian negotiators are unlikely to tell a direct lie, but like many others, they are not above creating a misleading impression out of technically true parts. And the system may convey an untruth even when no individual has knowingly done so. One memorable example occurred just before the Indian nuclear test in 1998. Bill Richardson, then U.S. ambassador to the United Nations, visited Delhi in mid-April 1998 and met with Prime Minister Vajpayee. In early May, the newly appointed Indian foreign secretary came to Washington on his first official visit. On May 11, the first group of weapons-related Indian nuclear tests took place, to America's surprise. The U.S. government took the test badly, and reacted badly as well to the seeming deception involved in the Indian government's decision to schedule both visits at a time when India was planning an action that would so directly fly in the face of one of Washington's most strongly held policies. In particular, the Indian foreign secretary's reputation in official Washington never recovered. He was considered to be either complicit in the deception or, more likely, out of the loop, and either one made him "damaged goods."

PUSHING HOT BUTTONS

In December 2013, the Indian deputy consul general in New York, Devyani Khobragade, was arrested shortly after dropping her children off at school and charged with visa fraud and underpaying her maid. The result was the most unpleasant crisis in U.S.-India diplomatic ties in decades, and it illustrates how many things can go wrong at once, and how easy it is for the reactions of both the Indian and the U.S. governments to deepen the crisis.

The charges arose out of the U.S. requirement that diplomats who bring household staff to the United States pay them the U.S. minimum wage and sign an undertaking to that effect. Khobragade signed, but also signed a second work contract with her maid that provided substantially less pay, apparently believing that she could offset the cost of the maid's housing and meals against the minimum wage. Disputes over servants' wages paid by U.S.-based foreign diplomats are not unusual. Few of them result in an arrest. Two earlier, broadly similar cases involving Indian consular officials in New York resulted in civil action in U.S. courts. Washington had alerted Indian officials to the possibility of trouble with Khobragade. No one in the Indian government, apparently, made the connection. From their perspective, no one believed that the U.S. government would take legal action because of something as trivial, in their view, as underpaying a domestic servant.

The arrest was guaranteed to cause shock waves in India—a woman diplomat being detained with criminal defendants for several hours after being "routinely" strip-searched. Khobragade's consular immunity was limited to official acts. The same is true of American consular officials abroad (including in India), but it is not unusual for the United States to request, and sometimes receive, broader immunity than its officials are strictly entitled to. To make matters worse, the arrest took place within hours after the newly appointed Indian foreign secretary had concluded her first official visit to Washington. The Khobragade episode earned not just the fury of the Indian government but the undying hostility of the new foreign secretary, who felt blindsided by the arrest.

Addressing the crisis proceeded along three lines, starting with the arrest itself. It took about a month to work out an arrangement that would permit Khobragade to leave the United States. The action was chiefly in the hands of the U.S. attorney for the Southern District of New York, ironically the Indian-born Preet Bharara. State Department officials are extremely cautious in dealing with law enforcement cases and worry about being charged with obstruction of justice. India demanded that the charges be dropped; the United States refused. Eventually, Bharara issued a formal complaint; the Indian government transferred Khobragade to the Indian mission to the United Nations, which made it possible for the United States to issue her a diplomatic visa conferring full diplomatic immunity; Khobragade was then formally indicted; the U.S. government asked India to withdraw her, noting that returning to the United States could subject her to rearrest; and Secretary of State John Kerry publicly expressed regret for the incident (short of the formal apology India had sought). Khobragade flew home on January 10, 2014.

Meanwhile, in Delhi, a second drama was playing out. MEA had mounted a major effort to identify potential retaliatory actions against the United States. They started with restricting U.S. diplomats' use of tax exemption cards and limiting American nondiplomats' use of the U.S. embassy's recreational facilities. They also included removing security-related traffic restrictions around the U.S. embassy in New Delhi, as well as other measures designed to snub the U.S. ambassador and make life uncomfortable for American Embassy staff. Perhaps the most painful, from the perspective of the embassy, was a crackdown on an apparently long-standing visa irregularity by the American Embassy School: it had for years employed teachers whose visa applications had listed them as "dependents," misleading the Indian visa authorities and breaching the ceiling agreed to by both governments on the number of teachers the school could bring in from abroad. When the United States asked for Khobragade's removal, the Indian government did the same to a U.S. diplomat.

The third process unleashed by the arrest concerned the future of U.S.-India relations. India and the United States were already dealing with multiple disagreements over commercial, nuclear, and visa issues. The effort to contain the damage started by trying to place the continuing discussions on the arrest and India's retaliatory actions in a channel where they could be addressed without poisoning the wider relationship. This effort engaged people on both sides who valued the long-term relationship their governments had begun building. As often happens when one issue has gone badly wrong, even this kind of procedural fix becomes a heavy lift. U.S.-India relations do not prosper without a regular infusion of high-level attention—and much of the high-level contact the United States would normally have had in Delhi was cut off. The Indian government blamed the U.S. ambassador, Nancy Powell, for the problem. Especially in view of the prior history of similar problems at the Indian consulate general in New York, the United States considered this grossly unfair. Several high-level visits from the United States to India were canceled or postponed because the Indian government could not confirm that the visitors would be officially received.

The case ground on for a couple of months. In mid-March, two months after Khobragade had left the United States, her indictment was dismissed on the grounds that she had enjoyed immunity at the time it was issued. She was reindicted a few days later; by then, she was back in New Delhi, where she worked, at least for a few months, in quite a senior job at MEA, as head of the Development Partnership Administration. MEA had taken care of its own.

A new Indian ambassador arrived in Washington in late December. In May, Ambassador Powell, whose planned departure date was drawing near, left New Delhi. By then, India had a new government and the United States and India launched a dramatic revival of their relationship. Ironically, Khobragade was reassigned by the ministry, leaving the Development Partnership job for something less prominent. And in the summer of 2015, she was again in the news. MEA took legal action against her because she had applied for U.S. passports for her children, who had U.S. citizenship through their father.

No one came out of this episode looking good. It pushed an unusual number of hot buttons, notably the dignity of the Indian state, the treatment of a woman diplomat, and the perception that the United States was seeking better treatment for itself than it was willing to accord India. Because the crisis involved the wages of a domestic servant, it brought up the different perspectives of Indian society, where any Indian diplomat would expect routinely to employ servants at home, and U.S. society, where having servants looks like entitlement. The United States handled it ineptly on several levels.

Viewed as an important and unfortunate episode in negotiations between Delhi and Washington, the Khobragade case demonstrates how easy it is for the U.S. government to be caught in a procedural trap from which it is very hard to find an exit—in this case the judicial process that started with the charges against Khobragade and her arrest. It also illustrates the passion India's diplomatic establishment can display when pushing back against what they see as an offense against India—and against one of their colleagues.[17] And it is a reminder that some of the criticisms leveled against the United States by Indians, especially the policy elites, during the Cold War years—that Americans are brash, inept, insensitive to India, overbearing, and arrogant—have not disappeared, despite a decade and a half of much better official relations. The fresh cast of characters that took office with the installation of a new government reversed much of the damage caused by this incident, but there is a more sobering lesson: Indian memories are long.

STRATEGY

Among observers of India's international and security policy there is a long-standing dispute over whether India has a strategic culture and how strong it is.[18] As we have seen, the power of India's attachment to "strategic autonomy," especially when coupled with a geographic perspective that has changed little since the days of the British Raj, creates a distinct strategic orientation. But the Indian government, like many others, is better at defining its long-term hopes than at spelling out and following the best route for reaching them. Similarly, it sometimes has difficulty distinguishing between higher- and lower-order objectives. Jagat Mehta, reflecting on his long diplomatic career, cited as one example India's effective blockade of Nepal to force a change in its overture to China, discussed at greater length in chapter 12. He questioned whether India's success in influencing Nepal's China policy had not been bought at too high a price in the form of lasting hostility.[19]

As India's profile in global affairs gets higher, its strategists and negotiators will face greater challenges. For relatively small countries, or for countries facing a clear existential threat, priorities are relatively easy to discern. Strategic interests are those bound up with one or two key interests or with an overpowering threat. Negotiators are charged with guarding what is essential and may give less weight to other things.

As India has become more powerful, its interests on the global scene have become more complex. Peripheral issues on which India took strong policy positions in earlier years are now more likely to bump into interests that affect the country in more visible, practical ways. Negotiators seeking to enhance their country's strategic autonomy now find themselves faced with choices and trade-offs between competing interests. This is fundamentally a problem of policy, but it will affect India's negotiators profoundly as they shape India's growing global role.[20]

CHAPTER SEVEN

Negotiating Security Issues

ON DECEMBER 26, 2004, a powerful tsunami ripped through the Indian Ocean, devastating a number of places in South and Southeast Asia. The relief effort featured intense cooperation between India and the United States, on a scale no one could recall having seen in the past. The Indian navy deployed thirty-two naval ships, seven aircraft, and twenty helicopters to support five relief missions, including work beyond India's borders in Maldives, Sri Lanka. and Indonesia. They were working alongside U.S. naval forces, which included a carrier strike group, an expeditionary strike group, and a hospital ship. This experience quickly came to symbolize the potential of the emerging U.S.-India security relationship. Indian officers spoke with pride about the speed of their response—nineteen ships were heading toward Maldives the day the tsunami struck—and the professionalism they shared with their American counterparts. They also saw up close some of the hallmark skills of the U.S. Navy in logistics and communications. "Naval diplomacy" with humanitarian applications became one of the favored forms of India's new regional diplomacy.[1]

Together with the Indian government's 2002 decision to escort U.S. ships through the Strait of Malacca in the wake of 9/11, the tsunami experience gave both countries' military services, and especially their navies, a taste of what a successful U.S.-India security partnership might bring. Achieving that partnership, however, is still a work in progress and, on the Indian side, a political minefield.

The security field showcases some of the toughest disconnects between the United States and India. Their concepts of their global roles do not mesh. The United States thinks of itself first and foremost as a leader and defender of freedom. Since World War II ended, the United States has expected that its good friends—"allies" is the much overused term—will share its basic threat perception and will work with it, if not across the board, at least on areas of mutual strategic interest. For India, all of the competing visions of its global role, as we have seen, are built around a consensus that stresses its historic greatness and commitment to strategic autonomy. The concept of "alliance" does not fit well into this framework, and deferring to the leadership of another country fits not at all. India guards its sovereignty with great vigilance and objects to arrangements that many other countries might find entirely acceptable. A number of U.S. politicians have a similarly prickly approach to sovereignty. This is more likely to accentuate the frictions over sovereignty issues than to resolve them.

A second philosophical difference is just below the surface. The United States develops strategies, as one senior U.S. official told the authors, for "changing everything but the weather." India has a narrower view of how much change it can effect in its basic strategic situation.

A third difference is the mismatch between the U.S. and Indian governmental structures dealing with defense, the most complicated bureaucratic interface between the two governments. The two defense establishments are primary actors in U.S.-India defense negotiations, with diplomats in a coordinating role, but as so often happens, the Indian Ministry of External Affairs (MEA) is closer to the center of the action than its U.S. counterpart.

This chapter explores three types of defense-related negotiations. First, we review the broad framework agreements intended to define and guide the U.S.-India security relationship. These agreements reflect the progress the two countries have made toward making defense a normal part of their interaction. At the same time, the sensitivities they evoke illustrate the hold that Cold War–era suspicions still have, especially on Indian attitudes and procedures. Next, we look at U.S. defense sales to India, where the two bureaucratic systems come together uneasily. Finally, we examine the two countries' negotiations over the agreements on equipment security, logistics, and related issues that normally come with a U.S. military supply relationship, a process bedeviled by different "red lines" on sovereignty issues. Chapter 8, on the U.S.-India agreement on civil nuclear cooperation, also addresses the issue of technology restrictions, which have been a perennial sore point in both nuclear and defense negotiations.

AGREEING ON A FRAMEWORK

India's defense cooperation with the United States during the Cold War years was severely restricted by both countries' policies. The most significant instance where the United States and India worked together came during India's brief and unsuccessful war with China in the high Himalayas in October–November 1962, which was discussed in chapter 2.

This episode illustrated some of the hallmarks of India's negotiating style. Although Nehru did make two formal, indeed desperate, requests for U.S. assistance, President John F. Kennedy's initial letter to Nehru on October 29, nine days after Chinese troops moved into Indian territory, effectively invited an Indian request, thus sparing India the need to make the first formal move. India had done its best to ensure that the answer would be "yes"; however, Foreign Secretary M. J. Desai and Finance Minister Morarji Desai had met with U.S. Ambassador John Kenneth Galbraith to alert him that India might have to ask for military aid and to urge that the United States not insist on an alliance. Galbraith had reassured them on this point, and Kennedy's willingness to forgo such political conditionality in exchange for U.S. help clearly came as a relief to Nehru. The sensitivity of this issue was underscored by the way the Government of India handled Nehru's November correspondence with Kennedy. It was sent with unusual secrecy, with MEA left out of the action except, apparently, for the foreign secretary. The then ambassador in Washington, B. K. Nehru, said years later in an interview that he had been embarrassed to have to deliver a message that deviated so starkly from India's nonaligned policy, so he had not shared it with any of his embassy staff. In another telling note, both the Indian and U.S. governments scrupulously avoided calling this action "aid." It was termed "procurement."[2]

This episode was both a success story and a cautionary tale. The success lay in the speed and responsiveness of the sometimes-lumbering U.S. supply machinery in sending military equipment to India. In spite of the Cuban missile crisis, which was taking place at the same time, the United States put together a military supply airlift within four days of receiving Nehru's first request, starting November 3. The military-to-military relationship seems to have been productive and friendly while the supplies were moving. However, the two sides subsequently saw the significance of this episode quite differently. For the United States, it was an example of finding common ground and working together with India. But the memory that this episode left in India was that there had only been a temporary "trickle" of military supply from the United States, less than the Indians had anticipated and which in any event was abruptly halted during the 1965 war with Pakistan. In other words, Indian analysts look back on this episode as a rather insignificant footnote to a basically unsatisfactory U.S.-India relationship, which compared unfavorably with India's experience with Soviet arms supplies. The experience tells us that no matter how smoothly the mechanics of military cooperation may work, what really matters is the underlying relationship at the national level.[3]

AFTER THE END OF THE COLD WAR, India and the United States recalibrated their relationship, and an important part of this process was a fresh attempt to work out agreed ground rules for military-to-military cooperation.[4] As this new relationship was crafted and implemented, what stands out is the difference between the way India and the United States organize their defense establishments. As we have already seen, the relationship between the Indian military and the Ministry of Defense (MOD) contrasts with the Pentagon, which is home both to civilian defense officials and to the U.S. military command structure. The U.S. chain of command runs from the Office of the Secretary of Defense through the Joint Staff to the combatant commands.

The policy role of the two ministries displays an even bigger contrast. The Pentagon is deeply involved in shaping U.S. national security goals and policies. Its civilian officials have critical policy roles and usually expect to spend their careers dealing with national security issues. Senior civilians—both career officials and political appointees—also provide staff for the U.S. National Security Council and are deeply involved in government-wide policy formation and in the most important negotiations. The Indian MOD is primarily responsible for budgets and procurement. It does not have an institutional role comparable to the Pentagon's in determining national security policy. Career civil servants from the Indian Administrative Service (IAS), who staff the ministry, often do not have a strong background in security issues and are therefore not necessarily the easiest "opposite numbers" for the kind of discussion on issues such as China, Indian Ocean security, or Pakistan that the United States sees as drivers of the U.S.-India strategic dialogue.

India also maintains a strong firewall between civilians and the military, in many ways higher and less porous than that of the United States.

Assignments of military officers to civilian departments or of civilian officials as advisers to military commands are common in the United States but rare in India, for example. But as previously noted, India's concept of "civilian supremacy" generally gives civilian bureaucrats the upper hand. In the U.S. system, civilian leadership relies heavily, though not exclusively, on politicians and senior political appointees both in the executive branch, especially the Defense Department, and in Congress, where the armed services committees of the two houses play major roles. The American and Indian sides look on each other as a mysterious labyrinth. This disconnect between counterpart organizations in the United States and India runs through the security negotiations that have taken place since 1990, aggravating the difficulty of meshing two quite different visions of the world and of the threat environment.[5]

The first step toward establishing a post–Cold War security relationship was a set of proposals presented by Lieutenant General Claude Kicklighter, commander of U.S. Army Pacific, to the Indian Chief of Army Staff, General Francis Rodrigues, in April 1991. The Kicklighter proposals, as they came to be known, concentrated primarily on exchanges of visits, training, and conferences. Their most ambitious provisions called for unit and combined training that went beyond the kinds of activities that had been carried out before. They also proposed an Indian role in regional conferences sponsored or cosponsored by the United States, a new concept for India.

Kicklighter's proposals were presented to the Indian army chief, but approval had to come from the MOD. This was a slow process. One participant recalls that the approval came through five days before the first scheduled meeting of the Executive Steering Committee, the seniormost U.S.-India body charged by the proposals themselves with conducting high-level strategic discussions.

In a sense, the remarkable thing about the Kicklighter proposals was how little negotiation took place. The proposals were carefully drafted to be constructive but as uncontroversial as possible. The Indian MOD approved them with practically no change, and the only real negotiations took place at the level of implementation. Some of the early accomplishments pointed the way toward the active pace of exercises that developed twenty years later. Noteworthy examples are high altitude combined training exercises and India's leadership role in hosting a 1993 multinational conference of armies in which Russia participated for the first time. Similar proposals were made and approved for naval cooperation within a year after the army program began, and eventually similar re-lationships developed for the air force.[6]

But in general, implementation moved slowly and carefully—some would say painfully. For India, a security relationship with the United States was still politically touchy, the result of four decades of very lim-ited U.S.-India security ties during the Cold War and of India's close relationship with the Soviet Union. Moreover, because of the military-to-military character of the Kicklighter proposals, the Indian govern-ment considered them a technical understanding and they therefore did not provide a full-fledged political "blessing" for U.S.-India military cooperation.

In 1995, four years after the Kicklighter proposals, India and the United States negotiated their first broad defense agreement, the Agreed Minute on Defense Relations. It was intended to establish a policy frame-work for a security relationship that had barely existed in the past. The negotiations reflected the beginnings of a strategic understanding be-tween the two countries as they came to terms with the breakup of the Soviet Union. They also, however, showcased the continuing political sensitivity in India of defense ties with the United States, and the mismatch between the responsibilities and operating styles of the two defense establishments.

Participants in the process recall that the decision to negotiate a for-mal agreement was boosted on the U.S. side by the appointments in 1994 of William Perry as secretary of defense and Frank Wisner, a high-flying career diplomat who had just completed several years as undersecretary of defense for policy, as U.S. Ambassador to India. Negotiations took place during a series of visits by mid-level civilian-military teams from the Pentagon. Civilian officials at the MOD were the principal negotia-tors for India, though successful visits to the United States by all the Indian service chiefs in the preceding year did a great deal to set a posi-tive tone.

The U.S. defense establishment found the process puzzling and some-what exasperating. They found the Indian side slow to respond, a prob-lem that crops up in many types of negotiations and that reflects in part the fact that Indian government offices are much more thinly staffed than their U.S. counterparts. What the U.S. negotiators regarded as routine drafting changes took months to turn around. The final drafting ses-sion, only a month before the visit by Secretary Perry that was to serve as the occasion for signing the documents, was punctuated by Indian requests for last-minute word changes that their American counterparts regarded as trivial.

After all that effort, the document itself was quite general. It established three vectors for cooperation: civilian to civilian; military to military; and defense production and research. It stipulated that the civilian channels would provide guidance to the other two, and set forth the consultations that would work out more specifically the areas for cooperation. The agreement was signed on January 12, 1995, by Secretary Perry and Indian Home Minister S. B. Chavan.[7]

The agreement did what both defense establishments needed it to do. It provided the high-level policy umbrella for the decisions on specific cooperation that were to be made by the consultative committees it set up. Writing some years later, the then defense attaché in New Delhi cited an impressive number of exercises, visits, and other joint activities that had been carried out.[8] The "scriptural citation" of a document signed by cabinet officers on both sides was important in permitting cooperation to go forward. Other countries have similarly found this kind of top cover important in working with India on security issues.

But implementation remained difficult and reflected a gap between the priorities of the two sides. The U.S. objective was to expand exercises and military-to-military activities, with interoperability as the big, long-term prize. For the Indian side, however, defense production and research was the most important feature of this agreement, and access to advanced technology was the primary objective. U.S. participants believed that there was also a gap in priorities within the Indian team: the Indian military also sought access to special courses, equipment, and doctrines, whereas Indian civilian officials focused almost entirely on coproduction. This gap between the objectives of the two sides colors security-related negotiations to this day.

The third in this series of broad agreements on defense cooperation, the Framework Agreement signed in 2005, was more ambitious than the first two. It started by acknowledging the two countries' "common principles and shared national interests," including a "common belief in freedom, democracy, and the rule of law."[9] It was signed six months after the tsunami relief effort and three weeks before the United States and India announced their intention to work toward an agreement making possible U.S.-India civilian nuclear cooperation, which will be described in greater detail in chapter 8. This period was the high point in the new U.S.-India relationship.

The content of the 2005 Framework Agreement reflected the strong political desire that had developed on both sides to cooperate and to give an increasingly public character to the emerging relationship.[10] U.S. officials argue that laying the groundwork for a new agreement started with a 2001 meeting of the Defense Policy Group that had been established by the 1995 framework. India's decision to escort U.S. vessels through the Strait of Malacca took place during this period and made a considerable impact on U.S. thinking. The exploratory work for the agreement was done, in back channels and very discreetly, by a mixed civilian-military team on the Indian side, including the deputy service chiefs, the MOD, and MEA.

This preparatory work started while the Indian government was still led by the Bharatiya Janata Party (BJP). By the time the 2005 Framework Agreement was ready, the Indian government had changed, but the new Congress Party leadership strongly supported the emerging U.S.-India partnership. Prime Minister Manmohan Singh was at the height of his political powers, as was Defense Minister Pranab Mukherjee, a political heavyweight but, like other Indian defense ministers, not one who had made a career out of defense issues.

The civilian officials below the political level, both in the MOD and in MEA, also appeared to their American interlocutors to have been empowered to move ahead with an ambitious document. The agreement defined thirteen broad types of activities the two defense establishments would undertake in pursuit of this shared vision and enshrined three channels for formal consultations between them. Some of the specific areas for cooperation listed in the document were strikingly more forward-leaning than those in the 1995 Agreed Minute. They included missile defense, for example. The 2005 Framework Agreement pledged to expand two-way defense trade "as a means to strengthen security, reinforce strategic partnership, and achieve increased interaction between the forces." The backing of the top of the Indian government made possible an expansive defense framework agreement, as it later helped deliver a nuclear agreement that was controversial in both countries. But unlike the later nuclear agreement, the 2005 pact did not impose legal obligations on either side and hence did not require the kind of exhaustive legal scrutiny that has stymied a number of other agreements. And, as with the previous defense agreements, the challenge of translating broad principles into implementation remained substantial.

In June 2015, soon after Narendra Modi completed a year as Indian prime minister, India and the United States signed another ten-year framework agreement. In effect, the 2005 agreement had become the standard for U.S.-India framework agreements, and the relatively smooth progress to signature was a barometer of the revival of U.S.-India relations. The 2015 pact included essentially the same areas for cooperation as in 2005 and a somewhat expanded list of forums for coordination between the two defense establishments. The most significant change was the higher profile given to technology transfer and to potential coproduction projects. The prospect of better access to technology garnered most of the coverage of the agreement in the Indian press, a useful reminder of India's priorities in defense cooperation. From the U.S. perspective, another 2015 addition was noteworthy: the reference to "exchanging experiences and practices in operating common defense platforms." This brought the notion of "interoperability," much prized in U.S. defense circles, into the approved areas for cooperation.[11]

The 2005 and 2015 agreements were both signed at the cabinet level and required clearance by the Indian Cabinet. In the U.S. system, both could have been handled by a flag officer or senior defense official. This reflects the greater caution that is built into the Indian system and the importance of having political buy-in for defense agreements, especially those with the United States.[12]

DEFENSE TRADE

Defense trade negotiations put into sharper relief two issues that had surfaced in these broad operating agreements: the two countries' different goals in defense negotiations and the asymmetry between the defense establishments. Then Deputy Secretary of Defense Ashton Carter captured the difference well when he quipped, in a September 2013 speech to the Center for American Progress, that his mission to troubleshoot U.S.-India defense relationships was called the DTI by both countries, but the two countries spelled out the acronym differently. For India, this stood for Defense Technology Initiative; for the Americans, it meant Defense Trade Initiative. The initiative soon came to be called by both names—Defense Trade and Technology Initiative.[13]

As with the defense framework agreements, India's primary goal in defense trade with the United States is to maximize the technological sophistication and domestic production of its defense equipment. This

objective grows naturally out of India's commitment to strategic autonomy and is supported with equal tenacity by governments of any party,
as well as by military officers and civilian officials. While there are no
differences over the goal, there may be internal differences within the
Indian government over the trade-offs required to achieve it. India's military officers are more sensitive to the need to bring new equipment into
use quickly. Defense production officials, and more generally civilian
defense ministry officials, tend to favor maximizing local production
even if doing so significantly delays the introduction of new technology
into the military inventory.[14] For them, establishing a more capable defense industry is seen as a critical contribution to strategic autonomy,
which can trump the military services' desire for a timely equipment
upgrade.

From the U.S. perspective, however, the long-term objective of defense
trade negotiations is to build a relationship. Ultimately, the United States
hopes to partner with India in handling future contingencies in the region, recognizing that doing so would clearly require an Indian political
decision when a potential case arises. Both the experience of negotiating
military purchases and the fact of using similar equipment, in the U.S.
view, would help make interoperability technically feasible and would
add to both sides' comfort level should it become necessary. The active
pace of military exercises is part of the same process of becoming
more accustomed to working together. For the United States, this is
regarded as a building block for pursuing shared Indian and U.S. strategic interests.

Indian defense leaders, like their American counterparts, speak of
India's becoming a "net security provider" in the Indian Ocean region,
a term they seem to interpret as an extension of India's quest for primacy in the region.[15] The concept of interoperability is regarded in some
Indian security circles as a euphemism for unwanted U.S. intrusion into
India's sovereign domain. Further complicating the U.S. concept of building a relationship, Indian practice is to make defense trade decisions one
transaction at a time.

Washington faces one unique problem in negotiating defense sales to
India: the perception that the United States is an "unreliable" supplier.
The issue grows out of the requirement that the U.S. government formally
notify the Congress of proposed arms sales above a certain threshold
($14 million for major defense items, and higher figures for other types
of equipment). The U.S. Congress can technically pass legislation amend-

ing or blocking the sale at any time before the transaction is consummated. Such legislation is unusual, but not unprecedented.[16] All Indian officials remember that after India's 1974 nuclear test, the U.S. Congress passed legislation incorporating retroactive conditions for nuclear fuel sales, obliging the U.S. government to terminate a thirty-year supply contract for nuclear fuel for a nuclear power plant at Tarapur, near Mumbai.[17] They also remember the U.S. cutoff of arms supply in 1965. Both reinforce the perception of unreliability.

This problem is intensified by the widespread view that U.S. export controls impose an enormous burden on India's defense purchases. This was undoubtedly true in earlier years. The procedures used in requesting export licenses were set up in the Cold War years, when there were significant obstacles to sales to India. However, as we will see, U.S.-India understandings on export controls have created a presumption of approval for many sales to India. Most of India's potential defense trade does not require a license, and of the items requiring a license, the overwhelming majority are now approved. Nonetheless, the perception has been hard to shake, reflecting both the hold of history and the opacity of the U.S. export control system.

Much of the U.S. effort in negotiating defense sales with India is directed toward overcoming the twin perceptions that the U.S. export control system is rigged against India and that the United States is an unreliable supplier. In two recent sales, the transfer of the USS *Trenton* and the sale of P-8 aircraft, the U.S. side made strenuous efforts to respond quickly to an Indian expression of interest. In the case of the *Trenton*, U.S. officials recall that their timely confirmation that the ship was available astonished their Indian counterparts. In the case of the P-8s, things began badly. An Indian admiral involved in the transaction recalled that the two governments had nearly completed negotiations for purchase of a different aircraft, a P-3C, when the U.S. side found that there were none to spare. However, when India inquired about the P-8I, the answer was yes. Speed, responsiveness, and perhaps most important, a transaction that put India into a privileged category made a big impact. As the admiral recalled, India was the first recipient of this aircraft outside the United States.[18]

India's defense purchases are governed by the Defense Procurement Procedures (DPP), which the MOD formally updates about once a year. These regulations are intended to foster transparency in an effort to eliminate corruption. As a practical matter, they are designed to reduce discretion to an absolute minimum, in the belief that discretion pro-vides opportunities for inappropriate influence. India's most famous defense procurement scandal, involving the purchase from Sweden of Bofors artillery pieces, helped bring down Rajiv Gandhi's government in the late 1980s. Its legacy lingers: MOD civilians, who have the major role in evaluating compliance with procurement rules, are especially skit-tish about any action that deviates from the procedural norm and might open them to accusations of corruption. After the Bofors scandal, it was twenty-seven years before the Indian government signed a new interna-tional purchase contract for artillery.[19] Following accusations against Air Chief Marshall S. P. Tyagi in a 2013 investigation into helicopter pro-curement from Italy, military officers, who are responsible for writing the technical specifications, will undoubtedly become more cautious as well.[20]

The procurement procedures also reflect the priority India places on acquiring technology and using it to build up its domestic industrial ca-pacity. At the heart of the procedures are three features that appear in virtually all international arms purchases: transfer of technology, co-production, and offsets.[21] The 2013 update to the DPP established five classes of procurement, starting with domestic purchase and manu-facture and ending with "Buy and make with transfer of technology" and, as a last resort, "Buy (global)." Any transaction other than a straight domestic purchase needs to be justified at high levels. The rules them-selves run to several hundred pages, and the policy guidance given to those who administer a purchase has normally tilted toward domestic production. Most importantly, any deviation from the procedures must be authorized by the Defense Acquisition Council, the most senior pro-curement decisionmaking body, headed by the defense minister.[22]

Because of the exacting requirements of the DPP, and because of the sensitivity of MOD officials about possible accusations of corruption, little negotiation can take place during the formal process of comparing competing bids. The most important negotiating on specific purchases consequently takes place either before they are formally open for bids or after the finalist or finalists have been selected.

India's planned purchase of 126 medium multi-role combat aircraft, one of the largest potential sales of military aircraft for many years, attracted six bidders, including two from the United States: Lockheed-Martin and Boeing. Both U.S. bidders were eliminated in 2011 in favor of two European finalists, and final negotiations with the French Rafale, the apparent winner, are still under way. This sale illustrates how the process works, how the Indian and American systems do and (often) do not mesh, and how the process reflects India's operating style and priorities.

The technical specifications for the equipment and the scope of technology transfer are largely set before India issues a formal request for bids. These are among the many areas where the Indian and U.S. systems do not mesh well. The Indian military services write the technical specifications for equipment they wish to buy, and their effort to include as much high technology as possible can lead to specifications that do not actually match products available in the marketplace. This problem can be mitigated by early professional contacts between supplier companies or the military representatives of supplier countries and companies and officers in the relevant Indian military service. But the United States does not process requests for release of information or approval of technology transfer without a formal expression of interest from the would-be purchaser, normally in the form of a Letter of Request. As we have repeatedly seen, the Indian government does not like to make the first move, and U.S. officials involved in defense trade complain that Letters of Request are hard to process through the Indian system.

In the case of the multi-role combat aircraft, both would-be U.S. suppliers made plans to include coproduction of the aircraft in their bids, knowing that they had no chance of success without it. Coproduction had not figured in previous U.S. sales of sophisticated equipment to India. The U.S. government announced before the formal bidding started that it would be willing to approve coproduction and to release the Active Electronically Scanned Array (AESA) radar system that the Indians were interested in. When the bid specifications were issued, the radar system was included.

Another feature of bid documents that can be contentious—and that U.S. bidders regularly try to influence in the pre-bid phase of the process—concerns the basis for price comparisons. U.S. equipment is relatively expensive, but U.S. suppliers believe they can offer a lower long-term cost for maintenance and upkeep. They therefore prefer to have bids evaluated on "life cycle costs" rather than the initial cost of the equipment. The DPP make no provision for life cycle costs, though the rules do not preclude using such costs as the basis for evaluation. Indian purchasers prefer to deal with firm, fixed costs and are skeptical that suppliers can really be held to an estimate of life cycle cost.

Another issue that can come up in this early phase is customization. Historically, most U.S. military equipment is designed for the needs of the U.S. forces, though suppliers are becoming more sensitive to international needs. The wide variety of conditions in which the Indian military needs to operate, combined with a strong sense of Indian uniqueness, makes it particularly important that equipment be tailored for their needs. One comprehensive review of U.S.-India defense trade regards this as an area where Israeli and French bidders excel in comparison with their U.S. counterparts.[23]

Once the bids reach the evaluation stage, the first decision the Indian purchasing officials must make is technical: which bids meet the specifications in the bid documents. Bidders not compliant with every one of the specifications may be disqualified, in contrast to the "best value" standard used in the United States. This practice creates a particular problem in cases where the specifications may not exist in one single piece of equipment.

In the combat aircraft purchase, ambiguous language in the specifications created a problem. The specifications referred to "reliable" aircraft, which representatives of at least one of the supplier companies interpreted as a preference (or perhaps a requirement) for more than one engine. However, the number of engines was not explicitly mentioned, and the finalists India selected were single-engine aircraft.

After the technically compliant bidders are selected, the least expensive among them is supposed to win the bid. In any competition for sophisticated equipment, these judgments will be more complex and less black-and-white than this description suggests. But the process of evaluating bids and asking for clarifications on both technical features and price opens up a second window for negotiation. This is also the point at which the suppliers and the Indian purchasers start to deal with formal paperwork, which can bring its own surprises. One retired U.S. military officer recalled a proposed sale of howitzers in the 1980s. The documents were ready to sign, the cost review was complete, and the negotiators on both sides had the necessary authority. A lawyer on the Indian side looked at the back of the sales document and found two disturbing statements: that the U.S. government could cancel the sale at any point before shipment, and that the U.S. government reserved the right not to refund money that had already been passed on to the supplier company. The general leading the U.S. delegation assured the Indians that this had "never happened." The Indians nonetheless were unwilling to sign. The

United States apparently stopped using that form after that incident, but it was too late for that sale, and the underlying problem was in any case still there.[24]

Military sales usually involve both the U.S. government and the supplier company. The relationship between them is confusing to Indian officials. This problem is aggravated by the two different systems the United States uses for military sales. For Direct Commercial Sales, the supplier company deals directly with the foreign government on all financial aspects of the sale; under the Foreign Military Sales (FMS) program, the U.S. government makes the sale. Each of these systems has some features that are incompatible with India's normal modus operandi. Commercial sales have the advantage that India can negotiate a firm, fixed price, as its procurement rules require. However, commercial transactions can give rise to the kind of problem that arose with the howitzer sale. FMS sales are in one sense a more familiar phenomenon, since most of India's other purchases are government to government. However, by law, the U.S. government can make neither a profit nor a loss on these sales, so the price can be adjusted upward or downward to achieve this goal, even at a late stage of the process.

With an increasing volume of Indian defense purchases from the United States, above $9 billion in value between 2008 and 2013,[25] both sides are becoming more familiar with each other's systems. But as always, the process of negotiating, even in a rule-bound system like the ones both India and the United States maintain, is not just an interaction between two systems: the personal connection matters, too. Working-level U.S. officials involved in defense trade lament that so few of them have had the opportunity to build up long-term relationships with their Indian counterparts. The United States regularly sends officers to the Indian Defence Services College, and Indian officers come to the United States for professional military education. But neither side seems to cultivate specialists in U.S.-India defense relations.[26]

At a higher level, the transition from Pranab Mukherjee to A. K. Antony as Indian defense minister in 2005 led to a perceptible cooling of the way the Indian MOD handled ties with the United States. Antony himself was much less personally involved than his predecessor. Under his stewardship, ministry officials made it more difficult for senior U.S. defense officials to be received at the top.[27] He also guarded zealously his reputation for financial probity—a very positive characteristic, but with the unfortunate side effect of increasing the already strong aversion to risk among his officials. Especially in an area like defense trade, where many important issues are subject to highly elaborate rules and procedures, a good personal relationship cannot ensure a mutually beneficial result, but without personal ties, that result may be much more difficult to obtain.[28]

WHAT GOES WITH DEFENSE SALES?

Defense sales pit two complex and somewhat hidebound systems against each other; the agreements the United States routinely signs with countries that buy its equipment embody a clash between U.S. and Indian views of sovereignty. The U.S. government is required to establish end-use verification arrangements for several different types of purchases. In the case of arms exports, the Arms Export Control Act requires the president to establish a system for end-use monitoring of the military equipment it provides.[29] In addition, most purchasers of U.S. military equipment also sign agreements covering the protection of U.S. communications security information (known as CISMOA) and providing for logistical support in an Acquisition and Cross Servicing Agreement (ACSA). From the U.S. perspective, these are all uncontroversial housekeeping agreements. In India, however, all three run into India's acute sensitivity over any real or perceived infringement on its sovereignty.

The only one of these issues that the United States and India successfully negotiated dealt with end-use-monitoring. An earlier agreement with the same broad purpose had been signed in 2004, covering items subject to U.S. export licenses that were potentially usable for both nuclear and non-nuclear purposes (so-called dual-use items). Formally called the India End Use Visit Arrangement, this agreement was part of a package of agreements formalized in 2004 as part of the liberalization of U.S. export controls applicable to India under the Next Steps in Strategic Partnership (discussed in greater detail in the chapter 8). This agreement was regarded as a success in the United States. It permitted the United States to meet its requirement for verification and made possible U.S. implementation of export control standards more favorable to India. It followed in a tradition of working around, rather than neatly complying with, procedural requirements that triggered India's sensitivities about sovereignty. However, it triggered a kind of catch-22 that has cropped up in other aspects of sensitive trade. During the negotiations, the Indian side requested that the requirement for post-shipment verification be explicitly mentioned on each export license. However, the then head of the Department of Atomic Energy refused to approve any transaction in which this requirement was mentioned. The Government of India continued to state that it considered the arrangement valid, but it proved impossible to implement.

The end-use monitoring required for military sales had the same purpose, but different legal authority and a different bureaucratic cast of characters on both sides. It was part of a system known in the U.S. government as "Golden Sentry." For three years, negotiations got nowhere. From the start, the Indian side resisted the whole idea. Indian officials made clear that they found the whole idea of "monitoring" an affront to India's sovereignty, and despite constant U.S. assurances to the contrary, they were convinced that the United States did not insist on it with its most favored defense partners. Opponents of the agreement charged in the press that these arrangements might be the first step in a long-range plan to draw India against its will into U.S. military operations.[30] The U.S. team was focused on the need to meet its legal requirement. At one point during the negotiations, the United States told India it had put a hold on new transfers until the agreement got signed.

At this stage, negotiations took place in New Delhi, in Washington, and in other locations where the officials involved met on the margins of other meetings. In New Delhi, the U.S. Embassy's political section worked with MEA, and the defense attachés worked with the Indian military. MEA seemed to the American side to take a harder line on the sovereignty issue. The usual exchange of drafts and counter-drafts moved slowly at best. More often, the Indians presented their objections, leaving it to the Americans to present alternative drafts. One U.S. participant recalled that this effectively put the U.S. team in the position of negotiating with themselves. Another commented that U.S. negotiators regularly got maneuvered into the position of wanting a result more than their Indian counterparts did. Another U.S. participant observed that negotiations came close to success in 2007, but as so often happens did not quite reach the finish line.

When the Obama administration took office in early 2009, Secretary of State Hillary Clinton decided to make this agreement a priority. This led to the real endgame, which took place at a higher level, in very close-hold talks between the leadership of the U.S. Embassy and the National Security Adviser. By then, U.S. officials had succeeded in persuading their senior Indian counterparts that there was no way to avoid end-use verification if they wished to purchase defense equipment from the United States—and that this requirement applied to all U.S. customers, including Britain and Israel, which also considered their relationships with Washington unique. The United States also noted that there had been at least a couple of cases in which an end-use verification clause had been included in Indian contracts for purchases of defense equipment. India did not regard these as precedents, but the "non-precedents" nonetheless were part of the picture.

A series of senior-level meetings ensued, typically one-on-one, over a period of five months. The Indian National Security Adviser also had occasion to meet senior U.S. Defense and State Department officials during this period, which provided an opportunity to reinforce the message he was receiving from New Delhi. In these negotiations, the Indian side was striving for language that it could present as being consistent with its view of Indian sovereignty. The key issues, not surprisingly, were India's insistence on advance notice of end-use verification visits, and U.S. flexibility as to where the visits would take place. Neither of these requirements was incompatible with the U.S. legislative language governing the monitoring requirement, but formally agreeing to them involved a fairly lengthy process on the U.S. side.

The prospect of Secretary Clinton's first official trip to India in July 2009 forced the pace of negotiations and proved to be the occasion for formalizing the agreement. Her star power undoubtedly helped produce a change in context and packaging that may have made the agreement go down more easily. On the final day of the visit, three agreements were formally recorded: the creation of a fund for cooperative scientific research; a Technology Safeguards Agreement, part of a package governing U.S. and Indian joint participation in space research; and the agreement that had been the subject of these negotiations, on the terms for end-use monitoring for U.S.-supplied military equipment. The safeguards agreement was an important breakthrough, ending a longstanding prohibition on U.S. space work with India. Also announced at the same time was the designation of two sites intended for U.S.-supplied nuclear plants under the U.S.-India nuclear agreement. The end-use agreement was not technically "an agreement." Rather, the two countries exchanged notes recording the standard language that would be included in every purchase contract subject to U.S. military end-use requirements.[31]

The end-use monitoring arrangement continued to attract high-profile press commentary. Some of the comments were aimed at reducing controversy; several articles noted that other countries also insisted on verification, albeit not with the same level of detail and legal intrusiveness as the United States. But some commentators focused on what they regarded as the violation of sovereignty involved in this arrangement. Brahma Chellaney, well known as a sovereignty hawk even by Indian standards, published a "fact sheet" that characterized the arrangement as one applicable to *"client states*—states that are under the U.S. security and nuclear umbrella."[32] (In fact, the requirement applies to all U.S. military sales.)

With this commentary on the public mind, Prime Minister Manmohan Singh made a formal statement to the Indian parliament a week after Clinton's departure, explaining the end-use arrangement. The heart of the statement was his assurance to India's legislators "that our Government has taken all precautions to ensure an outcome that guarantees our sovereignty and national interest." He went on to clarify that the verification procedures were designed to protect India's equities, highlighting the points that India had insisted on in negotiations: "India has the sovereign right to jointly decide, including through joint consultations, the verification procedure. Any verification has to follow a request; it has to be on a mutually acceptable date and at a mutually acceptable venue."[33] An agreement of this sort with the United States could not be treated as a routine matter; political explanations at the highest level were required.

The other two agreements that normally accompany military supply relationships with the United States both aroused high-octane suspicions that they were steps down a slippery slope threatening India's sovereign freedom of action. The Communications Interoperability and Security Memorandum of Agreement (CISMOA) deals with the protection of secure communications gear. For the United States, "interoperability" seemed a desirable and uncontroversial goal. For India, however, it sounded like sending the fox to guard the chicken coop. At several points in the defense procurement process, Indian officials had made clear that they preferred standard commercial equipment rather than secure equipment that they feared might be easily penetrated by the Americans. U.S. negotiators pointed out, to no avail, that the CISMOA would give India the ability to interoperate, not just with the United States, but with other NATO countries and Japan.

The agreement variously known as "acquisition and cross servicing" or "logistics support" also ran aground, primarily because of a fundamental misperception by India about the agreement's purpose and operation. U.S. officials familiar with this type of agreement describe it as an accounting mechanism, which permits both sides to run a "tab" for such support costs as fuel supply and use of facilities, settling the "tab" at agreed-on intervals. The agreement does not remove the requirement for the United States to obtain host country agreement, case by case, for any support that it might seek. Senior Indian military officers, however, describe the logistics agreement as tantamount to the establishment of U.S. bases. Nonofficial commentary describes it as a slippery slope, noting that since India rarely operates offshore, the only country that could benefit from this kind of facilities usage would be the United States. One U.S. official said that the issue was "like Kryptonite." Even officials in the Ministries of Defense and External Affairs who understood that these perceptions were incorrect did not want to touch it. The proposed agreements have gone nowhere.

IN JUNE 2012, U.S. Secretary of Defense Leon Panetta appointed his deputy, Ashton Carter, to oversee and troubleshoot the U.S.-India defense relationship. By all accounts, it was an inspired choice, illustrating the importance of consistent high-level attention and of good personal relationships in addressing U.S.-India issues. As deputy secretary, Carter had the standing to bring together all the U.S. players involved in a decision. His Indian interlocutors saw him as someone who had been interested in India and convinced of the importance of the relationship even before he came into government. This made it easier for him to gain their trust. It also smoothed over the protocol difference between him and his Indian opposite number, India's National Security Adviser. A U.S. deputy secretary ranks immediately below a cabinet officer and is considered the protocol equal to a Secretary in the Indian system; India's National Security Adviser formally has the status of a minister of state.

Carter's approach combined hands-on problem solving with an ambitious vision for U.S.-India security relations that fostered India's interest in building up its own technologically sophisticated production. He understood the Byzantine U.S. procurement system well, and his rank and convening power helped him push through decisions in Washington. He also worked hard to deal with the disconnects between the U.S. and Indian systems. The requests he made of India focused on specific issues, including the inflexibility of its rules on administering offsets. He also tried to tackle such long-standing problems as the slow process of approving Letters of Offer and Acceptance, noting that U.S. suppliers could not maintain all the terms of a bid indefinitely if India's decision process took a very long time. In the September 2013 speech cited earlier in this chapter, Carter listed some of his accomplishments in making the U.S. system more user-friendly for business to India. He noted that in the operation of U.S. export controls, India now benefited from a presumption of approval, and that it was in a group of only eight countries under the Strategic Trade Authorization, for whom "a small number of items" could be bought with no license required. He also mentioned his success developing a procedure for having the United States issue advisory opinions on export licenses before the sales contract had been drawn up. He described this as eliminating a "catch-22," giving both the Indian buyers and the American sellers a measure of certainty early in the process about what technology would ultimately be licensed by the United States.

More attractive, from the perspective of his Indian counterparts, were the visionary goals Carter sought for the defense relationship. In the same speech, he proposed that the two countries choose products for coproduction that would showcase both of their strengths. He also announced that he had proposed to his Indian counterparts that India and the United States work to coproduce a maritime helicopter, a naval gun, a surface-to-air missile system, and a scatterable antitank system. Almost as important was his decision to put the controversial agreements on communications interoperability and logistic support on the back burner. They had become irritants, and for the time being, were not worth the effort.[34]

This was all good news and illustrated the power of a senior international interlocutor with the personal and institutional credibility in India and in Washington to serve as champion for the relationship and power through some long-standing obstacles. The bad news, unfortunately, was a problem Americans and those who have dealt with them on complex issues will find familiar. At the end of 2013, Ashton Carter stepped down as Deputy Secretary of Defense and returned to private life. The U.S. government assumes that no one is indispensable and that officials can fill the vacuum that results when a principal negotiator leaves. But in dealing with India (and with many other countries as well), the departing negotiator's personal relationships—both inside the U.S. government and across international boundaries—are not easy to replace, especially when he has taken on the task of changing long-standing operating procedures and styles. Not surprisingly, Ashton Carter's appointment as U.S. Secretary of Defense about a year later was greeted with great warmth in New Delhi.[35]

Chapter 6 sketched out some of the characteristics of India's negotiating style. Looking at its security-related negotiations, a few themes described there come up with remarkable consistency. First and foremost, India is a sovereignty hawk. This is a central feature both of India's overall negotiating style, as we have already seen, and of its vision of its global role. Not surprisingly, defense-related negotiations display this characteristic even more than some other areas.

U.S.-India defense ties, like those of a number of other countries, operate within the framework of a broad agreement on "rules of the road." The experience of the past half century makes clear that these agreements in practice serve to ratify an underlying political relationship, not to substitute for it or create it. The 2005 defense framework agreement was possible only because the U.S.-India relationship was fundamentally changing, and the 2015 one reflected a new momentum in that relationship. Even with the added energy supplied by the civil nuclear agreement, however, the underlying relationship remains politically sensitive. The experience of successful military cooperation and security negotiations builds up confidence—but very slowly, and this process is always vulnerable to the political tensions of the moment or to changes in personnel. The suspicions that grew up during the long Cold War years are a stubborn feature of the landscape. And despite the considerable accomplishments of the new post–Cold War U.S.-India relationship, the concept of "partnership" has not yet been adapted to the needs of these two very different partners.

Looking at the actual conduct of negotiations, the relatively thin staffing of India's government means that all but the most important negotiations proceed slowly, with long periods of inaction between bursts of activity. When one puts this pattern together with the well-known U.S. preference for action and schedules and with traditional U.S. discomfort with long pauses between parts of a negotiation, one result is a frequent U.S. tendency to "negotiate with itself," offering several drafting proposals in succession. Especially when the interest in a particular agreement is asymmetrical, this pattern presents far more risks for the more eager party—typically the United States—than for the one willing to wait for a lengthy process to play out.

Finally, defense negotiations illustrate the vital importance of high-level attention and high-level "champions" when working on sensitive issues with India. The personal, sustained leadership of a senior U.S. official is the most effective way to navigate the differences between India's system and others, and to deal with the issues of sovereignty that are guaranteed to arise when security issues are in play. The negotiations leading to the civil nuclear agreement between the United States and India, discussed in depth in chapter 8, will illustrate this point powerfully.

CHAPTER EIGHT

Negotiating Nuclear Cooperation

ON JULY 18, 2005, the White House stunned India and the United States with the announcement that President George W. Bush and the visiting Indian prime minister, Manmohan Singh, had undertaken to work toward a series of agreements that would open the door to civilian nuclear cooperation between the two countries. This promised to resolve a problem that had bedeviled U.S.-India relations since the first Indian nuclear test over three decades earlier. In the process, the United States would be seeking controversial changes not just in U.S. policy but in law and in the functioning of international nonproliferation institutions that had largely been developed by earlier American governments. India would agree to unprecedented inspections of its civil nuclear facilities. It soon became clear that the process would be equally controversial within India.

The lengthy negotiations that led up to this announcement and those that followed it were the most complex and precedent-shattering that India and the United States had ever undertaken with one another. They combined bilateral and multilateral dealings by both countries and led to choices that neither country had anticipated making. They represent a unique passage in the transformation of U.S.-India relations. Nearly ten years later, participants from both sides look on this agreement as the most successful U.S.-India negotiation ever—even as they acknowledge that some of the early promise was not fulfilled. The civil nuclear agreement shows what can be accomplished when both governments are implementing a powerful shared top-level commitment and both top negotiators are empowered by their leaders to "get to yes." It also shows how deep are some of the differences in the ways both countries react, how their democratic impulses can impede agreement, and what they learned about one another during this long journey.

THE ROOTS OF THE NUCLEAR discord between India and the United States go back to the Treaty on the Non-Proliferation of Nuclear Weapons (NPT), which established a closed group of treaty-recognized "nuclear weapons states" limited to the five countries that had manufactured and exploded a nuclear device before January 1, 1967. The rights and responsibilities of nuclear weapons states and non-nuclear weapons states under the treaty were quite different. The United States and the other treaty-recognized weapons states retained their arsenals, but membership in the treaty prohibited them from helping a "non-weapons state" develop nuclear explosives. Non-weapons states joining the treaty undertook not to develop nuclear weapons and to put all their nuclear materials under international safeguards as a guarantee that this commitment would be kept.[1] U.S. policy and law went further, prohibiting all nuclear cooperation with "non-weapons states," as the treaty defined them, unless the receiving state placed under safeguards of the International Atomic Energy Agency (IAEA) all its nuclear materials and facilities, not just those involved in the proposed cooperation. This was referred to as "full-scope safeguards."

India exploded a nuclear device in 1974. The 1967 cutoff date for recognition as a nuclear weapons state was already built into the treaty, however, and the treaty's amendment provisions were virtually impossible to use, so India was locked into the treaty's "non-nuclear weapon state" category and its nuclear status was barred from recognition under the treaty. U.S. policy on full-scope safeguards ruled out nuclear cooperation unless India dismantled its weapons program and agreed to forgo any explosive capacity. India was not prepared to meet these conditions, which most Indians felt smacked of neocolonial discrimination. Full-scope safeguards had become the default requirement in the international institutions that NPT members, with the United States in the lead, had developed since the treaty went into effect. And tight strictures on trade in products that could be used in nuclear facilities had become a major inhibition on U.S. high-technology trade with India.

FIRST STEPS

India and the United States started working on a major transformation in their relations while the Clinton administration was in power in Washington and Atal Bihari Vajpayee of the Bharatiya Janata Party (BJP) led the government in Delhi. The decision to work toward this change was inspired both by the breakup of the Soviet Union and by India's economic surge. The U.S.-India standoff on nuclear issues was regularly raised by the Indian government as the most important obstacle to a genuine strategic relationship.

The U.S.-India dialogue during the late Clinton years was dominated by India's 1998 nuclear test. India wanted to establish a new relationship with the United States without giving up its newly declared nuclear weapon; Washington wanted to maintain the integrity of the nonproliferation system while opening up a serious strategic dialogue with India. The extended discussions between U.S. Deputy Secretary of State Strobe Talbott and Indian Foreign Minister Jaswant Singh did establish a genuine dialogue and led to the lifting of most of the sanctions the United States had been obliged to impose on India following the tests. Singh's main objective was to achieve "due and proper recognition" of India's nuclear capability and to have the United States acknowledge that India had broken none of its international undertakings.[2] He achieved both, at least implicitly. The United States, however, did not succeed in obtaining Indian agreement to join the Comprehensive Test Ban Treaty (CTBT).[3] The final nail in that treaty's coffin was driven in not by India but by the U.S. Senate, which voted decisively to reject the treaty. In any event, the Clinton administration was not seeking to open up nuclear cooperation with India. It had the limited goal of side-stepping the obstacle U.S.-India nuclear differences posed to a decent bilateral relationship.[4]

The George W. Bush administration wanted to craft a major partnership with India and concluded that removing the ban on nuclear cooperation was the only way to get there. This was a revolutionary goal. In its first term, the Bush administration started with more modest objectives, with two negotiations aimed at facilitating U.S. exports of high technology to India and strengthening Indian export controls. The United States had both commercial and strategic objectives: it wanted to expand exports from cutting-edge U.S. industries as well as strengthen strategic cooperation. Although this was not explicitly acknowledged in government-to-government dealings or even agreed on by the full interagency process in Washington, these negotiations were the initial step on the road to the nuclear agreement.

The first task was to create a High Technology Cooperation Group between the two countries and to agree on the principles governing its work. This would build on the cooperative structures that had begun in the late Clinton years, typically working groups composed of upper- and middle-level officials. Former U.S. officials involved in the high-tech trade issue recall that the request for a High Technology Cooperation Group came from India. Under Secretary of Commerce Kenneth Juster, who led the negotiations for the United States, wanted to expand the group to include a wide range of government agencies as well as the private sector. Juster recalled the initial meeting in late 2002 as a bit stiff and formal and the press release as minimal and bland.[5]

Three months later, an Indian team came to Washington to work out a statement of principles for the new group, sending a draft statement a few days ahead of time for their U.S. counterparts to review. Juster persuaded the U.S. team to confine its changes to the most important issues rather than wordsmithing the document. This helped change the negotiating atmosphere markedly, and the negotiation concluded in an afternoon. This time, the statement of principles and the accompanying press release were drafted with palpable enthusiasm and reflected both sides' acknowledgement of the issues most important to their counterparts.[6]

Both the good feeling and the speed of this agreement were decidedly different from many U.S.-India negotiations. Both sides emerged believing they could work smoothly with each other. Perhaps more significantly, both concluded that their counterparts were serious about the new relationship they were starting to develop and prepared to focus their effort on the issues most important to both sides. India's principal delegate was Foreign Secretary Kanwal Sibal, another indication of India's practice of keeping the Ministry of External Affairs (MEA) in the driver's seat wherever possible.

This initial agreement spelled out principles. It also led to a further easing of U.S. controls on the export of many dual-use technologies, those with both a commercial and military purpose. The next step was to reach an agreement on the substance of export controls on more sensitive items as well as space, civil nuclear, and missile defense items. This proved to be a much more complicated task.

This next phase started with strong momentum. Late in 2003, Deputy National Security Adviser Stephen Hadley and Under Secretary Juster traveled to New Delhi to present a proposal that became known as Next Steps in Strategic Partnership (NSSP). The core idea was a package deal: India would implement export controls and take other steps that would permit the United States to satisfy its legal and policy requirements that sensitive U.S. exports would not be misused or resold; and the United States, in a phased manner, would alleviate some of the burden of its controls on sensitive shipments to India relating to space, high-tech trade, missile defense, and civil nuclear cooperation. In mid-January 2004, after a series of meetings, the two countries announced the basic framework.[7] This created a sense of accomplishment but also some degree of disappointment among those in the Indian government who had been working on the issue. They felt that the agreement as announced did not live up to the proposals Hadley had made in Delhi, and that these had been watered down by the U.S. nonproliferation community. This sense in India that the United States was underperforming recurred at various points in the long nuclear negotiations, especially in the nuclear establishment and among foreign policy elites outside the government.

In fact, the negotiations were just beginning. Sibal's term as India's foreign secretary came to an end in November 2003, and he left to become Indian ambassador to Russia. What followed was a slowdown in the NSSP negotiations. Indian and American participants recall this differently. The U.S. side believed that the change in personnel had slowed things down; Indian participants attributed it to fallout from the disappointment mentioned above, coupled with the ever-present Indian concerns about anything that appeared to impair Indian sovereignty. Both recall that the negotiations had gotten bogged down in details.

The Indian election of May 2004 brought to office a new government led by the Indian National Congress, with Manmohan Singh as prime minister and former foreign secretary J. N. Dixit as national security adviser. Dixit had a well-established reputation for realpolitik-oriented strategic thinking, reflected in a Congress Party manifesto he reportedly drafted that put a realist cast on foreign policy. He came into office determined to transform the relationship with Washington and was well on his way to assembling a handpicked team at MEA to implement this project. His team included two of only three or four Indian Foreign Service officers who had worked on the U.S. relationship for over ten years. Ronen Sen, who took over as ambassador in Washington that summer, was a key member of the team, as were S. Jaishankar, who was specially recruited to be the Joint Secretary for the Americas at MEA in New Delhi, and Sen's deputy, Raminder Jassal.[8]

Early in the new Congress government's tenure, things came to a head. The Indian negotiator who had come to Washington and his U.S. counterparts have different recollections and seem to have been partly talking at cross-purposes. The Indian government sent its U.S. counterparts a list of over thirty issues India wanted to raise. The U.S. participants saw this approach as straight out of what they thought of as the "Indian playbook"—meticulous attention to detail and insistence on going through every word in every paragraph.[9] The U.S. negotiators basically said "no." They stated that the United States had already accommodated India's position on a number of issues that were now being reopened; they had tried their best to make the NSSP process succeed to the benefit of both nations, but they were not prepared to keep going over this material. The U.S. negotiator took the unusual step of sharing his speaking notes with the Indian government.

The Indian recollection is that, with the new government and its team now fully briefed and in place, they were prepared to be much more ambitious. They were concerned about losing sight of the forest for the trees and were looking to go beyond the confines of NSSP. The principal negotiator, who had traveled to Washington solo, recalls having been instructed not to come home until the negotiations were back on track.

After a two-day pause for reflection, negotiations resumed and were completed remarkably quickly. The negotiating dynamic had been reset, and the stage was set for a more ambitious approach. The agreement was signed in September 2004. In this last phase of negotiations, Americans involved in the process recall that the United States did address a few issues India had raised in the list that had initially been turned aside. The agreement included measures of considerable substantive and symbolic importance, including removing several units of the Indian Space Research Organization from the U.S. Department of Commerce's list of entities banned from trade with the United States. Interestingly, while the U.S. undertakings were spelled out in the press release, the details of changes to India's export control laws were not. The nuclear content of the agreement dealt primarily with establishing a "presumption of approval" policy for all dual-use items not controlled by the Nuclear Suppliers Group (NSG) that were intended for export to the "balance of plant" portion of an Indian nuclear facility subject to IAEA safeguards—in other words, for the part outside the nuclear core.[10]

THE NUCLEAR DEAL

By the time the second Bush administration started in 2005, both governments had prepared for a serious run at a nuclear agreement. India had handpicked its team and made clear to the United States that ending its "nuclear pariah" status without limiting its weapons program was its key requirement. The export control agreement embodied in the NSSP gave the United States the critical prerequisite for more ambitious negotiations. Washington had put together a policy framework for civil nuclear cooperation with India, including beginning to define what changes in law and regime obligations it would require.[11] Condoleezza Rice, who was more strongly committed to the idea of a nuclear deal than Colin Powell, had succeeded him as secretary of state. The nuclear issue had implicitly been put on the table. Senior officials had reflected together on what makes a partnership strategic and on the need to work on longer-term convergences of interests between the United States and India. They had made elliptical references to getting beyond the traditional, sterile discourse on nonproliferation. Indian participants in the process recall that President Bush and Prime Minister Singh had talked in general terms about a nuclear deal when they met in New York in September 2004. But the two governments had not talked about what kind of deal might be desirable or feasible.

The First Announcement

That bridge was crossed in the spring of 2005. Secretary Rice visited Delhi in March 2005, and she and Prime Minister Singh agreed to start negotiations. The first public indication that the United States and India were moving on a new track was a statement from an unnamed White House official that the United States wanted to "help India become a major power in the twenty-first century."[12] Under Secretary of State Nicholas Burns was named U.S. negotiator when Rice returned to Washington.

Both governments hoped to announce something during the state visit of Prime Minister Singh, planned for mid-July 2005. Two months is an extraordinarily short time for concluding even an agreement in principle on something as complex as this, especially where implementation will require changes in U.S. legislation. The negotiators were in a pressure cooker.

Between April and July 2005, Burns and his Indian counterpart, Foreign Secretary Shyam Saran, carried out an intense and very discreet series of discussions about what a nuclear agreement might entail. It was clear by this time that retreating to a less ambitious agenda would not make the negotiations much easier. Addressing technical problems like the long-standing issue of how to dispose of the spent fuel at the U.S.-supplied reactor in Tarapur would require the same kind of legislative heavy lifting that would be needed for civil nuclear cooperation, with much less payoff in terms of the strategic U.S.-India relationship. So they decided to go for a more comprehensive agreement. Both governments handled this phase in restricted channels. The many technical experts on nuclear issues in both countries were not in the room at this stage and the degree of coordination between them and the negotiators varied.

The Indian advance team for the prime ministerial visit arrived in Washington on July 14, 2005, three days before the prime minister, intending to negotiate the joint announcement. This was the first time that the two governments had formally embodied their discussions of a nuclear agreement in a document. Working under this kind of time pressure was highly unusual for both governments.

The negotiating team, as with the pre-visit talks, consisted of senior, nontechnical officials. Two key issues came close to scuttling the whole enterprise. The first was how the United States would acknowledge India's nuclear status. The solution here lay in creative drafting, avoiding NPT-derived phrases like "nuclear (or non-nuclear) weapons state," and including a comparison with the United States. The statement stipulated that "India would reciprocally agree that it would be ready to assume the same responsibilities and practices and acquire the same benefits and advantages as other leading countries with advanced nuclear technology, such as the United States."

The second near-killer issue was how to couch the limitations on U.S. cooperation. India had always rejected the idea of placing any limits on its military nuclear program. But the Indian team did acknowledge that the United States had a legitimate interest in ensuring that the new cooperation program would not expand India's military program. India agreed that it would formally designate certain of its nuclear facilities as "civilian" and that U.S. nuclear cooperation would be limited to these facilities. This commitment was embedded in a paragraph listing the obligations of "states with advanced nuclear technology," thus suggesting that this was something the "nuclear haves" did.

The rest of that paragraph recorded a series of Indian undertakings, including a commitment not to transfer enrichment and reprocessing technology to countries that did not have them, to place civilian nuclear facilities under safeguards, to negotiate an additional protocol with the IAEA, and to continue the moratorium on nuclear testing. Each one was carefully crafted to preserve India's position that all its commitments were voluntary and unilateral. Defining precisely what these promises meant was the arduous task of subsequent negotiations, either with the United States or with one of the nonproliferation organizations. Also included were some Indian commitments on export controls that had been foreshadowed in the earlier negotiations on NSSP.

But before the joint statement was released, the agreement had another near-death experience. The head of India's Department of Atomic Energy (DAE), Anil Kakodkar, who arrived after the advance team, said "no." India's nuclear establishment, having been on the receiving end of U.S. sanctions, was deeply suspicious of the whole enterprise and reluctant to engage with the United States. It was also in a position to trash a nuclear deal with Washington as a limitation on India's strategic autonomy. According to one participant, Foreign Minister Natwar Singh went over the agreement with Kakodkar, recording exactly what the latter could live with on each point. Things seemed to break down on the evening of July 17. The next morning, Secretary Rice and Burns met with Prime Minister Singh and he agreed to try again. The negotiators went back to work and reached agreement, but just barely: the Indian side agreed to the final word changes as the White House staff came to tell the group that President Bush was ready to receive them. The statement was released the same day.[13]

The Political and Commercial Dimensions

The nuclear negotiations then moved on to increasingly difficult and technically thorny agreements. At the same time, the public release of the statement—with no advance warning either to the U.S. Congress or to the Indian Parliament—put the process squarely into the political domain. From this point forward, the negotiating process expanded to include two new sets of players: both countries' legislatures and two international organizations, the IAEA and the NSG. In effect, there would now be three sets of negotiations proceeding at the same time: between the Indian and U.S. governments; between the governments and legislatures of each of the countries; and, in the final stages, between the governments and the international organizations. They were all essential parties to the deal, but this fact greatly complicated the process.

The next publicly visible move after the July 2005 announcement was Prime Minister Singh's formal statement to the Indian parliament, briefing the members on his visit to the United States and presenting the nuclear agreement in the context of much improved relations with Washington and India's national security. Formal statements like this one were the anchors of the Indian government's outreach with its parliamentarians. The subsequent history of the negotiations would probably have been smoother if these statements had been more energetically supplemented by individual contacts with both government and opposition members. But the statements did put a formal Indian government position on the record, in the name of the prime minister, making clear that the commitment to this effort came from the top.[14]

Because no agreement could be implemented unless the U.S. Congress passed the necessary legislation—two laws, as it turned out—outreach on Washington's Capitol Hill was even more important. The proposed nuclear deal was controversial, and at this early stage, the weight of expert and Congressional opinion was against it. In particular, those with a background in nonproliferation were deeply skeptical.

The Bush administration had not briefed anyone in the U.S. Congress in advance of the announcement. Since agreement was reached only at the last minute, there was really no basis for an advance briefing. But not surprisingly, resentment over the absence of prior consultations colored the reactions of many legislators. One key U.S. participant in this process recalls, however, that there was very broad congressional support for closer relations with India, based on the democratic heritage the two countries shared. He concluded that the Congress would need time to think about the idea.

The hearings in the Senate Foreign Relations Committee on November 2, 2005, put both perspectives on display. One of the administration witnesses, Under Secretary of State for Political Affairs Nicholas Burns, had been the principal U.S. negotiator of the July 2005 declaration, a position he retained through March 2008. The other, Robert Joseph, who was Under Secretary of State for Arms Control and International Security, had taken office only a few weeks before the July 18 statement and had therefore not been directly involved in the negotiations. Both officials presented the administration's strong support for the agreement. Among the nonofficial witnesses, two were former senior officials of the U.S. government, Ronald Lehman and Ashton Carter. Both saw opportunities for the United States in the proposal, but conditioned their support on strengthening India's contributions to international nonproliferation. The remaining two witnesses were strongly opposed.[15]

Rice and Burns made working with Congress on the civil nuclear agreement a top priority and dispatched senior U.S. government officials to brief individual members of the U.S. Congress. Burns recalled that in the nine months starting in July 2005, he had seen at least half the members of the Senate, on both sides of the aisle. These were serious meetings, and among the key participants were then Senators Barack Obama and Hillary Clinton, both relatively late converts to support for the agreement, and Joseph Biden, who also backed it.

Supporting the administration's advocacy was a business blitz, spearheaded by the U.S.-India Business Council and a broader group it put together, the Coalition for Partnership with India. The business groups highlighted the commercial benefits they hoped to achieve. Estimates of potential sales of nuclear reactors over ten years ran as high as $27 billion, with benefits of up to half a trillion dollars for the Indian economy over two decades.[16] Commercial opportunities can usually galvanize the U.S. government and the Congress, so the trade potential was a highly visible theme throughout the negotiating process.

India too was deeply engaged in outreach to the U.S. Congress, in close consultation with the U.S. administration. Indian-American organizations mobilized as never before and, by all accounts, had a significant impact. Indian officials also participated, both those based in Washington and visitors from Delhi, in close cooperation with the U.S. administration. Several of the Indian officials involved commented that direct advocacy with another country's parliament was a highly unusual experience for them. One noted that the Indian MEA normally resisted allowing Indian officials to engage in this kind of advocacy. Two others looked back on the experience with obvious relish, recalling how they had tried to get to know individual members and understand what they cared about, and to build their advocacy on that foundation. They tried to set up one-on-one meetings, feeling that the presence of note takers could be an inhibiting factor (and possibly observing, as one U.S. participant did, that sympathy for expanded ties with India was stronger among members of Congress than among congressional staff). Indian officials approached Capitol Hill groups that they hoped would be helpful—the Congressional Black Caucus, Jewish groups (with whom the Indian embassy kept close relations), evangelical groups. Visits to members of Congress in their constituencies were especially prized.

The Indian participants in this process noted that the first reactions they received were at best skeptical. For instance, Henry Hyde, Chairman of the House International Relations Committee, appeared reluctant at first to engage with the Indians, but warmed up over time. Not all of India's parliamentary encounters ended well: the Indians felt embarrassed by statements Representative Tom Lantos made about Iran. One of the participants in this process, in describing his approach, commented that it was crucial to do more listening than talking and never to win an argument. But in this massive three-year campaign, the Indian team showed tremendous skill, sophistication, and mastery of American—and U.S. congressional—culture. By the time the U.S. Congress took final action on the nuclear deal, Indian officials had, by one account, engaged in direct conversations with at least half the members of the House and the Senate. They made a major contribution to securing passage of the two pieces of legislation that the deal required.

Similarly, the U.S. team was in touch with India's parliamentarians. Burns, as chief U.S. negotiator, made it a point to meet the principal foreign policy-watchers in the leadership of India's opposition parties, especially the BJP, when negotiating sessions took place in India. Later in the long negotiating process, representatives of private U.S. and Indian-American groups visited India and made a point of urging the BJP to support the nuclear agreement.[17]

The U.S. side had less contact with the Left Front of communist and other leftist parties that were part of the Indian government's majority but also passionate opponents of the deal. The U.S. ambassador to India, David Mulford, and at one point Secretary of the Treasury Henry Paulson did see some of their leaders. As it turned out, the Indian government did not conduct as much initial spadework with either the opposition or the Left Front, which contributed to the agreement's near collapse later in the process.

The Indian and U.S. teams also collaborated in their press strategy, but this was a more uncomfortable process. The U.S. negotiators were convinced that regular and reasonably candid briefings of the press would be essential to a successful U.S. legislative effort. Burns had spent two years as State Department spokesman, and was highly skilled at dealing with the U.S. press. India's normal foreign policy process involves less interaction with the press than the U.S. team was accustomed to, so the idea of regular press briefings took some getting used to. The two foreign secretaries who participated in the post-2005 negotiations,

Shyam Saran and Shivshankar Menon, both decided to stay close to Burns in this process. They went over the key points for each briefing before it started. Often the briefings were carried out together and included both the Indian and the U.S. press, whether in Delhi or in Washington. Because Burns and his counterparts visited each other's capitals often (and not just for nuclear negotiations), they usually combined the nuclear briefings with a broader discussion of U.S.-India cooperation. This joint effort was yet another indication of how closely the two countries worked together. It probably narrowed, though it did not eliminate, the gap in how the press in the two countries covered the process.

Soon after the July 18 announcement, Iran's nuclear program came up for discussion in the board of governors of the IAEA. This proved to be yet another political land mine for the Indian government. On the one hand, the U.S. government made clear to the Indians that their vote on the proposed IAEA resolution criticizing Iran's "failures to meet its obligations" under its safeguards agreement would inevitably have a major impact on U.S. congressional attitudes toward nuclear cooperation. On the other, India's relations with Iran were important: Iran was a major energy supplier to India. Moreover, India's Muslims and many of its policy elites looked on Iran as the key indicator of whether India was maintaining sufficient "strategic autonomy" as it drew closer to the United States. India chose to vote with the United States to criticize Iran, an action interpreted by the Bush administration as a strong signal that it was serious about working with the United States. Twelve other countries abstained, including Russia and China. The U.S. nuclear negotiators breathed a sigh of relief, but the Indian government was politically pilloried for its vote.[18]

The Separation Plan

The next phase in U.S.-India nuclear negotiations was just getting under way when the Iran vote came up. In the 2005 agreement announced by President Bush and Prime Minister Singh, India had undertaken to designate formally which of its nuclear facilities would be considered "civilian," safeguarded in perpetuity and hence eligible for cooperation with the United States—the "separation plan." This designation was the jumping-off point both for India's subsequent safeguards negotiations with the IAEA and for its further nuclear cooperation agreement with the United States. For this and subsequent negotiations, India designated a somewhat broader "working group" that was responsible for negotiations. India's foreign secretary headed the group, and his principal colleagues were the National Security Adviser's office, the official responsible for the United States in MEA, and the head of the DAE. On the U.S. side, Burns remained lead negotiator and those with technical expertise, especially the Bureau of Nonproliferation in the State Department and the Department of Energy, now became key members of his team. On both sides, the negotiators had direct access to their national leadership. This was not particularly unusual in India, where foreign secretaries are often able to reach the prime minister and work in the same building. In the United States, however, direct access to the Secretary of State for a negotiator is not automatic. In both cases, it turned out to be critical in giving the teams the ability to explore unconventional solutions to negotiating problems.

The separation plan had to be an Indian plan, which would eventually be proposed to the IAEA. It also needed to be acceptable to the United States, although it would not be presented as a negotiated product. Getting there once again involved both internal and bilateral negotiations.

The natural cleavage in the U.S. government was between the regional experts, on the one hand, and the nuclear and legal experts, on the other. The U.S. side achieved an unusual degree of delegation discipline and buy-in to what was clearly a controversial negotiation. A longtime expert from the State Department's nonproliferation bureau, Richard Stratford, became one of the most active and creative members of the U.S. team, working hand in glove with those whose professional background meshed more comfortably with this pathbreaking negotiation. Indian participants recall some friction between the U.S. "nonproliferators" and the Indian skeptics about the nuclear deal, but once the U.S. government had set its course, there was rather less internal bloodshed than is often the case.[19]

The internal negotiations were tougher on the Indian side. India's foreign policy officials had come to share their leaders' commitment to reaching a nuclear cooperation agreement. They had the lead in dealing with the United States. They had to operate on somewhat less favorable terrain inside their government, however. The nuclear establishment basically did not want to deal with the United States and remained deeply skeptical, indeed hostile, throughout the negotiations for the separation agreement. The DAE had a regular representative on India's negotiating team, Dr. R. B. Grover. The Indian foreign policy officials worked hard to manage the stage setting in U.S.-India meetings so that the frequently harsher views of the nuclear officials were not expressed in ways that would make it impossible for the Indian government to propose or accept compromise language. They found ways of explaining particular sensitivities to the U.S. side, to avoid unnecessary confrontation. One U.S. participant in the negotiations believed that his Indian counterparts were trying to avoid having the senior Indian nuclear officials deal directly with the U.S. delegation leadership.

President Bush was set to visit India on March 1, 2006, so this date became the deadline for the separation agreement. The most visible issue to be worked out—and perhaps the most straightforward—was the number: which and how many of India's nuclear facilities would be covered. But two other issues took longer to resolve and had enormous significance for future elements of the nuclear agreement. The first was fuel security. The Indian government, having had the United States cut off fuel supplies a quarter-century earlier, insisted on an assurance that this would not happen again. The issue was a land mine for the American negotiators. The U.S. legislation that had interrupted supply in the past was still in effect. India was not prepared to have its unilateral undertaking to desist from another nuclear test transformed into a bilateral commitment, a position that ruled out some of the standard drafting devices the United States. would have preferred. In the end, the United States incorporated "assurances regarding fuel supply" into the nuclear cooperation agreement (known familiarly as the "123 agreement") that was next on the two countries' bilateral negotiating agenda. It also undertook to work with India to support Indian efforts to develop a strategic fuel reserve and to work with the IAEA on fuel security.

The second touchy issue was whether India would place its breeder reactors under safeguards. Here, India agreed to place "all future civilian thermal power reactors and civilian breeder reactors" under safeguards in perpetuity, but its existing prototype and test breeder reactors would not be safeguarded.

Negotiations on the separation plan took place in a series of meetings between September 2005 and March 2006. As with the previous agreement, they came close to collapse. A few days before the presidential visit, after a meeting where the American team felt it was being stonewalled, the delegation walked out of a dinner and headed back to Washington. This is highly unusual U.S. government negotiating behavior, the more so since the delegation's leaders were known as smooth operators not given to dramatic gestures. The United States saw this action as a way of focusing the attention of their opposite numbers; Indian participants downplayed the incident.

The Indian delegation leader called and urged the U.S. team to come back and try again. This second try, however, encountered the same kind of last-minute near-collapse as the July 2005 agreement. When President Bush's plane landed in Delhi, he was told that there would be no agreement. Burns and National Security Adviser Hadley went into the trenches again, negotiating till the wee hours with the Indian team. As had happened with the July 2005 statement in Washington, the final language changes were agreed minutes before the meeting between President Bush and Prime Minister Singh was to start.

The separation agreement figured in the joint statement concluding the Bush visit, but only in a very brief paragraph. The two leaders "welcomed the successful completion of discussions on India's separation plan and looked forward to the full implementation of the commitments in the July 18, 2005 Joint Statement on nuclear cooperation." Press briefings, one by President Bush and Prime Minister Singh and another later that day by Under Secretary Burns, filled in more details. Singh led off by stating that "India had finalized" its decision on which of its nuclear facilities were to be considered civilian and placed under safeguards—a formulation that underscored the plan's unilateral Indian character. Burns also described how the United States proposed to treat fuel supply assurances.[20] But the details of the program, including the number of plants to be safeguarded (fourteen out of India's twenty-two facilities) and the language embodying the fuel supply assurances, were first revealed in the prime minister's *suo motu* statement in parliament on March 7, which also laid the text of the separation plan on the table.[21]

The Hyde Act

For the balance of 2006, public action shifted to Washington, where the first piece of enabling legislation was now under formal consideration. The U.S. Congress zealously guards its prerogative not just to pass laws but to draft them. The administration did submit the text of a bare-bones bill; as often happens, the real congressional action was based on two different versions of the bill drafted in the Senate and in the House of Representatives, respectively. The features that caused the most controversy between the United States and India appeared in some form in both houses.

One provision that sparked outrage in India was a requirement that the U.S. president report annually to the Congress on, among other things, "whether India is fully and actively participating in United States and international efforts to dissuade, isolate, and, if necessary, sanction and contain Iran" for its nuclear program. This was a classic case of two democracies not understanding one another. In Washington, that provision was regarded as a standard dodge. It had been inserted in a successful effort to eliminate more intrusive language that could have explicitly conditioned nuclear cooperation on India's Iran policy. From Delhi, however, even the reporting requirement looked like an intrusion into India's sovereign domain.

Iran policy was not part of the negotiations, but it remained—and remains—an important part of the political background music both governments must deal with. It came up regularly at congressional hearings in the United States. In May 2007, seven congressional leaders, including Lantos, wrote an "open letter" to the Indian prime minister urging, among other things, that India "sever military cooperation with Iran." They were greeted with renewed outrage at this perceived intrusion on India's right to set its own foreign policy.[22]

The second provision that raised controversy in India stated that the authorization for nuclear cooperation would end if India detonated a nuclear device in the future. This was no surprise to either Indians or Americans—indeed, it even appeared in the administration's initial legislative draft—but its reiteration in the enabling legislation made the issue of India's testing moratorium a central one for the negotiations still to come on the nuclear cooperation agreement and in the multilateral arena.[23]

The multilayered campaign to strengthen congressional support for this legislation, which had started soon after Prime Minister Singh and President Bush announced their intention to work toward a nuclear agreement, reached its climax as the bill was going through Congress. Burns had met frequently with Representatives Hyde and Lantos to update them on the progress of the negotiations, as did Condoleezza Rice. It was a wild ride, but in the end a successful one. The Henry J. Hyde United States-India Peaceful Atomic Energy Cooperation Act of 2006, signed by President Bush on December 18, 2006, opened the door to making nuclear cooperation with India legal and set the basic legal ground rules that would govern it. Chairman Hyde, having been a skeptic at the start, took pride in having his name on the act, which was one of his last legislative acts before retiring from the Congress. The bill passed with overwhelming bipartisan majorities in both houses—a testament to how the weight of opinion in the United States had shifted in the preceding year and a half.[24]

The 123 Agreement

The next phase of negotiations saw two agreements being negotiated more or less simultaneously. The bilateral task was to negotiate a nuclear cooperation agreement, required under Section 123 of the U.S. Atomic Energy Act (hence the shorthand name "123 agreement") for any kind of nuclear cooperation. The multilateral one, which formally did not involve the United States, was for India to agree with the IAEA on an India-specific safeguards agreement and additional protocol.

Negotiating the 123 agreement took sixteen months and eight negotiating sessions, in New Delhi, Washington, and sometimes third countries. The teams that had worked on the separation plan continued into this phase. They already had the opportunity to learn about each other's operating styles and sensitivities. Participants on both sides agreed that this experience was critical to their ability to navigate the even more treacherous waters they now faced. As in the past, side by side with the discussions between the two governments, there were continuing negotiations. In the Indian government, these followed the same fault lines that had already become apparent in previous phases. The Prime Minister's Office and MEA were strongly committed to a successful negotiation; the DAE was more concerned about maximizing India's flexibility and preferred no deal to a suboptimal one. U.S. participants from both sides of the traditional policy division recalled an unusual degree of harmony and delegation discipline during this phase.

This time, the teams were negotiating an agreement for which there were multiple precedents on the U.S. side, with many agreements in place and publicly available.[25] The normal impulse of a U.S. negotiator would have been to start from a standard template. However, India was unique— it had a nuclear weapons program and was not an NPT-recognized nuclear weapons state—so none of the existing accords suited the particular Indian circumstances.

The Indian negotiators eventually concluded that their best bet would be to seek precedents for the kind of agreement they wanted, combing through previous U.S. agreements. One Indian official deeply involved in this process commented that U.S. openness about its previous agreements was one of the most attractive features of dealing with the United States. He noted that he still had a binder containing all the previous agreements, in case he needed them in the future. This agreement had to cover a long list of specific issues, several of which were guaranteed to be extremely troublesome.[26] Both sides came to the table having done extensive homework and prepared to exercise their highest drafting skills—but also prepared to be creative.

The initial meetings were devoted primarily to dealing with India's anomalous situation in the nuclear world. This was accomplished by limiting the scope of the agreement to India's safeguarded facilities. The United States made clear that nothing in the agreement could help the Indian military nuclear program, but also that the arrangement would not constrain other activities involving equipment or materials acquired outside the agreement with the United States.[27]

The second challenge was how to deal with the legal constraints placed on the United States by the Hyde Act. The act prohibited U.S. supply of enrichment and reprocessing equipment and also specified that further Indian nuclear tests would lead to termination of nuclear cooperation. The normal practice for U.S. negotiators would have been to include the language of the legal prohibition in the agreement. This, however, would put the Indians in a position of acknowledging that they were constrained by U.S. legislation, which was offensive to their view of sovereignty. It would also give an internationally binding character to India's testing moratorium, which India was determined to maintain as a voluntary, unilateral act.

The solution lay in finding non-legislative language that kept the United States in compliance with the Atomic Energy Act of 1953 and protected U.S. rights and responsibilities under the Hyde Act. The two negotiating teams by this time understood each other's concerns well and worked together in a remarkably collaborative fashion.

Two examples illustrate the kind of creativity that went into this process. The first was the issue of reprocessing. The United States does not export reprocessing equipment, and the Indians understood that their 123 agreement could not override this policy. However, they wanted to preserve India's option to reprocess fuel supplied by the United States, which was important as a way to demonstrate that India was obtaining full cooperation from the United States. The negotiations centered on the right to reprocess rather than the supply of equipment. The U.S. team leaned as far forward as it legally could on the principle of Indian eligibility, while deferring the practicalities. Thus, the United States gave advance consent for reprocessing U.S.-supplied fuel, but the agreement specified that in order to bring this right into effect, India would build a new national reprocessing facility dedicated to reprocessing safeguarded nuclear material under IAEA safeguards, with the precise arrangements and procedures to be agreed within one year after India requested the start of negotiations. This negotiation was in fact completed a few months ahead of schedule, after the Obama administration took office.[28]

The second example is Article 14, Termination and Cessation of Cooperation. The key question was how to reflect the Hyde Act's requirement that the United States end its nuclear cooperation if India detonated a nuclear device. The Indian government argued that it could best maintain its position that its testing moratorium was unilateral and voluntary if the agreement made no reference to testing. For the U.S. side, however, it was essential that it retain the right to react if India did test. The agreement handled this issue by including two full pages on the procedures to be followed if either party wished to terminate the agreement and cease cooperation—without specifying the grounds for such an action, and without ever mentioning testing. The termination process started with required consultations, lasting a year, the procedures for which in turn were spelled out in detail in Article 13. Underlining India's concern about its nuclear status, this article specified that "the Parties recognize that such consultations are between two States with advanced nuclear technology, which have agreed to assume the same responsibilities and practices and acquire the same benefits and advantages as other leading countries with advanced nuclear technology." The termination clause includes special provisions covering cases of alleged breach of the agreement and binds the parties to consider such extenuating circumstances as changes in their underlying security situation. The party seeking to terminate could cease cooperation if it concluded that agreement could not be reached in consultations, a provision that effectively would permit suspension of the agreement in a shorter period if necessary. The explanations that the two governments gave when the text of the agreement was released confirmed their view that the negotiators had squared the circle. India had preserved its right to test. The United States retained its right to respond, including suspending the agreement if the president so decided.

The third category of killer issues in the 123 agreement had to do with fuel assurances. The separation agreement had made broad undertakings about what the United States would do to support continuity of fuel supply to India's safeguarded reactors. The expectation was that these assurances would be spelled out in the 123 agreement. This proved to be the most difficult issue from a technical point of view and was hotly disputed within the U.S. government. The U.S. lawyers argued that the United States could not make fuel supply assurances legally binding; the Indian team cited President Bush's statement and his association with the separation agreement. In the end, the 123 agreement simply picked up verbatim the language that had been used in the separation agreement, without attempting either to make the process more specific or to spell out the legal character of these assurances.

Both teams were pushing hard to get the agreement finished in the summer of 2007. For all the amity between the teams, the divisions in the Indian team were still apparent as the 123 negotiations proceeded. On issues where India's nuclear officials opposed a compromise solution, resolution was often reached outside the negotiating room, through recourse to the prime minister.

The final negotiations took place in Washington in July 2007. The last session was a marathon. The Indian press reported on July 21 that the Indian negotiating team had extended its stay to try to overcome the remaining few issues.[29] The delegation included not just its customary head, the foreign secretary (by this time Shivshankar Menon had taken over this position), but also National Security Adviser M. K. Narayanan and the secretary of the DAE, Anil Kakodkar. Emblematic of the negotiating relationship that the two sides had developed was one participant's recollection of how the final drafting problems were resolved. There were four outstanding issues. Burns and Hadley met with Menon and Narayanan at the White House to break the logjam and decided that each side would get its way on two of the issues; and within a few hours, there was a complete draft.

The next day, front-page stories in India reported that the text was to be formally submitted to the two governments. Over the next week, unnamed Indian officials provided extensive briefings to the press, which recounted India's success in achieving its negotiating objectives.[30] On July 27, both governments released the text of the agreement and the

Indian government simultaneously briefed the parliamentary opposition.[31] The next day, the three most senior Indian officials who had been in Washington for the final talks held a joint press conference to support the agreement. This was an important milestone: DAE secretary Kakodkar, the greatest skeptic during the negotiations, was quoted several times stating that the agreement met India's objectives.[32]

On August 13, Prime Minister Singh formally briefed the Indian parliament. He covered all the expected points—India's expectations for full cooperation befitting a "state with advanced nuclear technology," the requirement for an India-specific safeguards agreement, fuel supply assurances, and his conclusion that the agreement preserved the integrity of India's nuclear program. He dealt forthrightly with the two most controversial issues: the handling of reprocessing (including a reference to the long-standing U.S. policy of not exporting enrichment and reprocessing equipment) and the provisions for termination. He wound up with a ringing restatement of India's commitment to an independent foreign policy.[33]

India Suspends Action

The moment of triumph was brief. The Indian government was peppered with questions about the agreement, focusing especially on those provisions of the Hyde Act that Indians found intrusive. A BJP spokesman called for renegotiating the agreement; the U.S. government publicly rejected that idea. Only five days after the prime minister's speech in parliament, the Politburo of the Communist Party of India-Marxist (CPI/M)—the largest party in the Left Front that was allied with the government coalition but not a member of the government—issued a statement describing the agreement as "not acceptable." The party warned the government of dire consequences, a threat to bring down the government, if it proceeded with the planned safeguards talks with the IAEA before the left's objections had been fully considered.

The next twelve months were perhaps the most dramatic instance on record of parliamentary involvement in a major foreign policy action taken by an Indian government. The details of how the face-off in India's political system played out in the Indian political system are spelled out in chapter 5. Manmohan Singh telephoned President Bush in October to say he was putting the agreement on ice. The shock in Washington was palpable. Many observers assumed that the deal was dead and bemoaned the massive investment of time and political capital in this enterprise.

The administration worked hard to keep it alive and to give Prime Minister Singh the time and space to deal with his opposition. With uncharacteristic discipline, the U.S. government maintained "radio silence" on the nuclear agreement, saying only that this was an internal political matter for India.

The IAEA Safeguards Agreement

The next step on the negotiating path was to work out an India-specific safeguards agreement with the IAEA. After a period of political regrouping, the left parties in India agreed that the negotiations with IAEA staff could carry on, provided the government did not bring a safeguards agreement before the IAEA Board. Formal negotiations began at IAEA headquarters in Vienna on November 22, 2007.[34]

The United States was not a party to these negotiations, though U.S. officials were active behind the scenes in asking other governments to support the process. Because of India's anomalous nuclear status, none of the standard formulations would fit the circumstances. The negotiators found the most useful precedents in the site-specific safeguards agreements in place in nuclear weapons states and wound up borrowing language from these agreements. The safeguards agreement specified the facilities in India that were covered—the same list as in the separation plan—and committed India to maintaining these facilities for non-military use. India was free to add facilities to the list of civilian facilities, but not to withdraw them. Those close to the process described the negotiations as straightforward. Not surprisingly, the resulting document picked up themes and turns of phrase that had recurred throughout the crafting of the nuclear deal, such as the recognition that India was "a state with advanced nuclear technology" and the stipulation that the agreement should not constrain activities at sites not covered by the agreement. Most importantly, the agreement was not to come into force unless the other agreements necessary to secure India's access to civil nuclear cooperation were also approved, a clear reference to the approval of the NSG. It was also linked to the fuel supply assurances referred to in the separation plan and the 123 agreement with the United States.[35]

The safeguards agreement had to be approved by consensus in the IAEA Board of Governors, who could not be formally asked to consider it until the Government of India had dealt with its political crisis. As noted in chapter 5, this took longer than the negotiations for the safeguards agreement. Having faced down the threat to bring down the government, Manmohan Singh requested a governors' meeting on the subject in July 2008. After all the drama of the political uproar in Delhi, the approval of the agreement on August 1 was something of an anticlimax, and its entry into force in May 2009 passed with little public notice.

By this time, however, public opinion in India was coming together in support of the agreement, despite all the political controversy it had aroused. Even left-leaning publications like *The Hindu* and numerous retired diplomats and other officials had come out in support. The end of the left parties' blocking of the agreement was greeted with quiet relief.[36]

The Nuclear Suppliers Group

The United States by this time was very close to its inexorable quadrennial deadline. The normal congressional session was supposed to end in September and a new president would be elected in November 2008, with President Bush's second term ending in January 2009.

Because of the need for legislation, the Congressional schedule became critical to completing the negotiation. Post-election "lame duck" sessions of Congress can occur but cannot be counted on, since the administration has no control over the congressional calendar. Moreover, unlike the situation in 2006, the Republican party that held the White House had lost control of the Senate. Thus the August 1 approval of the IAEA agreement left little time for the two remaining steps: obtaining agreement in the Nuclear Suppliers Group for a waiver of its normal requirement of full-scope safeguards, and passage of a second piece of enabling legislation. The U.S. administration was growing increasingly anxious about the time.

The U.S. negotiating team had talked about timing with their counterparts, but did not believe they had instilled a sufficient sense of urgency. The classic U.S. game of "good cop, bad cop" involves using congressional leaders to deliver unwelcome messages to foreign governments. In February 2008, two Democratic senators, Joseph Biden and John Kerry, and one Republican, Chuck Hagel, passed word to the top levels of the Indian government that unless the IAEA and NSG had both acted by May 2008, it would be impossible to complete the legislation and a new administration in January would inevitably want to renegotiate the deal before resubmitting legislation.

Deadlines punctuated this negotiating process from the start. As we have already seen, Indian negotiators have been known to delay difficult decisions until the last minute—the moment the president and prime minister are ready to begin their meeting, for example. The classic American use of deadlines more typically involves calculating when intermediate steps in a long process must be completed in order for the end result to be achieved in a timely fashion. This is often an ineffective tactic in negotiations with India. It comes across as another instance of the United States trying to make the world conform to its specifications. In this case, New Delhi's constraints were arguably more compelling than Washington's, since a false move could cost Prime Minister Singh his job. The Indian government carried on, recognizing that the congressional visitors were not bluffing, but ultimately not being driven by the suggested deadline.[37]

One very experienced participant described the negotiations in the NSG as the most brutal exercise in multilateral diplomacy he had ever witnessed. The NSG reaches decisions by consensus, so a single dissenting voice could scuttle the waiver. The United States, a founding member of the NSG, had undertaken to do its best to deliver a positive vote, not encumbered by conditions. For the United States to have credibility in pulling together the final moves in the NSG plenary, however, India also had to plead its own cause with the NSG members.

India's diplomatic persuasion actually started well before the formal process was initiated. One of the negotiating sessions for the 123 agreement was held on the margins of the NSG's 2007 plenary meeting in Cape Town, to facilitate informal contacts between the Indian negotiators and the NSG representatives. But the heart of India's outreach effort was bilateral. Foreign Secretary Shyam Saran and his successor, Shivshankar Menon, worked with all the NSG members, visiting most in their capitals. The most intense diplomacy was with countries that had given up their own nuclear options to join the NPT, as well as with China. Saran's experience with the Conference on Disarmament in the 1980s meant that he knew many of the players. Brazil was a key example. The Brazilian foreign minister was initially outraged: how could India ask Brazil, which had persuaded its own people to give up their nuclear option, to endorse an arrangement under which India would keep its weapons? But in the end, after at least one more visit from Delhi, the Brazilians agreed.

The United States, as it had promised, supplemented India's diplomatic efforts. U.S. participants recalled that seven or eight countries were at best dubious, and that is where U.S. efforts were concentrated. Australia was a particularly important one; others included Ireland, Sweden, Finland, Austria, and New Zealand. The United States also pressed China hard on this issue.

The NSG held two "extraordinary plenaries," in August and September 2008, to consider the India agreement. As the second of these got under way, eight countries were still seeking explicit conditions limiting the scope of the waiver. Three issues proved particularly thorny. The NSG agreed to drop a proposed clause that would specifically rule out supply to India of enrichment and reprocessing agreement. The negotiators worked out procedures acceptable to India for implementing consultations over the member countries' nuclear trade with India. Once again, the toughest was the issue of testing. As with the bilateral negotiations with the United States, India was adamantly opposed to creating an international obligation not to test.

In Delhi, the U.S. ambassador had been trying to reinforce the NSG campaign, and hosted a lunch for the ambassadors of countries that were still not persuaded to support the change in NSG rules. But the diplomatic campaign came to a head in a series of side meetings on the margins of the extraordinary plenaries. One of the U.S. representatives periodically asked for a show of hands on which countries still had problems with the Indian waiver request. He then stepped out of the room to telephone Secretary Rice, who in turned called the leadership of the countries involved—sometimes reaching them far into the night. The last three to come on board were Austria, Ireland, and New Zealand.

Eventually, all countries had agreed except China. India had made clear to China that any attempt to block the NSG waiver would become a major issue in their bilateral relationship. China's public comments had been characteristically opaque, referring to China's support for peaceful uses of nuclear energy but also its reluctance to damage the international nonproliferation regime. China normally does not like to deliver the only blocking vote. Knowing this, the U.S. strategy was to line up support from all the other countries before tackling China. As the objections from other countries started to disappear, the Chinese representative left the side meeting with a very junior official in charge—leaving his cell phone behind so that he could not be reached. Having sought instructions from Beijing, he indicated to the United States and India that China would support the current consensus and could accept the U.S. draft waiver resolution.

On September 5, India's Foreign Minister Pranab Mukherjee once more put a voluntary, unilateral testing moratorium on record, in what he was careful to describe as a *suo motu* statement. The waiver text, taking note of this statement, was formally presented to the NSG at 2:00 a.m. on September 6, and it passed shortly before noon the same day. India had its waiver and maintained its position that its testing moratorium was strictly voluntary. At the same time, the importance that all the NSG members attached to the moratorium—along with the similar statements that appeared in previous documents along the path to the nuclear agreement with Washington—made clear that, in reality, India would need to consider very carefully the consequences of ending it.[38]

The final step before India and the United States could finalize the nuclear agreement was passage of a second piece of enabling legislation by the United States Congress. There was an irony in this last legislative process. The U.S. Congress had wanted to see the text of the IAEA safeguards agreement and the NSG waiver before giving its final assent to civil nuclear cooperation with India. But by waiting until those agreements were available, the Congress effectively ensured that the commercial competitors of the United States were free to go ahead with sales while the U.S. suppliers had to wait for congressional action. It was all over with uncharacteristic speed: the legislation was introduced on September 23, 2008, passed four days later, and was signed in a glittering White House ceremony on October 8, 2008.[39]

AFTER THE AGREEMENT

A month later, Barack Obama was elected president, and he took office on January 20, 2009. By this time, the nuclear agreement was in place and Obama, along with his vice president and his secretary of state, had been part of the lopsided majority approving the legislation in the U.S. Senate. The remaining tasks involved negotiating an agreement covering the reprocessing in India of U.S.-supplied nuclear fuel and implementing the agreement as a whole.

To the surprise of some observers, the reprocessing agreement went through with practically no controversy. The 123 agreement, as noted, set up a negotiating timetable. The job was done in less than the required time, and the agreement itself signed on August 1, 2010.

Implementation meant making the arrangements for the actual supply of U.S.-origin nuclear reactors to India. This turned out to be a long series of procedural complications that continue as this book is being written. The agreement itself was a political and strategic prize, but the commercial prize for the United States lay in sales of nuclear equipment. During the previous negotiations, the Indian government had given the United States a "letter of intent" confirming its intention to make available two sites for reactors to be purchased from the United States. Shortly before Hillary Clinton's first visit to New Delhi as secretary of state, in July 2009, the Indian government announced that it had identified those sites, each suitable for up to eight reactors.

The pace of implementation slowed after that. If the negotiation of the basic agreement showed the Indian and U.S. governments at their most creative and productive, working out implementation arrangements illustrated how both governments have given each other heartburn for decades. Even with the legislative authorization in place, each nuclear export transaction from the United States requires complex assurances and certifications, a notoriously slow process. The parts of the U.S. government that handle this process were accustomed to treating India as a forbidden destination for nuclear trade. Some of the documents required negotiation with Indian nuclear officials. The combination brought together some of the most legalistic aspects of the U.S. system and some of the most inflexible characteristics of India's DAE. One example: the United States requires an assurance that nuclear material it supplies will not be transferred away from the original end-user without U.S. consent, even within India. The Department of Atomic Energy was unwilling to give these assurances in the case of transactions involving private companies or individuals. In this case, the U.S. side devised the solution: embedding the required assurances in the contracts with the purchasers involved, as part of the purchase contract, so that the DAE was not required to take any action.

Frustrated by the slow pace, the U.S. government in early 2013 requested a joint meeting of all the concerned officials from both governments. This effort seemed to loosen things up and gave the U.S. negotiators an opportunity to rebut some of the widely held misperceptions about U.S. requirements and whether India was being treated on a par with other countries. But it is hard to escape the conclusion that by this time, the special political drive that enabled the two governments to reach a very difficult agreement had abated, leaving their officials with fewer tools and less high-level support. It is difficult to tell to what extent these negotiating difficulties reflected DAE's traditional suspicion of the United States and to what extent they were expressions of India's acute sensitivities about anything that could be regarded as an infringement of sovereignty.

These teething pains were greatly increased by the nuclear liability legislation that India passed in August 2010. The legislation was intended to remove the discrepancy between India's liability regime and the Convention on Supplementary Compensation (CSC), an IAEA-sponsored instrument designed to standardize liability in the nuclear generating industry. The CSC put liability on the shoulders of plant operators. The Indian government originally put forward draft legislation that would have followed this pattern. However, it was introduced just as the Indian courts were releasing their final judgments on the country's worst ever industrial accident, the 1984 explosion of a Union Carbide gas plant in Bhopal, with a death toll estimated at over 3,000 people and possibly as many as 16,000. Inevitably, the news that senior figures in Union Carbide and on their Indian board of directors had suffered little or no punishment hijacked the nuclear liability bill, which, when it emerged from the legislative process, included a clause that appeared to put the suppliers of nuclear equipment at risk for unlimited liability in case of an accident.

The U.S. government pressed India to ratify the CSC and then conform its liability law to that convention. The Indian government agreed to ratify and talked about working things out on a case-by-case basis. But the reality was that this time, negotiations would not solve the problem in any relevant time frame. Amending the legislation would be a very heavy lift and quite impossible, at least until a new election had brought new members into parliament—and, of course, visible U.S. pressure would activate India's resistance to external dictation.

The liability legislation has been a problem for all of India's potential nuclear suppliers. Russia has sought to navigate around it by "grandfathering" Russian-supplied plants. France attempted to deal with it in the price—which predictably has given the Indians a bad case of sticker shock. The U.S. suppliers have tried to work out "pre-early works agreements" to set the broad terms of reference of eventual reactor sales. There has been talk of corporate structures that could effectively cap the exposure of the supplier companies. And in perhaps the ultimate irony, the nuclear disaster that struck Japan after the earthquake and tsunami of

2011 generated some domestic opposition to nuclear construction, slowing down a process that was already limping.

The advent of the Modi government caused a flurry of hope that a new parliament might be willing to amend the liability legislation, but this was quickly squelched when the government announced that an amendment was not in the cards. During President Obama's January 2015 visit to India, the two governments announced that they had reached a "breakthrough understanding" on nuclear liability, in the form of a nonbinding legal memorandum that purports to spell out how India's legislation comports with international liability norms, supplemented by an insurance pool to cover nuclear operators and suppliers for $250 million in damages in case of a future accident.[40] No one expects that this will be the last word on the subject.

SUMMING UP

A number of features made this series of negotiations unique in the history of U.S.-India relations. The primary one was the deep engagement of the leaders of both countries, both in deciding to undertake the negotiations and in the conduct of the talks themselves. It is hard to overstate the importance of this factor. The U.S.-India relationship is high maintenance and craves high-level attention. The strategic character of the issues involved was also a distinctive feature. For the United States, this was the most elaborate formative experience in dealing with a country that insisted on being treated as a fully equal partner despite a considerable power disparity. India was neither an ally nor an adversary. This was, moreover, both a bilateral and a multilateral negotiation.

India's negotiators had experience with leadership-driven initiatives. Their long relationship with Moscow was full of them, both broad (e.g., India's security understandings) and narrow (e.g., hardy perennials like the exchange rate to be used in counter-trade transactions). But this was the first such initiative with a democracy just as feisty as India's own, where both sides continued to carry a residue of suspicion from the Cold War years. Top-level commitment from the U.S. president and Indian prime minister were essential but not sufficient. What was new for India's negotiators was the need to do a deep dive into the U.S. political and bureaucratic system. The Indian team was struck by how much the U.S. negotiators were driven by detailed legal requirements and how this colored their view of what needed to go into the agreement.

For India, more of the hard issues were policy issues—which did not make them easier, but sometimes allowed a bit more scope for drafting solutions.

As with many other U.S.-India negotiations, this long drama brought together two countries that both consider themselves unique and deserving of special treatment. The tension between their expectations is a constant and colors their negotiating tactics. Every phase of these negotiations touched on the core values expressed in India's global visions and in its normal negotiating style: uniqueness, sovereignty, and strategic autonomy. These values clashed with the domestic and international legal structure within which the United States was operating.

Looking at these negotiations more tactically, three familiar patterns in Indian negotiating stand out: outstanding mastery of detail by India's top diplomats; a willingness to go to the brink if needed in defense of India's interests; and a complicated and contentious bureaucratic process in India. This last factor manifested itself in an unusual way. MEA and the Prime Minister's Office worked hand in glove. The DAE remained the principal skeptic about the agreement and the compromises and conciliatory language needed to bring the United States and India together. At several points in the negotiations, differences within the Indian government were only settled after the shape of an U.S.-India agreement on the disputed points had become clear.

The contrasts with other negotiations are more striking. Even before the nuclear deal was on the table, the speedy conclusion of the negotiations on the High Technology Cooperation Group and the Next Steps in Strategic Partnership reflected an unusual level of authority for the officials involved, which persisted throughout the long years of negotiating. The give and take between the two countries' negotiators, by all accounts, was more open-ended and less bureaucratic than is the norm in either government. And the compromises the two governments reached on key issues like India's nuclear status and its weapons program went far beyond what either government would previously have been comfortable with. This is only possible when there is a very strong political push to "get to yes."

The intense public spotlight on the negotiations was not unusual for India, where strategic discussions with the United States often spark outbursts from leftist and nationalist politicians. It was much more unusual in the United States, where the strong traditional U.S. commitment to nonproliferation was in tension with the more recent consensus that India is an important partner.

The multilateral aspect of these negotiations was also unique. Normally, multilateral diplomacy is a strong suit for India's Foreign Service but a specialty track for U.S. officials. In this instance, India was constrained to operate from the sidelines, not being a member of the NSG. It compensated with skillful bilateral approaches to the countries whose support was needed. The United States, on the other hand, has bilateral leverage that is not often mobilized in support of multilateral votes—but this time it was. These negotiations transformed U.S.-India relations, and not just because they opened the way for civil nuclear cooperation, removing a decades-long obstacle. At least as important was the learning experience that both countries went through on the way. This will certainly not eliminate the difficulties the two countries have had negotiating with one another—the challenging negotiations that took place after the basic agreement was in place are the clearest indication. But this experience provides both sides with tools they can use—if they have the determination and patience—to work through their inevitable problems.[41]

CHAPTER NINE

Negotiating Economics

WHEN PRIME MINISTER NEHRU visited the United States for the first time in 1949, the main economic issue on the agenda was the possibility of U.S. assistance. Some ten months earlier, the United States had launched the Marshall Plan for the reconstruction of war-torn Western Europe, and in January 1949, President Truman announced the Point Four Program of technical assistance that was the predecessor of the U.S. foreign aid program. Its purpose was to boost prosperity and economic growth in the developing world, both for its own sake and in the belief that prosperity would orient these countries more toward the West in the Cold War. India faced possible famine, which proved to be a recurring threat for nearly twenty years. Dealing with poverty was India's primary economic objective, and augmenting its resources for the effort was at the top of the country's international economic agenda. And India's place in the economic world was clear: it was one of the poor countries—a leader among them, to be sure, and a sophisticated spokesman for their needs, but a country that needed, and claimed, the kinds of "special and differential treatment" that the world's international economic agreements generally accorded to the third world.[1]

Fast-forward to the 1990s and beyond, and the transformation of India's economic agenda is striking. India's economy has always been a set of contradictions, with continuing deep poverty coexisting with great wealth, technological sophistication, and a vigorous and growing middle class. But high growth rates since 1990—roughly double the rates in earlier decades, with several years at three times the earlier rates—have changed the mix. India continues to be an aid recipient, but it has become much more selective both about the types of aid it receives and about those from whom it will accept assistance. Total aid is far smaller in relation to the size of India's economy. The country's international priorities and negotiations now start with trade, investment, and energy, and India is emerging as an aid donor. This shift in India's economy and in its priorities has created some ambiguity about India's international persona on economic issues. It remains a poor country and continues to defend vigorously its right to "special and differential treatment." However, it has also acquired a seat in some of the world's important economic councils.

Economic negotiations for India are first and foremost a domestic exercise. The principal negotiators are generally people whose main responsibilities are domestic: officials from the Ministries of Finance, Commerce, and Agriculture and occasionally, ministers who head those same ministries and who remain closely tied in with the concerns of their constituents. Far more than in security or diplomatic negotiations, then, economic negotiations bring India's domestic operating practices directly into contact—and often into contention—with those of other countries.

This chapter examines bilateral economic negotiations (chapter 10 shifts to multilateral negotiations, including India's multilateral trade negotiations). Here we look first at aid, starting with the early food aid negotiations, whose "hardball" negotiating history left a very mixed legacy for U.S.-India relations, and then discussing some cooperative programs that downplayed the "donor/recipient" dynamic. Next, we explore bilateral trade negotiations at the government-to-government level. Finally, we look briefly at an important milestone in the experience of U.S. businesses in India—the Dabhol power investment that engaged both the central government and the state of Maharashtra and ultimately wound up with all parties unhappy. Familiar leitmotifs of sovereignty, equality, complex governmental structures, and political trade-offs in both India and the United States run through this experience but take somewhat different forms when the subject matter is economic. India's great concern about any perceived derogation from its sovereignty or equality turns the standard vocabulary of U.S. aid and, to some extent, trade negotiations into a minefield. Trade, as its name suggests, typically involves more overt bargaining than other issues; this situation sometimes facilitates agreement, but it can also be an obstacle. And normal interactions in the business world bring the Indian and U.S. systems into frequent clashes.

ASSISTANCE AND COOPERATION

India was for many years by far the largest recipient of U.S. economic aid. The total provided by the United States between 1946 and 2012 came to $16.0 billion, with about half of it ($8.6 billion) in the form of food aid.[2] India was also the largest borrower from the World Bank, and the negotiations establishing the World Bank's soft loan window specified that India would initially receive 40 percent of the institution's annual funding. These numbers, and India's need for resources to lift a huge population out of poverty, ensured that aid would be at the top of its international economic agenda.

The U.S.-India aid relationship began inauspiciously. Nehru made his first visit to the United States in 1949. A severe grain shortage put food aid high on the Indian government's wish list, and the United States had just enacted its Point Four legislation providing the authority for foreign assistance. But this visit, especially its official components, turned into a classic exercise in misunderstanding. U.S. Ambassador Loy Henderson had recommended that the United States provide a $500 million aid program. The United States expected to be asked for aid. Nehru, having made clear on many occasions his distaste for asking, dropped hints about India's willingness to accept an offer, but ultimately, nothing came of it. The package Henderson had floated was rejected within the U.S. government some weeks after Nehru's departure.[3]

Within a couple of years, India became a regular recipient of U.S. aid. Faced with a failed monsoon and looming famine, the Indian ambassador in Washington, Nehru's sister Vijayalakshmi Pandit, requested 2 million tons of wheat in December 1950. At that time, such a grant required legislation whose passage was controversial in the U.S. Congress. This in turn was aggravated by a radio broadcast in which Nehru said, "We would be unworthy of the high responsibilities with which we have been charged if we bartered away . . . our country's self-respect or freedom of action even for something we badly need." Even as the congressional debate was in full cry, India voted against a British-backed U.N. resolution to brand China as an aggressor in Korea and abstained in a vote on an arms embargo against China and North Korea. India accepted much smaller offers of rice from China and of wheat from the Soviet

Union. These demonstrations that India would continue to make policy decisions as it pleased and to accept assistance from any available source generated some unhappiness in the U.S. administration, and even more in the Congress.

The U.S. legislative process provided its share of irritants to India, including congressional consideration of inserting new conditions into the bill. As U.S. officials explained to Ambassador Pandit, this is standard fare in the U.S. legislative process. To India, however, the conditions initially seemed like unacceptable violations of India's uniqueness and sovereignty. In the end, Nehru accepted a slightly watered-down version of the U.S. legislative conditions: Americans could observe the distribution of U.S.-provided wheat and a fund could be set up linking repayments to development projects in India, provided India controlled its utilization. In addition, Nehru asked U.S. Secretary of State Dean Acheson to provide a letter with assurances that nothing in the bill would "interfere with" or "influence" India's policy, foreign or domestic. After all this drama, on June 11, 1951, the Congress passed a bill authorizing $190 million in wheat as a long-term loan for India. Four days later, Nehru greeted Truman's signature warmly, as a "generous gesture."[4]

India soon became one of the largest recipients of U.S. aid, both food aid and project and technical assistance. Its public demonstration of what today would be called "strategic autonomy" and the dispute over congressional conditions foreshadowed the resentment that was to plague U.S. assistance to India for decades. U.S. insistence that the aid be accompanied by what Washington regarded as sound economic policies appeared in Delhi as arrogant and overbearing. Conditionality cropped up in all forms of U.S. aid (and in aid from most other donors as well, though other countries' conditionality generated less publicity). One high-profile example involved the proposal to finance a public sector steel mill at Bokaro, which President John F. Kennedy in 1963 had publicly supported. The U.S. Congress passed legislation banning any U.S. spending for the mill, largely because of its public sector ownership. Nehru, showing remarkable graciousness, wrote to Kennedy offering to withdraw India's request for the financing, an offer Kennedy gratefully accepted.[5] (The Indians later accepted a Soviet offer to build the mill, much to U.S. chagrin.)

The most painful exercise in dealing with aid conditionality came in 1965. Once again, the trigger was a deficient monsoon, and negotiations revolved around conditions for the massive food aid required to meet

India's desperate needs. In early 1965, the Indians had requested a two-year food aid program of 10 million tons of grain. Aid was by now an annual occurrence, so making a request was no longer the big issue it had once been. The surprise came from the White House: in June 1965, President Lyndon Johnson called for a "hard new look" at food aid for India, announcing that all new food aid shipments for India and Pakistan would henceforth need his personal approval. This became known as the "short tether" policy, a piece of American shorthand that Indians found particularly offensive, emphasizing as it did U.S. control and Indian dependence.

A month later, Johnson approved release of the first tranche—one million tons, roughly a two-month supply. From then on, he ran the India food aid program personally, with obsessive attention to detail and the single-mindedness born of a long career of playing hardball in the U.S. Senate, micromanaging shipping schedules and estimates of food supply on the ground in India.

The negotiations establishing the conditions for resuming aid took place between cabinet ministers. The Indian agriculture minister, C. Subramaniam, and his U.S. counterpart, Orville Freeman, met to work out the details of an agreement on policy reform. Subramaniam had been pushing for major agricultural reforms, so this exercise went in a direction that was not unwelcome from a policy perspective. But Johnson's "short tether" made the circumstances highly coercive. The Freeman-Subramaniam discussions were kept completely quiet, both men recognizing that publicity would open the Indian government to charges of knuckling under to American demands. They met in Rome, away from Indian media attention.

By November 1965, they had formalized an extraordinarily intrusive program whose implementation was required before the United States would release food aid. The program called for huge increases in agricultural production by expanding India's use of chemical fertilizers and high-yielding seed varieties, encouraging foreign direct investment in fertilizer plants, and removing government restraints on food distribution. The plan called for a 40 percent increase in Indian investment in agriculture, even if this meant reducing expenditures elsewhere in India's budget. It mandated the creation of implementing institutions. Several of these conditions impinged on the privileges of the Indian Parliament. The program went into effect. In Washington, White House pressure shifted from holding back shipments to accelerating them. Johnson, still personally micromanaging the India wheat aid account, invited Subramaniam to Washington.[6]

The following year, another monsoon failure brought a renewal of coercive U.S. tactics. By that time, India had a new prime minister, Mrs. Indira Gandhi. Before her first official visit to Washington in 1966, she told Indian journalist Inder Malhotra in words that could well have been used by many other Indian seekers of foreign aid: "Don't publish this, but my main mission is to get both food and foreign exchange without appearing to ask for them."[7]

Impressed by Mrs. Gandhi, Johnson allowed a little personal diplomacy to ease his "ship to mouth" policy for a time, but India soon found itself under intense pressure again as it negotiated a broader reform package, this time with the World Bank. India agreed to reforms, including a currency devaluation that generated major controversy. Relaxing supply constraints took a while this time. Johnson waited over a month after receiving recommendations from Freeman and from Secretary of State Dean Rusk that he ease up on shipments, sending emissaries to India to check up on implementation of agricultural reforms. Finally, Johnson authorized an allocation of 900,000 tons of wheat aid, and the food crisis ended.[8]

A number of U.S. officials, including Chester Bowles, then ambassador to India, found Johnson's tactics uncalled for, "an exercise in excess."[9] Coercion was possible only because of the desperation of India's food shortage. It brought about changes in India's agricultural policy, and these reforms in turn helped usher in major increases in India's ability to feed itself. There was speculation—and not just in India—that the hardball tactics were intended as retaliation for India's opposition to U.S. policy in Vietnam. But even an Indian analyst with no great sympathy for the United States argued that Vietnam had little if anything to do with the food aid issue, serving perhaps as a "decoy" to conceal the real U.S. determination to change India's agricultural policy.[10]

But however important the food supplies were, the short tether and "ship to mouth" policies also caused a lasting backlash against the United States and hardened India's determination not to be put in a position of such vulnerability again. The devaluation of the rupee contributed to a poor showing by India's Congress government in the 1967 election. Both Subramaniam and Planning Commission head Ashok Mehta were dropped as a result. At the end of the "ship to mouth" negotiations, Mrs. Gandhi telephoned Johnson. Dennis Kux records the observation of her press adviser, Sharada Prasad, who recalled hearing her talk cordially to Johnson. After hanging up the phone, Prasad remembered, Gandhi said angrily, "I don't ever want us ever to have to beg for food again." Subramaniam commented to Kux that Johnson's insistence on having personal control over wheat shipments was like the behavior of a provincial official during imperial days.[11] India's leaders gave public thanks for American aid—not just wheat, but other forms of assistance as well—but the experience of securing it surely reinforced the attraction of what Indians would now call "strategic autonomy."

Food aid negotiations illustrate the difficulty of reconciling India's concept of its historical role and its uniqueness with a donor's expectations of controlling the use of its resources. India's need for funding and its judgment that poverty entitled it to assistance were in tension with its sense of its proper dignity.

The 1974 negotiation that wound up one of the signature features of the U.S. food aid program was driven by the importance of this sense of dignity as much as by economics. Since the beginning of the food aid program, India had repaid its food aid loans in part in local currency, with a portion of the rupee account being reserved for use by the U.S. government. By the early 1970s, the United States owned rupees equivalent to some 20 percent of the Indian money supply. Usage of these accounts was restricted, but their size nonetheless stirred anxiety in India about the United States possibly destabilizing the Indian economy. Daniel Patrick Moynihan arrived in India as ambassador in early 1973, when U.S.-India relations were still close to the nadir they reached during the 1971 war that gave birth to an independent Bangladesh. At least one of his predecessors had been interested in writing off a substantial part of the rupee holdings, but nothing had happened. Indian Ambassador T. N. Kaul, in response to a question from President Richard Nixon during his presentation of credentials, suggested that solving the "rupee problem" would be a good way to improve relations.

With both sides interested in solving the problem, the action shifted to mid-level officials on both sides, and the U.S. team came up with a proposal to forgive future interest payments, write off one-third of the approximately $3 billion in U.S. holdings, and retain two-thirds for U.S. uses. Moynihan took advantage of a visit to Nixon's California home to get presidential approval for reversing those two numbers, proposing that two-thirds be granted back to India. Moynihan wrote in his diary that he had received exactly the instructions he hoped for: to begin by insisting on having the United States retain $1.5 billion, but to fall back if necessary to $1 billion. He made his case primarily on the grounds that any economic benefit the United States derived from the "excess rupees" was negated by the ill feeling they caused. Moynihan waspishly observed that this was the first time that "the President and the White House have rejected an interagency proposal concerning India on the grounds that it was not generous enough."[12] The two governments reached speedy agreement, with the negotiations revolving primarily around what uses would be permissible for the account to be retained by the United States. The most difficult negotiations revolved around Washington politics. House Speaker John McCormack wanted to use a portion of the rupees to endow a Christian medical school in Bangalore. In the end, the Indian government dropped its objections to the endowment and the agreement went through. On February 25, 1974, Moynihan was able to write to the Guinness Book of Records asking them to acknowledge the largest check in the world, slightly over $2 billion.[13] U.S.-India relations remained difficult, but one important irritant had been removed and both sides, in the end, took yes for an answer.

Nearly two decades later, in 1991, India faced a new economic crisis—not a monsoon failure this time, but a disastrous depletion of its foreign exchange reserves. This crisis is best known as the starting point of India's economic liberalization policy, which ushered in a period of unprecedented economic growth. For our purposes, it also illustrated how India had organized itself to avoid begging for help from an arrogant world. India had joined the International Monetary Fund (IMF) as a founding member in 1945, but had used the Fund's economic support resources only once, in 1981–82. With a mushrooming balance of payments deficit and rapidly dwindling reserves, the Indian government—a minority government headed by Chandra Shekhar—quietly began discussing possible support programs with the IMF. Resources on the scale India needed were going to require tough conditions and a currency devaluation, measures that had been politically toxic in the 1960s. To make ends meet, the Indian government leased twenty tons of confiscated gold to one of the nationalized banks, which physically transferred them to London as security for a bridge loan. In a country where a family's gold is the ultimate and highly personal form of savings "for a rainy day," the drama and symbolism of exporting the Indian government's gold is hard to overstate.

The following month, in June 1991, India elected a new government, with Narasimha Rao as prime minister and Manmohan Singh as finance minister. They promptly authorized both the economic reform conditions and the devaluation requested by the IMF. In economic terms, the most important action the government took was to start the deregulation process that has shaped India's economic progress over the intervening decades. From the perspective of India's negotiating sensitivities and tactics, however, the important thing was the way all parties to this negotiation collaborated to make clear that the program was made in India, for Indians, by Indians. India's Executive Director at the IMF, Gopi Arora, had made a very quiet trip to India during the election campaign. At the time, he explained in a conversation with one of the authors that he wanted to make sure that none of the major political candidates publicly opposed an IMF program during the campaign, since it was clear India was going to need the Fund. Arora succeeded. There was no whiff of IMF arm-twisting: both the government and the IMF treated the economic policy reforms as an Indian policy initiative, not as an IMF requirement.[14]

U.S.-INDIA TECHNICAL COOPERATION in the health field tells a happier story. Much of this work took place as part of technical assistance programs funded by the Agency for International Development or by one of the U.S. government health agencies. An important ingredient in its success, however, was that it was designed and carried out as professional collaboration between Indian and international experts, rather than as a program in which the U.S. experts were "helping" their Indian counterparts.

One program that came to be regarded within USAID as one of its "crown jewels" in India seemed very bland. In 1992, the government of India agreed to launch a National Family Health Survey funded by USAID. This was not an easy decision for a government concerned that survey data might be used in ways that could make it look bad. The first survey, however, proved useful to officials in the Health Ministry, who used it to identify gaps in immunization coverage and to unearth valuable data on malnutrition. Over the next decade and a half, two further surveys were carried out, with decreasing levels of U.S. funding and increasing levels of financial and professional commitment from India. The Indian government was able to solve long-standing problems using the survey's findings. The survey is now sailing on its own. Only old-timers remember that it started out as a USAID-funded project. Indian and foreign scientists involved in the survey have become colleagues, with professional relationships that extend beyond the survey itself.[15]

The experience of polio eradication in India was even more powerful. Polio was the second eradication program in which India played a major part. The smallpox eradication program, launched in 1966 under World Health Organization (WHO) auspices, began badly, with insufficient resources and an inflexible operating model more or less imposed on India and the other cooperating countries by international scientists. By 1974, India had over 188,000 cases of smallpox, or 86 percent of the worldwide caseload. Six years later, India was smallpox-free. A string of technological breakthroughs made the goal of eradication realistic. Success came, however, when the international program managers realized that they needed to tailor their approach to each particular affected country. In India, one critical ingredient turned out to be a relentless surveillance program, operated by Indian professionals who came to regard it as "theirs."[16]

Eradicating smallpox was a major boon for India's health, and a number of talented Indian scientists got their start working on smallpox. But the top-down nature of the program meant that it had little effect on the organization of India's public health system. However, when the WHO adopted the goal of eradicating polio, both international and Indian scientists were determined to go about it differently.

India was at first deeply skeptical about adopting the goal of eliminating polio. So were WHO officials stationed in India. Dr. Jon Andrus, an American doctor from the New Delhi WHO office, and Dr. Kaushik Banerjee, director of India's national immunization program, turned things around with a series of presentations on a successful 1993 immunization drive in neighboring Bangladesh. The next year, the minister of education for the Union Territory of Delhi, Harsh Vardhan, held a successful immunization drive, which got people's attention.

Over the next fifteen years, the program took off, the joint effort of the Government of India, state governments within India, and the WHO, with support from other bilateral donors and from Rotary International. The Government of India put serious resources into the effort. More importantly, Indian scientists were fully involved in running the campaign and were seen as the full professional equals of the international scientists who remained involved. They drove the changes in tactics that became necessary to overcome the inevitable setbacks. They effectively "localized" the campaign to deal with problems in particular places and communities. The National Polio Surveillance Program internalized the ethic of accountability and subjected its operational results to regular scrutiny. On January 13, 2011, the last naturally occurring case of polio was identified in India, and two years later, India was declared polio-free.[17]

This is an example of negotiation that served the interests of all sides—even though it did not involve parties sitting down at a table with bracketed texts. The success of these health programs was due in significant part to the way the participants chose to deal with one another across bureaucratic and national lines. The participants from outside India built on the professional skills of their Indian counterparts. Both created enduring relationships. The watchword was "cooperation" rather than "aid." The same approach was successful in other health efforts as well, notably the creation of India's National Institute of Virology and the development, both there and in the National AIDS Research Institute, of an internationally respected research capability.[18] The same model was successfully followed in other areas as well; agricultural research is a good example.

Interestingly, when India decided to become an aid donor, it consciously adopted an operating style that bore some resemblance to these collaborative efforts and was different from the way it saw donors relating to India. The name of its aid office—the Development Partnership Administration, launched in January 2012—was designed to make clear that this was to be a relationship of equals. India's distance from the aid-coordinating mechanism used by donors from the industrialized countries, the Development Assistance Committee (DAC) of the Organization for Economic Cooperation and Development (OECD), was based in part on what Indians saw as a rather intrusive set of data that DAC collected for purposes of comparing its members' programs—in other words, a potential challenge to sovereignty. But India also wanted to distinguish its program and style from those of other donors. This point came out over and over in the presentations made by advisers to India's aid program at a 2013 conference in Washington on the policies of the world's new aid donors.[19]

BILATERAL TRADE

Trade negotiations involve the domestic economy and local politics, with all the passion that entails, for both India and the United States. In some respects, U.S.-India trade disputes are magnified by the similarity between the two countries, both of which consider themselves and their requirements unique, neither of which is comfortable adopting practices because "everybody does," and both of which have feisty democratic systems in which the needs of constituents are far more compelling than maintaining a smooth trade relationship with a distant country. Trade disputes in both countries are frequently cast as attacks on national sovereignty (as we will see in chapter 10, this is especially true of multilateral issues).

But in other ways, the differences between the two systems are stark and hard to bridge. In India, trade is primarily the responsibility of the civil service. In theory, this gives trade negotiators the power to change policy. In practice, however, trade policy, like other well-established policies, is endowed with the sanctity of history and tradition. India's economy, in spite of the tremendous liberalization that has taken place since 1990, still has a strong state-centered tradition. Moreover, the principal sources of trade policy are domestic. Tariffs are a major source of government revenue, one that the Finance Ministry is reluctant to give up. Regulations designed to encourage the growth of domestic industry have deep roots in India's concept of how to boost its economic development, and India's senior bureaucrats have tremendous authority in implementing them.

India boasts highly energetic and visible business organizations. The two principal associations both have their roots in pre-independence India. The Federation of Indian Chambers of Commerce and Industry (FICCI), established in 1927, was initially dominated by manufacturing industries. The Confederation of Indian Industry (CII) grew out of older and smaller organizations focusing mainly on engineers and the industries associated with them, and took its present name and configuration after the economic reforms of 1990. Both now include members from across the range of Indian industry. There are also a large number of sector-specific organizations, the most prominent of which is the National Association of Software and Services Companies (NASSCOM), the industry association for the Indian information technology, business process, and electronic industries.[20] All three, and several other sector-specific organizations, publish studies on problems of interest to their members, maintain regular ties with the government officials most important to them, and present themselves as the public face of Indian business. FICCI and CII maintain active offices overseas and work in cooperation with international counterparts. They operate in a manner roughly analogous to the Chamber of Commerce in the United States. For all their high visibility, in contrast to their U.S. counterparts, they rarely confront the government over policy, especially not publicly.

Formal structures through which business leaders provide advice to the government do not appear to have the same role as in the United States. India established a Prime Minister's Trade and Industry Council in 1998, which included most of the most prominent names in India's major corporate sectors. However, it appears to meet relatively infrequently.[21] On the other hand, many senior industrialists have a cozy relationship with both national and state governments and find opportunities to emphasize the benefits that India could derive from protecting their particular sector of the economy.

Such contacts can be controversial, especially when written up in the media. A recent incident illustrates both the kind of conversations that take place and the kind of sensational coverage that business discussions with or about senior government figures can attract. In 2010, as India was rocked with an insider trading scandal relating to the government's auction of telecommunications spectrum, a relatively obscure Indian magazine, *Open*, published what purported to be transcripts of conversations between a socialite and lobbyist, Niira Radia, and various well-known business figures, including Ratan Tata, patriarch of one of India's oldest and most respected business conglomerates. The conversations consisted of frank assessments and advice, but also hinted at potentially troublesome connections among the parties. The news rocketed around the Indian media—both print and the Twitterverse.

Four years later, the question of whether the tapes revealed any criminal activity was still under investigation. Two lawsuits—public interest litigation and an action by Tata against the government for failing to protect the company's privacy—were working their way through the courts. The former minister of telecommunications who had presided over the spectrum auction scandal but had also admitted to meeting with two of the principal personalities involved in the tapes was facing criminal charges arising out of the telecom spectrum auction. The new government elected in 2014 had quashed the proposed appointment to the Supreme Court of a candidate who had been revealed in the tapes as too close to telecommunications interests. The story is still not over. It is easy to understand, against this background, why Indian business leaders generally treat their discussions with senior officials with great discretion, even if nothing improper is taking place.[22]

IN THE U.S. SYSTEM, in sharp contrast, the constitution makes international trade the responsibility of the legislature. Unlike counterparts in other countries, a U.S. trade negotiator cannot implement a trade agreement unless it is formally enacted into law. This is a unique arrangement, and one with which Washington's trade partners—India very much included—often have difficulty coming to terms. Add to this the much broader and more highly structured setup for giving U.S. business access both to the Congress and to trade negotiators who work for the executive branch, and the result is a system guaranteed to frustrate negotiating partners, who see little prospect of gaining and enormous risks of losing in any tentative deal with the United States.

Lobbying, or private sector policy advocacy, is a legal activity in the United States, but a highly regulated one. By contrast, the word is a synonym for corruption in India. The U.S. government maintains a number of formal advisory committees composed of business leaders. These committees operate under rules that require their meetings to be publicly announced in advance and their papers to be publicly available.[23] The U.S. government strives for openness in trade negotiations. Business leaders often come to the cities where negotiations are taking place and expect—and receive—regular and frequent briefings from the negotiators. This system makes exploratory or discreet negotiations hard to achieve.

The U.S. system also has a number of quasi-judicial features. U.S. trade legislation sets up a system for handling allegations of dumping or export subsidies that starts with an investigation by the Commerce Department. To outsiders, this has the look and feel of a prosecutorial undertaking. Legislatively required evaluations of whether another country is engaging in "unfair" trade, or is unduly burdening intellectual property, or is carrying out a number of other trade practices, require the U.S. government to formally designate those whose practices are considered unsatisfactory. These investigations and the formal naming that sometimes follow push India's "sovereignty" button even more vigorously than the tactics of U.S. trade negotiators.

The clash between the systems is beautifully illustrated by the Special 301 Report issued by the U.S. Trade Representative (USTR) on April 30, 2014.[24] The law giving rise to the report requires the U.S. government to submit to the Congress an annual review of intellectual property protection in the rest of the world and to designate countries whose practices warrant further U.S. monitoring or follow-up action. The United States and India have long-standing philosophical and commercial differences on intellectual property, which were significantly eased but not removed following an agreement that brought India into the WTO

Agreement on Trade-Related Aspects of Intellectual Property (TRIPS) and led to modification of India's patent law in 2006. As a result, India was regularly featured in these reports. There had been widespread speculation that Washington's unhappiness with recent developments (and especially the unhappiness of the U.S. pharmaceutical industry over India's issuance of a compulsory license) would lead India to be designated as a "priority foreign country," the category triggering the most intense U.S. attention.

As it turned out, India was listed, but in the same, less dramatic category in which it had figured in the past: the "priority watch list." But the details of the USTR announcement of its decision were revealing. The expected release date for the results of this annual investigation was in May 2014, just as India and the world awaited the results of an election that was widely expected to change India's government. In the run-up to this date, USTR was carrying out its investigation, which relied heavily on obtaining information from the Indian government. The Indian government pushed them away. In late February, Deputy USTR Wendy Cutler was advised to postpone an investigation-related trip, apparently at the insistence of the Indian Ministry of External Affairs. Some press reports argued that officials would be too busy to see her; the more candid ones described it as an Indian move to block a "U.S. investigation." The Indian press was full of stories about a "trade war."

Meanwhile, the officials in both the Indian and U.S. governments who were responsible for bilateral relations were trying to find a way through this clash of systems so that the two countries would not face an emotional dispute just as the new government in Delhi was taking office. The Indian embassy in Washington urged U.S. businesses that were reasonably happy with their situation in India to make this known and to encourage the U.S. government to find a less contentious way to handle the problem. It was probably not a coincidence that the Indian ambassador in the United States had previously served as India's principal negotiator for the nuclear agreement and had become deeply familiar with the way American businesses deal with the U.S. government.

In the end, USTR opted to postpone the problem. Simultaneously with the release of the formal report, it announced that it would conduct an "out of cycle" review of India's intellectual property practices six months after the annual report, stressing the U.S. desire to expand trade with India. The word "investigation" was inevitably still in play, and both India's commerce minister and its commerce secretary publicly announced that they would not cooperate with any "investigation" and that India's practices were compliant with its international obligations. But the deadline passed. The next visit of the Deputy USTR to Delhi was scheduled with no fanfare. By the time the "out of cycle" review and the 2015 annual report were released, the tone of the discussions had changed. India and the United States had agreed during Prime Minister Modi's visit to Washington to set up a working group to discuss their intellectual property differences, and the announcement of the 2015 report referred to the "increased bilateral engagement" of the two countries, with the hope of further progress to come.[25] The issue was not definitively resolved, but the negotiators had set up channels for managing it.

Most major U.S.-India trade negotiations take place in a multilateral setting, which as we will see in chapter 10 adds a large dose of complication, but some negotiations have been strictly bilateral. Indian negotiators pride themselves on maintaining good personal relations with their U.S. counterparts, but chafe, like the negotiators of other countries, at the rigidity caused by the dominant congressional role in U.S. trade policy. In their view, U.S. officials want immediate market access, but have limited ability to deliver when the solution requires legislation.

Trade officials on both sides, when asked about bilateral negotiations, recall a depressingly long list of perennial issues, many involving agricultural trade. Disputes over U.S. exports of almonds to India have been on the agenda since at least the mid-1980s. Indian negotiators speak of a dialogue of the deaf between officials and recall tactics on both sides as a kind of cat-and-mouse game, composed of half-measures that never quite get to the heart of things. Unblocking negotiations all too frequently would require one side, or sometimes both, tackling some untouchable aspect of their policy.

The U.S. effort to export cheese to India illustrates how the problem can be buried in fine print that no one has properly examined. With President Obama's 2010 visit to India fast approaching, Prime Minister Manmohan Singh made clear that he wanted a deal. Deep in what became a very intense negotiating process, someone discovered that U.S. cheese is often made with animal rennet, which makes it impossible for the Indian authorities to certify it as a vegetarian product. This looked as if it would put an end to any deal. In the end, the discovery of a handful of artisanal producers who made cheese with derived rennet—not an animal product—produced the desired "deliverable," although not much actual trade resulted.

Two relatively successful negotiations from the period since 2005 provide examples of how Indian and U.S. negotiators have found opportunities despite the differences of philosophy, perception, and economic interest that have plagued their trade relationship. The first of these negotiations concluded in 2007 and involved the simultaneous negotiation of access for Indian mangoes to the United States and for U.S. heavy motorcycles to India. India and the United States were looking for a "success story," an agreement that could energize their economic relationship. Recognizing the difficulty that usually attends multilateral negotiations, they were looking for a bilateral problem that could be solved.

The negotiators started with a list of about ten stubborn issues. In a process one of them described as "very frank," they eliminated any issue that either negotiator thought had little chance of success. That left the somewhat unlikely pair of products. India is the world's largest producer of mangoes, whereas U.S. mango production is practically nonexistent. And while India produces light motorcycles, it produces nothing that competes directly with heavy Harley-Davidsons, so the problem that is normally the biggest obstacle to trade agreements—competing production in the home market—was not a factor in either case.

The deal had to overcome some significant obstacles. Indian mangoes had been banned from the United States because of the potential presence of pests, including mango seed weevils and mango pulp weevils. The U.S. authorities were not prepared to waive their phytosanitary standards; some means of neutralizing or eliminating the pests would have to be found and approved in both countries. The answer was irradiating the fruit and shipping it in pest-proof packaging. The technical fix was facilitated by a procedure approved by the U.S. Department of Agriculture in 2006, for which Indian mangoes were the first fruit specifically authorized.[26]

U.S. heavy motorcycles did not meet Indian pollution standards. Eventually, the Indian authorities were persuaded that the Euro 3 standard, which the U.S. motorcycles met, would be acceptable. The motorcycles were also subject to fees and tariffs totaling 90 percent, which American suppliers considered prohibitive. Lowering the applied tariff (not just the much higher "bound tariff," which India had already promised to lower in trade negotiations) would be needed to unlock trade. The Indian Finance Ministry is always reluctant to cut tariff receipts, which constitute a significant revenue item, but in the end the ministry agreed.[27]

As with the nuclear negotiations (see chapter 8), there was a strong push from the top of both governments to build up U.S.-India relations. Significantly, the negotiations took place almost entirely within each government. American participants believed that when they were able to show some progress in the internal deliberations within the U.S. government, this spurred their Indian counterparts to push harder inside their system. On mangoes, the Department of Agriculture led the effort on the U.S. side, and it controlled and could therefore resolve the principal issue. When it came to motorcycles, the principal Indian actor was the Commerce Ministry. The absence of a competing Indian-made product solved the biggest problem, though the Finance Ministry had to accept losing money through the tariff reduction. The most unusual feature of the deal, indeed, was the decision to link these two products. Negotiators generally like the idea of linkages to come up with solutions in which each party can say it won something, but in both countries, the trade system—the bureaucracy, the structure of trade constituencies, and especially in the United States the structure of congressional committees— is intrinsically hostile to linkages. The "losers" tend to speak more loudly than the "gainers" in linked transactions. The absence of direct competition made this a relatively easy lift, and the linkage meant that everyone gained something from it.

The agreement was announced in Washington with considerable hoopla at the June 2007 annual meeting of the U.S.-India Business Council. The Indian Minister of Commerce, Kamal Nath, attended. Also at the meeting were enough mangoes to give one to each attendee (they were popular; a few people slipped out of the meeting with suspiciously bulging pockets). No motorcycles were given out. In the end, the mango deal generated some trade but more symbolism. The irradiation process was burdensome, and four years after mango trade opened up, India was shipping approximately 300 tons of mangoes per year to the United States, compared with 215,000 tons the U.S. imported from Mexico.[28] Motorcycles were more successful: India's imports from the United States of the heavy ones (over 800cc) tripled from $3 million to over $10 million in the first five years after the agreement went through.[29]

A second agreement, on air transport between the United States and India, illustrated the role that ministers can play in the Indian system. Most agreements are negotiated with Indian senior officials; in the words of one savvy American observer, "secretaries make things happen." For trade agreements, the likelihood that ministers will play a decisive role is somewhat higher. The air transport accord, signed in 2005, was an outgrowth of a U.S. push to establish "open skies" agreements with as many partners as possible, in contrast to earlier agreements that spelled out in detail what type of landing, cargo, and passenger carriage rules would apply, what cities were covered, with what frequency, and with what restrictions on pricing. India was regarded as a tough market for this kind of approach: it went against the state-centered grain, and at the time the agreement was negotiated, India's long-haul international air service was dominated by a state-owned company, Air India.

Karan Bhatia, then a U.S. assistant secretary of transportation, recalled sitting down with the Indian Minister of Civil Aviation, Praful Patel, in 2003 to talk about the advantages to India of a more liberal "open skies" agreement. This was not a new idea—sixty-six countries had already signed such agreements with the United States—but it was a sharp departure from the more state-centric model India was familiar with. Air India, not surprisingly, opposed changing the agreement, concerned about stronger competition from U.S. carriers.

In a long conversation, Patel heard Bhatia out and walked through the pros and cons of an open skies agreement. The U.S. official explained that without a new agreement, Indian carriers would be limited in their ability to set up direct flights to the United States from emerging centers of business activity like Bangalore and Hyderabad, and passengers from these cities would reroute themselves through nearby airports, like Singapore, that had a full panoply of direct flights. The result would drain business away from Indian carriers. Patel asked for time to think it over. The two went back and forth a couple of times, and Patel got word to Washington that he was prepared to negotiate.

The actual negotiations were carried out at the working level and went remarkably quickly. U.S. Transportation Secretary Norman Mineta agreed to go to India for the signing. There was one last drama: when Mineta's plane stopped to refuel in Alaska, his staff got a phone call from Delhi reporting that the Indian government had still not agreed to one technical issue. The traveling party dashed off a suggested solution. A very relieved U.S. Embassy officer met the plane and reported that the agreement was all set to sign.[30]

At the signing ceremony in April 2005, Mineta highlighted the importance of the agreement. He stressed the broad partnership that he hoped this agreement would unlock, including cooperation between the private sectors of both countries and between the aviation safety and regulatory organizations.[31] The person who made the agreement possible in this case was the Indian civil aviation minister. He had the vision and was willing to take the risk to sign India up for a new kind of agreement, in spite of the misgivings of the bureaucracy. The negotiations took place as the U.S.-India relationship was being reimagined, but before the negotiations leading to a nuclear deal got under way, making the relatively speedy result even more remarkable.[32]

THE EXPERIENCE OF NEGOTIATING a bilateral investment treaty (BIT) shows how much more difficult the process becomes when the goals are more difficult and the high-level commitment weaker. Both the United States and India have numerous such treaties in place. They provide for a mutually agreed level of protection for investments in the other country and establish ground rules for investors as well as for dealing with disputes. The United States, during the latter part of the George W. Bush administration, proposed negotiating a fresh treaty with India as part of the expansion of the two countries' relations. India's economic growth during that period, and the concomitant growth in investment in both directions, made this desirable.

From the start, however, negotiations went slowly. General statements of support contrasted with the absence of real progress in agreeing on the terms. Fundamentally, the two countries had different goals and expectations. The United States wanted to lock in robust free market protections; India wanted to avoid giving away too much. This difference was embedded in the standard texts that both had used for their earlier investment treaties. India, broadly speaking, followed the model that had been recommended by the OECD in 1967. In the intervening half-century, BITs concluded by OECD members had become more elaborate, with a stronger bias toward liberalization and more detailed definitions of investment and provisions for its protection. The United States and Canada were leaders in this trend toward longer and more elaborate BIT templates. In the U.S. model agreement released in 2012, five pages were devoted to definitions; the full text of most Indian agreements was about five pages long.[33] The United States had strong business and congressional support for a "high standards BIT," a phrase generally interpreted to refer to the more expansive type of agreement favored by Washington and Ottawa. The Indian negotiators' instincts were cautious, and became even more so with the advent of a series of highly publicized investment disputes. Both governments' internal procedures made both more rigid.

The process started with exploratory talks in February 2008, during the final year of the George W. Bush administration. Coverage in the Indian press, clearly based on an Indian government briefing, highlighted "ambitious" U.S. hopes for the treaty and concluded that negotiations would take a long time.[34]

The first formal negotiations were held in August 2009, after Barack Obama had taken office in Washington. At about that same time, the Obama team also decided to review the standard agreement template that the U.S. government was using as its point of departure for all new BIT negotiations. Technical discussions and even some formal negotiations continued. Senior U.S. officials continued to reiterate their determination to move forward with a treaty, and at one point Indian Commerce Minister Anand Sharma said that negotiations were "almost complete." But since it was publicly known that the U.S. negotiating draft was under review, there was little chance of successful engagement on contentious issues before that process concluded.[35]

The U.S. model treaty was completed in April 2012. Together with the text, the U.S. government released an explanation of the kind of market-oriented policies it hoped the treaties would enshrine. Four of the issues it highlighted were to become controversial. The first two, "most favored nation" (MFN) treatment and "national treatment," were standard fare in Indian investment treaties; the issue at this stage was their scope.[36] Similarly, India and the United States both allowed for arbitration to settle investment disputes, but had differences over how this should work. A fourth provision in the U.S. model treaty would place limits on local content rules and other "performance requirements." India generally does not include such provisions.[37]

With their model BIT now in the public domain, U.S. officials stepped up their enthusiastic and vocal support for a "high standards" BIT. Under Secretary of State for Economic Affairs Robert Hormats carried the torch on a visit to India; from the private sector, Ron Somers, president of the U.S.-India Business Council, also spoke out. About a month before the model treaty was released, U.S. Trade Representative Ron Kirk had used a congressional hearing to highlight the importance of these investment treaties and to note that the United States was negotiating with both China and India.[38]

Meanwhile, new problems emerged on the Indian side. A series of disputes under bilateral investment treaties cropped up in late 2011 and early 2012. One case involved an Australian investor who obtained a favorable judgment through the arbitration clause in the India-Australia treaty. When Indian courts did not enforce the judgment, the investor invoked the Australian treaty's MFN clause to try to use a provision in a third-country treaty that required India to provide "effective access" to the remedy proposed by the arbitrator. This raised alarm bells about the implications of arbitration, as well as criticisms by Indian officials of "treaty shopping." Another case, which received huge publicity, involved a tax dispute. The Indian tax authorities had assessed a retroactive tax against the British telecom giant Vodafone. The Indian Supreme Court ruled in Vodafone's favor, but the Indian government of the day then persuaded parliament to pass legislation effectively nullifying the Supreme Court judgment. Both cases sent shock waves through the investor community, but both also pushed the "sovereignty" button in India. In June 2012, the Indian government decided to review its own model BIT, an exercise it went through periodically. It was clear from the press coverage, however, that once the review was in process, the officials conducting it hoped future agreements would be less vulnerable to having foreign investors use either the MFN provisions or the arbitration clauses to limit the Indian government's sovereign discretion in future investment disputes.[39]

Discussions on the U.S.-India BIT continued, with roughly one formal negotiating round per year. The formal sessions consisted mainly of presentations on the U.S. model treaty and on India's early thinking about the model it was reviewing. In the summer of 2013, when trade and investment complaints had become a significant issue in U.S.-India relations, Finance Minister P. Chidambaram and Commerce Minister Anand Sharma came to Washington with a brief to resolve some of the long-pending issues. Chidambaram's press conference described India's major condition for moving ahead on the BIT: that India's judiciary "have the last word" on investment disputes, and that no arbitration process be permitted to supersede the judgment of an Indian court. In the end, Chidambaram and Sharma looked elsewhere for short-term relief for the U.S.-India commercial relationship, deciding instead to modify a recently enunciated policy on local content requirements for telecommunications equipment.[40]

The BIT remained on the U.S.-India agenda. In September 2013, Prime Minister Manmohan Singh and President Obama met at the White House and reaffirmed their commitment to a "high standards BIT."[41] Several investment initiatives were mentioned in the joint statement following Prime Minister Modi's Washington visit in September 2014, but it was silent on the BIT.[42] In May 2015, India released its model BIT, which had significant differences with the U.S. model, including no provision for most favored nation treatment.[43] The two sides had not yet reached the point of proposing specific language to bridge the substantive gaps between them. Despite statements of support and an effort to portray a bilateral investment treaty as a good way to inject good feeling into the relationship, there is little expectation of early action.

As noted previously, India and the United States had different primary goals for the BIT. Moreover, the U.S. government and business community wanted the treaty more than their Indian counterparts did. They were also handicapped by a procedural problem common in complicated governments. Both governments had developed new "model treaties" while the agreement was under discussion. This review and drafting process introduced major delays. It also hemmed in both countries' negotiators. Once a government has got all its major players to accept a particular text, no official wants to reopen the agreement—which is the inevitable result of real negotiations.

INDIAN GOVERNMENT MEETS INTERNATIONAL INVESTMENT: DABHOL

India is a difficult environment for foreign business. The World Bank's widely used survey, "Doing Business: Measuring Business Regulations," listed India at 142 out of the 189 rated countries in 2014. It was close to the bottom (below 184) for dealing with construction permits and enforcing contracts, and close to the top for protecting minority investors and getting credit (ranked 7 and 36, respectively). The number of procedures required to establish a new business in Mumbai, the country's commercial capital, is 13, compared to 7.9 for the rest of South Asia and 4.8 for the developing countries that are members of the OECD. The areas rated in the survey all involve working with government at some level—national, state, or local.[44] Even the biggest corporate boosters of investment in India acknowledge that tasks that might be routine elsewhere, such as obtaining electricity or registering property, are time-consuming and corruption-prone. Prime Minister Modi has set a goal of moving India up to the 50th slot by 2020; this is widely recognized as a heavy lift. These problems are certainly not unique to India, and they affect both Indian businesses and international ones. But they form the backdrop for other issues that are more directly related to the way Indian governments at all levels deal with foreigners.

With India's economic success since 1990, a growing number of international businesses have come to India, and their experience is an important dimension of India's integration into the global economy. Establishing and running an international business in India poses many challenges, but we will focus here on the ones that shed light on how the Indian government operates: the interface between U.S. businesses and the Indian government.

The experience of business showcases a number of features already familiar from other types of negotiations with the Indian government. These include the powerful role of India's bureaucrats, who come to their task with a strong sense of embodying the state; a tendency to expect more of foreign investors (especially those from rich countries) than of their own businesses; the impact of a highly complex federal structure in which state governments are the gatekeepers for many of the licenses businesses need in order to operate; and some of the more intangible characteristics noted elsewhere, such as Indian reluctance to settle for second-best solutions or to accept a negotiated agreement as the last word on the subject.

Businesses also run into some patterns not as prevalent in government-to-government negotiations. When foreign businesses are dealing with the government in India, they can encounter zealous and sometimes arbitrary enforcement of the rules. Procedural safeguards are hard to access. Businesses come to this type of situation as the junior partner, at least in the view of their Indian government interlocutors. Tax disputes have been a frequent source of problems, with both central and state tax authorities coming after foreign investors, sometimes with claims for retroactive taxes. Senior tax officials have little authority to overrule their more junior assessors on matters of legal interpretation.[45] This rigidity may leave bribery as the easiest avenue for obtaining relief from an assessment that appears unreasonable or overzealous.

Another frequent source of disputes is land acquisition, which requires a highly complex process. The central government's legal requirements for land acquisition have changed twice since 2013. The Manmohan Singh government enacted legislation that required the formal consent of a large majority of the landowners whose property is involved. The Modi government proposed legislation to loosen these rules, initially with an ordinance issued between parliamentary sessions; its effort to get legislation through the normal process has become badly bogged down. Land is politically high-voltage, and especially so at the state level. These are of course issues that affect both Indian and foreign businesses. One of the best-known land acquisition disputes involved one of India's leading companies, Tata, which sought to build its new minicar in Singur, in

West Bengal. The case came to a head in 2008, during an election for the state government. The fiery Mamata Banerjee, running for the chief ministership, threw her considerable political combat skills behind a protest movement objecting to the proposed acquisition. In the end, Tata backed out and established the auto plant in Gujarat. Banerjee won her election.[46]

Judicial processes offer relief from disputes—but they are famously slow and may also be used as an instrument of attack, either by business competitors or by government. Companies may suddenly find that a seemingly minor dispute—or one of which they were completely unaware—has escalated to a criminal complaint in a state court, with senior officials in the company being named. More generally, dispute settlement is a frequent sore point, as already seen in the discussion of bilateral investment treaties.

THE DECADE-LONG SAGA of the power generating plant at Dabhol, in Maharashtra, which started out as a story of exciting new opportunities and ended as a bruising cautionary tale, illustrates two of the most important and challenging aspects of international business dealings with the Indian government. The first is India's complex federal system. The project was from the start a matter of shared—and competing—responsibility between the national and state governments. Further complicating matters, elections took place at both the national and state level during the negotiation and implementation of the project, and opposing parties controlled those two levels of government during three critical years. The second feature is the difficulty of resolving disputes, either through arbitration or through the courts.

India's economic reforms of 1990 included a provision opening the power sector to international investment. Enron, an energy company that considered itself a bold, pathbreaking player, saw an opportunity. The project was approved for handling through the Government of India's new "fast track" procedure, under which the government would negotiate directly with the business involved rather than issuing a tender. By June 1992, land had been identified for a power plant and Enron had signed a memorandum of understanding with the Maharashtra State Electricity Board (MSEB), creating the Dabhol Power Company and undertaking to build the plant.

Normally, the next phase of the approval process would have been detailed technical negotiations with the Central Electricity Authority

(CEA). Apparently because of the project's "fast track" status, the CEA was persuaded to provide expedited clearance in principle, with full clearance to come later. Based on this and on the Finance Ministry's favorable view, the Foreign Investment Promotion Board cleared the project in December 1992. Meanwhile, the Maharashtra government, eager to move ahead but acutely conscious of its inexperience in projects of this scale, asked the central government to secure World Bank help. The World Bank's consultants came back in April 1993 with an assessment questioning the economic and financial viability of the project. The approval process nonetheless moved forward, with the final CEA clearance coming through in November 1993. Enron continued to work on the other technical clearances required by the project. There were 150, by one estimate.

The negative World Bank assessment contributed to the controversy that eventually engulfed the project. The nub of the problem, however, lay in the power purchase agreement signed in December 1993. MSEB and Enron agreed to a formula, denominated in U.S. dollars, under which the price could vary if input costs changed. Even more problematic was the "take or pay" contract, under which MSEB agreed to buy 90 percent of the rated capacity of the plant or pay the equivalent price, with Enron facing penalties for a delay in production. This became a central factor in the protests over the Enron projects and the lengthy subsequent negotiations it went through.

By early 1995, the financial structure of the project was set. The state government signed its guarantee of the project in February 1994 and the national government signed the required counter-guarantee in September. By January 1995, the U.S. government institutions involved, the Export Import Bank and the Overseas Private Investment Corporation, had signed financing agreements, and financing had also been lined up from international and Indian private banks.

In this early phase, Enron leaders spent ample time in India. According to one account, Rebecca Mark, chairman and CEO of the Enron unit responsible for the project, visited India thirty-six times during these negotiations. Participants in the process felt that they had established the all-important personal relationships at both the national and state levels to move the project ahead. The impatience for which American negotiators are famous, which often generates resistance, may on balance have been an asset in this case. The U.S. government had provided strong support to the project, including a visit by Energy Secretary Hazel O'Leary to India to press the Finance Ministry to sign the counter-guarantee. The U.S. government normally provides support for major investment projects, so this was not unusual. But both the U.S. government and major corporations lean toward a top-down approach, working with the highest levels of government they can reach. This tends to result in an approach that focuses primarily on the national rather than the state government.

In other respects, the seeds of further trouble had been sown. State elections in Maharashtra in January and February 1995 brought things to a head. Communal riots had convulsed the state in 1992–93. The outgoing state government faced a stiff challenge from a coalition of two nationalist parties, the Bharatiya Janata Party (BJP), the Hindu nationalist party that eventually also took power at the national level, and the Shiv Sena, a Marathi (Maharashtra) nationalist organization with a reputation for a tough street presence. Both campaigned against Dabhol: the Sena vowed to "push Enron into the Arabian Sea," and the BJP used its rallying cry of "swadeshi"—pushing for a homegrown solution to the power problem.

When the BJP–Shiv Sena coalition won, the stage was set for a confrontation. Enron and the U.S. government worked hard to change the new state government's mind on the project, and once again, a U.S. cabinet-level visitor took up the issue with the central government on a visit to New Delhi. The new state government established a cabinet subcommittee to assess the project, and by the end of May 1995 it had interviewed a string of experts and participants. It recommended canceling Phase II of the project and "repudiating" Phase I, which was already under construction. This was a complete reversal of the course the previous state government had taken.

The judgments behind this conclusion prominently featured the price, singling out the decision to denominate it in dollars; the high capital cost; and the environmental risks. Three findings by the subcommittee illustrate how difficult it is in India to deviate from the established way of doing things. The subcommittee concluded that the outgoing government had committed a "grave impropriety" by negotiating with a single supplier. The fact that this was the procedure envisaged in the fast-track system was not even mentioned in the report. The subcommittee also was "led to the irresistible conclusion" that the public record concealed secret, "off-the-record" negotiations that contained further improprieties. And the price formula, besides being regarded as too beneficial to Enron, was calculated on a different basis from the "fixed rate of return" model normally used in India.[47] If a project or decision is controversial—and this one was for reasons of both substance and politics—any procedure out of the ordinary can be turned into a reason for suspicion.[48]

In August 1995, the Maharashtra government issued a stop-work order to Enron, which complied. This turned out, however, to be the beginning of the next phase of negotiations. Sanjay Bhatnagar, who represented Enron in Mumbai at the time, recalled that the state's political leaders asked him why Enron had stopped work. An Indian company, he was told, would have come and talked to the state government first—the implication being that once in office, the state officials had to worry about power supply and would have found a way around the problem. By November, Rebecca Mark was back in India and called on Bal Thackeray, the flamboyant Shiv Sena leader. Thackeray and the Sena were ready to put things back on track.

The new contract, predictably, included a new formula for calculating the price. This one, based on prices in force at the time of the negotiations, would be more favorable to MSEB. Enron recognized that a price adjustment was necessary, and that it had to make the first move. Accordingly, it sent a letter to the state energy department offering to match the price in the last competitively bid project in the state. The offer, in other words, was designed to address the problem of the bidding procedure as well as the price issue. By February 1996, a revised agreement had been negotiated. Convincing the state politicians that the new terms were both acceptable and sufficiently face-saving took a little more time, as well as the persuasive powers of the secretaries in the state ministries, many of whom had been held over from the previous government. Within a few more months, the proposed revisions had been approved by the state government. Bhatnagar's recollection is that central government officials were sympathetic to this process, but basically powerless to make it happen at the state level.

Work resumed on both Phase I and Phase II of the project. The construction was greeted by violent protests and a flurry of legal challenges from Indian groups. The Indian government in 1997 approved an expansion of the natural gas terminal needed to bring gas from Qatar to Dabhol. In May 1999, Phase I of the project started generating power. Unfortunately, all the variable costs had gone up since the signature of the revised contract, so the price to MSEB was higher than they had calculated. Meanwhile, the political stars had realigned themselves once again: the BJP had come to power at the national level in 1998 and the Shiv Sena and BJP had lost power in Maharashtra the following year to a Congress-led government that had, ironically, campaigned against Dabhol.

In 2001, the next crisis struck. MSEB stopped making its payments to Enron and sought to cancel its power purchase agreement. By this time, Enron had decided to transform itself from a company that built and owned electrical plants into a company that basically traded in power. Rebecca Mark, the champion of the ownership strategy, had been forced out. High-level U.S. government efforts to resolve the problem and salvage the projects were unavailing. The Dabhol project ceased operating.[49]

Enron's experience underscores the importance of understanding who controls which decisions. This may be a moving target, with the locus of responsibility shifting in response to both political and institutional factors. Looking at the life span of the project, the central government established the policy that brought Enron and its international partners into it, and the central government wielded tremendous power over the technical approval process. But the aspects of the project that ultimately doomed it were mainly within the state government's jurisdiction. The state electricity boards have the basic responsibility for power generation and regulation in India. The price negotiation was carried out at the state level. However difficult it may be to negotiate with the central government, on this and many other issues, the strong identification of both political leaders and senior civil servants with the Indian nation normally creates a sense of institutional commitment when India has given an undertaking. It may be reinterpreted, but it will normally not be repudiated.

At the state level, however, the sense of institutional continuity is much weaker, and in the case of Dabhol it was basically absent. Taken together with the particular brand of revolutionary nationalism that animated the BJP–Shiv Sena government in Maharashtra, the situation left Enron vulnerable to having its contract ignored. A letter from Enron CEO Kenneth Lay says it well: "Our experience would indicate that contracts with governmental authorities in India really do not seem to represent anything more than a starting point for a later renegotiation and are broken by Indian governmental authorities whenever and as often as they prove inconvenient or burdensome." He was writing to Prime Minister Vajpayee, but what he describes is actually more characteristic of state governments.[50]

The third and final Enron negotiation was over the dissolution of the company and centered on the arbitration process. Arbitration is a normal feature of commercial contracts between foreign and Indian companies, but as Enron found, using it is at best extraordinarily difficult. Fali Nariman, whose reputation as a skilled business attorney is legendary, argued in a lecture that arbitration can be effective in India, but then went on to observe that "although Indian law favors dispute resolution by arbitration, Indian sentiment (encouraged by the fraternity of lawyers) simply abhors the finality attaching to arbitral awards!"[51]

Enron first announced its interest in arbitration when the Maharashtra government ordered it to stop work on the project in 1995, but the heart of its problems with dispute settlement took place after MSEB stopped making payments in 2001. The Maharashtra government's first move was to block arbitration through an injunction by the Maharashtra State Regulatory Commission, which appealed to the Bombay High Court to confirm that the commission had exclusive regulatory jurisdiction in the matters under dispute. The court did so. The matter was then appealed to the Indian Supreme Court, where it remained for the next five years. Meanwhile, the state government obtained an injunction from the Bombay High Court to prevent Enron from pursuing international arbitration regarding the state government's guarantee. The central government obtained a similar injunction from the Delhi High Court.

Enron and its American partners then approached the Overseas Private Investment Corporation (OPIC), claiming payment on their political risk insurance. This led to arbitration in the United States, where a panel under the auspices of the American Arbitration Association ruled that OPIC was required to pay Enron. It also ruled that the Indian courts and several Maharashtra state institutions had taken away Enron's rights by blocking its access to arbitration. This in turn triggered arbitration proceedings by the U.S. government against India under the U.S.-India investment guaranty agreement. Enron and its partners, which had routed parts of their investment in Dabhol through Mauritius, then sought arbitration against the Government of India under that country's bilateral investment treaty with India. This led to an International Chamber of Commerce ruling against India in April 2005.[52]

By this time, the project had collapsed, as had Enron, and negotiations over the financial settlement and disposal of assets were well under way. Settlements with Bechtel and GE, the remaining equity partners, were announced and formally approved by India's Supreme Court in July. Fali Nariman, who pointed out the Indian system's dislike for the finality of arbitration, was one of the lawyers who presented the settlement to the Supreme Court. His lecture on arbitration cited Dabhol as a success story—but said that success awaited only those who were prepared to consecrate a decade or more to obtaining results through arbitration.[53]

The Dabhol project was hardly typical. Its scale, complexity, and unfortunate political timing were unusual. Foreign investment in India's state-centered power sector was a new phenomenon. The decision to use gas being imported through a facility that had not yet been constructed would have made pricing unpredictable and controversial even under less turbulent circumstances. The principal investor, Enron, underwent a major change in its business focus midway through the project and wound up collapsing from causes that had nothing to do with India.

Some of the problems that dogged this project are common fare in other high-profile investments where private business is deeply involved with both the state and the federal government. India's complex federal structure and feisty political system can dish up surprises for international business, as they also do for other countries dealing with India. The willingness of the Indian government and even the courts to throw roadblocks in the way of arbitration, even when it is expressly provided for as a means of settling disputes, reflects more than just a commercial operator's efforts to get the best deal it can. It is another manifestation of the determination to protect the prerogatives and primacy of the Indian state that runs through both India's global vision and its government's negotiating style. In the Dabhol case, the arbitration that actually went forward was initiated by a foreign government, against India's national government, under a treaty to which India was a party. As we have seen, Indian officials negotiating a similar treaty with the United States want to prevent future investors from taking advantage of such provisions in the countries through which their investments may flow.

CHAPTER TEN

Multilateral Negotiations

MULTILATERAL NEGOTIATIONS, widely regarded as the most prestigious aspect of the Indian diplomat's craft and career, attract the "best and the brightest" of these diplomats. The subject matter is often global in scope and the arena may have global participation, providing a chance to exercise India's influence on a worldwide stage. Global forums bring to mind the heady days when Nehru spoke for India to the world, his soaring rhetoric and moral vision lifting India above the daily struggles of poverty and regional disputes. Global organizations are also a way of measuring India's rising role in the world, and it has been a consistent objective of Indian foreign policy to achieve major power status in the major organizations. The most visible example is a permanent seat on the UN Security Council.

Several senior and retired Indian diplomats have observed that multilateral negotiations were the setting where they really learned the negotiating craft. One diplomat with particular experience in the UN world commented that the real challenge of multilateral negotiations was that India's opposite numbers did not necessarily have a commitment to relations with India, unlike bilateral counterparts.[1]

However, there is a built-in tension between developing an international consensus, as multilateral negotiations often seek to do, and India's rigorous view of foreign policy independence. Indian officials often express their support for a rules-based international system and the institutions that create the rules, but there is great resistance to adding to those rules. Historically, India has been a "rule-taker" rather than a "rule-maker." In recent years, India's stronger economy and higher international profile have given it an opportunity to join the countries that shape international norms. Making this switch, however, is not a sudden event—it is a process, and often involves taking public positions that trouble one or another country that India cares about. India's enthusiasm for involving the United Nations in international disputes does not extend to issues in its immediate neighborhood. When multilateralism and strategic autonomy conflict, the latter usually wins. This is hardly unique to India, but it jars with some of the messages India sends to the rest of the world.

The skills that serve Indian diplomats well in bilateral negotiations also figure in their multilateral work. Indian officials often play leadership roles in multilateral meetings, though they say that they do not particularly seek out such positions. Their proficiency in English makes them a natural choice for drafting assignments and pulling together the threads of a confusing, multisided debate. The habit of meticulous research on the history of issues, so characteristic of the Indian Foreign Service, can be a huge advantage in multilateral gatherings where their international colleagues may not have the details at their fingertips. Indian diplomats take great care to learn the rules of procedure in the organizations where they work, typically through on-the-job experience with senior officers rather than formal training.

Indian diplomats argue that one of their particular skills in multilateral negotiations is "bridging," finding common ground between different groups or parties. This perception is not necessarily shared by other participants. David Malone, a retired Canadian diplomat who had served both as high commissioner to India and as Canada's representative at the United Nations Economic and Social Council, argued that while India's diplomats were unquestionably brilliant, hardworking, and experienced in the ways of multilateral negotiation, their style was sometimes better at winning oral arguments than garnering negotiating victories.[2]

India's hard-line reputation is not just a matter of style. Some of the international norms that are crafted and implemented in other multilateral settings—especially on trade and climate change, which have considerable political visibility at home—present direct challenges to Indian interests. While Indian negotiators usually articulate their objectives in positive terms, their primary requirement, not infrequently, is to block an undesirable result. India's negotiators have demonstrated on many occasions that they are prepared simply to say "no" in order to avoid a deal they find unfavorable. They have been willing, in the process, to put at risk the support of countries that might otherwise assist India in assuming a bigger role in shaping the global system. Many of India's international friends wonder whether this calculus of costs and benefits will change as India becomes more prosperous and more internationally prominent.

This account of India's management of multilateral negotiations starts with a look at the feature that most clearly distinguishes multilateral from bilateral negotiation: working in coalition with other countries. When two countries bargain, it is easy to define the sides, even if each country has its own complex set of internal relationships. In multilateral negotiations, the path to success requires a working coalition. There are often many sides to a negotiation, and defining "one's own side" can be complicated.

We then look at India's efforts to obtain leadership positions in multilateral organizations. We explore how India works in some specialized multilateral forums, each with its own habits of business and patterns of coalition building. These include the UN Security Council, climate change negotiations, the World Trade Organization, and disarmament negotiations. Finally, we look briefly at some of the more restrictive groups in which India is either active or seeking admission, such as the G-20, nonproliferation export control organizations, and BRICS.

WORKING WITH COALITIONS

India's "magnetic north" is the commitment to an independent foreign policy, usually articulated as "strategic autonomy." This is not incompatible with coalition building, but neither is it an altogether comfortable fit.

For nonaligned India, the traditional place to look for partners in multilateral negotiations was in the large groups of developing countries, the Non-Aligned Movement (NAM) and the Group of 77 (G-77), which now numbers over 130. These groups reached their zenith during the 1960s and 1970s, as the collective voice of the third world facing off against the richer countries, especially the West. When the groups acted collectively, they formed an imposing bloc in UN-based organizations where the rule is "one country, one vote." This made them especially effective at blocking a result that a critical mass of their members opposed or at setting forth general principles without spelling out their implementation. The large groups were a natural fit for the United Nations General Assembly and the UN Conference on Trade and Development (UNCTAD). The G-77 and NAM are still active in the broad developing country caucuses, especially at UN headquarters in New York. One Indian diplomat commented that these groups are "where the troops are rallied." Indian diplomats with multilateral experience point out that New York is the one place where one can count on a "friendly forum."[3]

Starting in the early 1990s, India began looking for alternative coalition possibilities that could more effectively advance the goals of a rising India. As one Indian official put it, the nonaligned had become less of a movement and more of a forum.[4] The large groups were more useful for articulating what their members opposed than what they favored. India began to focus more on coordination within somewhat smaller groups that could align their objectives more easily. The precise configuration of these smaller developing country groups varied from one forum to another. The dynamic was still one of developing country solidarity, and there were relatively few instances in which India shifted coalitions in dealing with different issues. In the words of two academic analysts, these were still, for the most part, "bloc" style rather than issue-based coalitions.[5]

Obtaining recognition of new groups was sometimes a challenge. One Indian official recalled the experience in Geneva of creating a group of twenty-two countries, termed the "Development Agenda Group." Initially, the meeting chair, as well as the U.S. representative, refused to use the group's name, referring only to the speaker's country. After some months, however, the U.S. delegation sought out the Indian official involved and the group, as the Indian official recalled, was grudgingly accepted as part of the Geneva landscape.[6]

Indian officials have also developed negotiating partnerships with other individual countries whose economy and global position are on the rise. As we will see especially in discussing climate change, China became an important partner, in spite of its strategic rivalry with India. Brazil was a partner with particular importance in trade negotiations. Russia has been important, based in part on traditional India-Russia ties, as has South Africa. These five countries, in different combinations, often form the core of the smaller groups that India now likes to work with.

China and Brazil illustrate how unusual India's coalition-building style is, however. Both are more willing than India to compromise with

Western powers to get a result they can live with. India remains more reluctant to move in that direction, especially on economic issues, and hence is more likely to find itself isolated in the negotiating endgame. If India is trying to block an unfavorable result, it may not mind isolation; if it is trying to achieve a positive result, standing alone can be costly.

Neither the developed nor the developing countries necessarily take monolithic positions in the global negotiations in which India participates. On climate change, India has sought to use the difference between the U.S. and European positions to fend off commitments on carbon emissions, to which the Europeans were far more receptive than the United States. On both trade and climate change, on the other hand, India complains about developed countries' efforts to split the developing country group.

India's participation in regional organizations has provided less scope for coalitions. The extreme example is the South Asian Association for Regional Cooperation (SAARC), which includes India and seven other immediate neighbors.[7] The organization's operating rules require consensus for almost any decision, a response in part to India's concern about the smaller members banding together against it. This has limited what the organization can accomplish, at least in its formal sessions, though a good deal of useful business takes place during tea breaks.[8]

A SEAT AT THE HIGH TABLE

Leadership roles in multilateral organizations are regarded by India's foreign policy establishment as an important indicator of India's global recognition. The one to which the Indian government has been formally committed for the longest time is a permanent seat on the UN Security Council. The UN Charter makes this a difficult process. The five permanent members are specified by name in the charter. Amending the charter requires a two-thirds vote in the General Assembly and ratification by two-thirds of the UN membership, including all the current permanent members.[9] The last increase in the number of nonpermanent Security Council seats from six to ten, implemented in 1965, was under discussion for ten years, which illustrates how slow the process is.[10]

Since the early 1990s, India has sought the needed support from both permanent Security Council members and the full UN membership. The campaign was both persistent and oddly hesitant, consisting mainly of putting India's Security Council ambitions on the agenda for senior-level visits with leaders of other countries. Among the five permanent members of the Security Council, whose concurrence is essential, Russia, France, and Britain were the first to offer public support. The United States, long hesitant, came on board when President Obama, during his 2010 visit to New Delhi, pledged U.S. support for a permanent Indian seat in a "reformed" Security Council, a pledge reiterated during Prime Minister Modi's 2014 visit to Washington. None of the four permanent council members that offered support was in any hurry to see the council expand, however, and none pushed to accelerate the slow reform process, described below.

That left China, which as we have seen was also the last holdout in India's effort to persuade the Nuclear Suppliers Group to change its rules and authorize safeguarded civilian nuclear trade with India. After top-level meetings with India, China has issued cryptic statements endorsing "full Indian participation" in the United Nations, but has stopped short of offering formal support. So India had promises of support—but little action—from four of the permanent members and politely phrased nonsupport from China.

The General Assembly, which is responsible for formal action regarding changes in the UN Charter, had established a committee in 1993 to consider reforms of the Security Council. Its official name was imposing: Open-ended Working Group on the Question of Equitable Representation on and Increase in the Membership of the Security Council and Other Matters Related to the Security Council. The "never-ending working group," as cynics referred to it, became part of the annual ritual, focusing on two sets of issues: expanding the membership and reforming council procedures. In 1997, the then president of the General Assembly, Malaysian diplomat Razali Ismail, pressed the issue. He circulated in the General Assembly a draft resolution that also formed the nucleus of later expansion proposals discussed in the General Assembly. It called for five new permanent members and four new non-permanent ones. Geographic distribution was proposed for all the new members. New permanent members would not have veto power, and the existing permanent members would be "urged" to restrict use of the veto to certain major issues.[11] Razali's consultations led him to believe that his proposals had the support of two-thirds of the General Assembly membership. However, in a pattern that repeated itself later, it quickly became clear that only a handful of members were prepared to back up their support with a vote.[12]

In the mid-1990s, India made the important tactical decision to team up with Germany, Japan, and Brazil in the belief that moving ahead in a group would improve the chances of getting the necessary two-thirds of the General Assembly. The first two had garnered U.S. support during the 1990s. There was no U.S. push to action at the time, and in the aftermath of the second Iraq war, the United States tacitly backed away from its support for Germany. By 2004, the group, now called the G-4, was soliciting support among General Assembly members for a draft resolution. Among the broader General Assembly membership, Indian officials also looked for support to the L-69, a newer group composed primarily of developing countries and dedicated to Security Council reform. Indian diplomats were convinced that there was strong General Assembly support for expanding the Security Council, that securing the needed two-thirds vote in the General Assembly would basically be a popularity contest, and that India was popular.

In fact, the G-4 proposal faced significant opposition in the General Assembly. Three centers of opposition were particularly important. The S-5 or "five small countries" (Switzerland, Singapore, Jordan, Costa Rica, and Liechtenstein) opposed expanding the council and wanted to reform only Security Council procedures. A second group called Uniting for Consensus professed to seek a proposal that could win unanimous General Assembly support, but was actually brought together by opposition to specific members of the G-4. Pakistan opposed India's candidacy; Italy opposed Germany; and Argentina and some other Latin Americans opposed Brazil. China, which was not formally part of the Uniting for Consensus group, opposed Japan. The third center of resistance was a large group of African countries committed to a formula that would include two African seats with a veto, in contrast to the single seat in the G-4 proposal.

The G-4 submitted a draft in July 2005 during the General Assembly's annual debate on the Security Council. The draft document bore a strong resemblance to Razali Ismail's 1997 paper.[13] The resolution's twenty-seven sponsors were an unusual group: the two smallest countries in South Asia (Bhutan and Maldives); one permanent Security Council member (France); three countries that had been part of the Soviet Union (Georgia, Latvia, and Ukraine); ten NATO members; six small Pacific island states; and four Latin American countries. Russia, interestingly, was not a sponsor. Indian officials close to the process recall great optimism that the resolution would gain the needed two-thirds. In the end, it became clear that it could not win a formal vote, so the debate ended without one.

The G-4 continued to raise the issue every year, gathering a trickle of additional supporters. By 2011, the G-4 claimed to have 100 supporters in the General Assembly, close to the required 128. None of the existing permanent Security Council members, however, had made a serious push to support expansion. Without their active support, it is all but impossible to enact an expansion proposal. A group called Intergovernmental Negotiations on Security Council Reform had inherited the mantle of the Open-Ended Working Group, and the G-4 continued to make joint statements at its meetings. But even within the G-4 differences of view had arisen, with Germany and Japan apparently contemplating semi-permanent seats with no veto.

In short, after two decades, India's campaign for a permanent seat had, in the view of its diplomats, come tantalizingly close to success at least once, but ultimately failed. Indian UN hands continue to play the long game, but beyond regular and somewhat formulaic references to permanent council membership during high-level visits, there is little evidence that the quest has been a priority for the top leadership of the Indian government. There does not appear to have been an all-hands-on-deck effort to lobby General Assembly members in capitals or to push back against members of the groups opposing the G-4 proposal. The UN Security Council seat did not feature in the manifesto of the victorious Bharatiya Janata Party (BJP) during India's 2014 election campaign. One veteran of India's UN mission described India's campaign as "a bureaucratic effort."

For the first fifteen years of India's active quest for a permanent seat, it was not on the council at all. Its absence may have been an important factor hindering its case. Its presence on the Security Council in 2011–12 did nothing to convert the tepid support among the Permanent Five into more active backing; indeed, India's record on the council probably added to the doubts some of them already had about the likely impact of a permanent Indian seat. Interestingly, one of the by-products of India's time on the council was a growing consciousness in India that this prominent position would force the country to make highly visible policy choices that were bound to offend countries it cares about.[14]

The lack of a powerful political push from the country's top leadership and the relatively thin diplomatic and political resources India devoted to this campaign contributed to this unsatisfactory result. The main reason, however, lay in two more fundamental factors: the fact that

India's inherent global power was not compelling enough to persuade the five original permanent members that they needed India's permanent participation to make the council effective and, perhaps as a result, the shallowness of the support India enjoyed among the UN's other members. India considered itself a natural candidate. The tenor of the decades-long discussions in the General Assembly's working group and intergovernmental negotiations indicates that there is wide, if not deep, support for Security Council reform, but no agreement on the specifics. India had not mobilized compelling arguments to convince skeptics to push India's candidacy. India's tactics displayed a reluctance to make requests that we have seen elsewhere, counting instead on India's standing as a leader of the developing world to deliver at least the needed General Assembly vote. But given the requirement for the support of the five current permanent council members, more effective tactics in the General Assembly might not have been enough in the end.

INDIA'S NEXT TWO CAMPAIGNS for international leadership positions were more focused. The dynamic Shashi Tharoor, who had worked for the United Nations for many years, entered the race for UN Secretary General in 2006 with the support of Sonia Gandhi, president of the Congress Party. Tharoor gave a very public face, as well as his usual eloquent voice, to his campaign. But despite his memorable effort, the Indian bureaucracy was not deeply engaged. Moreover, the real campaign for secretary general takes place behind closed doors. The first step in selecting the secretary general is a "recommendation" by the UN Security Council, where the support of the five permanent members is a requirement. In that setting, Tharoor was out-campaigned by Ban Ki-moon. The Republic of Korea had made the election of the first ever Korean UN Secretary General one of its top foreign policy priorities and had lobbied all over the world, especially with the Permanent Five. When the "straw votes" were taken in the council, Ban was the only candidate with no negative votes. Tharoor finished a strong second, but he had three negative votes, including one of the permanent members.[15]

India's successful campaign for Secretary-General of the Commonwealth of Nations in 2007, by contrast, was both personal and national. The candidate, Kamalesh Sharma, was an experienced diplomat who had also served in senior UN jobs and was India's high commissioner in London at the time he put his hat in the ring for the Commonwealth position. He recruited a "campaign manager" and organized an elaborate campaign, traveling all over the Commonwealth. He was determined to meet all member governments on their home turf and mobilized active support both from the Ministry of External Affairs (MEA) and from the political leadership, up to the prime minister. Being an MEA insider, he was able to make sure that Indian High Commissions lobbied their host governments. He paid particular attention to "swing" votes, such as small island states and some of the African and Caribbean countries. The Commonwealth Secretary-General is elected by the Commonwealth Heads of Government, so broad support extending to the top of member governments was essential. The campaign took the better part of a year. Sharma sailed through.[16]

OPPORTUNITIES FOR VISIBLE Indian leadership in other multilateral organizations have not generated as strong a campaign as one might have expected. The selection of a new International Monetary Fund (IMF) managing director in 2011 and World Bank president in 2012 generated much speculation that this would be the moment to challenge the half-century-old convention whereby the United States chooses the leader of the World Bank and Western Europe does the same for the IMF. In the event, candidates from Colombia and Nigeria made a bid for the World Bank presidency, and Mexico fielded a candidate for the IMF leadership. There were no contestants from India, although a number of high-powered former officials had the kind of economic background that would suit both organizations. The reasons are not clear; some of the notional candidates may not have wanted to leave Delhi, and in the wake of the Shashi Tharoor defeat, the government machinery may not have been keen to mount another uncertain effort. In the end, the United States and the Europeans retained their traditional positions.

In both these institutions, voting strength in the board of directors, which makes or ratifies all important decisions, is determined by quotas based on a country's economic profile. In both institutions, India once was guaranteed a permanent seat on each board representing only itself, a privilege generally reserved for the five largest members of the institutions. As the membership expanded and India's quota share shrank in relative terms, India kept its seats on the boards of both, but had to be reelected every other year as the leader of a group comprising several other countries in South Asia. In recent years, India has participated in discussions aimed at revising national quotas, in the hope of raising its voting share above the current 2.3 percent. It was willing to entertain the cost of an increased quota. India did not take a particularly aggressive position, however. There was none of the drama that regularly accompanies India's trade negotiating tactics.

An important reason for this difference is that the management structure of these institutions is politically invisible in India, in stark contrast, as we will see, to the subjects under discussion in global trade talks. The institutions, moreover, are not fundamentally negotiating organizations. The aid projects and economic support packages they provide are based on extensive staff evaluations. As we saw in chapter 9, negotiations on specific programs are essentially bilateral, between the Indian government and the institution's senior staff, and take place out of public view. While the board must approve each program, contested board votes are exceedingly rare. China has supported quota revision more aggressively than India, with a much larger economy to back it up. In practice, quota expansion could benefit China more than India. Further complicating the situation, the western European countries are widely considered to have more board seats than their economic size and the institutions' focus on developing countries would warrant. The IMF reform plan approved by the board in 2010 would have reduced the number of European directors by two, in favor of emerging economies. Unsurprisingly, the Europeans resisted. Five years later, the U.S. Congress appropriated the funding for the necessary U.S. contribution to a quota increase, bringing this change into effect.[17]

In short, India has taken a low-key approach to IMF and World Bank quotas. India and China have not thus far made an issue of the de facto veto enjoyed by the United States in both institutions, but it clearly adds to their unhappiness. It was also undoubtedly a factor in their decision to create a BRICS Development Bank in 2014, which has been characterized in the Indian press as a step forward bringing India, China, and more generally BRICS into the global limelight.

Indians have a very high profile in the running of the IMF and World Bank, however. Their staff relies heavily on impressive numbers of skilled Indian economists and development experts. Whereas the executive directors who make up the institutions' boards have generally been senior or recently retired officers of the Indian Administrative Service (IAS), many of the Indian economists on the institutions' staff are not from the civil service. Their influence within the IMF and World Bank, according to one keen observer, seems to reflect their personal standing rather than any effort to mobilize India's "team" within the organizations. Nor is there much effort to build up India's cadre of World Bank and IMF hands in a strategic fashion. One knowledgeable Indian official contrasted India's policy with China's practice of systematically grooming senior staff for years for the day when China would wish to put forward a candidate for one of the top jobs in the IMF or World Bank.[18] India has arguably more talent in the relevant specialties, but the same kind of grooming does not take place. Indians with a distinguished record in these institutions are more likely to turn up in a senior job in New Delhi. The selection of Raghuram Rajan as Governor of the Reserve Bank of India, India's central bank, is a case in point. He is not a member of the IAS. He had a distinguished career in academia, mainly in the United States, and had previously served as chief economist of the IMF and as chief economic adviser in the Indian Finance Ministry. The World Bank's current chief economist, Kaushik Basu, has a very similar profile and also served as chief economic adviser to the Government of India. Similarly, Montek Singh Ahluwalia served as India's finance secretary, in four other secretary-level posts in the Indian government, as head of the Independent Evaluation Office of the IMF, and as deputy chairman of India's Planning Commission.[19]

The World Trade Organization, by contrast, is the one global organization in which India achieved "insider" status. WTO negotiations were led for decades by a small, informal group of countries whose representatives worked out the outlines of a deal in which the rest of the membership eventually concurred. The "quad," as the group was called, originally consisted of the United States, Canada, the European Union, and Japan. In 1999, as the Doha Round of trade negotiations was struggling to get off the ground, Australia, India, and Brazil were added to the group.[20] This gave India the status it had been looking for in other international organizations. One former U.S. negotiator recalled that the United States hoped that including India in the deliberations in the "green room" would make India more of a champion of the negotiating process and a more active voice in seeking solutions acceptable to all the WTO's members. However, it does not seem to have had much impact on India's negotiating style. Nor is there much evidence that the relationships India built up in these small group consultations resulted in identifying common ground for the trade agreements under negotiation. We will explore this experience and possible reasons for it later in this chapter.[21]

INDIA ON THE SECURITY COUNCIL

India was a founding member of the United Nations, joining even before its independence from Britain, and was a prominent member from the start. Nehru hoped that the United Nations would embody, and eventually realize, his dreams of world peace and freedom. The Ministry of External Affairs staffs India's delegations to UN headquarters in New York and the organization's decentralized offices in Geneva and elsewhere. These assignments are much sought after, both for their own sake and for the advantage they bring in securing future assignments in cities like Brussels, Paris, and Vienna that host both bilateral and multilateral missions. But despite the increasing resources devoted to multilateral issues (detailed in chapter 5), India's mission to the United Nations is thinly staffed. In 2012, an Indian staff of twenty-four compared with a Brazilian mission of forty-two. The contrast is even greater when one considers that India had increased the size of its mission to staff its Security Council responsibilities.[22]

India has served seven times on the Security Council. Its most recent term, in 2011–12, followed an unusually long gap of twenty years, reflecting both India's reluctance to go after a temporary seat when its real goal was a permanent one, and a decisive loss to Japan in the Security Council election in 1996.[23] By the time it rejoined the council, as we have seen, India was deeply engaged in seeking a permanent Security Council seat and wanted to use its two years in a non-permanent slot to demonstrate its credentials.

Indian officials familiar with UN diplomacy observe that the dynamic of participating in the Security Council is different from other UN work and is driven more by broad global perspectives. The most frequently cited example is India's prickly view of sovereignty and consequent opposition to Security Council decisions that could be considered "interventionist."[24] India also wanted to block unacceptable actions, in particular by keeping the Security Council out of India's immediate neighborhood.

India found its two most recent terms on the Security Council frustrating. The permanent members did almost all the drafting, a role that Indian diplomats often played in other settings. As a result, much of the serious negotiating of the text of resolutions and formal statements was precooked by the permanent members, leaving the others with relatively few options for shaping the outcome. Moreover, the permanent members knew the procedural rules better than others and had staff that specialized in the Security Council. The regional groups and negotiating caucuses that play such an important role in the General Assembly do not operate in the smaller Security Council.

India's time on the council did give it an opportunity to showcase its contributions to the work of the United Nations. India is one of the three largest contributors of troops to peacekeeping missions and has established a peacekeeping training facility. As a Security Council member, India chaired the Committee on Counter-Terrorism, and it had already been active in the global response to maritime piracy. On these issues, which do not criticize specific countries or raise the specter of intervention, India's actions and policies are generally in line with the Security Council center of gravity, including the Western permanent members.

India's desire to present itself as a desirable, indeed inevitable, permanent member of the Security Council, however, may be more heavily influenced by country-specific issues, which have traditionally had pride of place on the council's agenda and generate the most passion among its permanent members. This applies particularly to resolutions on the Middle East. During India's term, multiple resolutions came up involving Libya, Syria, and Iran. India has traditionally been very reluctant to oppose the Arab countries and Iran, a reluctance intensified by sensitivity about its own Muslim population. Relations between the Western and non-Western permanent members were troubled at the time India served, and the fissures were acute on the Middle Eastern issues. One of the rare unanimous council statements, on Libya, was put together during India's presidency. In general, however, Indian diplomats gave their U.S. counterparts the impression of trying to impress the General Assembly rather than the permanent Security Council members. There seemed little scope for the bridging role India considers its skill. In any case, playing that role would have been sure to anger one or another constituency important to India. Even on the thematic issues, India has had a hard time getting together with UN activists on problems like children in armed conflict and protection of civilians.

For the first year of India's 2011–12 term, it was joined on the council by both Brazil and South Africa. These three countries sent their UN ambassadors to Syria in the early stages of Security Council deliberation on that crisis, but their mission did not lead to any Security Council action.[25] Indian officials complained that the council was proceeding based on a flawed understanding of the problems in Libya and Syria. Looking back on this experience, Indian UN hands argue that India must serve more frequently on the council in order to be taken more seriously there, and indeed India is already seeking support for a candidacy in 2020.[26]

CLIMATE CHANGE

Negotiations on climate change take place under the United Nations Framework Convention on Climate Change (UNFCCC) and center on a series of global conferences. Unlike many of the UN Security Council debates, however, climate change affects India's economic interests in concrete and direct ways. India is vulnerable to the ravages of climate change and hence stands to gain in the medium and long term from its mitigation. However, the cost of reducing carbon emissions, the principal means of prevention that is under international negotiation, imposes a heavy short-term burden on a country still struggling with widespread poverty. The danger of demands for commitments weighs more heavily on India with each passing year: China has now become the world's greatest emitter of greenhouse gases, and India is in third place, following the United States.

Over two and a half decades of climate negotiations, India's objective has been consistent: to avoid binding commitments to reduce emissions while insisting that developed countries, which have been industrialized for much longer, both reduce emissions and bear the cost of measures that developing countries might undertake. In practice, this means that India has argued strongly in favor of keeping the Kyoto Protocol to the Framework Convention on Climate Change as the legally binding climate agreement: it is the only international instrument that mandates emissions cuts by developed countries.

Indian diplomats underline the developed-versus-developing country character of environmental negotiations. However, there have been important splits within both groups. Among the industrialized countries, the United States has been more reluctant to undertake binding commitments to reduce emissions than the EU. The U.S. position is based in significant part on the difficulty it would face in implementing any such pledge. Despite the major role the United States played in negotiating Kyoto, the U.S. Senate refused to ratify it because it imposed no emissions commitments on developing countries.

Among developing countries, on the other hand, those for which environmental damage poses an existential threat (principally small island nations such as Maldives and more recently the Philippines) have been more willing to make a deal that they believe might strengthen developed countries' emissions reductions. Some participants, such as Brazil and Indonesia, have high emissions principally because of their extensive forests and the impact of deforestation. They therefore have different concerns when it comes to defining emissions commitments. And some developing country participants have been more willing than others to bet on the ultimate willingness of aid donors to help bankroll their environmental pledges.

India has a two-pronged coalition strategy in climate change negotiations. At one level, it seeks to keep together the largest possible bloc of developing countries—in practice, the G-77—to oppose demands for emissions commitments by developing countries. At another level, however, the G-77 is too large and unwieldy for detailed negotiations, and India's interests and negotiating skills line up most closely with other large developing countries. The G-77 has also, in the view of India's negotiators, been vulnerable to European efforts to divide the group, luring smaller developing countries away from the larger ones.

Indian diplomats have therefore looked for smaller groups to carry the negotiating load. Negotiators going back to the early days of environmental negotiations have described BASIC—Brazil, South Africa, India, and China—as their most important coalition. Besides the similarity in their approach, these countries generally show up at most of the smaller working groups that take place between the full annual conferences. In recent conferences, BASIC has been supplemented by a somewhat larger (twenty to twenty-five countries) but less well-defined group known as the Like Minded Developing Countries. Like BASIC, this group consists primarily of medium-to-large-size countries; unlike BASIC, it includes strong representation from energy producers and from the Middle East. Its composition can shift slightly from one issue to another, and it has been useful on narrower, more specific issues.[27] Both groups, in the view of Indian diplomats, have turned out to be strong enough coalitions to last through to the end of the major environmental conferences. Both figured in the acrimonious negotiations on the working draft to be presented to the 2015 conference on climate change—together with the G-77.[28]

In general, India has not found regional groups particularly useful. The Association of Southeast Asian Nations (ASEAN) has worked together, but there has been no Asia-wide group that operated jointly on substantive issues at the environmental conferences. In any event Asia includes both developed and developing countries, which does not fit well with India's objectives or negotiating strategy.

India has participated in global environmental negotiations at least since the 1991 conference that gave birth to the UNFCCC. MEA shares responsibility for climate negotiations with the Ministry of Environment and Forests. Chandrashekhar Dasgupta, at the time India's deputy permanent representative to the United Nations in New York, presided over India's delegation to the 1991 convention that drafted the UNFCCC. The diplomats, as he saw it, were negotiators; his colleagues from the Ministry of Environment and Forests were "implementers" and a source of technical expertise. His continuing involvement over nearly two decades from various positions, including at least one post-retirement job, illustrates another feature of India's management of negotiations it cares deeply about: continuity among a handful of key players.

Early in the process that eventually produced the UNFCCC, Dasgupta submitted as a "non-paper" the draft of a complete convention. Both the text and the negotiating process followed patterns that have continued to characterize global environmental talks in the intervening three-plus decades. The text required developed countries to reduce emissions by a set percentage; exempted developing countries from the requirement for binding emissions cuts; provided for voluntary contractual undertakings on emissions reduction by developing countries; and required the developed countries to support the poorer countries both technically and financially. Many of these ideas were already in circulation, but Dasgupta argued that by putting them into a text at the start of the process, he put the developing countries—and India—in a stronger position than they normally held during global conferences. Since then, these same ideas have been at the heart of the debate on how to craft a global environmental bargain.

The Indian text, inevitably, also exposed fissures within the developing country group. Oil exporters, for example, had misgivings about obliging their developed country customers to cut emissions. India's decision to work with smaller groups was one result—and one that lasted for decades in one form or another.[29]

In time, UNFCCC conferences became an annual event. India's environment minister chaired the Indian delegation at these events while much of the negotiating load between conferences was taken up by MEA.

The basic dynamics on display in the 1991 meetings continued. So did India's practice of working with a small group of large developing countries while keeping the broad developing country bloc intact. The presence of a minister as head of delegation, however, inevitably made the domestic politics of the issue more prominent.

Climate negotiations have been a frustrating enterprise. The annual UN climate conferences moved gradually toward greater acknowledgment that climate change needs to be addressed by all countries, while preserving a distinction between developed and developing countries, with language that was extensively debated and examined for shades of meaning. The phrase "common but differentiated responsibilities" figured in the 2014 Lima declaration. Like similar phrases from earlier conferences, it was hailed by weary negotiators as a step toward the new global instrument they hoped to conclude in 2015 in Paris, with developed country representatives stressing "common" responsibilities and those from developing countries emphasizing "differentiated" ones. Indian environmental reporters saw Lima as a triumph for India's policy of keeping the G-77 together; observers from the West emphasized the strains that had appeared within the developing country group and the apparent progress toward accepting the need for developing countries to cap emissions.[30]

India seemed to be exploring a change in its negotiating approach as it prepared for the Copenhagen conference in 2009. Unlike most of the earlier climate change conferences, this one included a summit meeting in the last few days (the "High Level Segment"). India's environment minister, Jairam Ramesh, a dynamic politician known for his eloquence and his often unconventional approach, had signaled a hard line the summer before the conference, when U.S. Secretary of State Hillary Clinton visited India. Visiting Washington in late September 2009, Ramesh met with the U.S. climate change negotiator, Todd Stern, as well as with a "who's who" of Washington personalities.

Ramesh came with what seemed like an olive branch. In several public speeches and presumably also in private, he stated that India would be "a deal maker, not a deal breaker" in Copenhagen. He made clear that binding commitments were still off the table as far as India was concerned, but floated a number of proposals that he hoped would make it easier for the United States and other industrialized countries to forgo commitments by India and other developing countries. After he returned to India, Ramesh reinforced this message in a letter to the prime minister, which not surprisingly, in India's overheated media environment, was leaked in what he described as distorted form.

His words stirred up a good deal of dust in India. Dasgupta refers to the "confusing signals" sent out by the environment minister. Press reports suggested that two veteran negotiators had threatened to pull out of India's Copenhagen delegation. Ramesh continued to talk of "deal making" as he reached Copenhagen. By the time the heads of government arrived in Denmark, it was apparent that the negotiating parties had not reached agreement. The Indian delegation, together with those from Brazil, China, and South Africa, put together a draft they hoped would be the basis for a consensus document. It included a common commitment to limiting global temperature increase to two degrees Celsius and incorporated Ramesh's formulation on "nationally appropriate mitigation actions," voluntary national commitments by developing countries.[31]

The Copenhagen Accord, as it came to be called, was thrashed out in a remarkable meeting including the heads of government from the United States, India, and China. Dasgupta, in his last appearance as an Indian negotiator, describes in his oral history how President Obama slipped into a meeting chaired by the Danish foreign minister, tapped Dasgupta on the shoulder, and asked him to let Indian Prime Minister Singh know that Obama wanted to meet him and would be meeting his Chinese counterpart as well. According to Dasgupta's account, when Prime Minister Singh told Obama that India could not accept binding commitments, Obama replied that Singh should be carefully listened to.[32] In the end, the Copenhagen Accord was "taken note of" by the conference, but was not able to achieve a consensus.[33]

Ramesh's effort to add creativity and a bit of honey to India's negotiating position did not extend to the next government. At the 2014 Lima conference, India's chief representative was Prakash Javadekar, Minister of Environment and Forests in the Narendra Modi government that had taken office earlier that year. The statements he made were entirely consistent with the traditional Indian position, despite the change in the party in power. In his speech to the other ministers at the conference, Javadekar positioned India as the champion of the world's poor: "We in India are committed to protecting the interests of the poor. We did it in WTO for ensuring food security of our people."[34] Interestingly, one of India's most experienced environmental journalists stressed that India was prepared to take this position "even at the cost of standing alone at multilateral forums," a phrase that did not appear in the transcript of the minister's speech but that accurately described the stand India had taken in the World Trade Organization (which we will examine later in this chapter).[35] This reflects both the role India had undertaken in the negotiating context and the political message its politicians wanted to deliver at home.

One new element that may become more significant in future climate change negotiations is the triangular relationship among the United States, India, and China. This was hinted at in Copenhagen; indeed, one journalist argued that the Chinese leader was the principal force blocking consensus around the accord.[36] More significantly, the United States and China reached agreement in November 2014 on a set of climate change goals that each would observe. India did not officially comment on the deal. President Obama and Prime Minister Modi also agreed in January 2015 on a program of cooperation on climate change, prominent features of which included clean energy cooperation and phasing down the use of hydrofluorocarbons.[37] This suggests the possibility of India, China, and the United States playing off each other's policies in a multilateral setting. A comment Jairam Ramesh made during the excitement over his "deal maker" comments is pertinent here: he observed that India needed to "learn to dialogue bilaterally and negotiate multilaterally. That's what I call walking on two legs."[38]

THE WORLD TRADE ORGANIZATION

Indian negotiations with the United States are often contentious, and as we have seen, multilateral trade negotiations may be the most contentious of all. For India, they have a higher domestic profile and involve a wider array of domestic and bureaucratic constituencies than the other categories we consider in this chapter. They have a similarly intense domestic political impact in the United States. In practice, U.S. and Indian efforts in multilateral trade negotiations frequently collide.

India's Commerce Ministry has the lead on trade negotiations. India's permanent representative to the World Trade Organization (WTO), based in Geneva, is an IAS officer from the Commerce Ministry. The commerce secretary, the senior IAS officer in the ministry, is the key trade official in Delhi involved in international trade issues in intense detail. The Indian Foreign Service (IFS) also plays an important part. Foreign Service officers are occasionally seconded to the Commerce

Ministry to staff trade positions. In an assignment pattern that is fairly typical for this portfolio, the deputy representative to the WTO in late 2014 was a Foreign Service officer with several prior postings in Geneva. IFS officers are regularly assigned to staff-level positions in Geneva and follow trade issues both between and during regular negotiating sessions. Such assignments are seen as a good way to groom officers for more senior multilateral positions.

WTO negotiations escalate to the political level, especially in the final stage, and India's delegation is typically headed at that point by the commerce minister, who is clearly the major decisionmaker. Sometimes the minister follows a script worked out by the secretary; at other times the minister may overrule the bureaucracy. U.S. trade representatives for the past two decades have worked closely with both ministers and secretaries of commerce. Most recent commerce ministers have learned the technicalities of trade in depth. Trade negotiations have intense constituency interest for any Indian elected to parliament.

India was one of twenty-three founding members of the General Agreement on Tariffs and Trade (GATT), the precursor to the WTO, in 1947. GATT was never part of the UN system. Its members (or Contracting Parties in the language of GATT) agreed on a set of common principles enshrined in the Articles of Agreement. The most important of these was the promise, with a few exceptions, to grant other members most favored nation (MFN) and national treatment. In other words, tariff concessions granted to one member would automatically be extended to all members, and internal taxes and regulations should not fall more heavily on imports than on domestically produced goods.[39] Countries joined GATT by "binding," or committing themselves not to exceed, a schedule of tariffs. The multilateral trade negotiations GATT sponsored at intervals produced agreements further lowering members' trade barriers. The specific undertakings they embodied were negotiated bilaterally, between "principal suppliers," but applied to all members and became an integral part of members' GATT obligations.[40]

The Articles of Agreement included special provisions for developing countries, authorizing them to deviate from some of GATT's normal obligations on a number of grounds, including their need to boost the standard of living of their population. These provisions were tremendously important to India, but became a regular source of frustration in its negotiations with other countries, notably the United States. Especially in the early years, India stressed its entitlement to preferential trade in trade negotiations. The United States was pursuing an agenda of trade expansion and market opening, which often clashed with India's goals.

The decision to replace GATT with the more formal WTO in 1995 was part of a larger round of trade negotiations. Member countries, responding to pressure especially from the United States, crafted a package of agreements, many of which aimed to bring under international trade rules areas that had previously not been covered, such as trade-related aspects of intellectual property, investment, and general principles of services trade, known to trade aficionados as the "Singapore issues."

India had resisted expanding the scope of the trade system from the start, in keeping with its generally skeptical approach toward creating new international obligations that might impinge on its economic policy. Before the formation of WTO, India had organized a group of ten countries to resist adding these new areas to the trade rules. In the run-up to the Doha Round, it led the Like Minded group of developing countries in resisting demands for a new round until earlier agreements important to them had been implemented. In the end, India found itself isolated and reluctantly joined the WTO. This decision aroused an uproar in parliament, with the government accused of selling out India's interests. This undoubtedly left scars on future negotiators.[41]

In 2001, the WTO members' trade ministers met in Doha, Qatar, to discuss launching a new trade round. India and several other developing countries resisted this idea, and especially resisted building the new round on "Singapore issues." India's commerce minister, Murasoli Maran, was quoted as having told the UN Secretary General that it was in India's interest that the Doha meeting fail to reach agreement on a new round.[42]

Exhaustive and exhausting negotiations eventually reached agreement on terms of reference for the round that would place the needs of developing countries "at the heart" of its work program and would embed "special and differential treatment" for developing countries in the schedules of concessions and rules negotiated in the round.[43] But the possibility of negotiations on the so-called Singapore issues was still more than the Indian delegation was prepared to accept, and Maran refused to join the consensus. According to one account, what followed was a dramatic exercise in high-pressure tactics—a showdown involving the United States, the WTO Director-General, and the host nation, Qatar, eyeball to eyeball with Maran. In the end, an isolated Maran agreed to some modest face-saving language changes that strengthened the role of public health in intellectual property decisions and appeared to place further hurdles in front of negotiations on the "Singapore issues."[44]

The Doha Round was a tremendously complex undertaking, involving product-specific negotiations (especially on nonagricultural products) and an ambitious agenda of norm-setting negotiations to complete the expansion of trade rules that had started with the creation of WTO. India was an active participant in all aspects of the round. By far its most important issue was agriculture, which was largely left out of normal trade rules under GATT. Agricultural subsidies had long been the subject of intense and bitter disputes among the industrialized countries, especially between the United States and the European Union. For India, agriculture was a life-and-death issue, economically and especially politically. The round's procedures stipulated that agreements needed to be a package deal—"nothing is agreed until everything is agreed"—making the stakes even higher for the agricultural negotiators.

Two episodes in the Doha Round agricultural negotiations provide a snapshot of India's approach: the negotiations leading to the temporary breakdown of the round in 2008, and the showdown over India's agriculture subsidies and the Trade Facilitation Agreement in 2013–14.

Much of India's effort was intended to resist what the United States was trying to do. In the early days, India sought to take advantage of the long-standing U.S.-EU discord over agriculture and to work with the EU, but eventually this strategy was superseded by a more familiar one, working with the larger developing countries: Brazil, South Africa, and to some degree China. The close collaboration with Brazil continued despite the gap between Brazil's and India's goals: Brazil's main interest was in opening other agricultural markets whereas India's chief objective was to retain the right to close its own market by raising agricultural trade barriers in case of need. India supplemented this strategy by collaborating with groups of twenty to thirty developing countries similar to the Like Minded group. These groups were particularly important as partners in floating negotiating proposals.[45] Besides these developing country groups, India was part of the small steering group of four to seven countries that met regularly to try to pull the whole negotiation together. Indians were also part of the daily gathering informally known as the "Breakfast Group," which included all of the most actively involved ambassadors but no WTO staff.

Key Indian and U.S. negotiators involved in the agriculture discussions already knew each other from years of bilateral negotiations, and participants from both sides felt they had been able to establish productive personal relationships with their counterparts. Indian trade officials adopted some American habits much faster than their Indian diplomatic colleagues, such as calling their counterparts by their first names. They took pride in trying to steer decisions toward the most favorable corners of the U.S. government. Indian negotiators admired their U.S. counterparts' candor and willingness to make a deal, something they felt was less characteristic of some of their other negotiating partners.

Both sides' officials, however, were painfully aware of the institutional disconnects between the two systems. In many ways they had "mirror image" perceptions of each other's agricultural support systems and negotiating constraints. Each was frustrated with the other side's inability to address political obstacles, a problem Indian officials blamed, often correctly, on the limited authority of the U.S. executive branch. Each side was frustrated with the other's unwillingness to make the first move. One Indian participant described the prevailing Indian perception of the U.S. position as "give me your market, but it will take us three years to change the rules."[46] Indian officials complained about the absence of U.S. institutional memory when top officials were replaced, which seemed to happen more often on the U.S. side. U.S. officials, as we have seen, often make the opposite complaint—that their Indian counterparts had the negotiating history memorized, leaving the looser U.S. system at a disadvantage.

In July 2008, the Doha Round was already three years past its original deadline for completion. Ministers from member countries gathered in Geneva to try to meet a fresh deadline for establishing the "modalities" for agricultural negotiations and the outlines of a deal on agricultural subsidies. The main protagonists in the subsidy negotiations were the United States and the European Union, but India's concern about its farmers' incomes and maintaining food security programs for its large impoverished population made it a significant player as well. In the run-up to the Geneva meeting, the Indian press had been full of urgent pleas from farm and political groups, urging trade officials not to sign a WTO agreement, which they equated with capitulation. The small steering group, which now included both India and Brazil, maintained an intensive pace of meetings. The GATT tradition, carried over to the WTO, was that compromises were reached in this small group.

Negotiators had prepared a daunting package of papers embodying elements of the deal that would go into effect if the agricultural piece fell into place. U.S. Trade Representative Susan Schwab, the lead U.S. negotiator, thought a deal was within reach and recalled that India's professional negotiating team had used their knowledge of trade rules very creatively to try to reach agreement.

It was not to be. India's lead negotiator, Minister of Commerce and Industry Kamal Nath, who had returned to Delhi for a crucial vote in parliament,[47] returned as the conference was reaching its climax. He deflected Schwab's hint that there might be additional U.S. flexibility, noting that he had none. The missing ingredient, from India's perspective, was a "special safeguard mechanism" that would permit developing countries to restrict agricultural imports under special circumstances. In the small group meeting, Nath responded to the proposed compromise saying, "I reject everything!"[48] Participants from both sides noted that the problem was not an inflexible personality. Rather, it was the iron law of Indian politics that required politicians to protect the Indian farmer, coupled with a strong Indian aversion to compromising on issues they regard as central. For an Indian politician, it is far better to return home having held out for the maximum position than to come back with half a loaf.

India was not solely responsible for the breakdown. Post-mortem press conferences made clear that the United States and the EU had also reached an impasse on their long-standing agricultural subsidy dispute. WTO Director-General Pascal Lamy and Kamal Nath directed their ire at the United States; Schwab and her colleague from the U.S. Department of Agriculture blamed both the EU and India for failure to offer meaningful market opening. But the inflexibility of India's politics and the willingness of one of its senior politicians to simply say "no" meant that there were no counterweights to the other problems that afflicted the negotiations. Interestingly, the Brazilian negotiator—veteran foreign minister Celso Amorim—shocked his Indian counterparts by lauding the package.[49]

THE NEXT CRITICAL EPISODE started at the WTO ministerial meeting in Bali in December 2013, with agriculture once again in a starring role. After twelve years, the Doha Round still had no concrete results; the ministers decided to try to conclude an agreement on simplifying the procedures for handling trade at the border, known as the Trade Facilitation Agreement (TFA), which they hoped would serve as "low hanging fruit."

This agreement in turn was the product of several years of detailed negotiations spelling out border procedures that member countries would follow in importing and exporting goods. India was deeply involved in crafting this agreement, drafting important sections of the text. Its government very much wanted some of its key provisions to go into effect. Procedurally, however, India was determined that the TFA remain flexible enough that it and other developing countries would not be caught up in dispute settlement proceedings based on failure to implement some of its more complicated provisions. U.S. negotiators also believed that India wanted to keep the TFA negotiations from being concluded too quickly, seeing this agreement as potential leverage should they not achieve their objectives in the agricultural negotiations.

The Bali ministerial meeting was to be the moment of decision. Negotiating staff had narrowed the gap on agriculture. The key provision was the length of time during which WTO members would refrain from challenging developing countries whose agricultural stockpiles exceeded the proposed new ceiling of 10 percent of the value of agricultural production. The U.S. and other major agricultural exporters were asking for a two-year time limit, or "peace clause." India Commerce Minister Anand Sharma insisted on an indefinite time frame, though there were reports that India might be able to live with four years.[50] U.S. negotiators believed the future viability of the WTO was at stake.

After marathon meetings with U.S. Trade Representative Michael Froman and the trade minister of the host country, Indonesia, they settled. The Indian press reported that an Indian text had been the basis of the agreement.[51] The Ministerial Decision on Public Stockholding for Food Security Purposes, as it was called, included a four-year "peace clause." It was reached in tandem with a ministerial decision to conclude the TFA negotiations and begin the procedures needed for the TFA to enter into force. This was a cross-sectoral package—trade facilitation and agriculture.[52] Negotiators like such agreements, but the Indian system, like the U.S. system, is uncomfortable making one important constituency happy at another's expense. India had resisted linkages involving agriculture for many years, fearing that India's modest position in global trade would put it at a disadvantage on crucial issues of agricultural trade.

Some months later, when the time came for the members of WTO to formally adopt the two agreements, India had a new government. Prime Minister Narendra Modi had campaigned on his promises to make the

Indian economy hum, but he had no exposure to or interest in international organizations like the WTO. His powerful finance minister, Arun Jaitley, was a former commerce minister and as an opposition parliamentarian had lambasted the previous government for "selling out" India's trade interests. The Indian representative to the WTO said his government would refuse to adopt the agreements, claiming that promised efforts to find a permanent solution to the problem of public stockholding for food security had not materialized. In the WTO, in practice, consensus is required to make a negotiating text official, so this effectively meant that neither the TFA nor the agricultural agreement could proceed to the next phase, required for entry into force.

The news sent shock waves through Washington. The agreement India was blocking, from the U.S. perspective, had been negotiated in accordance with India's request; the Indian action called into question the viability of the multilateral trade system. The Indian position was taken up by the cabinet, which did not bend.

India had practically no support within the WTO for its hard line. A handful of members were eventually persuaded to speak up in support, but in reality India was the lone holdout. It was a stand reminiscent of the heroic solo resistance described in India's epic literature that Amrita and Aruna Narlikar cite as archetypes for India's multilateral negotiating behavior.[53]

In July 2014, India was able to work through the G-33 to put forward a new proposal that would have exempted developing country stockholdings altogether from WTO restraints. The July meeting broke up without agreement. The Brazilian director-general of the WTO was visibly frustrated as he worked through the summer and into the autumn to find a face-saving solution and urged that the Bali agreement not be reopened.

The issue came up inconclusively during Prime Minister Modi's visit to the White House in September 2014. Modi told American audiences he supported a rules-based trading system—but insisted that India would not unblock the TFA without receiving satisfaction on agriculture. Politically, however, he would have had trouble settling the issue during a White House visit: that setting would have opened him up to charges of caving in to U.S. pressure. U.S. and Indian officials worked the issue behind the scenes, enlisting the help of Indian officials familiar with the United States. India's ambassador to the United States, S. Jaishankar, and Finance Minister Jaitley, who had been ill during much of the summer, were brought into the picture. Discussions continued at the WTO in Geneva to ensure the necessary consensus.

In November 2014, Modi and President Obama met once more, on the margins of a meeting of the East Asian Summit, and announced that they had settled the issue. The Bali agreement was upheld. It included slightly tighter language on the agreement not to challenge public stockholding in developing countries and on an effort to find a permanent solution within a year.[54] The six-month crisis had resulted in very little change to the agreements negotiated at Bali, but the Indian government had taken a public stand.

India's negotiating partners and academic observers agree that India often resorts to a "just say no" approach to multilateral negotiations. Several studies argue that this is a tactic adopted by countries that feel overmatched in negotiations and grows out of India's political culture.[55] These explanations certainly reflect part of the reality. But there may be a more compelling explanation. Indian negotiators—as well as Indian elites—have never been convinced that trade negotiations offered great economic benefits to India. In these two cases, brinksmanship protected India's core equities. The Bali agreement was better than what India had turned down at Doha, and the revised agreement a year later was very slightly better, from India's perspective. The costs to India were, from the point of view of India's trade officials, relatively modest: India reaffirmed its position as a very difficult negotiating partner and probably reduced the likelihood of obtaining U.S. support in some of its efforts to join new international organizations. But many Indians discounted the likelihood of such support in the first place, and two commerce ministers reaped the political benefit of taking a heroic stand against the world's most powerful countries.[56]

In the larger national context, however, the Modi government has made expanded economic relations a tremendously high priority. The animosity stirred up by this seemingly arcane issue may have been more than they expected. The next few years will provide some clues as to whether the Indian government is adjusting its calculus of the costs and benefits of a hard line.

THE COMPREHENSIVE TEST BAN TREATY

Our final look at India's multilateral negotiations addresses disarmament, one of the relatively few subjects on which the Indian foreign service has built up a cadre of specialists. While India opposes nuclear proliferation from a disarmament perspective, as we saw in chapter 8, it remains strongly opposed to the privileged position for recognized nuclear weapons states set up in the Non-Proliferation Treaty (NPT), sometimes referred to as "nuclear apartheid."[57] India's role in negotiating and then not joining the Comprehensive Test Ban Treaty (CTBT) illustrates how Indian security interests override some of its common negotiating procedures and strengthen its tendency to say "no" when its objectives are not met.

Negotiations on a CTBT started in early 1994, under a mandate from the UN Conference on Disarmament. At the outset, the idea had Indian support, and the best possible pedigree: Nehru himself broached it in the United Nations in 1954. India's work in the ad hoc committee where the discussions took place displayed the familiar characteristics of its approach to multilateral negotiations: drafting skill; a good eye for the time to make a point; meticulous attention to historical and drafting detail; and equally careful research on the legal background as it affected India's position. The principal negotiator on the CTBT, India's ambassador to the UN organizations in Geneva during the critical endgame of the negotiations, Arundhati Ghose, had extensive multilateral experience. Her deputy was one of MEA's disarmament experts. Ghose was stretched thin and had to represent India in half a dozen other organizations covering everything from intellectual property to health, in addition to the disarmament role. As Ghose ruefully observed in an oral history interview, "Every concerned ministry in Delhi wanted me to attend every single meeting!"[58]

The stage for India's transformation from supporter to bitter opponent of the CTBT was set by two developments: the indefinite extension of the NPT in 1995, which made permanent the two-tiered NPT system; and the development of simulation technology that enabled the nuclear weapons states to conduct subcritical tests by computer even without physical tests. These two developments led the ambassador to conclude that the emerging final negotiating phase was a "trap." Indian UN negotiators often have considerable latitude in determining how to operate, but Ghose sought high-level instructions from Delhi in late summer 1995. The prime minister approved a hard line: unless the body of the treaty included an "equalizer" on disarmament—a commitment by the nuclear weapons states to disarm—India could not accept the text. India also found the verification procedures intrusive and feared they would ultimately be a back door forcing India into the NPT. But the central problem was India's view that the CTBT text would effectively box India in.[59]

India put out this position at high levels and in multiple forums over the next few months. The chairman of the Indian Atomic Energy Commission went public in a speech at the International Atomic Energy Agency (IAEA); the foreign minister and prime minister both mentioned it at the United Nations General Assembly. In January 1996, Ghose decided to amplify India's publicly stated position by making specific reference to "India's security interests."[60]

Over the next few months intense bilateral negotiations took place with the key delegations in Geneva, Russia, the United States, and China. Ghose recalled that John Holum, head of the U.S. Arms Control and Disarmament Agency, complained that her insistence on nuclear disarmament was a "pipe dream." With characteristic feistiness, she responded that "your CTBT" was also a pipe dream.

Ghose's government, meanwhile, was bringing her back for consultations more often than usual—monthly, she recalled—and on one occasion brought her back to New Delhi to hear the parliamentary debate on the CTBT. For a ministry that is generally cash-strapped, this was an unusual effort to make sure an ambassador in the middle of a difficult negotiation was fully sensitized to Indian political reaction. The BJP government, she said, had been briefing the opposition on the negotiations.

The ad hoc committee had undertaken to complete its negotiations in time to transmit the finished text—which had to be adopted by consensus, under the committee's rules—to the United Nations General Assembly in September 1996. The endgame was fully under way by June of that year. Under the normal rotation of the chairmanship of this committee among the regional groups that operate at the United Nations, it was the Western group's turn to provide a chair, and that job fell to a Dutch diplomat. Recognizing that the group was not likely to reach consensus, he decided to present a "chairman's text," reflecting his best understanding of country positions based on intensive bilateral consultations he carried out. His text, inevitably, drew objections, particularly from the NAM members (known in that setting as the G-21).[61] Ghose felt that the text had ignored India's positions and recommendations.

By the time the chairman's text was formally submitted to the committee, India had signaled its objections. Called to New Delhi once again, Ghose received instructions from the prime minister: India would oppose the treaty text, thus depriving it of the consensus needed to pass the Conference on Disarmament (CD). Iran joined India in the "no" column.[62] Because of the lack of consensus, the CD was only able to send the treaty to New York by having Belgium present it as a "national paper," a procedure India objected to as illegal, but could not block. In the General Assembly's vote, India was joined by two other "no" votes—Libya and Bhutan.[63]

The conditions for entry into force of the treaty provided the final dispute of these negotiations. After experimenting with several different formulas, the chairman decided to use the IAEA's list of countries with advanced nuclear technology as the group whose ratifications were required to bring the treaty into operation. These of course included India, as well as Pakistan, Iran, and North Korea. India took passionate exception to what it regarded as a coercive tactic, one that it believed had been masterminded by its adversaries, Pakistan and China. In a classic example of the meticulous research Indian diplomats deploy in important negotiations, their Geneva delegation argued that it was contrary to the law of treaties to impose obligations on a state through a treaty that state has already said it would not sign.

In these negotiations, India was playing a solo game. It had tried to line up support from the group of developing countries that were participating in the CD, the G-21. However, with the exception of India and Pakistan, all were parties to the NPT and were therefore reluctant to get too involved in supporting an Indian position that was basically designed to preserve India's options outside that treaty.

Two years later, the United States and India engaged in talks aimed at repairing the damage to their relationship from India's 1998 nuclear weapons test. The U.S. Senate had rejected the CTBT. For both philosophical and policy reasons, Washington was looking for a way to obtain Indian and Pakistani signatures on the treaty and, in the process, create pressure on the Senate to reconsider its rejection. Indian Prime Minister Vajpayee and his foreign minister (and negotiator with Washington), Jaswant Singh, wanted to deal delicately with this issue. Vajpayee addressed the treaty in his 1998 speech to the United Nations General Assembly: "India . . . is now engaged in discussions with key interlocutors on a range of issues, including the CTBT. We are prepared to bring these discussions to a successful conclusion so that the entry into force of the CTBT is not delayed beyond September, 1999. . . . In announcing a [testing] moratorium, India has already accepted the basic obligation of the CTBT."[64] Vajpayee's words left a little space for the Indian government to reconsider and provided some comfort to Washington. However, both sides surely understood that the chances of either the United States or India ratifying the treaty were vanishingly small. India had said "no" in the CTBT negotiations; in this critical negotiation with Washington, India's answer in practice was still "no," but delivered with a spoonful of honey and a smile.

JOINING THE CLUBS

India's economic surge since 1990 has raised the question of whether India should be represented in some of the more selective groups on the international scene. The picture that emerges is one of considerable ambivalence—both on India's part and on the part of other countries.

The East Asia–centered organizations in which India is either a member (East Asian Summit and Asian Regional Forum) or a dialogue partner (ASEAN) fit smoothly into India's strategic outlook as the embodiment of India's "Look East—Act East" policy. India has not altogether fit into the "club" of the ASEAN-related organizations, however, partly because the Southeast Asian countries are more comfortable than India is coordinating economic policies. The comparison with China is ever present in East Asian regional institutions. The other countries want India inside the tent as a counterweight to China, but also want to downplay the rivalry.

On the other hand, India's interest in the Asia Pacific Economic Cooperation (APEC) forum has thus far gone unrewarded. The organization combines Asian countries (going as far West as Thailand) with countries from the other side of the Pacific Rim. The United States kept India out in 1997, insisting on a ten-year moratorium on new members. The other members were not enthusiastic enough to push back. While no one has publicly given reasons, India's hard line and brinksmanship in trade negotiations and still quite state-centric economy seem to be the main issues. And from India's side, the problem is a familiar one: opinions in the Indian government are divided on the value of joining APEC, and in any case, having been turned down once, India does not want to ask until it is sure that the answer will be "yes." President Obama's statement in Delhi in January 2015 that the United States "welcomes India's interest" in joining APEC signals a shift, but it is not clear whether or when action will follow.[65]

Among the smaller global organizations, India joined the G-20 early in the global financial crisis and has participated in its deliberations about maintaining global financial health and stability. Modi attended a G-20 meeting in Australia six months after becoming prime minister. This is clearly an important forum, in which former prime minister Manmohan Singh's credentials as an economist served him well.

The group that inspires the greatest interest among Indian policy elites is BRICS, the group of emerging nations that a Goldman Sachs report turned into an acronym (Brazil, Russia, India, China, South Africa). The group meets every year and is at least implicitly looked on as the only one with the potential to provide some counterweight to the economic power of the United States. Its decision to start a development bank, noted earlier, suggests a degree of operational ambition; the fact that the bank and other potential activities will have to be financed by China may turn out to be a complicating factor. But at present, BRICS is the international association that best reflects India's view that the world ought to be more multipolar.

Mexico and Korea have joined the Organization for Economic Cooperation and Development (OECD), traditionally a rich countries' club with members from Western Europe, North America, and Japan. So far at least, no one has suggested that India follow suit. India itself is not keen on exploring membership. The OECD countries have developed a robust set of normative agreements on how they will handle such issues as foreign investment, and India has misgivings about the intrusiveness of these foreign standards.

The most interesting story among these organizations, and the only one that involves actual negotiations, concerns the export control groups that were set up to discourage the spread of various kinds of armaments. Four organizations were set up, each with its own membership and purpose. The Nuclear Suppliers Group (NSG), founded in 1974 after India's initial nuclear test, coordinated member countries' policies on the sales of supplies and equipment related to nuclear plants. The Australia Group, founded in 1985, is an informal group that harmonizes members' export control policies so as to prevent the spread of chemical and biological weapons and their precursors. The Wassenaar Arrangement performs a similar function for small arms transfers. Finally, the Missile Technology Control Regime (MTCR), established in 1987, coordinates export control policies for missiles considered capable of delivering weapons of mass destruction.

There had been obstacles to Indian membership from both sides. India had serious misgivings about being caught up in anything related in any way to the NPT and was not interested in subjecting itself to intrusive procedures. The member countries saw India as a troublesome actor on proliferation issues and were not eager to bring it inside the tent.

With the conclusion of India's nuclear agreement with the United States, including the NSG's approval of a waiver of its normal strictures against commercial commerce with India, attitudes changed. India became interested in joining the four groups. Having gone through an exhaustive review of its export policies with the U.S. government, as described in chapter 8, India expected to be able to get through the scrutiny imposed on behalf of these organizations relatively easily. The United States concluded that membership in these groups would bring India into the parts of the nonproliferation system that were not off-limits by the terms of the NPT. It would also help anchor India's commitment to strong export controls in a larger international setting. President Obama publicly mentioned his support for India's membership in the organizations when visiting India in November 2010.

Since then, work has proceeded slowly on advancing India's membership. What is instructive for our purposes is not so much the details of the organization-specific negotiations as the way India approached the process as a whole. For India, membership was desirable, but certainly not essential. Among the four organizations, India's strong priority was membership in the NSG, which for years had stood as a symbol of India's exclusion from a system that it regarded as discriminatory—and which also provided a forum where not only big powers like China but smaller ones, like a handful of developing countries and the smaller European nations, could sit in judgment. The issue of status, in other words, was a significant element for India.

India's view from the start was that it should be admitted into all four organizations as a package deal. The United States, as had happened in the NSG's consideration of the nuclear deal, was working with India to broker the admission. It believed there was no way to avoid a one-by-one approach, working on each organization's membership criteria and then developing the necessary consensus among the members. This process was distasteful to India, not least because it put India in the position of making a request to an organization some of whose members were unenthusiastic.

In 2015, India intensified its diplomacy, engaging one-on-one especially with the members of the NSG and the MTCR. Press reports cited in particular the Modi visit to Ireland, Indian President Pranab Mukherjee's visit to Sweden, and the foreign secretary's visit to Switzerland, with a string of further engagements planned at the prime ministerial level. A meeting of the MTCR in October 2015 ended without discussion of India's membership. But the push continued. During a visit by the Italian NSG chair to India in November 2015, he referred to his hope for forward movement during the next NSG plenary meeting, in June 2016.[66] The final outcome is not yet clear: China could oppose moving India forward, and other issues regarding India's anomalous nuclear status are not fully resolved at this writing. But this campaign bears the hallmarks of India's multilateral diplomacy in those cases where the prime minister is engaged and the objective is to approve something rather than simply block an undesirable result.

CHAPTER ELEVEN

Negotiating with Pakistan and China

THE PRECEDING CHAPTERS HAVE illustrated India's negotiating style primarily by drawing on its interactions with the United States. They reflect the fractious relations between the two countries, especially during the Cold War years, as well as the increasingly important and positive part America has played in the much changed foreign policy India has pursued since then.

In this chapter and the next, we will examine a few examples of how India deals with countries whose roles in its global vision are markedly different from the one it assigns to the United States. We start with Pakistan and China, which by virtue of geography, history, and their nuclear arsenals represent the two principal strategic threats to India. Both have a relationship with India that is to an important extent adversarial. Both, in different ways, challenge India's assertion of preeminence in its immediate region. Pakistan has to a large extent built its identity on resisting India's dominance. China inherits thousands of years of history as the dominant power in East Asia, a role it expects to perpetuate. It has teamed up with Pakistan to keep India in check while cultivating much improved economic relations with India and, as we have seen, making common cause with it in many multilateral forums.

PAKISTAN

A great deal has been written about the relationship between India and Pakistan, those "distant neighbors" as Indian journalist Kuldip Nayar called them in his 1972 study of their bilateral ties. In chapters 2 and 3 we looked at India-Pakistan relations in the context of India's longtime quest for regional preeminence and strategic autonomy. Here we focus more closely on process: how New Delhi has dealt with Pakistan to achieve its goals.

India's policy and negotiating approach to Pakistan are driven by its commitment to primacy in South Asia. Pakistan's situation is unique. Unlike the smaller South Asian neighbors, Pakistan has built its foreign and security policies on the assumption that it will always have a hostile relationship with India. It is determined not to accept India's assertions of regional primacy and pushes back whenever it can against Indian claims of a global standing superior to its own. India dismisses and even ridicules such Pakistani efforts to assert equality. This different view of their respective roles is a constantly recurring theme in their diplomatic encounters, along with a well-developed practice on both sides of sticking to time-honored positions and language, lest a modest change be seen as an unreciprocated concession.

The animus between India and Pakistan dates back to the bloody partition that ended the British Raj in 1947. This hostility has persisted despite promising developments in the relationship that have occurred from time to time—and which always proved short-lived. In the early decades of Indian and Pakistani independence, some observers forecast that once the generation of leaders who had lived through the horrors of partition had left the scene the two countries would develop a less inimical and more "normal" relationship. The more optimistic thought this might even come in time to replicate U.S.-Canadian ties. But no lasting improvement has taken place. Indians and Pakistanis may get along famously when they meet informally to watch their national teams confront one another in international cricket matches, and leaders of the two countries have from time to time found this cricket rivalry a convenient occasion for meetings in an atmosphere of unusual bonhomie with their counterparts from across the border. Typically, these encounters spark hope that such "cricket diplomacy" will lead to progress at the negotiation table. But the enthusiasm usually does not last long before a grimmer reality again sets in.

There is a widely held view in Pakistan that India has never been reconciled to partition and is determined either to undo it or to break up Pakistan into small, weak states that will more readily accept Indian subcontinental dominance. In fact, most Indian leaders now accept that

Pakistan is here to stay. As Prime Minister Atal Bihari Vajpayee tried to demonstrate in 1999 when he spoke at the monument in Lahore commemorating the 1940 resolution calling for the creation of Pakistan, not even leaders of Hindu nationalist parties question Pakistan's separate status today. But most Indians consider Pakistan a hostile, nuclear-armed, revanchist state that threatens Indian interests in Kashmir and elsewhere. In their view, Pakistan conspires with other countries to impede India's ascent to global power and causes problems for India both in international forums and on India's own soil. The memory of the Pakistan-masterminded attack on Mumbai in 2008 and Pakistan's subsequent reluctance to deal harshly with the people India rightly claimed were responsible continue to rankle. As noted in chapter 3, the Manmohan Singh government dealt with that incident with considerable restraint. No Indian government is likely to be as willing to do so again, least of all Narendra Modi's.

India's diplomacy toward Pakistan is not influenced by any significant "peace party." There are no influential lobbies in India calling for making the compromises that could help bring about better relations. Many Indians would welcome less hostile ties, but not if they cost India such concessions as a settlement of the Kashmir dispute that gave India significantly less territory there than it now controls. A good many business people see profit for themselves in improved trade relations. But there is no evidence that they are prepared to mobilize seriously to bring the government to be more forceful and imaginative in moving in that direction. "Better relations with Pakistan" is not a slogan that cuts much ice either with influential Indians or with rank-and-file voters. Indeed, it could be dangerous for one's political health to be labeled a Pakistan sympathizer.

Should an Indian government take significant initiatives to improve ties, it could probably persuade most politically aware Indians to go along, within limits. But its hand is unlikely to be forced. Many Indians hailed Prime Minister Modi's "statesmanship" in inviting his Pakistani counterpart to New Delhi for his inauguration. But few seem to have found fault with his government's abruptly canceling high-level India-Pakistan diplomatic talks a few months later. Indian leaders take no domestic political risk in adopting a tough line toward Pakistan.

Forms of India-Pakistan Diplomacy: Composite Dialogue

In the mid-1990s, India developed its conciliatory "Gujral Doctrine" for dealing with neighboring states.[1] Pursuing that doctrine its author, Prime Minister Inder Kumar Gujral, and his Pakistani counterpart,

Nawaz Sharif, held bilateral talks and developed a comprehensive structure to resolve disputes between the two countries. This structure has become the standard approach of the two countries to their bilateral diplomacy.

The dialogue process involves more or less simultaneous consideration of a basket of issues ranging from the very difficult, most obviously the Kashmir dispute, to the seemingly easier ones, such as drug trafficking and small differences between the two countries over the location of the India-Pakistan boundary at Sir Creek close to the Arabian Sea.

The foreign secretaries of the two countries supervise the formal negotiations and take the lead in the more sensitive of them, such as discussing a Kashmir settlement and devising confidence-building measures to enhance peace and security. Armed clashes and other incidents have interrupted the process. The longest hiatus followed the 2008 Pakistan-based attack on Mumbai. Efforts to resurrect the dialogue in 2014 under a different name soon ended when the newly installed Modi government objected to a meeting that the Pakistan high commissioner in New Delhi had with Kashmiri separatists and canceled a session about to take place.

The composite dialogue had some modest "confidence building" successes, such as the establishment of bus service between the Indian and Pakistani sides of Kashmir in 2005. But this required major pressure by the Indian prime minister's office on the bureaucracy, and in the end the arrangement was so hemmed in by restrictive regulations that it made little lasting difference for the people of Kashmir it was designed to help. The service was suspended in 2015 when India accused Pakistani drivers of bringing in drugs.[2]

The dialogue also led to a promising initiative in 2012 to open up trade between the two countries. This was heralded by visits by each of the two trade ministers to the other's capital. Again, a political push was needed to make progress. But the absence of consistent pressure from the two prime ministers and their cabinet colleagues led the initiative to fizzle out. The incoming Modi government had urged Pakistan to wait for it to take office before announcing Pakistan's grant of "nondiscriminatory market access" to imports from India. But the Pakistanis were still dragging their feet when the Modi government canceled high-level official talks, referred to previously, and another promising development failed to materialize.[3]

In short, the composite dialogue process has needed a major political effort even to make relatively small steps forward and has made no lasting progress even on what appeared to be the most tractable problems.

More fundamentally, the process was handicapped from the start by the difference in the negotiating strategies the two governments adopted. The Indians have favored dealing first with the easy issues, which they argue will establish a diplomatic climate that will facilitate dealing with the tough ones. The Pakistanis, for their part, have always feared that once the easy issues were successfully dealt with the Indians would back away from efforts to resolve the Kashmir issue, and Pakistan would have used up all its bargaining chips. Kashmir is key for the Pakistanis. After the latest break in the talks, the Pakistanis declared they would not resume them unless Kashmir was on the agenda.

Back-Channel Talks

One initiative on Kashmir that India and Pakistan undertook in the mid-2000s seemed to bring the two countries to the brink of an agreement. This effort had been sparked by the "out of the box" ideas for a settlement that Pakistan President Pervez Musharraf informally outlined in media interviews. Musharraf's compromise formula offered concessions to India that went well beyond anything that Islamabad had ever proposed. The subsequent negotiations that they sparked—after some Indian foot-dragging—were conducted by special emissaries who were formally authorized by their leadership to carry them out, and who operated quietly beyond the view of the media. Their discussions were never part of the composite dialogue machinery. This back-channel format has been the most promising formula for getting beyond the well-worn path trod in previous years. An Indian official with deep experience dealing with Pakistan observed that the approach he found most effective involved giving Pakistan the space to draw its own conclusions, rather than putting an Indian stamp on ideas. That is not a tactic that comes easily to Indian officials, but the back channel may be a format that makes it easier for both sides.[4]

Crisis Management

India's strong preference in dealing with its neighbors, and especially with Pakistan, is to avoid any third-party involvement in the process. UN envoys participated in India-Pakistan peace efforts in the late 1940s; the United States and Britain attempted to facilitate a settlement in the early 1960s; both efforts came to naught and left a lasting bad taste in India's mouth. The Tashkent talks hosted by the Soviet Union that ended the 1965 India-Pakistan War and the World Bank negotiating effort that produced the Indus Waters Treaty were more successful, but India's distaste for third-party engagement remains strong. It prefers to deal with Pakistan directly and from a position of superior power, as it did, for example, in the Simla negotiations ending the 1971 war in which Bangladesh split from Pakistan.

The only exceptions since the 1960s involve crisis management negotiations. On three occasions, the United States, working in one case with Britain, involved itself in a brewing crisis between India and Pakistan. The first was in 1990, when military movements in the border areas between the two countries seemed to be headed toward a confrontation. In the early stages of the emerging face-off, the U.S. ambassadors in New Delhi and Islamabad, on their own initiative, undertook the task of trying to evaluate rumors about military movements, providing their findings, which were generally reassuring, to their respective host governments. This troubleshooting initiative may have been the most important contribution to averting a serious miscalculation. It was followed by a high-profile visit to the region by the then U.S. deputy national security adviser, Robert Gates, bearing a stern message about the importance of de-escalating and offering U.S. help in working out confidence-building measures. India and Pakistan rejected the U.S. facilitating role, but proceeded to negotiate a package of de-escalatory measures bilaterally.

The second crisis management effort took place during the Kargil operation, described in chapter 3. This time, President Bill Clinton's active telephone diplomacy with Indian Prime Minister Vajpayee persuaded the latter that the United States was sympathetic to India's security requirements, and Clinton's dramatic July 4 meeting with Pakistani Prime Minister Sharif led Pakistan to withdraw its forces from Kargil.

During the third crisis, the ten-month mobilization of Indian and Pakistani troops along the boundary that followed the terrorist attack on the Indian Parliament in December 2001, the Indians and Pakistanis were arguably more concerned about a broader war than in the preceding two crises, though it seems clear that neither side wanted war. In this case, U.S. diplomatic intervention came relatively slowly, about five months after the initial precipitating incident and a few weeks after a second attack on an Indian army facility in Jammu that killed a group of Indian military dependents. U.S. Secretary of State Colin Powell and his deputy, Richard Armitage, were persuaded that war was preventable and decided to take action. Armitage went to Pakistan in late May 2002 and extracted from President Musharraf a pledge to do his best to prevent future infiltration from Pakistan-controlled territory into Indian-controlled territory. He then went on to India, relayed Musharraf's undertaking—and then made it public. Musharraf had agreed that his pledge should be relayed to the Indian government but was apparently taken by surprise at the public confirmation. As Armitage intended, this had the effect of making it harder for Musharraf to back away from the undertaking. U.S. efforts were coordinated with those of Britain; wags commented that these two countries conspired to have an unending parade of VIPs visit New Delhi and Islamabad over the summer, making a sudden move to war potentially embarrassing. In October, the Indian government ended its mobilization. It had accomplished its purpose; infiltration had decreased during the summer. In those circumstances, the drain on the army's manpower and resources was too costly to continue the mobilization.

In all three cases, the U.S. government saw a greater risk of war than its Indian or Pakistani counterparts, and the United States took the initiative to get involved. Significantly, the United States dealt separately with each country: it did not facilitate meetings between the two. In the 2002 crisis, both the United States and India made use of dramatic gestures to try to increase pressure on the other participants. India's statements about "imminent war" were, according to longtime security analyst P. R. Chari, intended in part to goad the United States into pushing Pakistan harder. The U.S. decision to evacuate dependents and nonessential staff from its embassy and consulates in India was designed in part to get India's attention. In all three cases, participants had a good idea what the end of the crisis would require; the U.S. role made it a bit easier to find the path there.[5]

India's willingness to accept the U.S. role reflected the change in U.S.-India relations after the Cold War. It was made easier by the fact that no three-way meetings were involved. In the absence of an acute crisis, it is hard to imagine that India would have accepted U.S. involvement.

Summit Meetings

Direct meetings between the two prime ministers have typically taken place on the margins of sessions of international forums such as the annual summit meetings of the United States General Assembly and the

South Asian Association for Regional Cooperation (SAARC). These encounters often receive considerable public attention; their accomplishments are usually less than commentators looking for progress had hoped for.

More rarely, the leaders of the two countries hold formal summit meetings not linked to a broader gathering. Some of these summits have been truly historic, such as those at Tashkent in 1966 and Simla in 1972 that ended India-Pakistan wars. Prime Minister Vajpayee's dramatic trip to Lahore to meet with Nawaz Sharif—which he made using a newly established bus service between India and Pakistan—led to a decision to resume the bilateral composite dialogue and, as noted, provided an occasion for Vajpayee, the leader of a Hindu nationalist party, to make clear to the Pakistani public that India accepted the separation of the two countries. Like most exercises in "cricket diplomacy," many other formal summits have accomplished little other than to establish a better atmosphere for serious bilateral exchanges later. Some have even set back bilateral relations.

Day-to-day Indian-Pakistani diplomatic relations are handled by the two countries' high commissions in Islamabad and New Delhi. India assigns some of its top Foreign Service officers to Pakistan, and relations at the New Delhi end are always dealt with by the foreign secretary. By most accounts, assignments to Pakistan can be very difficult, and many Indian diplomats seem to come away with a more unfavorable feeling toward the host government and people than they had before they were sent there. (The same phenomenon is common among Pakistanis assigned to New Delhi.)

Despite intrusive surveillance and other handicaps they face, Indian diplomats posted to Pakistan are well informed about developments there. They are aided in their missions by intelligence officers operating under diplomatic cover. (These officers are from time to time declared persona non grata; New Delhi reciprocates if it hasn't itself begun the process.) The Indian Foreign Service does not nurture Pakistan specialists. It almost certainly reckons that its officers are already familiar enough with the country's policies and ways.

Water—and Creating Shared Assets

Arguably the most successful India-Pakistan agreement ever was the Indus Waters Treaty, signed in 1960. As discussed in chapter 2, the negotiations were brokered by the World Bank. The success of the agreement derived in part from the fact that it divided the six rivers of the

Indus system so that India had exclusive rights to three and Pakistan had rights to the remaining three. Much of the negotiating dealt with the rules for the use of waters from Pakistan's rivers that flowed through Indian-controlled territory before reaching Pakistan. The treaty established a binational Indus Water Commission that was to meet at regular intervals, but did not require the disputants to work together in the day-to-day management of the rivers. Despite periodic disputes that have led the parties to take action under the treaty's dispute settlement mechanisms, the treaty's basic provisions have held for over half a century. This has led observers to wonder if creating a genuinely shared economic asset—in this case, the substantial water supply and power potential of a great river—is a way to create the cooperation that has been so hard to sustain. So far, however, the Indus Waters Treaty remains the only example of this kind of success. Some commentators worry that with increasing water shortages in both Pakistan and India the long-standing treaty could itself be in some jeopardy.

Countering Pakistan's Quest for International Support

A continuing theme in India's policy toward Pakistan has been its effort to isolate Pakistan and keep it from finding a powerful foreign partner to compensate for its inherent comparative weakness. This policy led New Delhi to react angrily to Pakistan's linkup with the United States in the 1950s and 1980s, when Washington designated Pakistan a frontline state in the struggle against communist imperialism. As noted in chapter 3, the Indians adopted a more relaxed position in the 2000s after the 9/11 attacks led Washington to turn again to Pakistan, this time to help it in Afghanistan in the U.S. Global War on Terrorism.

India's complaints about U.S. policy toward Pakistan have reflected both its concern that the United States will back Pakistan in international forums, as it did for many years in UN consideration of the Kashmiri dispute, and its fear that Pakistan will use American-supplied arms to balance the larger Indian forces. India welcomes evidence that the United States is not equating it with Pakistan and has at times tried to persuade Washington to pursue policies or adopt symbolic measures that demonstrate higher American regard for India than for Pakistan. With the strengthening of U.S.-India relations since 2000 and India's growing self-confidence as a rising global power, New Delhi appears to have concluded that such efforts are no longer called for.

India has similar concerns about the "enduring entente" between Pakistan and China, though it recognizes more clearly than it has in its dealings with the United States that it can do little about Beijing's policies. For many years India tried to counter Islamic Pakistan's natural advantage in dealing with Muslim countries in the Near East. More recently India has come to worry about the possibility that Moscow will supply arms to Pakistan and perhaps support it diplomatically. This interest in avoiding the presence of an outside equalizer in its relations with Pakistan can also be seen in New Delhi's traditional preference for strictly bilateral equations in relations with its other South Asian neighbors, all of them weaker and less challenging to India's drive for security and regional preeminence than is Pakistan. (As we note in chapter 12, the government led by Narendra Modi has taken a kindlier view of multilateral cooperation with India's smaller neighbors, especially on economic issues.)

India and Pakistan's Internal Politics

India prefers civilian regimes in Pakistan to military ones. The Indians are well aware of the Pakistan army's animus toward them and its conviction that India poses an existential threat to their country. Of the four wars India has fought against Pakistan, all but one were triggered by the Pakistan military. Despite this record, India has not tried to meddle in Pakistan's national politics to promote civilian leadership. But it does encourage separatist and other dissident movements in the smaller Pakistan provinces to make life difficult for the Punjab-dominated army and government. Pakistan has done the same in Kashmir and in Indian Punjab, where in the 1980s it supported an armed rebellion calling for a separate Sikh state.

The Multilateral Connection

India and Pakistan occasionally make common cause in multilateral institutions where they share common interests. This is particularly true in trade negotiations. Both countries are members of some of the same negotiating coalitions. They both are strong defenders of "special and differential" treatment of developing countries.

Some of the approaches India takes in multilateral forums have provided Pakistan an opportunity to piggyback on these positions for its own purposes. Arms control and nonproliferation negotiations are an example. Pakistan has used India as an excuse to avoid pressure on such issues as joining the Non-Proliferation Treaty (NPT), arguing that it will join as soon as India does. It took a similar position on the Comprehensive Test Ban Treaty (CTBT). The same logic sometimes works in reverse. Pakistan has refused to support the Fissile Material Cutoff Treaty (FMCT) in the UN Conference on Disarmament, largely because of its concern that the proposed terms of reference will grandfather in India's larger stockpile of materials. This action has deprived the text of the consensus needed to move forward to actual treaty negotiations. India is in no hurry to move ahead; Pakistan's blocking move is convenient.[6]

As we saw in chapter 10, Pakistan has also opposed Indian efforts to become a permanent member of the UN Security Council and other moves by New Delhi to gain greater status in world bodies. The two countries routinely vote against one another's bids for two-year seats on the council and other sought-after positions in the UN structure.

India, for its part, has vehemently opposed Pakistan's call for renewed United Nations interest in helping to settle the Kashmir dispute. It can be reasonably sure that India's efforts will succeed. It can also be certain that Pakistan will continue to demand that the issue be resolved in accordance with the resolutions passed by the UN in 1949 and 1950, and that these Pakistani pleas will go nowhere.

The Underlying Imbalance

In the years following partition, India's advantage of size was to some extent mitigated by Pakistan's strong outside backers and relatively good economic performance. Since about 1990, India's economy has surged while Pakistan's has lagged, and Pakistan's international relationships have become more complicated. India will undoubtedly see this as an advantage to be cultivated. It may not affect India's negotiating tactics immediately, but it is likely to affect the dynamics of Pakistan's relations with China, one of its principal international friends, and will change the environment in which India-Pakistan negotiations take place.

CHINA

In dealing with Pakistan, India is the more powerful party. Pakistan is unwilling to acknowledge India's greater weight, but India holds the territory Pakistan wants and its army and economy are several times the size of Pakistan's. With China, the asymmetry is reversed. The Indian political leadership, and especially the defense establishment, regard China as their country's primary strategic challenge and are still affected by India's defeat in the 1962 border war. China's long-standing relationship with Pakistan, and especially its role in the development of Pakistan's nuclear arsenal, accentuates this sense of threat.

The border issue has been a constant in India-China relations from the start, and we will look at India's approach to negotiating with China through this issue. Efforts to settle the border have been going on, slowly and irregularly, since 1950, and their failure was the principal cause of the 1962 war. These negotiations pit two "civilizational powers" against each other. While the precise impact of culture on negotiation and communication is often unclear, both countries take pride in their standing as the embodiment of a great civilization. The dynamics of this still-incomplete process reflect the power disparity between the two countries, a strategic rivalry that is more important for India than for China, nationalist political opinion in both countries, and especially in the early years, India's difficulty in dealing with China's tactics, which rely heavily on long-term patience and ambiguous communications to create a record of China's position.

The View from Delhi and Beijing

Indians are acutely aware that China's economic rise started a decade and a half before India's, and has moved faster. Militarily, China's size, ambition, and nuclear arsenal make it India's most serious long-term security challenge. Indian rulers from ancient times to the present have considered the mountains to their north to be their prime security barrier, so geography makes a threat from China particularly sensitive. China's long-standing strategic connection with Pakistan accentuates this danger. Chinese military modernization has surged ahead in recent years. In the international arena, China has the status India believes it should have: permanent member of the UN Security Council, possessor of nuclear weapons legitimized by the NPT, and widely acknowledged member of the small group of nations that runs the world.

From India's perspective, the present economic relationship and India-China multilateral cooperation are the most beneficial areas of India-China ties. Bilateral trade grew from an annual $2.5 billion in the three-year 1999–2002 period to $67.4 billion in 2010–12, twenty-seven times the earlier figure. China became India's largest trading partner in goods in 2008. India's imports from China, however, are almost three times as great as its exports there. Whereas China exports manufactured goods, India's exports are heavily concentrated in raw materials.[7] Their global competition for energy and, closer to home, water resources may become more significant in the future. On the other hand, India was quick to join the new Chinese-sponsored Asian Infrastructure Investment Bank, hoping for funding for its massive infrastructure needs. In other words, looked at through the prism of the three principal drivers of Indian foreign policy, China represents a challenge to India's regional primacy; it fits into India's nonaligned framework and desire to encourage a multipolar arrangement of geopolitics; and it represents an economic opportunity, although China is currently well ahead of India in economic power.

Seen from Beijing, the picture looks quite different. India is not a serious threat, and their rivalry, self-evident in India, is barely acknowledged in China. China's relations with Pakistan are intended to keep India off balance, and some degree of India-Pakistan hostility is strategically useful to China. Chinese observers profess to accept increasing Indian engagement in East Asia and downplay Indian concerns about the growing Chinese presence in the Indian Ocean. However, the natural order of things, in the Chinese view, is that India would have important (but not exclusive) influence in South Asia, leaving China preeminent in East and Southeast Asia.

India's recent economic growth and larger international profile has apparently led to greater seriousness in China's engagement with India and an upgrading of the bureaucratic status of the Chinese embassy in New Delhi. Nonetheless, India-watchers in China believe India is a long way from being able to fulfill its ambitions, which they uniformly characterize as "unrealistic." The tone of condescension is hard to miss. Chinese analysts and officials particularly dislike India's practice of comparing itself to China. In the Chinese view, their disparity, still growing, needs to be reflected in the results of negotiations, which explains China's unwillingness to offer India terms that might have been acceptable a few decades ago.

The Border in the Early Years: Negotiations and War

The background of the India-China border dispute, going back before India's independence or the existence of the People's Republic of China, is described in chapter 2. The nature of the disagreement in the eastern sector, the only one that included important settled areas and the one where Nehru seemed most confident of India's position, was different from the center and west. However, China had not accepted any of the border lines claimed by India. Efforts to resolve the location of the border and to manage the two countries' relationship across it have gone on intermittently during the intervening nearly seven decades.

The first phase of this effort ended with the India-China border war in 1962, following twelve years of slow-motion communicating and signaling between the two governments. Most of this effort took place against the background of Nehru's desire for good relations with the newly created People's Republic, and his dream that the two Asian giants could work together to bring about a world order with greater justice and a stronger voice for poor countries. Nehru directed the effort personally for India and dealt extensively with Zhou Enlai.

For the most part, China set the tactics and Nehru reacted. China relied heavily on signaling with nonverbal gestures and communicating with cryptic and ambiguous messages, rather than explicitly negotiating. China's 1950 invasion of Tibet had brought Indian public attention to the border problem. In November 1950, Nehru asserted in parliament that the India-China boundary in the east was the McMahon Line, negotiated by India's colonial authorities in a conference including China and Tibet, but never accepted by the People's Republic. But despite several meetings between India's ambassador in Beijing and Zhou Enlai, India did not raise the issue with China. And even after India in 1951 took control of Tawang, an area close to the McMahon Line with particular significance for Tibetan Buddhists, the Chinese did not raise the border issue. India's ambassador in Beijing, K. M. Panikkar, advised his government that India should interpret Zhou's silence as acquiescence, a recommendation that made Nehru uneasy with good reason. Ambiguity and the pattern of waiting for the other side to speak first were familiar techniques in China's dealings with its other negotiating partners, as described in Richard Solomon's classic study on Chinese negotiating behavior.[8] The subsequent history of the border dispute featured recurring missed communications of this sort, where China either remained silent or dropped hints so subtle as to be easily missed, obscuring a conflicting position that would become critically important later on.[9]

Starting in 1953, the issue came out from under its veil with India's publication of an official map showing the boundary it claimed. The following year, Zhou visited India—again, neither side brought up the border—and India signed an agreement relinquishing its rights in Tibet. India and China agreed to base their relationship on the Five Principles of Peaceful Coexistence, the *Panchsheel*. Following a dispute over a grazing ground in the middle sector of the border, Nehru brought up the border issue in a meeting with Zhou later in 1954, noting the boundary alignment in China's maps. Zhou downplayed the significance of the maps, saying they were "old" and did not reflect consultations with the neighbors. Nehru, referring to India's claims and maps, noted that "our frontiers are clear."[10] Zhou's ambiguous response deflected the issue again. China was in control of the negotiating environment, as it generally tries to be.[11]

In 1957, on a visit to Delhi, Zhou mentioned the McMahon Line. The conversation was about the section of the line that formed the China-Burma boundary, but Nehru took it as Chinese acceptance of the line as a whole.[12]

The border dispute now began to create facts on the ground, as China's construction of a road through Indian-claimed territory in Aksai Chin, in the western border area, became widely known. India had already begun strengthening its presence in the areas it claimed, especially in the east; the pace now picked up. Nehru was inclined to supplement this signaling on the ground by raising the issue of the road with the Chinese, along with other border disagreements, but because the road was not in the most clearly defined part of the border, he did not protest. India did protest later that year, however, when the Chinese government published a map showing large parts of the central and eastern border areas within the "approximate boundaries" of China.

The Chinese response to this protest and to a later one stated that China would decide a "new way" of drawing the boundary after surveys and consultations with neighbors. This led to an exchange of correspondence in which Nehru argued, apparently based on Zhou's comment in 1957, that Zhou had made it clear that China was prepared to accept the McMahon Line. Nehru challenged the Chinese maps appearing to claim large parts of territory that he considered unquestionably Indian. In reply, Zhou said that the entire boundary was not formally delimited, argued that China had not raised the issue previously because "conditions were not yet ripe," and challenged the Indian maps. After nearly a decade in which both sides were positioning themselves without actually discussing the problem, the issue was now joined.[13]

With the 1959 uprising in Tibet and the Dalai Lama's flight to India, India-China relations plummeted. China reached for some of the tougher weapons in its negotiating arsenal, publicly accusing Nehru of an "imperialist" Indian policy. China's now strong assertion of border claims that Nehru had downplayed left Nehru feeling betrayed. Moreover, he now faced an unprecedented uproar in parliament that was to grow over the next three years, with pointed and emotional questions, which he handled personally during the parliament's Question Hour.[14]

Against this backdrop, and in the wake of serious clashes along the border, India and China made some moves to explore tamping down the crisis and eventually resolving the issue. It was more than a decade since India had first focused on the border issue. The process started with the April 1960 Nehru-Zhou summit—not "negotiations," Nehru insisted, and certainly not accepting the Chinese assertion that the entire border needed to be delimited, but "discussions." India was aware that Zhou was interested in proposing a swap, with China keeping its claims in the west and India in the east. However, an Indian Supreme Court decision over an unrelated border issue between India and East Pakistan had held that the Government of India could not give away any Indian territory without a constitutional amendment authorizing it, making that idea much harder to implement. India floated an alternative, whereby India would retain sovereignty of the land it claimed in the east and China would retain full use of its claim in the west.[15] Some observers recalled an acrimonious discussion, with both sides apparently convinced that the other was misleading them. No agreement was reached. The effort to identify a common statement of principles—characteristic of Chinese negotiations for long-running or complex issues—also failed. Nehru, on the advice of Jagat Mehta, then a young diplomat, refused to accept the word "dispute" in the six points proposed by Zhou. In the end, the two leaders, unable to reach agreement, decided to assign Indian and Chinese teams to study the historical record of the two countries' claims. The teams worked diligently and produced a report in six months that left each side convinced of the rightness of its own cause.[16]

Some observers believe that this was the most promising opportunity to resolve the border problem. Zhou, apparently seeking to salvage something out of his efforts, issued a press statement that was conciliatory in tone and emphasized both sides' determination to maintain the status quo peacefully and refrain from patrolling near the border.[17] Despite the statement's words about pursuing a border settlement by peaceful means, its failure was followed, tragically, by the 1962 war, which upended India-China relations and left the border still undecided.

From the perspective of India's negotiating style and global role, this twelve-year process shows India initially quite uncertain about how to handle a dispute with a country with which it did not have the power to compel a solution. Srinath Raghavan argues that even in this early phase, Nehru was conscious of a power disparity between China and India.[18] Indian tactics relied on signaling through the movement of administrative and military personnel, wordsmithing ("discussions" instead of "negotiations," no reference to a "dispute"), and for a number of years, not explicitly raising difficult issues (like the border). India was blindsided by China's tactics and its use of silence and strategic patience. Nehru's political difficulties after 1959 hemmed him in. Nationalist sentiment in China also played a part. The slow-motion character of this encounter undoubtedly was influenced by the fact that by the time the issue was joined, neither side was in a hurry to settle.

After 1962, Enlarging the Context

For a decade and a half after the war, the border rarely figured in discussions between India and China. By that time, China had settled many of its other border issues. The China-Burma settlement in 1960 essentially followed the line in force during the colonial era. The 1961 agreement with Nepal followed the watershed principle and the traditional border except where the two governments disagreed about where that lay. In welcoming the Nepal agreement, India said it would like to resolve its dispute with China by following the same principles.[19] The 1963 settlement with Pakistan, in which China gained territory that India claimed in the old princely state of Jammu and Kashmir, added a new complication to the India-China face-off.[20]

India and China restored diplomatic relations in 1976. A visit by then foreign minister Atal Bihari Vajpayee three years later was best remembered for Vajpayee's decision to cut short his time in Beijing when China invaded Vietnam. But before the visit aborted, Vajpayee was able to convey to his hosts that he wanted India and China to resume serious discussions, and the Chinese side quoted from the 1960 Zhou statement. Talks took place, in a familiar slow-motion process, until they were interrupted by a serious confrontation near the Line of Actual Control in 1986.

The real relaunch of discussions came later, when Prime Minister Rajiv Gandhi visited Beijing in 1988. By this time, however, the border discussions had changed character and were placed in the context of the broader relationship. The two sides were still seeking a border settlement. Later newspaper accounts, quoting retired Chinese participants during Rajiv Gandhi's visit, state that Gandhi had turned down a version of the swap that was apparently discussed in 1960. But as a practical matter, both countries' priority was now to keep the border quiet. The formal joint statement following the visit made this clear through its pledge of working "through peaceful and friendly consultations." In addition, the two sides pledged to develop the rest of the relationship, an understanding generally interpreted as insulating the border from other issues. Finally, they established a joint working group to talk about the border. While this was not the first time the issue had been handed to a working-level group, it was a decisive move away from the overwhelmingly summit-level process that had been in force before the war.[21]

This pattern has continued for the intervening two and a half decades, and the emphasis on managing the border has become stronger. The two governments have created more elaborate structures for addressing the border and reached agreements on how a border settlement should be negotiated. The process for examining the border became better defined and more broadly based, especially with the creation of a working group responsible for keeping the boundary peaceful that yielded an agreement on confidence-building measures. The Agreement on the Maintenance of Peace and Tranquility along the Line of Actual Control in the India-China Border, signed in 1993, was the instrument for keeping the peace along the line to which Chinese forces had withdrawn following the 1962 war. The agreement amplified statements from earlier agreements with more detailed undertakings. For example, both sides pledged not to step over the line and agreed on a procedure to follow, including joint verification of the line, in case this was breached. They undertook to keep both sides' military forces to a minimum and to determine their distance from the line through mutual consultations.[22] A 1996 agreement spelled out in some detail confidence-building measures intended to reduce the risk of unintended incidents, which included pledges to limit specific kinds of heavy military equipment, to exchange data on the forces and armaments to be reduced, to avoid military exercises involving more than one division or at least to conduct them parallel to the border rather than moving toward it, to avoid air intrusions through similar restrictions, and importantly, to conduct flag meetings on a regular basis.[23]

By 2003, little progress had occurred toward a settlement, and the two sides decided to create a new format that would ensure more high-level attention. During a visit by Indian Prime Minister Vajpayee to Beijing, China and India signed a Declaration on Principles for Relations and Comprehensive Cooperation. This long document included the pledges of peace and tranquility that had become standard fare in India-China declarations of this sort. It also established working groups on economic, financial, and cultural issues. Both countries undertook to appoint special representatives "to explore, from the political perspective of the overall bilateral relationship, the framework of a boundary settlement." These envoys, the National Security Adviser for India and a State Councilor for China, became the central high-level personalities in the formal China-India dialogue, not just on the border but more broadly.

In the next twelve years, the envoys met for eighteen rounds of talks. In 2005, they agreed on a statement of principles. It was the first successful framework statement of that sort, though many of the ideas in it had figured in earlier joint declarations. Significantly, it made explicit the idea that had been implicit since Rajiv Gandhi's visit to Beijing that "the differences on the boundary question should not be allowed to affect the overall development of bilateral relations."[24] With this framework agreement in hand, the envoys were supposed to proceed to the second and third phases of the planned border talks: developing a framework and implementing it. Ten years later, they continued to work on the framework.

By 2005, the India-China relationship was already undergoing major change. China's economic surge was twenty-five years old; India's had been under way for fifteen years. Trade, which had been a trickle, was expanding to the point where China was soon to be India's largest partner for goods trade. Both countries now approached the border talks with greater confidence, which paradoxically would make a border settlement more difficult to achieve. China thought it should be able to get more than it had been willing to settle for in the past. As one longtime Indian participant put it, "as long as both sides feel the political future belongs to them," neither country's political leaders saw any reason to back away from claims they had maintained for six decades.[25]

The talks continued to produce a greater measure of understanding and a fairly impressive array of agreements opening up new areas of cooperation and establishing a process for dealing with the border. In 2013, when Prime Minister Manmohan Singh visited Beijing, India and China signed a Border Defense Cooperation Agreement that expanded on the confidence-building accord reached earlier. They also signed an agreement on border rivers, a potential harbinger of issues to come. Other agreements dealt with the broader relationship. The first meeting of the special envoys after Modi became prime minister was expected to focus on defining the Line of Actual Control, in a further effort to prevent conflict in border zones.[26]

Not surprisingly, these agreements were not the whole negotiating process, and arguably not even the most important part of it. During the period from 1988 to 2015, China's practice of negotiating with signals and facts on the ground continued. Incidents continued to occur from time to time on the border. A particularly serious one took place in April 2013, six months before Manmohan Singh visited Beijing, when Chinese troops entered Daulat Beg Oldi, a strategic location near the Line of Actual Control in the western sector. Senior levels in both governments negotiated the Chinese withdrawal under terms that were not publicly discussed but were reported to include India's destruction of its own bunkers in another border area. Another incident occurred just at the time of Chinese President Xi Jinping's visit to India in September 2014. When asked how to interpret this border incident and others, one veteran of the process said, "You can't know without testing." As he noted, that takes time.[27]

Other challenges to the border issue did not involve armed confrontation. China issued periodic reminders of its claim to the Indian state of Arunachal Pradesh, often again on the eve of high-level visits from China to India. It protested every time an Indian prime minister visited there. China also challenged an Asian Development Bank project in that state. Residents of Arunachal Pradesh planning to visit China on Indian government business were refused regular Chinese visas in their official passports and received "stapled visas" on a separate paper. These things took place side by side with other manifestations of Chinese disagreements beyond the border area. One example was the 2012 warning issued by the Chinese navy to an Indian ship drilling for oil under a concession from Vietnam in the South China Sea, important parts of which are disputed by several riparian countries.[28] Talks on the border and the comprehensive relationship were also influenced by the ups and downs in China's policy toward Kashmir, which went from strongly pro-Pakistan to relatively neutral and back to a more pro-Pakistan stance, and by the growing indications of Chinese help for Pakistan's nuclear weapons program.

India had come to expect these tactics and had developed a nonverbal "vocabulary" for responding. The process was not foolproof, and not all the Chinese actions lent themselves to mirror-image reciprocity. The problem of "stapled visas," for example, was eventually resolved quietly. Incidents along the Line of Actual Control were darkly viewed by the strategic community, but diplomatic and political observers were more inclined to see them as predictable efforts to probe for Indian weakness. In spite of incidents that violated the letter of several agreements, Indian diplomatic observers considered that the effort to manage the border was basically a success.

The Indians too pushed the envelope. One interesting example, which attracted remarkably little public commentary, was India's decision to open up an office in Taiwan in 1995. The Indian government quietly informed China and selectively advised them about some of the details. In the words of one retired senior official, "We had a good idea what they wanted to know and what they didn't want to know." India-Taiwan trade increased, airline links were established, and a tax treaty was concluded. At least one prominent member of parliament, future prime minister I. K. Gujral, visited Taiwan. Beijing said little. This could of course suddenly become an issue, after a long period of Chinese silence.

THE MODI GOVERNMENT: NEW DEPARTURES TOWARD PAKISTAN AND CHINA

Narendra Modi came into office as Indian prime minister as an avowed hawk. He spent his political career espousing a tough policy toward Pakistan. He spoke of China as a security threat, but also as an economic example. In his first year in office, Modi's policy has been more complex than this description would suggest. His priorities have been relations in the neighborhood and ties with the major powers, with a particular focus on Asia. There is not yet a long Modi negotiating record, but one can discern both continuity and change in his initial contacts with the two countries that represent a strategic challenge for India. As we have seen, his first moves toward both were welcoming ones, inviting Pakistan Prime Minister Nawaz Sharif, along with the leaders of the rest of India's neighbors, to his gala inauguration and receiving the Chinese foreign minister three weeks later. Their paths then diverged.

With respect to Pakistan, the fist shows through the velvet glove. When Modi came to office, there were high hopes that India and Pakistan would implement a proposed opening of bilateral trade that had been prepared by the previous Indian government. The focus on economics seemed right in Modi's "sweet spot" and that of his Pakistani counterpart, Nawaz Sharif. The Pakistan army was believed to have second thoughts about the deal, and a series of lethal incidents on the contested Line of Control in Kashmir soured the atmosphere.

Then Modi's government abruptly canceled the scheduled talks between Indian and Pakistani foreign secretaries in August 2014. The reason given was a meeting between the Pakistan high commissioner in Delhi and a group of Kashmiri separatists. Similar meetings had regularly taken place before high-level, government-to-government encounters; previous Indian governments took them as unfortunate but routine. Against this background, India's cancellation of the talks was widely interpreted by both Indians and Pakistanis as Indian insistence on setting the terms of any government-to-government dialogue. The new foreign secretary, visiting Islamabad some months later, delivered the Modi government's message about the good things that might result from a cooperative Pakistani stance, showcasing its economic generosity to the rest of the region. But it came with a stern insistence on Pakistan cutting off support for militant groups operating across the line. Modi's December 2015 stopover in Pakistan moved away from hardball diplomacy. But it again underscored India's assertion of its prerogative, as the region's great power, to set the South Asian diplomatic agenda.

CHINA FITS INTO all three of Modi's priority categories. Modi is determined to bring to India the sort of investment and economic growth that China has mobilized. Modi's initial approach to China featured the same kind of economic appeal he was making to the other major global powers, looking for expanded trade ties and massive investment. Modi had visited China several times as chief minister of Gujarat. Once he became prime minister, he reached out early: Xi Jinping visited Delhi in September 2014, shortly before Modi's visit to Washington. The Chinese leader received extraordinary hospitality, including an invitation to a birthday celebration for Modi in Gujarat.

Modi's return visit to China in May 2015 showed his approach at its confident best, the leader of one of Asia's giants visiting the other giant and laying the groundwork for an Asian Century. Some of the message was familiar, notably the pledge to settle the border on a mutually agreeable basis and prevent it from damaging the rest of the relationship. More surprising was Modi's candor about some of the issues India faces with China, asking that China rethink its claim to Arunachal Pradesh.

The joint statement's economic message skipped the often ritualistic numeric goals for trade expansion, but included references to the two countries' business enterprises doing more together. The twenty-four new agreements included a large number designed to strengthen cultural and people-to-people ties, including an undertaking to grant electronic tourist visas to Chinese citizens.[29]

But the Modi government had also delivered some unmistakable cautionary messages to China. Present at the gala inauguration were the representatives of the Dalai Lama, described as guests of Modi's Bharatiya Janata Party (BJP). A visit to Hanoi in October 2014 was the occasion for Modi to publicly confirm India's willingness to sell arms to Vietnam—not a new policy, but receiving higher profile publicity than such deals had previously earned.[30] Importantly, Modi had the initiative. These gestures were backed up at the policy level by Modi's moves to deepen relations with the United States, Japan, and Australia, countries that China would look on as potential counterweights to its influence in East and Southeast Asia. When President Obama visited New Delhi in January 2015, for example, he and Modi released a "Joint Strategic Vision" for the Indian Ocean and Asia-Pacific. It was drafted in an inclusive way, but provisions like the commitment to settle maritime disputes peacefully placed India close to the United States on the Asian security interests of greatest concern to both.[31]

Both with Pakistan and with China, the boldness of the Modi government's first moves was not surprising, coming from an insurgent politician who had just won a tremendous election majority. The factors that have driven Indian policy and tactics, strengthening India's primacy in the neighborhood and a commitment to strategic autonomy, are still at the heart of Modi's policy. But the style does represent a change from the more measured and careful approach that generations of Indian leaders have adopted. Negotiations with India's smaller neighbors, described in chapter 12, show a similar shift.

CHAPTER TWELVE

Negotiating with Smaller South Asian Neighbors

INDIA'S STYLE IN DEALING with its South Asian neighbors other than Pakistan has ranged over time between the high-handed approach practiced by Indira Gandhi and the more conciliatory policies promoted by I. K. Gujral. Narendra Modi has added an important economic focus in his approach to these countries. But India's basic goals have remained constant: the neighboring governments accepting Indian regional preeminence—which they often resentfully regard as a demand for hegemony—and limiting relationships with major outside powers that in India's view could detract from its own primacy.

India's policies have been unapologetically realist, and its negotiating style has often had a tough edge. India has generally welcomed its neighbors' adopting democratic practices and observing human rights along Indian lines, but it does not seek to export these values to them. It has at times bluntly played favorites among political rivals inside these nations, as it did in the 2014 Bangladesh parliamentary elections when it openly supported Sheikh Hasina's Awami League. But India has lived for extended periods with autocratic regimes that it viewed with serious misgivings or outright disfavor, and has sometimes reached important agreements with such governments.

Yet while India's longtime objectives of regional preeminence and the security of its borders have not changed, New Delhi has come to recognize that the earlier policy of seeking to prevent any meaningful political or security relationship between its neighbors and major outside powers needs to be replaced by one in which it wins an active competition for influence with these outsiders, most importantly China.

BANGLADESH

India may have expected to reap long-term gratitude from Bangladeshis for its military intervention in their struggle for liberation from Pakistan in 1971. What it got instead was a classic big neighbor/small neighbor relationship. Bangladesh recognizes that its ties with India are crucial for its political and economic well-being, but it is uncomfortable with its inferior position in the bilateral power balance and tends to blame Indian overreach when things go wrong. The major negotiations between India and Bangladesh showcase both India's long-standing insistence on strict bilateralism in its discussions of water and transit issues and the way this policy began to shift after 2010 toward a willingness on New Delhi's part to bring other regional countries into these discussions.

Domestic politics and political parties are never far from the surface in India-Bangladesh negotiations. In four and a half decades of Bangladeshi independence, successive Indian governments have been more willing to accommodate Dhaka when the Awami League—the party that brought Bangladesh to independence with Indian help—was in power there.[1] The relationship has been particularly warm when the Indian National Congress was in charge in New Delhi. More recently the Bharatiya Janata Party (BJP) government led by Modi has also given sympathetic attention to Bangladesh, which Dhaka has reciprocated. In the past decade, the relationship has been complicated by politics in the Indian state of West Bengal and to a lesser degree in states in India's northeast. These state politics have had a powerful impact on the way the central government has dealt with Bangladesh.

Bangladeshis who have negotiated with India report that in most circumstances they find elected Indian political leaders easier to deal with than the Indian bureaucracy, which they regard as rigid, unsympathetic, and condescending. One retired senior Bangladeshi diplomat observed that Indian bureaucrats are very hard on Bangladesh: "They just say no." Another former official with deep experience in Bangladesh-India negotiations put it more pungently: "You need a backbone of titanium, nerves of steel, and the skin of a hippo." Occasionally, dealing with Bengali officials from India has smoothed over the rough spots, thanks to the cultural and linguistic bonds between Bengalis on both sides of the border.

More often, Bangladeshi observers comment, where problems have been resolved it is because a politician has weighed in.[2] But India's political leaders can also be very tough when they find it necessary. During some river water negotiations the Indians have gone as far as to withhold from Bangladesh vital water flows that they had earlier agreed to provide.

The themes that most clearly stand out in Indian negotiations with the Bangladeshis are the problem of linking different issues on the bilateral agenda, the role of political parties based exclusively in West Bengal and other Indian states that border Bangladesh, and as already noted, the political affiliation of the leadership in both countries. Until recently, another constant was India's insistence on a strictly bilateral approach, with no third-party involvement.

These themes are illustrated by negotiations between the two countries on three important issues: their dispute over the waters of the Ganges River system and other rivers that flow across India into Bangladesh; the problems posed by the anomalous way their common border was drawn; and Indian interest in the development and use of transit routes across Bangladesh territory linking its "mainland" with its isolated and underdeveloped northeast.

River Waters

Predating Bangladeshi independence, the Ganges waters dispute was sparked by India's unilateral decision in the early 1950s to build a massive barrage at Farakka, designed to divert for its own uses a substantial part of the river's flow before it crossed over into what was then East Pakistan.[3] Until about 2010, India insisted that the two riparian states work out the division of waters without international involvement.

India's status as upper riparian, its control of the barrage, and its superior national power gave it a strong bargaining position. When independent Bangladesh brought the Farakka issue before the United Nations General Assembly, India successfully opposed the move. Bangladesh eventually recognized that its efforts to mobilize world opinion would not succeed and accepted the bilateral approach. An Awami League government signed a treaty with India in 1996 resolving this part of the water dispute. Predictably, the Bangladeshi opposition blasted the government for giving away too much for too little in return.[4]

Since then, the Bangladesh government has had to face the unpleasant fact that its only chance to win a more sympathetic Indian bargaining position is to link the river waters issue to the settlement of another dispute where it holds better cards. In recent years this strategy has focused on Indian interest in obtaining transit rights across its territory.

The most recent water negotiations started during the preparations for the 2010 visit to New Delhi of Bangladesh Prime Minister Sheikh Hasina, leader of the Awami League. Indian Prime Minister Manmohan Singh was interested in resolving some of the long-standing problems with Bangladesh. In preparing for this meeting, the Bangladeshis suggested that the two countries tackle the two biggest remaining water disputes not as "division of water" problems but as "common river basin management" problems. It took intervention by the Indian prime minister's office to persuade the relevant Indian ministries to accept the "management" concept. One reason this issue required high-level intervention was that the logic of this phrase, as both sides understood, would eventually lead to bringing in additional countries on management of certain rivers. The Bangladeshis wanted to start by including Nepal in discussions on the Ganges and Bhutan on the Brahmaputra.[5]

The result was a major change in India's policy of strict bilateralism, introduced gradually and almost by stealth. The joint statement issued at the conclusion of Sheikh Hasina's visit set forth an ambitious agenda for cooperation, with particularly detailed discussion of rivers and a call for a new meeting of the Indo-Bangladesh Joint Rivers Commission.[6] Participants on both sides recall that the concept of "basin management" was accepted at that time. It was put into the public record in the framework agreement for cooperation signed during Manmohan Singh's much-ballyhooed 2011 visit to Dhaka. The breakthrough on including third countries was not explicitly mentioned. It did, however, make its way indirectly into the report of a roundtable on restructuring the Joint Rivers Commission, a group including senior officials from both sides, which referred to a "gradual multilateral approach." By early 2015, Bangladeshi officials and political figures from both the country's major parties had come to regard this change as a promising breakthrough in relations with India.[7]

IN VISITING DHAKA, Singh had bigger ambitions than a cooperation agreement. He wanted to transform India-Bangladesh relations with a package deal that would include agreements on a third river basin, the Teesta River (a Ganges tributary), a transit agreement, and a treaty rationalizing the land border (discussed in the next section). This trio of pacts was designed to celebrate and enhance the good relations that the two countries had developed during the three years Hasina had been in power and to recognize the domestic political risks she had taken in making improved India-Bangladesh relations a major, well-publicized objective of her government. The Indians, for their part, had helped sweeten the deal by extending a US$1 billion line of credit to Bangladesh and affording duty-free access to almost all Bangladeshi products, most importantly textiles.[8] But the three-agreement package ran into difficulties that were related both to India's internal politics and the problems the two countries faced in linking several different issues that had different constituencies. It was left to Singh's successor, Narendra Modi, to try to deal with them.

Land Boundaries

The anomalies along the land boundary between India and Bangladesh date to the 1947 partition, when tiny bits of land were cut off from their national "mainlands" on either side of the newly drawn border. The issue stemmed from the complicated patterns of landholding in eastern India, where areas directly ruled by the British that became part of what was then East Pakistan were entangled among territories held by a princely state that had acceded to India. The problem had apparently not been foreseen by those who had hastily prepared the terms of the partition agreement.

The Indian and Pakistani governments were unable to resolve the problem. But after Bangladesh became independent, Indira Gandhi and Bangladesh leader Sheikh Mujibur Rahman agreed to exchange the cut-off areas: 111 Indian enclaves surrounded by Bangladeshi territory comprising some 17,000 acres were to be transferred to Bangladesh, while 51 Bangladesh holdings surrounded by Indian territory, totaling about 7,000 acres, would go to India.[9] The Bangladesh government ratified the treaty promptly. Dhaka has generally been more interested in settling the issue than New Delhi, and the territorial exchange involved did not raise as many hackles in Bangladesh as in India. Mrs. Gandhi's government had not yet secured parliamentary passage of the constitutional amendment required for such transfers before the assassination of Mujib in 1975 changed the political equation.

The terms of the land boundary agreement were, in a sense, waiting to be dusted off, and during Singh's 2011 visit to Dhaka, he and Sheikh

Hasina signed a protocol reactivating the main provisions of the draft 1974 treaty. As has been the pattern when the Indians sought a compromise settlement, an Awami League government was again in power in Dhaka and Congress was in power in India. However, strong parliamentary opposition in India, led by the BJP and eastern India-based regional parties, stymied this initiative, and the treaty remained unratified when Congress was defeated in the May 2014 election.

Some BJP members in eastern India feared the political repercussions of a seeming "giveaway" of Indian territory, and some were concerned about setting a precedent that could be used to justify a "giveaway" involving Pakistan. Nonetheless, Singh's successor Narendra Modi reversed the position his own party, the BJP, had taken on the proposed land border agreement when it was in opposition—a good illustration of the way opposition parties in India (and elsewhere) can change their negative tune when they take power. He was eventually able to overcome resistance in the Congress Party, which had with equal cynicism moved in the opposite direction. Both houses of the Indian Parliament unanimously passed the necessary legislation and the two countries exchanged the ratification documents during Modi's official visit to Dhaka in June 2015. The transfers began soon afterward.

Transit across Bangladesh

India's interest in using Bangladeshi roads, railways, and waterways to facilitate access to its northeastern states has been heightened by its growing effort to develop greater connectivity with Southeast Asia, an area of increasing importance for Indian trade, investment, and security. For a half century, only limited shipments of goods by special arrangement have been allowed. Even those governments in Dhaka most sympathetic to India have been wary of the strong concern many Bangladeshis feel about the political, security, economic, and (more recently) environmental implications of sizable Indian traffic flows across their country. When a transit agreement was proposed in the late 1990s, Bangladeshi opposition figures aroused public opinion by accusing the government of granting India a "corridor." In negotiations with the India on the issue, governments in Dhaka have contended that Bangladesh's fragile transportation network is inadequate. As noted, this is one issue where Bangladesh holds the high cards, though its own increased interest in connectivity in all directions has probably reduced their value.

Linkage

Bangladesh was not willing to agree to a transit agreement without India's solving one of the issues on Dhaka's agenda, however. Prime Minister Singh understood this and planned to include in the package an agreement that Bangladesh sought on water rights in the Teesta River. This was a bilateral issue—there are no third countries in the Teesta basin. However, local Indian politics intervened in the person of the West Bengal chief minister, the Trinamool Congress leader Mamata Banerjee, whose party's political activities are confined to her state. She blocked the agreement because she felt it would damage the interests of some of her farming constituents. New Delhi did not contest the point. In explaining the failure to reach an agreement with the chief minister, senior Indian officials repeatedly stressed that any such pact would have to be acceptable to the concerned Indian states. This development led the Bangladeshis to renege on the transit pact.[10] As the Dhaka press headlined: "No Teesta, No Transit." And though the land transfer agreement was signed, the Manmohan Singh government failed to secure passage of the necessary constitutional amendment, as we have seen.

The final chapter in this negotiating saga, interestingly, once more cast the Modi government as the solver of long-standing problems between India and Bangladesh. In April 2015, the Bangladesh government announced that it had concluded negotiations on a new transit agreement with India, under which Bangladesh would be able to transport goods from Nepal and Bhutan across Indian roads, railways, and waterways. India would have the same facility for transporting goods to Myanmar across Bangladesh.[11] What had changed was not the negotiating technique but the policy: the Modi government was prepared to use economic agreements as the lead element in an approach that cast India as an engine of regional economic growth. The process had its tentative beginnings with the new approach to regional river management (as described previously). The Modi government brought it into the open.

Modi's June 2015 official visit to Dhaka added further substance to India-Bangladesh connectivity. Bangladesh agreed to open two important harbors as transshipment points for sea-borne Indian cargo moving between the Indian mainland and the northeastern states. Additional bus services connecting Bangladesh with Kolkata and several of these states were launched. Agreements were reached to increase power and pipeline connectivity. An Indian economic zone is to be set up to increase Indian investment in Bangladesh.

But the West Bengal chief minister persisted in opposing the deal on the division of the waters of the Teesta that she had torpedoed when Singh had visited Dhaka four years earlier. This latest failure led some Bangladeshi critics to argue that India had come out the winner in the Modi visit. They recalled the slogan "No Teesta, No Transit" raised during Singh's trip. Now India had won the transit rights, but the Teesta issue remained unresolved. They were not mollified by a handsome Indian $2 billion credit to Bangladesh to support infrastructure, twice the amount of the credit the Singh government had provided.

Other Issues

These issues do not of course exhaust the list of problems between New Delhi and Dhaka. The relationship and its domestic underpinnings in both countries are also shaped by the massive illegal migration into eastern and northeastern India of Bangladeshis searching for better economic prospects, widespread smuggling in both directions that has sparked deadly clashes between the two countries' paramilitary forces along the border, Islamic extremists' use of Bangladeshi territory as a base for operations in India, communal violence in both countries, and other long-standing problems. But these important issues have not led to sustained, high-level negotiations that match those revolving around river waters, land boundaries, and transit. Indeed, no negotiations can be possible on what is probably the most important of these—illegal Bangladeshi migration—until Dhaka abandons its longtime claim that no such migration is taking place.

SRI LANKA

The classic problems of a big neighbor/small neighbor relationship have been exacerbated in India-Sri Lanka ties by the presence in the island nation of a substantial aggrieved minority with ethnic links to India. From the time in the late 1940s when India and, a few months later, Sri Lanka won independence from Britain, this "Tamil problem" has been the most important issue confronting Indian foreign policymakers in their dealings with Colombo. Sri Lanka illustrates Indian diplomacy at its most active, remarkably deeply involved in the details of Sri Lanka's internal governance and constitution-writing, including three years of maintaining a substantial Indian Peace Keeping Force (IPKF) in the island. In the end, India was unable to resolve this issue to its satisfaction. Its perception that Sri Lanka's relations with foreign countries threaten its own security have also vexed bilateral ties and figured in one important negotiation. As with Bangladesh, India's relations with Sri Lanka and its diplomatic style in dealing with the island nation have varied over time and have been influenced by the political equations in both countries.

The Tamil Issue

As we saw in chapter 5, Indian diplomacy in dealing with Sri Lanka has been complicated by pressures mounted by several political parties based in Tamil Nadu state. It was made even more difficult by fear of Tamil encirclement on the part of the island's Sinhalese majority. Tamils represent just under 20 percent of the country's population, divided between the Sri Lankan Tamils, who live in the island's north and east, and the group called Indian or Estate Tamils, whose forebears were brought from India as plantation workers in the nineteenth century and live mainly in the central highlands.[12] The Tamil dimension in India-Sri Lanka relations was particularly acute during the quarter-century Sri Lankan civil war (1983–2009), but it continues to roil relations and is likely to remain a major focus in New Delhi's dealings with Colombo.

Soon after it became independent in 1948, Sri Lanka stripped the Indian Tamils of their citizenship rights, declared them Indian citizens, and tried to force their repatriation to India. The Nehru government steadfastly refused to accept Sri Lanka's position and for sixteen years the issue seemed intractable. It was only after Lal Bahadur Shastri became prime minister in 1964 that India made major concessions in reaching a bilateral agreement with Mrs. Sirimavo Bandaranaike's government on the issue.[13] With the signing of the agreement and a follow-up accord in 1974, the problem of the Indian Tamils on the island largely faded as an issue in New Delhi's foreign policy.

The Sri Lankan Civil War

The event that engaged India, and soon led to negotiations intimately bound up with the island's political future and foreign policy orientation, was the outbreak in 1983 of a quarter-century-long civil war in which insurgents drawn from the large and discontented Sri Lankan Tamil community sought to break up the country. The war ended in 2009, but the postwar fate of these Tamils remains an important issue for New Delhi, especially because of its impact on the politics of India's Tamil Nadu state.

The twenty-five initial years of Sri Lankan independence had been marked by a succession of failed efforts by the majority Sinhalese community and the Sri Lankan Tamil group to reach a political settlement. At stake were such key issues as regional autonomy, the country's official languages, education, land distribution, and government employment. Several agreements between government and Tamil leaders were negotiated but badly implemented. Intercommunal violence mounted. It reached unprecedented heights in July 1983 with the massacre of Tamils in the Colombo area and the flight of many of the survivors to the relative safety of the Tamil-dominated north and to India and other foreign countries.

Reacting to this virtual pogrom, which understandably aroused widespread condemnation in India, Prime Minister Indira Gandhi sent an angry message to the Sri Lankan government that included an offer of her government's good offices. She was already on bad personal terms with Sri Lankan President J. R. Jayewardene, whose pro-Western foreign policy orientation Mrs. Gandhi considered antipathetic to Indian interests. Possibly fearing an Indian invasion, Jayewardene quickly accepted her offer, sent his brother to New Delhi for preliminary talks with the Indians, and agreed to receive the Indian foreign minister in Colombo.[14]

India's objective in dealing with the crisis was to bring about a negotiated political settlement acceptable to all of the island's communities within the framework of a united Sri Lanka. Mrs. Gandhi spelled out her government's policy in a statement to the Lok Sabha in August 1983 that stressed support for Sri Lankan independence, unity, and integrity. She reiterated India's policy of noninterference in the internal affairs of other countries. But she also spoke of "the close ties between the peoples of the two countries, especially India's links with the Tamils," and warned Jayewardene against permitting "any extraneous involvement in Sri Lankan affairs, which would complicate matters."[15]

J. N. Dixit, who became India's high commissioner in Colombo in May 1985, recalled that after Rajiv Gandhi succeeded his mother as prime minister in October 1984, he modified what Dixit termed Mrs. Gandhi's "pro-Tamil militant slant" to "bring a measure of balance and impartiality in our attitude to the Sinhalese-Tamil conflict."[16] But concern about the impact of its Sri Lanka policy on the politics of Tamil Nadu remained a major consideration for the Indian government.

In 1984 and 1985, New Delhi launched three major efforts to bring about a settlement. It was an extraordinarily intrusive engagement in Sri Lanka's most intimate problems, involving diplomatic mediation, intelligence operations, and extensive contact with political parties in both countries.[17] The first two episodes involved bringing representatives of the Sri Lankan government and the plethora of Tamil and Sinhalese-based parties together, with high-level Indian officials on hand to urge them on. In the third, Indian representatives moved between the Sri Lankan participants. During the proximity talks, Prime Minister Rajiv Gandhi and President Jayewardene met at Bangalore in South India on the margins of a session of the South Asian Association for Regional Cooperation. This Indian participation in the three rounds of talks was publicly billed as a facilitating role, but the Indian emissaries and the Indian high commission in Colombo went well beyond that by helping to develop compromise formulas and twisting the arms of Sri Lankan leaders of all factions to accept them. New Delhi assigned some of its top diplomats and officials to these efforts.[18]

India accompanied these diplomatic efforts with threatening statements, the provision of arms and training in South India to Tamil insurgents (importantly including the most hard-line of the militant groups, the Liberation Tigers of Tamil Eelam—LTTE), and asylum to Tamil political leaders and large numbers of refugees. India also tried to take advantage of its patronage of the Sri Lankan Tamil parties (and the threat to withdraw it) to press the Sri Lankan government and other leaders, both Tamils and Sinhalese, to accept Indian-sponsored suggestions for compromise. Senior Indian officials were in frequent contact with Sri Lankans across the political spectrum. Indian High Commissioner Dixit played an extremely active role in arranging and participating in these exchanges, meeting with Sri Lankan officials and political leaders of all stripes and seeking to influence New Delhi's policies.

These Indian-sponsored efforts eventually failed. The two sides were too far apart. The degree of power to be devolved to the Tamil-majority areas proved a particularly tough issue to resolve, and although several imaginative formulas were devised, none could win acceptance from the contending factions.[19] New Delhi's efforts were complicated by political pressure exerted on it by Tamil Nadu–based political parties sympathetic to the Sri Lankan Tamils' cause.

By the time the mediation effort failed, the LTTE, an avowedly secessionist group, had become the dominant voice among the Sri Lankan Tamils. The LTTE had no qualms about either decimating its rival parties to consolidate its leadership of the Tamil struggle or killing Sinhalese and Muslim civilians. Encouraged by divisions within Tamil ranks, the Sri Lankan government became increasingly aggressive and in early 1987 launched an offensive in the northeast that climaxed with an economic blockade and bombardment of Tamil forces in Jaffna, the major northern city. This action drew a stern warning from Indian Prime Minister Rajiv Gandhi, who told Jayewardene in a top-secret personal message: "Escalating violence will compel us to think afresh about the whole situation, consequent on Sri Lanka's rejection of the path of negotiations."[20]

India, in other words, was blaming Sri Lanka for the breakdown of the negotiating process. New Delhi would not resume its own diplomatic efforts unless the Sri Lankans called off their military offensive. It continued to demand in public forums that the Sri Lankan forces stop killing innocent civilians and that Colombo "satisfy the legitimate aspirations of the Tamil population of Sri Lanka through the devolution of appropriate powers within the framework of Sri Lanka's unity. . . ."[21] New Delhi also stepped up its angry complaints about the assistance in arms, military training, and intelligence operations the Sri Lankan government was receiving from the United States, China, Pakistan, Israel, the South African apartheid regime, and other foreign sources. Tamils in India called even more stridently for forceful action by the Gandhi government.

As the Sri Lankan army continued its attacks against rebel-held areas in the north and east over India's repeated objections, New Delhi adopted more drastic measures, dispatching a flotilla of fishing boats to convey humanitarian assistance under the auspices of the Indian Red Cross to the trapped Tamil population in Jaffna. When these boats were turned back, India used its air force to drop food and fuel shipments on the city. It shrugged off international criticism of this action.[22] More important, it radically changed its negotiating strategy. Instead of continuing to try to play—with scant success—the role of facilitator or mediator, India decided to become a direct participant in negotiations designed to bring about a settlement.

After weeks of forceful Indian negotiations with the Jayewardene government, this fresh approach led to the signing of the controversial

Indo–Sri Lanka Accord in July 1987. Arguably, Jayewardene accepted the agreement only because he reckoned that the alternative was a protracted civil war and the breakup of the Sri Lankan state. The accord was resolutely opposed by some of his most influential government colleagues, the leading Sri Lankan opposition party, and many other important Sinhalese political and religious leaders. Although the Indians were able with some difficulty to persuade LTTE leader Velupillai Prabhakaran to go along with the agreement, he did not formally endorse it and soon disavowed it.[23]

The agreement called for a prompt cessation of hostilities, surrender of arms by militant groups, and the return of Sri Lanka's military to barracks.[24] India undertook to help if Sri Lanka needed assistance in implementing these provisions. It was this clause that led to the dispatch to Sri Lanka of the IPKF. Gandhi and Jayewardene reasserted the desire of their two governments "to preserve the unity, sovereignty, and territorial integrity of Sri Lanka." The Sri Lankans were obliged to acknowledge that the island was a "multiethnic and multilingual plural society" in which each ethnic group had a "distinct cultural and linguistic identity which has to be carefully nurtured." Sri Lanka also agreed to set up a new Tamil-majority province in the northeast that—though the agreement did not say so—would be a Tamil homeland within the framework of the Sri Lankan state. Two days later, Jayewardene declared his government's intention to devolve power to provincial units in the Sinhala-majority part of the island as well. This agreement became the basis of the thirteenth amendment to the Sri Lankan constitution.

India also used the accord to solidify its preeminent position in South Asia and to strengthen its security against challenges from the outside. Sri Lanka agreed not to use its territory for purposes hostile to India and accepted a series of limitations on foreign activities there in provisions that clearly if not explicitly targeted the United States, China, Israel, and Pakistan.

Despite the forceful high-level diplomacy New Delhi brought into play to fashion the 1987 agreement, the pact failed to settle Sri Lanka's ethnic conflict or, in the long term, to promote India's broader regional interests. The Indians had badly misread the LTTE's intentions, and its denunciation of the pact came as a surprise to them. The IPKF, which had been dispatched to the island to peacefully disarm Tamil insurgents, found itself transformed into an expeditionary army whose objective was to suppress the insurgents militarily. To the Indians' further un-happy surprise, the IPKF soon lost the support of Tamils both in Tamil Nadu and in northern and northeastern Sri Lanka. Many in both groups considered it a mercenary force and provided assistance to the LTTE.

In battling the rebels the IPKF was largely on its own: much of the Sri Lankan military had been sent south to deal with a second civil war, this one against the Janata Vimukti Peramuna (JVP), a radical Sinhalese revolutionary group that was seeking to fundamentally change Sri Lanka's political, economic, and social structure. At Sri Lanka's request, Indian Air Force planes helped transport Sri Lankan units from the northern front to the south.[25]

The IPKF continued its fruitless mission until Jayewardene's newly elected successor as president, Ranasinghe Premadasa, unceremoniously asked New Delhi to withdraw the forces, to the Indians' mortification. By the time the last IPKF units left in early 1990, India had sent 80,000 troops to Sri Lanka; 1,200 of them had died. In conversations with the authors, some Indian military commentators called it "India's Vietnam." The provincial autonomy arrangements for the Tamil northeast that Indian diplomats had so carefully negotiated collapsed with the IPKF's departure.

Badly burned by its peacemaking experience, India avoided playing any major diplomatic or military role in further efforts to bring about a negotiated Sri Lankan settlement. Reflecting on the failed Indian intervention a few years later, Dixit, by then Indian foreign secretary, told the authors that in light of this unhappy experience New Delhi was no longer able to play such a role in Sri Lanka.[26] It reengaged in a significant way only after the war ended with the Sri Lankan army's annihilation of LTTE forces in 2009.

NEPAL

Nepal's geographic setting on the southern slope of the Himalayas between India and China puts the landlocked country at the heart of New Delhi's security concerns. Prime Minister Nehru made these concerns most explicit in an address to parliament in December 1950, soon after the newly triumphant Chinese Communists moved their forces into Tibet. "From time immemorial," Nehru declared, "the Himalayas have provided us with magnificent frontiers. . . . We cannot allow that barrier to be penetrated because it is also the principal barrier to India. Therefore, much as we appreciate the independence of Nepal, we cannot allow anything to go wrong in Nepal or permit that barrier to be weakened, because that would be a risk to our own security."[27]

Spurning his hard-line Congress Party colleague, Deputy Prime Minister Sardar Vallabhbhai Patel, who called for the annexation of Nepal and the other two Himalayan monarchies, Bhutan and Sikkim, Nehru had sought instead to replicate the special position the British Raj had enjoyed with them. India signed separate treaties of peace and friendship with the three in 1950. The India-Nepal Treaty of Peace and Friendship stopped short of establishing a formal bilateral military alliance.[28] But the text of secret letters between the two governments later made public makes clear that New Delhi considered that the 1950 treaty placed Nepal within India's defense perimeter.[29]

Although India has other important interests in Nepal and the way it has dealt with Kathmandu has changed over the years, the priority India gives to its security against a perceived Chinese threat continues to be the driving force in its policies there. This security issue has strongly influenced the way India negotiates with Nepal and explains New Delhi's willingness to play diplomatic hardball when it concludes a strong approach is called for.

One example of these tough tactics was India's decision in 1989 to take advantage of its virtual stranglehold over the Nepalese economy to force Nepal to back away from a contract to purchase a small supply of arms from China. The embargo the Indians instituted to achieve their goal came at a time when they were becoming increasingly exasperated by broader Nepalese policies. The consequent economic hardship heightened widespread popular Nepalese dissatisfaction with the country's authoritarian political system that had promoted these policies and helped bring about the launching of a more democratic political system, much to New Delhi's satisfaction.

The China Card

Writing in 2001, J. N. Dixit, who by then was India's foreign secretary and would soon become its national security adviser, listed as New Delhi's leading "point of worry" in its relations with Kathmandu Nepal's efforts "to play China against India."[30] This Nepalese attempt to extract concessions from India by drawing closer to China (or threatening to do so) has long been part of Kathmandu's broader effort to reduce the role India plays in its affairs and win international recognition as a genuinely independent country.

Many in the Nepalese political class had quickly become dissatisfied with the 1950 India-Nepal Treaty, which they considered an unequal agreement that gave India an unacceptably dominant position in their country. Nepal's growing contact with other countries through common membership in the United Nations and other organizations, along with the establishment in Kathmandu of resident foreign diplomatic missions and economic programs, lessened the country's sense of isolation and encouraged it to seek to develop its own international standing and personality. Increasingly sensitive to what they perceived as condescending Indian behavior and unwarranted interference in the country's foreign relations, politically aware Nepalese came to resent the way the Indian government and the ruling Indian National Congress played favorites in the country's domestic politics (except when this involvement favored their own faction).

India, for its part, has been disappointed that despite the cultural, ethnic, and religious ties between the two countries and the many special economic and other favors it has bestowed on Nepal, the unappreciative Nepalese failed to offer full support for India's security and foreign policies, not least with regard to China and Tibet. It had, of course, been China's occupation of Tibet and its subsequent actions there that had greatly heightened the importance of Nepal to the security of India.

Against this background, King Birendra's 1973 proposal that Nepal be recognized internationally as a "Zone of Peace" met strong Indian opposition. New Delhi feared that the arrangement—which to India's dismay the Nepalese touted with some success for years in world forums— could become a threat to Indian security by undercutting the 1950 India-Nepal Treaty and placing Kathmandu's relations with New Delhi on a par with those it had with Beijing.[31]

The Dispute over Trade and Transit Treaties

One issue that gradually became a particular irritant in bilateral relations was India's role in Nepalese international trade. Before the 1950s, all of Nepal's demand for foreign goods was met by Indian agents and shops. These imports were shipped across Indian territory into Nepal without the two countries regulating their movement. As trade increased,

New Delhi and Kathmandu signed a trade and transit treaty in 1960. This provided free and unhindered passage into Nepal for Indian goods and imports transiting India from third countries.

This treaty was periodically renewed. But the Nepalese dissatisfaction with it grew. They resented the fact that the treaty covered both trade and transit. They argued that while trade was a matter of convenience, transit was a permanent right for a landlocked country and should be dealt with separately.

The Indians resisted this view. They were concerned that drawing up separate treaties would lead to an even greater quantity of third-country products being imported without regulation into Nepal and then being re-exported to India. New Delhi's autarkic economic policies, which included strict limits on imports, put such re-exported products in great demand in India. Indian resistance to separate treaties was interpreted in Nepal as a diminution of the country's sovereignty. It was only after a very hard fought battle within the Indian government that agreement was reached in 1978 to accept Nepal's demands.[32] The two treaties and an accompanying Indo-Nepalese agreement to control smuggling were renewed for brief periods and eventually scheduled to expire in 1989.

The India-Nepal Agreement on Arms Assistance

In 1965, New Delhi and Kathmandu signed an agreement, described as secret but widely known, in which India undertook to supply arms, ammunition, and equipment for the entire Nepalese Army. It also agreed to replace the existing Nepalese stock with modern weapons as soon as available and to maintain and replace the equipment it provided. Kathmandu would be "free to import from or through the territory of India arms, ammunition, or warlike material and equipment necessary for the security of Nepal." In the agreement, the Indians noted that the American and British governments had given India to understand that if there were any shortfalls in the supply of arms and equipment provided by the Indians, they would fill the gaps to the extent of their ability. India and Nepal agreed that the arrangements spelled out in the agreement "shall have no bearing on the independent foreign policy of either government."[33]

India did not always agree to provide the weaponry that Nepal sought. It had reportedly turned down several requests for anti-aircraft guns, which it concluded the Nepalese army did not require.[34] Nepal continued to procure its arms from India until 1988, when China agreed to sell it light arms, ammunition, uniforms, and sixteen anti-aircraft guns reportedly worth around $20 million in all. The arms reportedly began arriving by truck from Tibet in March 1988. India considered this sale unacceptable—as small and unthreatening as it appeared. They regarded it as a breach of the 1950 Treaty of Peace and Friendship and the 1965 agreement on arms assistance.

The Nepalese ignored Indian warnings not to go ahead with the deal. They were neither willing to give guarantees to purchase no further Chinese arms nor prepared to ensure that materiel already purchased would not be used against India. And as the Indians must surely have known, sometime in 1988 Nepal signed an agreement with the Chinese to exchange intelligence information, a development New Delhi could hardly have regarded with equanimity.[35]

New Delhi struck back. It sought to use Nepal's economic dependence on India to force it to scrap the arms purchase from the Chinese and rely exclusively on India for weapons.[36] More broadly, India wanted to underscore its own primacy in South Asia and discourage Nepal from challenging it.

India used the trade and transit treaties to advance these goals. When these agreements were about to expire and Nepal refused to sign a single treaty to replace the separate trade and transit treaties that had been negotiated in 1978, India announced there would be no further extensions and informed Nepal in March 1989 that the treaties would definitively expire three weeks later. When they did, the Indians closed all but two crossing points and made passage through them difficult. As Professor John Garver has concluded, "India's general attitude was that if Nepal wanted a special economic relationship with India, and the generous treatment that implied, it would have to accept a special security relationship.[37]

The Indian blockade had a devastating impact on the Nepalese economy. Nepal depends heavily on India for essential supplies such as kerosene and salt and for the transshipment of important foreign goods. Although some Nepalese spoke of developing supply routes across the Himalayas or using air transport, neither of these approaches was practical. Nepal's desperate efforts to win the support of foreign governments for breaking the economic blockade failed. No outside powers saw it in their interest to become involved. The Indians held firm. The authors, who at that time dealt with South Asia policy in the U.S. State Department, recall the Nepalese ambassador's plaintive, unsuccessful efforts to persuade the United States to urge India to lift the blockade.

Reaching a Settlement

As New Delhi probably foresaw, the Indian blockade and the resulting economic problems heightened already widespread popular discontent with Nepal's autocratic monarchy. India, for its part, seriously faulted the regime, not so much for its undemocratic character—the Indians had lived for decades with Nepalese autocratic rule—as for its pursuit of policies India found inimical to its interests. India could only have been delighted when government-organized anti-Indian rallies designed to inspire Nepalese patriotism turned into anti-government protests.

In February 1990, a pro-democracy movement was launched in Nepal that quickly won strong support in India. The Nepalese government's attempts to suppress it were widely criticized in India, where Prime Minister Rajiv Gandhi and his successor, V. P. Singh, condemned such efforts as state violence. As the demonstrations mounted in number and intensity, King Birendra of Nepal asked opposition leader Krishna Prasad Bhattarai to form a government. The new prime minister quickly proposed to the Indian government a restoration of the March 1989 status quo and conclusion of new trade and transit agreements. Even more important for India, he also asked the Chinese to hold up the final shipment of arms.

Visiting New Delhi in June 1990, Bhattarai signed with Prime Minister V. P. Singh a communiqué that restored the status quo ante April 1, 1987 in relations, "before the recent bilateral tensions emerged." Both sides "undertook to respect each other's security concerns, not to allow activities in the territory of the one prejudicial to the security of the other, and to have prior consultations, with a view to reaching mutual agreement on such defense-related matters which, in the view of the other country, could pose a threat to its security."[38] In December 1991, the two countries signed separate trade and transit agreements as Nepal had called for.[39]

Despite this concession, India had basically prevailed. Indeed, New Delhi's tough policy to force the Nepalese to back down on the arms issue and more broadly accept India's leadership role on security matters had brought it an extra dividend in the installation of a sympathetic democratic regime in Kathmandu. As noted, Indian governments have cared relatively little about the character of governments in their neighborhood (and elsewhere). What was important for New Delhi was that the leaders of the new Nepalese democracy were more likely to take into account Indian security concerns than its autocratic predecessor had been.

A Changed Nepal

In the quarter century since this India-Nepal confrontation, the Nepalese political scene has greatly changed. The monarchy has been abolished and a prolonged uprising by radical Maoist forces ended with the Maoists joining the Nepalese government. These and other political developments in Nepal have changed the India-Nepal political equation.

India's abiding focus on the security of its northern frontier continues to be the prime feature of its policy toward Nepal. But as noted in the discussion of post–Cold War developments in chapter 3, New Delhi seems to have concluded that it can no longer exclude Chinese influence from its smaller neighbors but can instead serve its interests better by altering its tactics.

Nepal's recent experience shows both the potential and the limitations of this changed approach. Over the past decade India has grown to tolerate if not welcome a substantially increased Chinese role in Nepal in trade, transport, military supply, infrastructure development, and high-level official visits. The red line it has always drawn in the high Himalayas against perceived threats from a strong and rising China is a bit fainter. However, India still looks on Nepal as a potential pathway for danger, and its traditional response of playing hardball is still part of its toolkit.

THE MODI GOVERNMENT: A NEW LOOK?

Narendra Modi became Indian prime minister as an avowed hawk. His policy and negotiating style with India's smaller South Asian neighbors, however, combines a fundamentally realist approach with a style that showcases more seduction than threats. We have already seen the significant changes his government has made in the management of land boundary and transit problems in Bangladesh. In Sri Lanka, India had already made financial support part of its approach when that country's civil war ended in 2009, but its proposed infrastructure funding was plagued with implementation problems. In 2015 Modi spent several days in Sri Lanka, the first bilateral summit there since 1987, visiting both Colombo and Jaffna, in the heart of Tamil northern Sri Lanka. Economic cooperation, once again, had a high profile. The basic message of the summit diplomacy in each place was clear: India wants to be a regional leader whose economic success benefits the whole neighborhood, and it is prepared to listen to its neighbors' views in the process. Maintaining India's preeminence is still the goal, but with more honey than vinegar.

The new Modi look has a tougher side as well, however. In Nepal, Modi's first moves were clearly part of the campaign to use India and specifically its economy as a magnet for better regional relations. He visited Nepal in August 2014, three months after taking office, and set about working on a long-stalled plan for trading electric power between the two countries. In April 2015, India was first on the spot with generous relief after a devastating earthquake struck the most heavily populated parts of Nepal.

Nepal's approval on September 20, 2015 of a new constitution, long years in the making in an often troubled constituent assembly, changed the tenor of India's diplomacy with Nepal. Days before the constitution was promulgated, the Indian foreign secretary visited Nepal. Press reports indicated that his main message was that the constitution's protections for Nepal's ethnic minorities along the Indian border were unsatisfactory, and that these provisions should be revised in consultation with India. Once the document was formally approved, India reacted coolly. Suddenly, truck traffic along the India-Nepal border came to a halt, in particular tankers carrying fuel. From Nepal, this looked like a replay of the 1989 blockade. India blamed the stoppage on disturbances inside Nepal and denied any official blockade. At this writing, protests against the constitution continue in the border areas and broader Nepalese unhappiness with what is seen as Indian coercion is intensifying. A visit by the Nepalese foreign minister to Delhi got nowhere. In late October, Nepal reached agreement with China for short-term supply of 1.3 million liters of fuel.[40] The crisis had started, in other words, with Indian unhappiness about a Nepal domestic issue, but its inevitable escalation brought China into the picture. There are reports of some trucks getting through from India but the end of the story remains unclear.

The Nepal crisis underscores both Nepal's uniquely sensitive location and India's continuing willingness to use hard tactics. A recent border incident involving Myanmar provided another example of a tough India approach. The Indian army confirmed on June 9, 2015, that it had conducted a raid inside Myanmar on camps of rebels operating in India's small northeastern states, apparently a response to an incident five days earlier that killed twenty Indian soldiers. India has long worked with governments in Myanmar to rein in militants active in India's northeast. Publicly available information is murky, but it will not escape the attention of any of India's South Asian neighbors that India was prepared to take matters into its own hands and cross the border.[41]

CHAPTER THIRTEEN

India in a Changing World

THIS ANALYSIS OF INDIA'S global vision and negotiating style started with the "tryst with destiny" Jawaharlal Nehru promised his countrymen as twentieth-century India became independent. Over the next seventy years, Nehru's vision had a powerful impact on India's foreign policy. He sought a democratic state, with strong institutions, embodying India's unique culture. Those objectives are still at the heart of India's government. Nehru inherited and built on the regional preeminence that the British Raj had seen as India's due. He saw in nonalignment both a new definition of international morality and a means to maximize India's freedom of action. Nonalignment remains the dominant vocabulary for Indian foreign policy, and preserving freedom of action—strategic autonomy—is one of its key principles.

After 1990, the vision of India's global role that guided its foreign policy underwent two important adjustments. First, deregulation and a decade of rapid growth made India's economy a source of national power and a driver of foreign policy. Second, this economic change and the end of the Cold War shook up India's extra-regional relationships, making the United States an important partner.

The election of Narendra Modi as prime minister intensified the post–Cold War adjustment. Modi is a strong leader and starts out with a single-party governing majority, something India had not seen since the height of Congress Party power under Nehru and his daughter. In his first year in office, Modi has displayed a dramatic and assertive foreign policy style and has articulated high ambitions for the country. But fundamentally, his vision for India's role in the world builds on the same elements as the one that has guided policy since 1990. The economic foundation of India's future and the economic driver of its foreign policy stand out in sharper relief than under his predecessors. Modi is likely to be less coy about his interest in enhancing India's power. Under him, non-alignment has continued to morph into maximizing India's options, or strategic autonomy. In maintaining India's primacy in South Asia, Modi has relied more on enticement of the smaller neighboring states than most earlier governments. By contrast, his approach to Pakistan, reflecting his party's traditional position, is both tougher and more changeable than some of his predecessors. In his first year, he gave lower priority to global organizations, though this could change. But these are evolutionary adjustments, not revolutionary moves.

As India navigates a changing world, its international modus operandi will largely follow the patterns described in the preceding chapters. Three aspects of the global landscape, however, may in time lead India's foreign policy and negotiating style to adapt in more significant ways: the opportunities created by its growing economy; the challenge of an increasingly assertive Chinese role both in the region and globally; and changes in the U.S. role, especially in Asia. India's own ambitions for global leadership could also lead to adjustments both in its goals and in the negotiating tactics it adopts to reach them.

THE ECONOMY: WILL INDIA TAKE ANOTHER BET ON GLOBALIZATION?

In India as elsewhere, foreign policy starts at home. India's ability to deal with the challenges of a changing world will continue to depend on its ability to maintain a strong and stable political system and effective leadership to work it. It will also depend on how its economy fares.

India's recent history is encouraging. The economic reforms of the 1990s and 2000s dramatically increased economic growth, tripled the share of international trade in India's economy, and removed important regulatory barriers to private business. Significantly, these changes were followed by a dramatic drop in the poverty rate, which fell from 45 to 22 percent between 1994 and 2012.[1] As India made its basic reform decisions, its foreign exchange reserves were nearly gone, as we saw in chapter 3. India took a chance on reforms and globalization. This paid off handsomely, not only in economic terms but in establishing India as a powerful regional country with credible potential to become a major global power. India's expanding relationships with the United States, Japan, Korea, and Southeast Asia, for example, would not have occurred on anything like the scale they did without the economic boom. A thriving economy facilitated India's decision to expand a program of development partnership, or economic aid, to give a new dimension to its foreign policy.

Resuming the growth path India achieved before the 2008 financial crisis is the starting point if New Delhi seeks to expand its global role further. This objective should be achievable, though it will not come easily. Modi has set soaring goals, such as moving India's position to the top third of the World Bank's "Doing Business" index and revving up manufacturing through the "Make in India" program. His government's dominant position in the lower house of parliament enabled him to move part of his economic agenda forward during his first year in office. But like previous governments that tackled a major reform agenda, Modi's will need to overcome obstacles deeply embedded in India's institutional and political culture. India's administrative institutions are strong, but even with strategic changes in their leadership they follow strongly ingrained practices that will not change easily. India's political institutions continue to be oriented toward rural constituencies and patronage. And a pro-business agenda remains controversial in India.

A growing economy would pay off, not just at home, but also in India's foreign policy. It would make it easier for India to build up the institutions needed for a larger international role. Of particular importance would be increasing the size of the Indian Foreign Service, including a stronger economic and commercial cadre. India's major government services would benefit both from greater specialization (for example, on such subjects as defense and international economics) and from greater flexibility in how they are assigned in the institutions that manage India's international economic relations. Even a major increase in the current budget of the foreign affairs agencies would be tiny in relation to the overall funding needs of the Indian government.

Defense reorganization is another piece of unfinished business. The many studies of India's defense organization that now sit on groaning shelves (see chapter 5) suggest a wide measure of consensus about how to make India's military better able to meet the challenges of a more complicated world. Similarly, there have long been complaints within the Indian government about the slow process of defense procurement. None of these institutional reforms would break the budgetary bank, but lively economic growth would make it easier to tackle the more pressing obstacles to these reforms: political and bureaucratic inertia.

An economically resurgent India would enjoy greater freedom of action in its relationships across the globe. The growth surge of the 1990s and 2000s had a strong impact on India's management of its economic relationships. Its decision to conclude free trade agreements with Japan, Korea, and the Association of Southeast Asian Nations (ASEAN) broke with decades of reluctance to open India's market. In all three cases, India's negotiating tactics remained cautious, but the decision to go for free trade agreements was a bold one. Thus far, the free trade agreements have had relatively limited impact on trade flows, but they have opened up that possibility.

Looking ahead, India's policymakers will face a choice: whether to embrace new opportunities from greater engagement with the global economy or continue to pursue a policy that is more modest and carries less political risk. The foreign policy blitz with which Modi began his government focused heavily on bringing in investment, with major packages announced with the governments of China and Japan. India has continued trade negotiations with the EU and Canada. However, its two most important trading partners do not figure in these negotiations. China, a manufacturing powerhouse, has a massive and growing trade surplus with India. The United States insists that its free trade areas cover a far higher percentage of trade than the countries India has reached agreements with, which would almost certainly mean granting trade access for products India considers sensitive. Opening trade to both would bring into the Indian market a degree of competition it has not faced in the past; on the other hand, reduced barriers to Indian exports would give them a boost. Negotiating with either one would be an extraordinarily difficult enterprise, especially in the wake of the Obama administration's difficulties with the proposed Trans-Pacific Partnership. For India, opening trade with China and the United States would present political risks in a country that still regards foreign competition with suspicion. But as other global trade liberalization efforts move ahead, if India decides that it needs to expand trade with these two countries, it may need to take a fresh chance on unblocking its own export success.

India has been even more reluctant to deepen its embrace of globalization in the multilateral arena, as we have seen. Its resistance to including new aspects of trade in the World Trade Organization is an understandable effort to moderate the pace at which global rule-setting and global competition come into the Indian economy. And it has basically sought to keep agriculture off-limits for international trade rules. The United States, Europe, and Japan took a similarly restrictive approach to agricultural trade for decades after the international trade architecture was set up following World War II. Fighting to avoid greater integration with the international economy and negotiating by brinksmanship is the path of least resistance, but will impose opportunity costs on a growing Indian economy.

This is not a simple choice—or a binary one. One could imagine a future government looking for other tools to meet its domestic objectives, in order to smooth a path to greater globalization. Enhancing the livelihood of farmers and maintaining a safety net under the domestic food supply are legitimate goals. They might more effectively be met, however, by developing new domestic tools, such as boosting investment in smaller towns that will attract surplus agricultural labor. The farm sector would benefit as much by the creation of jobs outside agriculture as by stimuli for agriculture itself. Improving agricultural incomes through domestic policies could open the door to a more supple international negotiating strategy that might boost India's exports. The trade-off here is between trade goals and domestic political imperatives. If Modi retains and expands his ability to mobilize domestic support, both in national institutions and at the state level, and if he is able to bring out creative impulses in the star performers of the often change-resistant civil service, he will have better odds of developing this kind of policy.

THE CHINA CHALLENGE

Changes in the way China uses its growing power will have a tremendous impact on how India conceives of and manages its international role. China's ability to block India from obtaining the kind of status that China enjoys by virtue of its permanent membership on the UN Security Council and its nuclear status as recognized by the Non-Proliferation Treaty (NPT) is always in the background of the two countries' rivalry. More importantly, China's deepening economic and military profile in South Asia will challenge India's security and standing in its immediate region. The countries of Southeast Asia have welcomed a more prominent Indian presence. At the same time, they are wary of competition between the two Asian giants. China's looming presence in that region both invites and potentially constrains India's ability to expand its footprint further east.

Growing Chinese Presence in South Asia

In India's immediate region, South Asia and the Indian Ocean, China has become a much bigger player in the past decade. China's trade with the region grew by a factor of 16–20 between 2005 and 2010.[2] Its economic assistance to countries in this region also rose dramatically. The largest and most striking example was Xi Jinping's April 2015 visit to Pakistan, when he reportedly promised $46 billion in support for infrastructure, including transit facilities in Indian-claimed territory in Kashmir. China's military presence and interest has been growing elsewhere in South Asia as well. The visit of two Chinese submarines to Colombo in the fall of 2014, the second one a nuclear-powered Han-class vessel, set off alarm bells in Delhi.[3]

Security in the neighborhood will be a critical priority for any future Indian government, and maintaining India's position of primacy will remain the preferred means of achieving it. However, India will need to adapt how it defines and pursues primacy. With India's smaller neighbors, the Modi government has already made a start, pushing for regional economic integration, with India's economy helping its neighbors achieve their own aspirations. As we have seen, the objective is squarely in line with past policy, but some of the tactics represent a departure from the hardball negotiations that were standard fare for many years. With Bangladesh and Nepal, for example, the Modi government strengthened the previous government's willingness to look at their intertwined river basins on a trilateral basis rather than insist on a bilateral format in which India would have the overwhelming preponderance of bargaining power. Modi's formal speech to the South Asian Association for Regional Cooperation (SAARC) in November 2014 sketched out an enticing vision of a better connected region. He apparently hoped to counteract decades of suspicion in the region about their largest neighbor's intentions and the means it was using to achieve them.[4]

If China continues to expand its power in the Indian Ocean region and the smaller South Asian countries try to play China off against India, Modi's policy shift and India's greater prosperity will expand India's choices and improve its bargaining position. India can expand its economic enticements, broaden the regional approach and strengthen India's

ties around the periphery of the Indian Ocean, or return to hardball negotiations—or some combination of the three. Establishing the credibility of economic enticements gives these options greater strength. On the
other hand, the crisis in India-Nepal relations in late 2015, described in
chapter 12, suggests that India may still be quick to reach for tough tactics in cases where the China factor is in play.

INDIA'S APPROACH TO Pakistan is important both for its own sake and
in the context of China's expanding footprint in South Asia. At this
writing, Pakistan remains outside India's new regionalism. A few months
after taking office, the Modi government took a tough line toward
Pakistan, following the prescription favored by strategic analysts on the
hawkish side of the spectrum and in his own Hindu nationalist party.
The cancellation of India-Pakistan talks in August 2014 showed that India
plans to insist on controlling the terms of negotiation. The Modi government has said that curbing militant and terrorist activity by Pakistan
would be the minimum price for resuming serious discussions. India has
signaled that if this happened it might extend its economic outreach to
Pakistan. Its generous economic dealings with its smaller neighbors are
partly designed to offer Pakistan an example of the advantages better
relations with India could bring. It is too early to tell whether Modi's
surprise visit to Pakistan represents a "Nixon to China" moment.

But absent this kind of transformation in India-Pakistan ties, the
Modi government's approach to Pakistan, in contrast to its ability to expand its options in dealing with the rest of its South Asian neighbors, is
more likely to freeze or even worsen the India-Pakistan dispute than to
resolve it. This approach may be the most that the Modi government
considers feasible, but it leaves India open to provocations by spoilers
that could undo all its efforts in the region.

The worst-case scenario could be a new India-Pakistan conflict, resulting either from a miscalculation by one side or the other or from an
Indian response to terrorism coming from Pakistani territory. India lacks
good options for responding to this sort of provocation, especially given
the inevitable uncertainty about where Pakistan's nuclear "red lines"
lie. Potential military responses are uncomfortably poised between militarily meaningless actions, like disabling militant camps in Pakistan-
controlled territory, and moves that could risk nuclear war, such as attacks
on important military installations. Nor are the potential alternatives
to a military response well developed. India has accepted U.S. crisis

management help in the past, but looking to foreigners is always a tough call and would go down badly with some of Modi's political supporters. The possibility of conflict with Pakistan continues to be a "wild card" in India's future, the one contingency that in the worst case, if the two countries wound up in a nuclear war that neither one presently wants, could render meaningless the concept of regional primacy—and indeed the whole idea of security in the region.

Another challenge to India's regional security comes from the China-Pakistan connection. That relationship, as we have seen, has a long history, a tight connection to Pakistan's military and nuclear posture, and emotional resonance in both Beijing and Islamabad. Unsurprisingly, Pakistan has doubled down on this strategic relationship, which it has always used to support its rejection of India's claim to regional primacy. Chinese President Xi Jinping's April 2015 aid pledge was the largest aid commitment Pakistan has ever received by an order of magnitude. No quid pro quo was mentioned, but clearly this undertaking reflects heightened expectations on Beijing's part, and Pakistan would almost certainly try to meet them.

From China's strategic perspective, a certain level of India-Pakistan tension is useful, though Beijing has made clear on at least one occasion that it does not wish to see tensions turn into war.[5] Thus, India can expect no cooperation from China if it sets out to improve the tenor of India-Pakistan relations and has little to offer China that would change its approach. It can at most hope that China will quietly urge the Pakistanis to pull back from the brink, as China did following Pakistan's move into Kargil, in the Indian-controlled part of Kashmir, in 1999.

The best antidote to this Chinese strategy would be a serious peace overture between India and Pakistan. Taking such an initiative goes against the logic that usually guides India's negotiations with Pakistan, and such a policy change could only be made at the energetic insistence of the prime minister. The closest parallel was the overture toward Pakistan started by Prime Minister Atal Bihari Vajpayee in 1998, and restarted by him a few years after the Kargil conflict. Significantly, Vajpayee, India's only other prime minister from the Bharatiya Janata Party (BJP), was the subject of generous public admiration by Modi shortly before the 2014 election campaign. The trade initiative that was ripe for conclusion as Modi took office would be the obvious place to start. However, as Modi's first year in office ended, neither Modi's government nor the Nawaz Sharif government and its key army constituency in Pakistan had any appetite for the kind of diplomacy needed for peacemaking, let alone for the concessions that a deal would require.

China and India in East Asia

In Southeast and East Asia, unlike South Asia, China is already the largest regional power; the United States has played a traditional balancing role; and India has been deepening its involvement over the past three decades, but is still a much less powerful actor. India has been moving toward a policy of implicit balancing against China, especially under the Modi government. As we have seen, this policy involves an increasingly close and substantive Indian relationship with the United States. This includes close consultations on China and East Asia; growing economic and security ties with Australia and Japan; and increasing trade ties, including free trade areas, with ASEAN and Korea. It is supported by the strengthening of the Indian navy and growing U.S.-India naval ties.

The "Look East" policy of the early 1990s was the original vehicle for the vital economic part of this policy. The Modi government doubled down on this approach and gave it a new name: "Act East." Like its predecessors, the Modi government worked hard at improving ties with China at the same time, and these efforts, coupled with the fact that China had become India's largest partner for goods trade, permitted India to distance itself from any public acknowledgment that it was balancing its relations with the United States and China against one another.

If China's economy continues to surge, one can expect increasing Chinese pressure on countries in Southeast Asia to treat it as the preeminent power in that region. Indeed, there are indications that China is already moving down that path. China's unwillingness to look at the complex conflicting sovereignty claims in the South China Sea on a multilateral basis is a case in point—and an attitude that will be familiar to the architects of India's traditional policy in its own subregion. The "default response" from India would be to continue building up its relationships with countries active in China's neighborhood, including the United States, while denying any attempt to balance with other regional powers against China.

A Chinese economic slowdown might ease or postpone these pressures—or might lead China to take a more aggressive posture. In the first case, a strong Indian economic performance could provide opportunities to expand its footprint in the region. But this option cannot be created at the last minute: it would depend critically on Indian economic policy decisions made at least five years ahead of time. If, on the other hand, China chose to display its military muscle to distract attention from a faltering economy, finding the right response would require steady nerves and strong diplomatic ties in Southeast Asia and with the United States.

At first blush, in short, the environment in East Asia seems made to order for India's "strategic autonomy" approach. New Delhi seeks good relations with all powers active in the region, including both the United States and China, but aligns itself with none. India's regional security interests, however, are much closer to those of the United States and the rest of its de facto balancing coalition than to those of China. In particular, India shares with all these countries a desire not to have China emerge as the dominant power in Southeast and East Asia.

However, China is both a security challenge for India and an important economic partner, and it is in some respects a significant global partner as well. An example is their joint membership in BRICS. The question for Indian policymakers will be how much these other ties with China influence or constrain their choices. The idea behind India's concept of strategic autonomy is that, by avoiding excessive identification with any one powerful country, India can maximize its freedom of action. But in this case, India's desire to maintain an unstated balancing coalition for security purposes may come at a cost to its other equities with China, and vice versa.

POSSIBLE CHANGES IN THE U.S. GLOBAL ROLE

Indian strategic commentators also worry about the possibility of a reduction in the U.S. position in the world, and specifically in East Asia. New Delhi was uneasy with the "unipolar moment" that followed the Cold War because the United States was too powerful. At the same time, its quest for better relations with Washington came about *because* of U.S. power. A strong United States would help speed India's economic rise and facilitate India's move toward a larger footprint in global institutions. Especially in East Asia, it shared many of India's strategic interests and thus served as a tacit counterweight to China.

India and the United States spent the first decade and a half of this century trying to define their partnership in terms both were comfortable with. Given their very different global visions, especially the U.S.

concept of its leadership role and India's devotion to strategic autonomy, this effort remains a work in progress and is likely to continue to be so. For New Delhi it has, however, been premised on the United States remaining the single most powerful actor on the world scene and a critical player in the Indian Ocean and East Asia. India maintains an independent policy toward China and the East Asian countries, but it does so in the knowledge that the U.S. strategic approach is compatible with its own, especially on those points where India and China disagree. Indian policy also presupposes that Washington will continue to play a major role in East Asian security matters.

These common strategic interests color the way India and the United States deal with the other drivers of their relationship—the growing trade and investment ties, with their inevitable disputes, and the policy differences that run through many of their multilateral relationships, especially on trade. One especially tricky driver is the impact of the confidence each of them has in the moral superiority of its political systems. Both countries like to think of themselves as unique and as countries that have a right, even an obligation, to seek the good of mankind. An Indian journalist years ago commented to the authors that "we are two such preachy peoples." The self-righteousness that each (not incorrectly) perceives in the other has often been a handicap in the relationship.

If the United States remains economically vibrant and deeply engaged in Asia, and if it recovers some of the domestic political effectiveness of earlier years, it will exert a strong pull on Indian policymakers. But if it continues to struggle with such basics as passing a budget and funding its international policies, India may try to supplement its efforts to balance China with a kind of "insurance policy," in which it is less willing to count on Washington.

REDEFINING NONALIGNMENT AGAIN?

In the last two scenarios—a more aggressive Chinese posture in South and Southeast Asia, or a diminution in U.S. influence globally and especially in Asia—the response most in tune with India's vision and foreign policy history is to balance its regional and global relationships. The building blocks for such an "insurance policy" are already on display. India is cultivating economic and security ties with all the major actors in the Indian Ocean and Southeast Asia (except Pakistan); it plays up its relations with the United States when Chinese policy becomes more aggressive; it plays up its ties with the BRICS countries and strongly supports the Chinese-sponsored Asian Infrastructure Investment Bank, both to benefit from the bank's resources and to strengthen ties with Beijing in case Washington falters.

India may have trouble hedging against all possible contingencies. Hedging against the consequences of both potential U.S. weakness and disengagement and Chinese assertiveness at the same time would be hard to do effectively. If Russia opted to become more deeply involved in East and Southeast Asia, it would be an obvious participant in such a policy. However, Russia's biggest power moves have been in Europe, the Caucasus, and the Near East. Russian policymakers seem acutely aware that China has passed them in its ability to bring power to bear in East Asia, and a serious Asia policy would require resources that, for the present, Moscow would have difficulty mobilizing and be reluctant to spend.

India twice significantly redefined its nonalignment policy: in 1962, when it accepted military assistance from the United States and Britain after the Chinese invasion; and in 1971, when it signed an alliance with the Soviet Union a few months before the Bangladesh war. On both occasions, India perceived an acute threat to its security. The kind of scenario in which India might once again reconsider its basic orientation is more likely to come from an acute and specific crisis rather than the gradual evolution of global or regional trends.

Two potential examples involve China. One is deeper Chinese involvement in a future India-Pakistan war, as discussed previously. The other is water. Almost all the rivers that supply northern India as well as Pakistan and Bangladesh rise in Tibet. China is widely reported to be planning several hundred dams on the upstream end of several of these rivers. In November 2014, it inaugurated the first of six planned power stations at a large new dam in Tibet, on the upper reaches of the river known in India as the Brahmaputra. This generated a torrent of analytical commentary, with experts in China arguing that this was a run-of-the-river project that should not worry India, and observers in India divided between caution and alarm. Official commentary from Delhi was sparse. A 2010 statement by the then Indian foreign minister that he had been told the project would be "small" gave little reassurance to analysts who thought they saw a replay of the disingenuous communications India received from China before the 1962 war.[6] India and China have agreed to exchange hydrological information, which may help them manage future concerns about water flows. However, they have no agreement that places limits on China's use of these shared rivers or requires consultation before building new dams (unlike the situation with Pakistan, where the obligations of the two sides regarding the rivers they share are spelled out in the 1960 Indus Waters Treaty). This could be a potential danger point for a sudden and dramatic deterioration in India-China relations, with the possibility of upending how India thinks about regional primacy and pursues strategic autonomy. This is also an area where Pakistan's interests partly align with India's—both are lower riparians to China—but this fact does not alter the danger of an India-China confrontation.

WHAT KIND OF GLOBAL LEADERSHIP?

Leadership figures in the "common core" of India's foreign policy vision, the views that are widely shared across the political and intellectual spectrum. However, it is a very general vision of leadership: recognition of India's uniqueness, acknowledgment that India deserves a major role in the world, and an aspiration to have the architecture of global power accord India substantial weight. In the Indian foreign policy debate, discussions of leadership are longer on symbolic achievements—such as a permanent seat on the UN Security Council—than on the uses to which India would like to put a future leadership position.[7]

Historically, India has exercised leadership in two ways. It has sought to contribute ideas to the global debate, with nonalignment being the leading example. It has also been a leader in large groups of developing countries, such as the Non-Aligned Movement (NAM) and the G-77, groups that were in effect seeking to act as the opposition to a rich-country-dominated system. These groups won some modest substantive victories. One example was the creation of trade preferences for developing countries through the Generalized System of Preferences (GSP), in response to deliberations in the UN Conference on Trade and Development (UNCTAD) in the 1960s. In specific negotiations, such as the environmental negotiations discussed in chapter 10, these groups were able to block outcomes that India and its coalition partners opposed. But many of these victories were largely rhetorical. They did not fundamentally change the system.

India's negotiating style, as we saw in the last several chapters, fits in with this type of leadership role. It is more defensive than offensive, and better at blocking or delaying unwanted action than it is at forging ahead.

It has helped India avoid entangling alliances it did not want. In its "opposition" role, India did not need to do much heavy lifting to keep the members of these large developing country groups united on the broad goals being discussed. When the challenge of keeping a large group together became more onerous, India began doing its most important work with smaller and more manageable coalitions.

THUS FAR, BOTH INDIA'S foreign policy and its vision of the country's future role have emphasized India's pursuit of its own interests, largely though not exclusively as a solo player. Looking ahead, India may need to develop new forms of leadership. A speech by Indian Foreign Secretary S. Jaishankar in Singapore in July 2015 suggests that its concept of leadership may be changing. The speech focused on India's relations with the United States and China, and how they fit into the changing power dynamics in Asia. India aspired, he said, "to be a leading power, rather than just a balancing power." The next sentence got to the heart of the matter: "Consequently, there is also a willingness to shoulder greater responsibilities," Jaishankar said. In other words, he, and with him the Indian government, was focusing not just on the appearance of leadership but on the contribution expected of leaders.[8]

Especially if it seeks to establish itself as a powerful player throughout South and Southeast Asia, India will need to systematically cultivate a larger group of countries that are prepared to work with it on a long-term basis across Asia—or indeed across the globe. Modi's outreach to some of India's smaller neighbors has already, as we have seen, expanded India's options for attracting them as willing participants in regional initiatives built around India's leadership. Building up economic ties with the ASEAN countries might be the next opportunity.

To turn diplomatic outreach into an opportunity for leadership requires resources. Despite the pledge in Jaishankar's speech, this is likely to be the most important hurdle in India's way, should the country decide to move more strongly in this direction. For example, turning the Modi government's initiative into a more lasting bond with India's smaller neighbors could involve mobilizing either private or public sector investment and negotiating mutually favorable trade deals. This would represent a major change in the way Indian officials have approached trade negotiations in the past and would not come easily. Using India's economic assistance program as a vehicle for cultivating these countries would also probably require a further increase in both funding and capacity.

Another way to make leadership efforts credible and lasting is to embed them in institutions. One existing example is the Indian Ocean Naval Symposium (IONS), founded by the Indian naval chief in 2008 and consisting of Indian Ocean riparian countries that meet every other year. Strengthening India's leadership position in the wider Indian Ocean area would benefit by adding economic links to the navy-to-navy ones already underway. India's strength in humanitarian relief efforts, on display in the 2004 tsunami in Sri Lanka and Indonesia and the 2015 earthquake in Nepal, would similarly be a good complement to building up the kind of mutual benefit on which long-term regional leadership depends. This too, of course, requires resources. And the late 2015 crisis with Nepal is a reminder that, despite Modi's economic outreach, some of India's smaller neighbors still bridle at an approach they consider overbearing.

Another new institution is the planned BRICS Development Bank mentioned in chapter 10, although it may do more for China's leadership standing than India's. India already has impressive institutions in academia, management training, public health, and other fields that could be a springboard for a stronger global leadership role.

The idea of systematic and long-lasting cooperation with another country, especially a powerful one, is regarded with some suspicion by Indian foreign policymakers. The examples given here would not be particularly controversial, because they involve politically balanced groups of countries. But they would require a long-term effort at building a coalition that was intended to work, not just on a single issue in a single conference, but on a fairly wide range of issues. Coalition-building is certainly part of India's negotiating toolkit, but not a particularly comfortable part.

The bigger question is how a future Indian global leadership role would affect its relations with the world's most powerful countries. The moves that come most naturally to India, absent an overpowering threat to its core strategic interests, are hedging and balancing, with India avoiding becoming too entangled in any one relationship. Ultimately, however, if India embraces a global leadership role, it will no longer have the luxury of simply avoiding awkward choices: it may, more often than is now the case, need to choose close relationships and decide how much to invest in them.

SUMMING UP

Contemporary India's international aspirations, policies, and tactics form a rich tapestry. Four strands stand out especially strongly, shaping India's foreign policy visions and its government's style of negotiating. The first is exceptionalism. Consciousness of India's unique civilization and 5,000-year heritage has shaped the way Indian leaders think about their country and their expectations of how the world should treat it. India's foreign policy and international aspirations are not a transposition of ancient cultural habits into a modern setting, and while one can find cultural roots for occasional aspects of India's negotiating style, the impact of more recent history is more powerful. But recognizing the power of India's heritage is the starting point.

The drive for primacy in South Asia, central to India's foreign policy, its aspirations, and the way it negotiates with neighbors, is the second strand. It reflects the country's basic security needs, embedded in its geography, and has done so in one fashion or another going back both to India's distant history and to the strategic imperatives of the British Raj. Even Indian leaders remembered as idealists became realists when confronted with a challenge to their regional standing. Different governments have adjusted the way they pursue regional primacy and have shifted the way they define their danger signals; hardball negotiating tactics with India's neighbors have selectively given way to a gentler approach, but the goal is unchanged.

The other two strands are of more recent origin. Nonalignment was embedded in India's foreign policy DNA and its global aspirations by Nehru. As he originally conceived it, and as it has increasingly been interpreted by more recent governments, the real imperative is maximizing India's freedom of action, often articulated as "strategic autonomy." Nonalignment—avoiding entangling alliances—is a means to that end. It has been particularly important in shaping the way India negotiates with major powers, especially the United States.

The final strand is India's economic needs and its potential for economic power. In the early years of independent India, the economy was a constraint, and India's obligation to improve the life of an impoverished population was seen as a limitation on its global role. From the 1990s onward, the economy began to look like an opportunity and an emerging source of power. Expanding India's economic success has become a central feature of its foreign policy and, especially in the year since Modi took office, a critical part of its aspirations. Since the economic surge began, India has undertaken economic negotiations it never dreamed of before, including creating free trade areas, but has lost none of its determination to scrutinize carefully the impact on India's economic welfare and to maintain its strategic autonomy.

The visions that have competed to guide India's foreign policy have evolved with changes in the world, the region, and in India itself. "Nonalignment First" had its strongest influence in the early years; economic growth and the end of the Cold War gave birth to "Broad Power Realism"; and Modi's strong emphasis on economics is bringing in a new version of the "Hard Power Hawk" perspective, one that treats economics as a critical source of power. One can imagine further adjustments in the future: if India's outreach to Southeast Asia is successful, for example, the notion of India's regional role may adapt to include a stronger presence east of the subcontinent. Elements of the three competing visions continue to leave their imprint on policy.

These basic drivers have been remarkably persistent, however. Looking into an unknown future, the first two—exceptionalism and regional primacy—will surely remain guiding stars for India's foreign policymakers. Economic success will to a large extent determine the scale of India's global role. It could also have an impact on India's negotiating style, as India's policymakers and business leaders become more accustomed to India as a confident economic player.

Nonalignment and the drive for strategic autonomy will continue as a powerful heritage for policymakers. But of the four drivers, this one will pose the most difficult choices for India's future leaders. The world in which they will operate is increasingly integrated, economically and in many other ways. If India does pursue a bigger international leadership role, its policies will become more deeply interdependent with those of other countries. It will need to make choices that it has been able to avoid until now. It may in the end continue to see a solo role as its preferred international pathway. But the whole concept of autonomy, or maximizing one's options, is harder to define for countries playing a major role in a globalized world.

Notes

CHAPTER 1

1. Jawaharlal Nehru, *India's Foreign Policy: Selected Speeches September 1946–April 1961* (New Delhi: Publications Division, Ministry of Information and Broadcasting, 1961), pp. 13–15.

2. Lalit Mansingh, "Negotiating Bilaterally: India's Evolving Experience with the United States," in *American Negotiating Behavior*, edited by Richard H. Solomon and Nigel Quinney (Washington: United States Institute of Peace, 2011), p. 252.

3. Jawaharlal Nehru, *The Discovery of India* (New York: John Day, 1946), p. 44.

4. B. K. Nehru, *Nice Guys Finish Second* (New Delhi: Viking Penguin, 1997), p. 381.

5. Nehru, *The Discovery of India*, pp. 209–19.

6. Ainslie Embree, *Imagining India: Essays on Indian History* (Oxford University Press, 1989), pp. 13–18; from an essay first published in 1985.

7. Nehru, *The Discovery of India*, pp. 58–85.

8. Roger Boesche, *The First Great Realist: Kautilya and His Arthashastra* (Lanham, Md.: Lexington Books, 2002), pp. 79–89.

9. Vincent A. Smith, *The Oxford History of India*, 3rd edition, ed. Percival Spear (Oxford University Press, 1961), pp. 117–43.

10. Nehru, *The Discovery of India*, pp. 114–15.

11. Raymond Cohen, *Negotiating Across Cultures: International Communication in an Interdependent World* (Washington: United States Institute of Peace, 2004), p. 93.

12. Shashi Shekhar, "Narendra Modi's Foreign Policy Vision," *NitiCentral*, October 18, 2013 (www.niticentral.com/2013/10/18/narendra-modis-foreign

-policy-vision-147714.html); Narayan Lakshman, "Vasudhaivam Kutumbakam Is India's Philosophy," *The Hindu,* September 28, 2014 (www.thehindu.com /news/national/vasudhaiva-kutumbakam-is-indias-philosophy-modi/article 6453203.ece).

13. The central figure in the negotiations with the 560-plus princely states, Sardar Vallabhbhai Patel, is looked on by Prime Minister Modi and his party as a revered figure in India's history and the model for what national security leadership should be. The most comprehensive history of that process is V. P. Menon, *The Story of the Integration of the Indian States* (Calcutta: Orient Longman, 1956).

14. For a penetrating analysis of this phenomenon, see C. Raja Mohan, "Modernizing the Raj Legacy," *Seminar,* January 2012 (www.india-seminar .com/2012/629/629_c_raja_mohan.htm).

15. Jagat S. Mehta, *Negotiating for India: Resolving Problems through Diplomacy* (New Delhi: Manohar, 2006), pp. 36–37; Mohan, "Modernizing the Raj Legacy," *Seminar.*

16. Charles H. Heimsath and Surjit Mansingh, *A Diplomatic History of Modern India* (New Delhi: Allied Publishers, 1971), pp. 15–21.

17. Quoted in Coral Davenport and Ellen Barry, "India Emerges as Key Player in Paris Talks," *New York Times,* December 1, 2015, p. A5.

CHAPTER 2

1. The unchallenged power of the Royal Navy in the Indian Ocean meant that the Raj could safely ignore the security of its maritime boundaries. Independent India does not enjoy that advantage.

2. *Vital Speeches of the Day,* "The Pursuit of Peace," vol. 16, no. 2 (November 1, 1949), p. 48.

3. Jawaharlal Nehru, *India's Foreign Policy: Selected Speeches, September 1946–April 1961* (New Delhi: Publications Division, Ministry of Information and Broadcasting, 1961), p. 47.

4. Michael Brecher, *India and World Politics: Krishna Menon's View of the World* (New York: Praeger, 1968), p. 8. Interestingly, Brecher also cited Menon's view that nonalignment was "materially speaking, a weak man's policy. In a sense . . . it is like [Mahatma] Gandhi's non-cooperation. In his weakness he invented an instrument which was stronger than anything else."

5. Speech to the Indian Council on World Affairs, in Nehru, *India's Foreign Policy: Selected Speeches, September 1946–April 1961,* p. 42.

6. S. Gopal, *Jawaharlal Nehru: A Biography,* vol. 2, *1947–1956* (Harvard University Press, 1979), p. 139.

7. Michael Brecher, *Nehru: A Political Biography* (Oxford University Press, 1959), p. 566.

8. Speech at the Bandung Conference, April 1955, quoted in S. Gopal, *Jawaharlal Nehru,* vol. 2, p. 139.

9. S. Gopal, *Selected Works of Jawaharlal Nehru, Second Series,* vol. 1 (Harvard University Press, 1976), 440–43, cited in Gopal, *Jawaharlal Nehru,* vol. 2, p. 139 and pp. 145–47. See also Nehru's March 22, 1949 speech in which he

said, "We can be of far more service without [aligning ourselves with power blocs] and I think there is just a possibility . . . that at a moment of crisis our peaceful and friendly efforts might make a difference and avert that crisis." Nehru, *India's Foreign Policy: Selected Speeches, September 1946–April 1961*, p. 47.

10. Nehru, *India's Foreign Policy*, p. 589.

11. Quoted in A. N. Mukherjee, *Sino-Indian Relations and Communists* (Calcutta: Institute of Political and Social Studies, 1960), p. 1.

12. A suzerain is defined as a dominant state controlling the foreign relations of a vassal state, but allowing it sovereign authority in its internal affairs.

13. The Indians were particularly concerned about the impact of Washington's decision to deploy the U.S. Seventh Fleet to protect the Kuomintang regime on Taiwan from the threat of a Communist Chinese invasion. India was also troubled by Moscow's boycott of the UN Security Council following the council's unwillingness to transfer the Chinese seat there from the Chiang Kai-shek regime to the victorious communists.

14. The West was represented by Canada, the Soviet bloc by Poland.

15. Interestingly, the conference included representatives from some of the Soviet Central Asian republics. Neither Nehru nor any of his successors ever spoke out against Moscow's control over these areas. They accepted the myth that these Asian territories were integral and equal parts of the Soviet Union and did not regard them as colonies.

16. Letter to the chief ministers, April 26, 1954, quoted in Gopal, *Jawaharlal Nehru*, vol. 2, p. 191.

17. S. Gopal, *Jawaharlal Nehru*, vol. 2, p. 184.

18. Jawaharlal Nehru, *Letters to Chief Ministers*, vol. 3, *1947–64* (Oxford University Press, 1985), p. 324, letter of July 2, 1953.

19. As Nehru and many others foresaw, Pakistan did use the American arms against India, when the two countries went to war in 1965. Washington was unable to prevent this confrontation, but did cut off further arms shipments to Pakistan (and to India).

20. Other considerations also came into play. India's satisfaction with the U.S. position in the Suez crisis of 1956 and its discomfort with the simultaneous Soviet invasion of Hungary; its increasingly dire foreign exchange shortage; Washington's enhanced support for Indian economic development following the post-Stalin Soviet Union's offer of generous aid programs to India and other leading nonaligned powers; the increasingly troubling rumbles on the disputed Sino-Indian border; and what New Delhi correctly regarded as the Eisenhower administration's willingness to accept the legitimacy of nonalignment—all figured in the changing equation. The surprisingly warm personal relationship between Nehru and Eisenhower that developed during the prime minister's December 1956 visit to the United States also contributed to improved U.S.-India relations and to a more balanced Indian approach to nonalignment.

21. India and Pakistan occasionally raised broad proposals designed to break through their persistent enmity. Nehru suggested a no-war pact, which the Pakistanis rejected because it froze what was for them an unacceptable status quo in Kashmir without providing a satisfactory framework for resolving that dis-

pute. Pakistan President Ayub Khan, for his part, urged joint India-Pakistan defense arrangements to counter China. Nehru said this would imply forsaking India's nonalignment policy and rejected the offer.

22. These leaders included most notably Sukarno of Indonesia, Nasser of Egypt, Nkrumah of Ghana, and Tito of Yugoslavia. All but Tito, who led a European nation, had played prominent roles at Bandung.

23. Telegram to R. K. Nehru at Cairo, June 6, 1961. Cited in S. Gopal, *Jawaharlal Nehru: A Biography*, vol. 3, *1947–64* (Harvard University Press, 1984), p. 185.

24. The selection of participants was made at a preparatory conference in Cairo in June 1961. The Indians sought to define nonalignment broadly to include some of the European neutrals such as Sweden and Austria. As it turned out, all of the countries that participated were Asian or African, aside from Yugoslavia and Fidel Castro's Cuba. Three other Latin American countries sent observers.

25. It is worth noting, however, that in December 1961, the prime minister, under considerable political pressure at home and from third-world leaders, contributed to the demise of Western colonialism when—to the consternation of the West and the delight of many former colonial countries and communist ones—he sent Indian troops to liberate Goa from its Portuguese rulers. Nehru's Western critics saw this as another example of Indian hypocrisy.

26. Reflecting this concern, Nehru persuaded the conference to address letters to President Kennedy and Premier Khrushchev warning them of the danger of war. Nehru himself, accompanied by Indonesian President Sukarno, personally delivered the one to Khrushchev in Moscow.

27. Belgrade Declaration of the Heads of State and Government of Non-Aligned Countries, September 6, 1961.

28. For an excellent study of Nehru and the Belgrade Conference as viewed by U.S. Government officials, see Robert B. Rakove, *Kennedy, Johnson, and the Non-Aligned World* (Cambridge University Press, 2013), chap. 3.

29. The two sides also dispute a much smaller area along Tibet's border with the Indian state of Uttar Pradesh in the middle sector of the Himalayan range, but this region did not figure significantly in either the negotiations or the war.

30. Ashley J. Tellis, *India's Emerging Nuclear Posture* (Santa Monica, Calif.: Rand, 2001), p. 147.

31. The Indian government has never authorized the declassification of these messages. *Foreign Relations of the United States (FRUS)*, 1961–63, vol. XIX, South Asia, carries the text as it appears in S. Gopal. *Jawaharlal Nehru: A Biography*, vol. 3 (Harvard University Press, 1984), p. 229.

32. State Department telegram 2172, November 20, 1962, to New Delhi, *FRUS*, 1961–63, vol. XIX, South Asia.

33. S. Gopal, *Jawaharlal Nehru*, vol. 3, p. 229.

34. Ibid. Gopal cites a television interview of Nehru released November 8, 1962.

35. The conventional wisdom has long been that the Kremlin had concluded that it could not afford to oppose Beijing or threaten the unity of the world communist movement while the USSR and the United States confronted one another

in the Cuban missile crisis. (The missile crisis coincided with the Sino-Indian War.) More recently, some scholars have argued that Moscow's shift to a pro-Chinese position on the border issue predated the Cuban crisis and was prompted by ideology, not realpolitik. They cite Khrushchev's statement to the Chinese ambassador to Moscow just before the People's Liberation Army launched its attacks: the Chinese were the USSR's brothers and the Indians only its friends; if India attacked, the Soviet Union would stand by China; there is no place for neutrality. See, for example, Srinath Raghavan, *War and Peace in Modern India* (London: Palgrave Macmillan, 2010), pp. 302–03.

36. Note, for instance, Indian Foreign Secretary T. N. Kaul's unapologetic comment that it was "okay for the nonaligned to seek arms and assistance from countries willing to give it without strings, political or military, and without giving up a policy of nonalignment. See T. N. Kaul, *Ambassadors Need Not Lie* (New Delhi: Lancer International, 1988), p. 16.

37. After the cease-fire, Nehru suggested to the Kennedy administration that if the Chinese returned, India would agree to send her tactical aircraft into combat and the United States would undertake the defense of Indian cities. Washington turned down this proposal and suggested that the Indians approach the British, who also declined.

38. See Dennis Kux, *India and the United States: Estranged Democracies* (University Press of the Pacific, 1993), p. 154.

39. Department of State telegram 2329 to New Delhi, November 25, 1962, *FRUS*, 1961–63, XIX, document 211. The message was sent by President Kennedy.

40. For a detailed study of the negotiations, see Howard Schaffer, *The Limits of Influence: America's Role in Kashmir* (Brookings Institution Press, 2009), pp. 77–96.

41. Memorandum of Kennedy's conversation with Indian Ambassador Brij Kumar Nehru, December 17, 1962, *FRUS* 1961–63, vol. XIX, South Asia, p. 439.

42. Howard B. Schaffer, *Chester Bowles: New Dealer in the Cold War* (Harvard University Press, 1993), chap. 16, details the difficulties that developed between the United States and India. Bowles was ambassador to India from July 1963 to March 1969. Howard Schaffer was a political officer on his embassy's staff.

43. Indian Ministry of External Affairs, *Annual Report 1964–65*.

44. Indian Ministry of External Affairs, *Annual Report 1966–67*. The report offered no similar encomiums to the United States.

45. See P. N. Dhar, *Indira Gandhi, the "Emergency," and Indian Democracy* (Oxford University Press, 2000), p. 170. According to Dhar, who headed Prime Minister Gandhi's secretariat at the time, "Several key persons in the decisionmaking process in the foreign office and the prime minister's secretariat had expressed their doubts on the desirability of India entering into such an arrangement with the USSR. The prime minister herself had serious reservations. She was concerned about India's image as a leader of the Non-Aligned Movement." No doubt to assuage such misgivings, the treaty stated that "the

USSR respects India's policy of nonalignment and reaffirms that this policy constitutes an important factor in the maintenance of universal peace and international security and in the lessening of tensions in the world." For a more recent and more comprehensive account of the genesis of the treaty, see Srinath Raghavan, *1971: A Global History of the Creation of Bangladesh* (Harvard University Press, 2013), chap. 5.

46. For a good review of India's relations with its smaller neighbors, see Surjit Mansingh, *India's Search for Power* (New Delhi: Sage, 1984), pp. 262–315.

47. B. S. Das, the top Indian diplomat assigned to Sikkim at the height of the political crisis there, provides a fascinating firsthand account of events leading to the principality's becoming a state of the Indian Union. Krishna V. Rajan, ed., *The Ambassadors' Club: The Indian Diplomat at Large* (New Delhi: Harper-Collins, 2012), pp. 22–33, "Sunset for the Chogyal."

48. Kux, *India and the United States*, p. 337.

49. For an excellent summary of U.S. policy toward India during the Carter and subsequent Reagan administrations, see Thomas Perry Thornton, "American Interest in India under Carter and Reagan," *SAIS Review*, vol. 5, no. 1 (Winter–Spring 1985), pp. 179–190.

50. Desai had been forced out of office in July 1979. His replacement as prime minister, Charan Singh, another Janata Party leader, was unable to secure a parliamentary vote of confidence and headed a caretaker government that Mrs. Gandhi's Congress Party defeated in an election in January 1980.

51. Mansingh, *India's Search for Power*, p. 5.

52. These protests had some justification. Important items in the long list of military hardware that Washington supplied the Pakistanis were far more useful to them in confronting India than they were in containing Soviet aggression.

CHAPTER 3

1. See Indian Ministry of External Affairs, *Annual Report 1988–89*.

2. Although the government of Prime Minister Narendra Modi (elected 2014) was technically a coalition and included members of smaller parties allied with the Bharatiya Janata Party in the National Democratic Alliance, the BJP by itself held a majority of the seats in the Lok Sabha. But in its initial years this alliance did not hold a similar majority in the indirectly elected Rajya Sabha, Parliament's upper house. This situation may be remedied over time as fresh elections take place: one-third of the Rajya Sabha is chosen by the legislatures of the Indian states every two years. In any event, failure to secure a majority in the Rajya Sabha does not pose a threat to the government's ability to remain in power.

3. The BRICS countries are Brazil, Russia, India, China, and South Africa.

4. In making the decision to remain aloof, the Indians were moved importantly by their concern for the fate of the many Indian citizens working in Kuwait and Iraq. In 1990–91 the short-lived Chandra Shekhar government temporarily permitted the refueling of U.S. transport planes in India en route to the Persian Gulf, but withdrew this permission when it came under attack at

home. For a useful discussion of the way India grappled with the Iraq issue, see Rudra Chaudhuri, *Forged in Crisis* (London: Hurst, 2014), chap. 7.

5. In 1995, Prime Minister Narasimha Rao, who had earlier ordered the development of nuclear weapons, instructed the nuclear establishment to conduct a test. Preparations for the test were discovered by the Americans. Confronted by the United States, Rao called off the tests, in effect maintaining India's policy of nuclear ambiguity.

6. For an excellent discussion of the Indian decision to test, see C. Raja Mohan, *Crossing the Rubicon* (New Delhi: Viking, 2003), chap. 1.

7. One senior American diplomat who was not surprised was Frank Wisner, who had been ambassador to India during the first administration of President Clinton and had an unusually sharp understanding of Indian foreign policy imperatives. In an oral history statement recorded a couple of months before the explosions in the Rajasthan desert, Wisner presciently told his interviewer: "We've hoped that we could talk the Indians out of becoming a nuclear power. We can't do it. They won't accept it. They consider it essential to their national security and even more to their national pride." Oral History Statement of Ambassador Frank Wisner, recorded March 22, 1998, Association of Diplomatic Studies and Training, Frontline Diplomacy: Foreign Affairs Oral History Collection, U.S. Library of Congress (www.loc.gov/collections/foreign-affairs-oral -history/). Despite his pessimistic outlook, Ambassador Wisner played a major role in the first Clinton administration's effort to dissuade the Indians from going the nuclear weapons route.

8. The text of the June 4 joint communiqué is at www.fas.org/news/pakistan /1998/06/98060404_tpo.html.

9. The text of the June 6, 1998 resolution is at www.mofa.go.jp/mofaj/gaiko /naruhodo/data/pdf/data6-1.pdf.

10. Washington was particularly upset that Indian Foreign Secretary Raghunath, visiting there a week or so before the tests, had remained mum about them. The possibility that the foreign secretary was himself kept in the dark did not reduce senior American officials' ire. The Indians publicly denied the allegation made by the State Department spokesman that they had sought to mislead the United States.

11. The text of Vajpayee's letter as published in the *New York Times* is at www.nytimes.com/1998/05/13/world/nuclear-anxiety-indian-s-letter-to -clinton-on-the-nuclear-testing.html.

12. Since Vajpayee himself held the foreign affairs portfolio, Jaswant Singh played the role of de facto foreign minister.

13. Strobe Talbott, *Engaging India* (Brookings Institution Press, 2004), p. 78. Talbott's book is the best study of the Talbott-Singh negotiations as seen from the American side. Jaswant Singh's memoirs, *A Call to Honour: In Service of Emergent India* (New Delhi: Rupa, 2006), presents an authoritative Indian account. Interestingly, Talbott wrote the foreword to Singh's book.

14. The text of Vajpayee's September 28, 1998 speech is at http://asiasociety .org/india-usa-and-world-let-us-work-together-solve-political-economic-y2k -problem.

15. Talbott, *Engaging India*, p. 81.

16. Mohan, *Crossing the Rubicon*, p. 25.

17. The media reported that it was the first time senators had defeated a security-related pact since the Treaty of Versailles had been voted down eighty years earlier.

18. Singh, *A Call to Honour*, p. 264. Jaswant Singh, for his part, recalled later that in his talks with Talbott he was not aiming to reach a watershed in U.S.-India relations. He had sought, he told us in a February 2013 interview in New Delhi, "due and proper U.S. recognition of the reality of India and the potential for improved relations." He explained that this "reality" was that the United States and India were potentially natural allies, as Vajpayee had publicly stated at the time. Singh defined this to mean that U.S.-India relations should have enough substance to them to absorb the challenges that would naturally occur. Singh said he had the prime minister's support throughout the talks. Vajpayee had left the negotiations to him. He had found the parliamentary opposition difficult to deal with and spoke of them with contempt: they were ill-informed, used debates and parliamentary questions to embarrass him and the BJP, and frequently accused him of selling out Indian interests. He said he had "got used to it." (Authors' interview with Jaswant Singh, February 2013.)

19. See Howard B. Schaffer, *The Limits of Influence: America's Role in Kashmir* (Brookings Institution Press, 2009), pp. 156–65.

20. As the visits to the two countries were in the planning stage, the Indian embassy in Washington had tried to persuade the White House that Clinton should visit only India. Embassy officials later admitted to us that they had been mistaken: the sharp contrast between the ways Clinton dealt with the two countries dramatized the changed priorities in U.S. South Asia policy more powerfully than a visit to India alone could have.

21. The two countries designated 2014 as "the year of friendly exchanges" between them in observation of the sixtieth anniversary of their declaration of Panchsheel in the era of Sino-Indian good feelings.

22. These apprehensions appear to be shared by the Indian public. A 2014 Pew Research poll found that 72 percent of respondents believed that the Sino-Indian border dispute could lead to another conflict. See timesofindia.indiatimes.com/india/72-of-Indians-fear-border-issue-can-spark-China-war/articleshow/38397343.cms.

23. Beijing continues to annoy the Indians, too, by taking measures that demonstrate that it differentiates between Kashmiris and other Indian citizens. India rejects such actions.

24. This concern peaked immediately after the 1998 Indian nuclear tests, when at a summit meeting in China President Bill Clinton and Chinese President Jiang Zemin issued a lengthy joint statement on South Asia in which they declared their hope that the United States and China could "jointly and individually contribute to the achievement of a peaceful, prosperous, and secure South Asia." The complete text of the statement is at www.china-embassy.org/eng/zmgx/zysj/kldfh/t36228.htm.

CHAPTER 4

1. We are particularly indebted to Kanti Bajpai for his seminal work in distinguishing among the major schools of thought on India's foreign and security policy. Our categories are similar to his, but not identical, and we have chosen to focus on somewhat different features of them, but his was the pioneering work. It is particularly well expressed in "Indian Strategic Culture," in *South Asia in 2020: Future Strategic Balances and Alliances*, edited by Michael Chambers (Carlisle, Penn.: Strategic Studies Institute, 2002), pp. 245–304.

2. Amitava Tripathy, "Prospects of India Becoming a Global Power," *Indian Foreign Affairs Journal*, vol. 6, no. 1 (January–March 2011), pp. 58–69.

3. K. S. Bajpai, ed., *Democracy and Diversity: India and the American Experience* (Oxford University Press, 2007), p. xv.

4. See chapter 2 in this book; see also, for example, Michael Brecher, *India and World Politics: Krishna Menon's View of the World* (New York: Praeger, 1968), p. 326.

5. Sunil Khilnani et al., *Nonalignment 2.0: A Foreign and Strategic Policy for India in the Twenty-First Century*, National Defence College and Centre for Policy Research, New Delhi, 2012 (www.cprindia.org/sites/default/files/Non Alignment%202.0_1.pdf), p. iv.

6. Sumit Ganguly and Eswaran Sridharan, "The End of India's Sovereignty Hawks?" November 7, 2013 (www.foreignpolicy.com/articles/2013/11/07/the _end_of_indias_sovereignty_hawks_human_rights).

7. George Washington University, "India as a Global Power: Contending Views from India," conference held January 23, 2012; video files at www.rising powersinitiative.org/events/audiovideo-recordings/.

8. "The Last Word—Did U.S. Use Cash to Buy Congress Trust Vote?" CNN-IBN TV (http://ibnlive.in.com/news/the-last-word-did-cong-use-cash-to-buy -trust-vote/146399-3.html).

9. Jawaharlal Nehru, *India's Foreign Policy: Selected Speeches September 1946–April 1961* (New Delhi: Publications Division, Ministry of Information and Broadcasting, 1961), p. 25.

10. This figures prominently in George Tanham's classic *Indian Strategic Thought: An Interpretive Essay* (Santa Monica, Calif.: RAND National Defense Research Institute, 1992), pp. 23–24. See rand.org/pubs/reports/2007/R4207.pdf.

11. Barack Obama, Address to the Indian Parliament, *The Hindu*, November 8, 2010 (www.thehindu.com/news/national/article874394.ece).

12. Informal remarks by Ambassador Neelam Deo, Stimson Center, Washington, D.C., August 14, 2012.

13. Occasionally, India has tried to mobilize a UN committee to criticize Pakistan, but these are rare exceptions. One example was the complaint India lodged against Pakistan in the UN Security Council Sanctions committee on June 25, 2015; it will probably not be repeated soon, since China blocked any action by the committee. See Dr. Abdul Ruff, "UNSC Sanctions Committee Drops Indian Complaint against Pakistan over Lakhvi's Release," *Asian Tribune*, June 26, 2015 (www.asiantribune.com/node/87242).

14. See, for example, Inder K. Gujral, *Continuity and Change: India's Foreign Policy* (New Delhi: MacMillan and Ministry of External Affairs, 2003), pp. 20–22 and 36–38.

15. Nehru, *India's Foreign Policy: Selected Speeches September 1946–April 1961*, especially pp. 29, 42, 589; Mani Shankar Aiyar, remarks to conference on "India as a Global Power: Contending Views from India," George Washington University, Washington, D. C., January 23, 2012, video files at www.risingpowersinitiative.org/events/audiovideo-recordings/; Rajiv Sikri, *Challenge and Strategy: Rethinking India's Foreign Policy* (New Delhi: Sage, 2009), pp. 258–63; Gujral, *Continuity and Change*, especially pp. 24–28 passim.

16. Khilnani et al., *Nonalignment 2.0* (www.cprindia.org/sites/default/files/NonAlignment%202.0_1.pdf), p. 69.

17. Sikri, *Challenge and Strategy*, p. 189; Gujral, *Continuity and Change*, p. 26; see also Muchkund Dubey, *India's Foreign Policy: Coping with the Changing World* (New Delhi: Pearson, 2013), p. 3.

18. Sunil Khilnani, "India as a Bridging Power," paper presented at the Foreign Policy Centre, London, 2005, p. 9.

19. Gujral, *Continuity and Change*, p. 108; Aiyar, remarks to conference on "India as a Global Power," George Washington University, January 23, 2012, video files at www.risingpowersinitiative.org/events/audiovideo-recordings/; Dubey, *India's Foreign Policy*, pp. 50–58; Sikri, *Challenge and Strategy*, pp. 1–92.

20. See, for example, Sikri, *Challenge and Strategy*, pp. 139–43.

21. Sikri, *Challenge and Strategy*, pp. 105–11.

22. This is especially well described in Sikri, *Challenge and Strategy*, pp. 220–33.

23. Aiyar, remarks to conference on "India as a Global Power," George Washington University, January 23, 2012.

24. This came out clearly in a presentation on India's approach to economic development aid by Dr. Sachin Chaturvedi of the Research and Information System for Developing Countries, a New Delhi think tank, at a seminar hosted by the Asia Foundation on "Asian Approaches to Development Cooperation," Washington, D.C., April 23, 2013.

25. Admiral Raja Menon and Rajiv Kumar, *The Long View from Delhi: To Define the Indian Grand Strategy for Foreign Policy* (New Delhi: ICRIER, 2010); and Rajiv Kumar and Santosh Kumar, *In the National Interest: A Strategic Foreign Policy for India* (New Delhi: Business Standard, 2010).

26. See, for example, C. Raja Mohan, "India's Strategic Future: Why India Needs to Move from 'Strategic Autonomy' to Strategic Cooperation with the United States," November 4, 2010 (www.foreignpolicy.com/articles/2010/11/04/indias_strategic_future).

27. Kumar and Kumar, *In the National Interest*, p. 13, 34–44.

28. C. Raja Mohan, *Crossing the Rubicon* (New Delhi: Viking, 2003), pp. 27, 58.

29. Mohan, *Crossing the Rubicon*, p. 260.

30. Radha Kumar, "Back to Reality, India's National Interests and Multilateralism," The Stanley Foundation, February 2014.

31. Kumar and Kumar, *In the National Interest*, p. 13.

32. Mohan, *Crossing the Rubicon,* pp. 142–72.

33. See, for example, Prem Shankar Jha, *Crouching Dragon, Hidden Tiger: Can China and India Dominate the West?* (New York: Soft Skull Press, 2010).

34. C. Raja Mohan and Ajai Sahni, *India's Security Challenges at Home and Abroad*, NBR Report No. 39 (Seattle: National Bureau of Asian Research, March 2012), pp. 45–46.

35. Rajiv Kumar and Santosh Kumar, *In the National Interest*, p. 15–16; Menon and Kumar, *The Long View from Delhi*, p. 44.

36. Radha Kumar, "Back to Reality."

37. Kumar and Kumar, *In the National Interest*, p. 14.

38. See, for example, the admiring reference to Mao's dictum that a rising China should not exercise leadership, in Mohan, *Crossing the Rubicon*, p. 153.

39. Sanjaya Baru, *Strategic Consequences of India's Economic Performance* (New Delhi: Academic Foundation, 2006), especially pp. 29–57.

40. Baru, *Strategic Consequences of India's Economic Performance*, pp. 76–77. Chinese scholars have applied this calculation to India and concluded that China's power outweighs India's by 4:1. Authors' interviews in Shanghai and Beijing, May 2011.

41. For a masterful discussion of some of the early episodes in India's campaign to integrate former princely states, see Srinath Raghavan, *War and Peace in Modern India* (London: Palgrave MacMillan, 2010), chaps. 2–5.

42. See, for example, Bharat Karnad, *India's Nuclear Policy* (Westport, Conn.: Praeger, 2008), pp. 5–7.

43. Speech to conference on "India as a Global Power," George Washington University, Washington, D.C., January 23, 2012.

44. Brahma Chellaney, "The Forgotten Nuclear Deal," *Japan Times*, posted July 20, 2015 (chellaney.net).

45. Brahma Chellaney, "World's Geopolitical Center of Gravity Shifts to Indian Ocean," *Nikkei Asian Review*, posted July 1, 2015 (http://chellaney.net /2015/07/01/worlds-geopolitical-center-of-gravity-shifts-to-indian-ocean/).

46. Bharat Karnad, "Republicans Better for India," *Indian Express*, October 19, 2012 (newindianexpress.com/opinion/article1305812.ece).

47. B. Raman, "Pakistan: Thus Far and No Further," *Raman's Strategic Analysis* (blog), December 3, 2008 (ramanstrategicanalysis.blogspot.in/2008 _12_03_archive.html).

48. Karnad, *India's Nuclear Policy*, pp. 124–25.

49. Bharat Karnad, "BJP Rajnath's Wrong Steps," *Security Wise* (blog), July 22, 2013 (bharatkarnad.com/2013/07/22/bjp-rajnaths-wrong-steps/).

50. See, for example, Bharat Karnad, "China Respects Hard Power," *Indian Express*, September 7, 2012 (newindianexpress.com/opinion/article602025 .ece).

51. Sanjaya Baru, "The Singh Doctrine," *Indian Express*, November 6, 2013 (www.indianexpress.com/news/the-singh-doctrine/1191321/0); see also Indrani

Bagchi, "Manmohan Singh Outlines His Own Take on Panchsheel," *Times of India*, November 5, 2013 (articles.timesofindia.indiatimes.com/2013-11-05 /india/43693495_1_indian-subcontinent-indian-foreign-policy-indian -economy).

52. Interview with authors, February 2013.

53. Runa Das, "Strategic Culture, Representations of Nuclear (In)Securities, and the Government of India: A Critical Constructivist Perspective," *Asian Journal of Political Science*, vol. 17, no. 2 (August 2009), pp. 136–39.

54. Private roundtables with authors at the Institute for Peace and Conflict Studies, New Delhi, and at Gateway House, Mumbai, February 2013.

55. Besides the sources specifically noted, material in this chapter draws on the authors' experience as U.S. diplomats; on our interviews in January and February 2013 with Lalit Mansingh, Yashwant Sinha, Jaswant Singh, Geoffrey Pyatt, Kishan Rana, and K. S. Bajpai; and on interviews with groups of younger scholars at Gateway House, Mumbai, and the Institute for Peace and Conflict Studies, New Delhi.

56. J. N. Dixit, *Makers of India's Foreign Policy: Raja Ram Mohun Roy to Yashwant Sinha* (New Delhi: HarperCollins, 2004). Dixit was high commissioner in Sri Lanka as the island's ethnic conflict was in crisis, and he was remembered there for his high-pressure approach, including air-dropping supplies in the mainly Tamil north against the express request of the Sri Lankan government. (See chapter 12.)

CHAPTER 5

1. The Ministry of External Affairs (MEA) recently moved part of its operations to an attractive newly built red sandstone structure named for Prime Minister Nehru about a half mile from its South Block headquarters. But all top officials remain at South Block and can be counted on to do their utmost to avoid being shifted away from that symbolic seat of power.

2. The others are the ministers of Defense, Finance, and Home Affairs.

3. After Nehru, several prime ministers concurrently served as their own ministers of external affairs, all for relatively short periods. Three prime ministers had headed MEA before later attaining the PM position.

4. For an excellent account of the foreign policy workings of the Prime Minister's Office during Manmohan Singh's first government (2004–09), see Sanjaya Baru, *The Accidental Prime Minister: The Making and Unmaking of Manmohan Singh* (New Delhi: Penguin/Viking, 2014). Baru served in the PMO as Manmohan Singh's media adviser during his first term.

5. The American practice of awarding ambassadorships to major political figures and campaign contributors is rarely found in India. Some IFS officers are asked upon retirement to stay on as ambassadors to major countries and are technically "politically appointees." But there are at most only a small handful of noncareer diplomats, including some politicians and a few retired military or senior civil service officers, who have served as chiefs of Indian missions abroad.

6. See this chapter's section on the Indian Administrative Service for statistics that illustrate the difficulty in passing the exam.

7. These and subsequent statistics in this chapter are drawn from the *Annual Report of the Ministry of External Affairs 2013–14* (http://mea.gov.in/Uploads /PublicationDocs/23873_EXTERNAL_AFFAIR__Eng__AR_2013-14.pdf), supplemented by information supplied by an IFS officer familiar with the recruiting process.

8. A lesser "B Branch" of the IFS includes some 250 officials who hold diplomatic rank as first or second diplomatic secretaries. But they are outside the service's main career ladder and cannot ordinarily aspire to its more senior positions. They and other professionals such as legal and treaties specialists and interpreters usefully fill out the sides of the IFS pyramid.

9. American scholar Daniel Markey, now at the Johns Hopkins School of Advanced International Studies in Washington, presents strong arguments for expansion of the IFS in "Developing India's Foreign Policy 'Software,'" *Asia Policy*, no. 8 (July 2009), pp. 73–96.

10. "Inside the Indian Foreign Service," in *Foreign Service Journal*, journal of the American Foreign Service Association, Washington, D.C., October 2002. For a more recent, insightful Kishan Rana critique, see his article "The Indian Foreign Service: The Glass Gets Fuller," in *Foreign Service Journal*'s June 2014 issue.

11. Interviews with authors, February 2013. This number does not include those senior officers who voluntarily retired from the service after they had been passed over for foreign secretary and other top positions.

12. Three IFS women officers have become foreign secretary. Only one woman has held independent charge of MEA as foreign minister, the incumbent Sushma Swaraj, a prominent leader in the Bharatiya Janata Party (BJP). Indira Gandhi held the position twice when she was prime minister.

13. Authors' interviews, especially with Kishan Rana, February 2013.

14. The IFS does not count assignment to the Indian mission to the United Nations as service in the United States.

15. Conversation, New Delhi, February 2013.

16. Authors' interviews with IFS officer involved in management, 2013 and 2014; Ministry of External Affairs, organizational chart (http://mea.gov.in /Images/pdf/MEAOrganogram_January_29_2015.pdf).

17. See, for example, Dr. Subash Kapila, "India's National Security council—A Critical Review," South Asia Analysis Group, May 10, 2000 (www .southasiaanalysis.org/paper123#sthash.LhpUOpmA.dpuf), and Amitabh Mattoo, "Securing India—It is time the national security architecture was overhauled," *The Telegraph*, January 28, 2010 (www.telegraphindia.com/1100128 /jsp/opinion/story_12031858.jsp).

18. All five national security advisers to date have been men.

19. The officials who have held the NSA position are Brajesh Mishra (1998–2004), J. N. Dixit (2004–05), M. K. Narayanan (2005–10), Shivshankar Menon (2010–14), and the incumbent, Ajit Doval, who took over following the accession of BJP leader Narendra Modi as prime minister in May 2014. Mishra, Dixit, and Menon had been senior IFS officers; Dixit and Menon both became

foreign secretaries and Mishra held the powerful position of principal secretary (PS) to the prime minister concurrently with his role as the first NSA before the NSA/PS position was bifurcated in 2004 on his retirement. All three had headed diplomatic missions in countries crucial to Indian interests. Narayanan and Doval were members of the Indian Police Service who had risen to become Intelligence Bureau chiefs.

20. Mishra is something of an exception. After retiring from the Foreign Service and serving for several years with the United Nations, he joined the BJP and became close to its leader, Atal Bihari Vajpayee. When Vajpayee became prime minister in 1998 he appointed Mishra India's first NSA (as well as his principal secretary). Mishra thereupon resigned from the party.

21. Number cited by retired NSA Shivshankar Menon, in Brookings Institution, "India's Role in the World: A Conversation with Shivshankar Menon, Washington, D.C., October 7, 2014." Transcript is on the Brookings website (www.brookings.edu/~/media/events/2014/10/07%20india%20role/20141007 _menon_india_transcript.pdf).

22. Brookings Institution, "India's Role in the World: A Conversation with Shivshankar Menon."

23. The IAS is one of three "All India Services." The others are the much smaller but important Indian Police Service (which we have seen is a recruiting pool for national security advisers and intelligence chiefs) and the Indian Forest Service.

24. The Indian fiscal year April 1, 2012–March 31, 2013.

25. Statistics drawn from the Annual Report of the Government of India Ministry of Personnel, Public Grievances, and Pension for 2013/14 (http:// persmin.gov.in/AnnualReport/AR2013_2014(Eng).pdf). IAS officers are also recruited into the service by promotion from the civil services of the Indian states, ordinarily much later in their careers. These officers typically do not reach the higher echelons of administration.

26. The only IAS position as such in MEA is that of financial adviser.

27. For a study of career progressions in the IAS, see John-Paul Ferguson and Sharique Hasan, "Specialization and Career Dynamics: Evidence from the Indian Administrative Service," *Administrative Science Quarterly*, vol. 58, no. 2 (June 2013), pp. 233–56 (http://asq.sagepub.com/content/early/2013/04/11 /0001839213486759.full.pdf+html).

28. Chandra also served with great distinction as India's ambassador to the United States in the late 1990s during the Kargil crisis. In retirement he chaired a blue-ribbon committee that made suggestions about the organization of the Indian armed forces. (The recommendations were subsequently ignored by the governments of Manmohan Singh and Narendra Modi.)

29. The International Institute for Strategic Studies, *The Military Balance 2015* (London: Routledge, 2015), pp. 247–53.

30. As an alternative to the three-year term, the chairman may hold the position until the time he reaches age sixty-two, whichever comes first.

31. Ashley Tellis, *India's Emerging Nuclear Posture: Between Recessed Deterrent and Ready Arsenal* (Santa Monica, Calif.: Rand, 2001), p. 284.

32. At the same time, the chiefs of the three military services enjoy considerable autonomy over their own internal affairs, such as operation planning, threat assessments, force structure, and staffing responsibilities. Coordination between the services on these matters is far more limited than in the U.S. system.

33. For an excellent recent discussion of Nehru's attitude toward the Indian Army and his concern about a military coup, see Steven I. Wilkinson, *Army and Nation: The Military and Indian Democracy since Independence* (Harvard University Press, 2015), chap. III, "Protecting the New Democracy."

34. Authors' conversation with a U.S. Defense Department official, July 2013.

35. Nitin Pai, "The Case for Military Diplomacy," Centre for Land Warfare Studies (CLAWS), April 19, 2011 (www.claws.in/561/the-case-for-military -diplomacy-nitin-pai.html).

36. The Parliamentary Standing Committee on Defense, an all-party body, has joined many other critics in calling for the designation of a single chief of defense staff (Wilkinson, *Army and Nation*, p. 155). The committee argued that many leading democracies had adopted the system without harm to their civilian leadership.

37. The earliest of these was the appointment by Prime Minister V.P. Singh in 1989 of a Committee on Defense Expenditure headed by Arun Singh, former minister of state for defense, ostensibly to rationalize military spending but actually to conduct a comprehensive inquiry into the entire defense setup. No action was taken on the committee's report and its recommendations were never disclosed. There followed the appointment by the BJP-led Vajpayee Government of a Kargil Committee chaired by the highly regarded retired IAS strategic guru K. Subrahmanyam, which filed its report in 1999 (http:// nuclearweaponarchive.org/India/KargilRCB.html), and a broader and more comprehensive follow-up study prepared by a Group of Ministers Committee, also Vajpayee-appointed, in 2001 (http://pib.nic.in/archieve/lreleng/lyr2001 /rmay2001/23052001/r2305200110.html). A third commission headed by Naresh Chandra submitted its report in 2012. The report was never publicized or acted on, but like the earlier studies, it is believed to have included the creation of a single chief of defense staff among its recommendations. For an excellent study of reform efforts over the years, see Anit Mukherjee, "Failing to Deliver: Post-Crises Defence Reforms in India, 1998–2010" (New Delhi: Institute for Defence Studies and Analyses), Occasional Paper No. 18, 2011.

38. Indian Parliament, "Parliamentary Committees" (http://www.parliamen tofindia.nic.in/ls/intro/p21.htm). In discussions in New Delhi, we often found that MPs were more likely to be more impressed by committee activities than were foreign policy practitioners and political commentators.

39. Even less powerful are the Indian Parliament's consultative committees. These committees are chaired by ministers and have been accurately dismissed by one keen observer of the parliamentary scene as "talking shops" (Inder Malhotra, conversation with the authors, New Delhi, March 2013).

40. Krishna Bose, *An Outsider in Politics* (New Delhi: Penguin, 2008), pp. 164–65.

41. Parliamentary questions can be "starred" (requiring oral replies) or "unstarred" (receiving written answers).

42. Rama Lakshmi and Emily Wax, "India's Government Wins Parliament Confidence Vote," *Washington Post,* July 23, 2008, www.washingtonpost.com /wp-dyn/content/article/2008/07/22/AR2008072200161.html.

43. National Security Advisory Board (www.nsab.gov.in/).

CHAPTER 6

1. Jagat S. Mehta, *Negotiating for India: Resolving Problems through Diplomacy* (New Delhi: Manohar, 2006).

2. See, for example, Sunil Khilnani, "India as a Bridging Power," paper presented at the Foreign Policy Centre, London, 2005, p. 15; see also Michael Brecher, *India and World Politics: Krishna Menon's View of the World* (New York: Praeger, 1968), p. 8, and Charles H. Heimsath and Surjit Mansingh, *A Diplomatic History of Modern India* (New Delhi: Allied Publishers, 1971), p. 61.

3. The culture of frugality does not prevent official corruption; indeed, the fact that officials receive much of their official compensation in kind, in the form of official housing and transportation, means that ill-gotten gains, when they exist, can be more easily hidden from public view.

4. Nandan Nilekani, one of India's premier software entrepreneurs and the architect of the pathbreaking national identity card system India put in place in 2009, went one step further and applied the name to a makeshift vehicle cobbled together in parts of the north Indian countryside. Nilekani, *Imagining India: The Idea of a Renewed Nation* (New York: Penguin, 2009), p. 450.

5. K.S. Bajpai, ed., *Democracy and Diversity: India and the American Experience* (Oxford University Press, 2007), p. xv.

6. Stephen P. Cohen, *India: Emerging Power* (Brookings Institution Press, 2001), pp. 84–91; Richard H. Solomon, *Chinese Negotiating Behavior* (Washington: United States Institute of Peace, 2005), pp. 57–71.

7. M. Rama Rao, "Political Parameters, Guiding Principles for Resolving India-China Border Dispute," *Asian Tribune,* April 12, 2005 (www.asiantribune .com/news/2005/04/12/political-parameters-guiding-principles-resolving-india -china-border-dispute).

8. Mehta, *Negotiating for India,* pp. 81–82.

9. Chester Bowles, *Ambassador's Report* (New York: Harper & Brothers, 1954), p. 199; Dean Acheson, *Present at the Creation* (New York: W. W. Norton, 1969), p. 355.

10. Interview with authors; comment on the AIDS designation issue is from Teresita Schaffer's personal experience.

11. See, for example, R. S. Misra, *The Philosophical Foundations of Hinduism: The Vedas, The Upanisads, and the Bagavadgita: A Reinterpretation and Critical Appraisal* (New Delhi: Munshiram Manoharlal Publishers, 2002), esp. pp. 1–18.

12. See Ainslie Embree, *Imagining India: Essays on Indian History* (Oxford University Press, 1989), pp. 13–14.

13. In the Indian languages, different words are used for the large caste groups and these more occupational categories, but the two are not altogether separate. Some of these occupational ties reinforce the ritual purity status that gave birth to the caste system.

14. A useful discussion of the dynamics of upward mobility for groups can be found in Ashutosh Varshney, *Battles Half Won: India's Improbable Democracy* (New Delhi: Penguin, 2013), chap. 7. Among the mechanisms that bring this mobility about, he cites "Sanskritization," or adoption of practices more characteristic of higher-status groups; Westernization, which starts with learning English; and, interestingly, entrepreneurship—including entrepreneurship by sub-castes, who would previously have been considered too high status to engage in such activities. As one might expect, however, this is not a linear process. A social scientist who had studied marriage patterns among call center workers in Bangalore told the authors that a surprisingly large number of them opt for traditional arranged marriages so as not to strain ties with their families. Anand Giridharadas recounts a similar example in *India Calling* (New Delhi: Fourth Estate, 2011), p. 69.

15. Rodney W. Jones, "India's Strategic Culture," paper prepared for Defense Threat Reduction Agency, Advanced Systems and Concepts Office, Comparative Strategic Cultures Curriculum, October 31, 2006 (www.fas.org/irp/agency /dod/dtra/india.pdf), p. 4.

16. C. Raja Mohan, *Crossing the Rubicon: The Shaping of India's New Foreign Policy* (New Delhi: Viking, 2003), p. 260.

17. This solidarity was shared only up to a point by other parts of the Indian government. Press and private comments included a certain amount of gloating over the supposedly snobbish Foreign Service receiving its comeuppance—a reaction that will sound familiar to many countries' diplomats whose friends at home believe they are living the high life.

18. Skeptics include George K. Tanham, *Indian Strategic Thought: An Interpretive Essay* (Santa Monica, Calif.: RAND, 1992); and Rodney W. Jones, "India's Strategic Culture." On the other side of the debate are Sunil Khilnani et al., *Nonalignment 2.0: A Foreign and Strategic Policy for India in the Twenty-First Century*, National Defence College and Centre for Policy Research, New Delhi, 2012 (www.cprindia.org/sites/default/files/NonAlignment%202.0_1.pdf); Rajiv Kumar and Santosh Kumar, *In the National Interest: A Strategic Foreign Policy for India* (New Delhi: Business Standard, 2010); and Admiral Raja Menon and Rajiv Kumar, *The Long View from Delhi: To Define the Indian Grand Strategy for Foreign Policy* (New Delhi: ICRIER, 2010).

19. Mehta, *Negotiating for India*, pp. 29–30; Jagat S. Mehta, *Rescuing the Future: Bequeathed Misperceptions in International Relations* (New Delhi: Manohar, 2008), pp. 224–27.

20. This chapter draws on the authors' experience as diplomats and on interviews with Lalit Mansingh, Jaswant Singh, Yashwant Sinha, Nancy Powell, Meera Shankar, Leslie Haydon, K. Shankar Bajpai, Naresh Chandra, C. Raja

Mohan, Walter Andersen, Karan Bhatia, Susan Schwab, Carla Hills, Frank Wisner, and Geoffrey Pyatt, as well as several other serving officials between October 2012 and March 2015.

CHAPTER 7

1. S. Amer Latif, "U.S.-India Military Engagement: Steady as They Go" (Washington: CSIS, 2012), pp. 1–2.

2. Dennis Kux, *India and the United States: Estranged Democracies 1941–1991* (University Press of the Pacific, 2002), pp. 204–7. S. Gopal's summary of the two letters is included in *Foreign Relations of the United States 1961–1963,* Volume XIX, South Asia, document 203, November 19, 1962. The FRUS entry notes that the Indian government has not declassified the original messages. (See also chapter 2.) See also Rudra Chaudhuri, *Forged in Crisis: India and the United States since 1947* (London: Hurst, 2014), pp. 81–100; B. K. Nehru, *Nice Guys Finish Second* (New Delhi: Viking/Penguin Books India, 1997), p. 404.

3. Charles H. Heimsath and Surjit Mansingh, *A Diplomatic History of Modern India* (New Delhi: Allied Publishers, 1971), pp. 470ff; Howard B. Schaffer, *Chester Bowles: New Dealer in the Cold War* (Harvard University Press, 1993), pp. 244–45; Olson, "Indo-U.S. Military Cooperation," thesis submitted to the National Defence College, New Delhi, 1993.

4. A Military Assistance Program continued for three more years after the 1962 effort, but this ended with the India-Pakistan War of 1965, and military cooperation remained extremely limited until the end of the Cold War. See Olson, "Indo-U.S. Military Cooperation."

5. Authors' interviews with U.S. and Indian current and former defense officials, February 2013 and July–August 2013; Col. Steven B. Sboto, U.S. Army, *India and U.S. Military Cooperation and Collaboration: Problems, Prospects, and Implications,* thesis submitted to the National Defense College, New College, New Delhi, 2001; Olson, "Indo-U.S. Military Cooperation," pp. 43–50; Brig. Anil Chait, VSM, "From Estrangement to Engagement: Threats and Opportunities in Indo-U.S. Relations and the Roles of their Armed Forces," USAWC Strategy Research Project, March 6, 2006.

6. Olson, "Indo-U.S. Military Cooperation," pp. 43–50.

7. At the time, Indian Prime Minister Narasimha Rao held the defense portfolio. Since it would have been inappropriate under Indian practice for him to sign as the counterpart to a defense minister, the task fell to Chavan.

8. Col. Steven Sboto, "Indo-U.S. Military Cooperation: Taking Stock," *FAO Journal,* December 2003 (www.zoominfo.com/CachedPage/?archive_id =0&page_id=818481703&page_url=//www.faoa.org/journal/sboto1203.html &page_last_updated=2009-01-19T08:48:43&firstName=Steven&lastName =Sboto).

9. "New Framework for the U.S.-India Defense Relationship," June 28, 2005 (www.rupe-india.org/41/app5.html).

10. Siddharth Varadarajan, "U.S. cables show grand calculations underlying 2005 defence framework," *The Hindu,* March 28, 2011 (www.thehindu.com

/news/the-india-cables/us-cables-show-grand-calculations-underlying-2005 -defence-framework/article1576796.ece).

11. U.S. Department of Defense, "Framework for the U.S.-India Defense Relationship," June 3, 2015 (www.defense.gov/pubs/2015-Defense-Framework .pdf); PTI, "India, U.S. Ink New Defence Framework Accord," *Economic Times*, June 3, 2015 (economictimes.indiatimes.com/news/defence/india-us-ink -new-defence-framework-accord/articleshow/47532025.cms).

12. This section draws on the authors' experience as diplomats as well as on interviews with Col. Steven Sboto and Col. Russell Olson, former defense attachés in New Delhi; Adm. (ret) Sureesh Mehta, former Chief of Naval Staff; Commodore Uday Bhaskar, Indian Navy; Claudio Lilienfeld and Christopher Clary, former Defense Department officials; A. Peter Burleigh, former U.S. charge d'affaires in New Delhi; Cara Abercrombie, Defense Department official; Peter Lavoy, former Deputy Assistant Secretary of Defense; and unpublished writings by these and other former officials of both countries.

13. U.S. Department of Defense, news transcript, September 20, 2013 (www .defense.gov/transcripts/transcript.aspx?transcriptid=5313).

14. In one example, the Light Combat Aircraft that India started working on in 1983 was first formally inducted into the air force order of battle thirty years later, in 2013. Authors' experience in the U.S. State Department.

15. See, for example, the 2011 statement by India's Defense Minister A. K. Antony at a naval summit in 2011, in Sujan Datta, "India Takes on Ocean-Cop Role, Tests China," *The Telegraph,* Calcutta, October 13, 2011 (www.telegraph india.com/1111013/jsp/frontpage/story_14618394.jsp).

16. Richard F. Grimmett, "Arms Sales: Congressional Review Process," Congressional Research Service, February 2012, p. 1 (www.fas.org/sgp/crs/weapons /RL31675.pdf).

17. The issue was a newly enacted requirement that a country purchasing nuclear fuel from the United States maintain safeguards on all its nuclear facilities. As is explained in detail in chapter 8, India was unwilling to institute these "full-scope safeguards." The retroactivity of this requirement is what led to the charge of unreliability.

18. Interview with authors, April 30, 2013.

19. "India Buys New Artillery 27 Years after Bofors," New Delhi Television (NDTV), May 11, 2012 (www.ndtv.com/article/india/india-buys-new-artillery -guns-27-years-after-bofors-209582).

20. Neeraj Chauhan, "CBI names former air chief Shashi P. Tyagi in Agusta kickbacks scandal," *Times of India*, February 26, 2013 (http://timesofindia .indiatimes.com/india/CBI-names-former-Air-chief-Shashi-P-Tyagi-in -Agusta-kickbacks-scandal/articleshow/18682556.cms?referral=P).

21. Offset refers to purchases by the supplier company from related industries in India. The normal offset requirement is 30 percent of the value of the contract.

22. S. Amer Latif, "U.S.-India Defense Trade: Opportunities for Deepening the Partnership" (Washington: CSIS, 2012); Ministry of Defence, Government of India, *Defense Procurement Procedures 2013: Capital Procurement.*

23. Latif, "U.S.-India Defense Trade," pp. 15–16.

24. This account was recounted by one of the U.S. participants. Ironically, one country that did fall afoul of both these stipulations was Pakistan, whose 1990 purchase of F-16s was blocked before shipment when the United States imposed sanctions over Pakistan's nuclear program in October of that year. The United States also refused to refund Pakistan's initial payments for the planes, on the grounds that the U.S. government no longer had the money, having passed it on to General Dynamics. About a decade later, under pressure of a lawsuit by the Pakistani government, the U.S. government found a way to refund the money. Five years after 9/11, the United States approved a new sale of F-16s to Pakistan.

25. Statement by U.S. Assistant Secretary of State for Political-Military Affairs Andrew Shapiro, quoted in Andrea Shalal-Esa, "U.S. Aims to Expand India Arms Trade by 'Billions of Dollars,'" Reuters, April 18, 2013 (www .reuters.com/article/2013/04/18/us-usa-india-weapons-idUSBRE93H10B 20130418).

26. One interesting example is Adm. Walter Doran and Indian Adm. Arun Prakash, who had been classmates at the Indian Defence Services College in 1979, and who were, respectively, U.S. Commander of the Pacific Fleet and Commander of the Indian Navy a quarter century later at the time of the Indian Ocean tsunami. Their relationship undoubtedly contributed to the smooth functioning of the pioneering U.S.-India cooperation on tsunami relief. Latif, "U.S.-India Military Engagement," p. 1.

27. "U.S. Admiral caught in ministry protocol for appointments," *Rediff News*, June 26, 2013 (www.rediff.com/news/report/us-admiral-caught-in-ministry -protocol-for-appointments/20130626.htm); Sandeep Unnithan, "Lone Dissenter," *India Today*, April 9, 2011 (http://indiatoday.intoday.in/story/defence -minister-a-k-antony-reins-in-military-ties-with-the-us/1/134697.html).

28. In addition to the sources cited in individual footnotes, material in this section draws on the authors' interviews with Adm. (ret) Sureesh Mehta, former Chief of Naval Staff; Commodore Uday Bhaskar, Indian Navy; Capt. (ret) Kenneth Spurlock, USN, former chief, Office of Defense Cooperation, U.S. Embassy New Delhi; Leslie Hayden, U.S. Embassy, New Delhi; Col. (ret) Woolf Gross, former Assistant U.S. Army Attaché, New Delhi, and former Northrop Grumman official; Claudio Lilienfeld, Vikram Singh, and Christopher Clary, former U.S. Defense Department officials; Cara Abercrombie and S. Amer Latif, U.S. Defense Department officials; Peter Lavoy, former Deputy Assistant Secretary of Defense; and unpublished writings by these and other former officials of both countries.

29. US Code Title 22, chap. 39, subchap. IIIA, sec. 2785.

30. See, for example, "Hillary Clinton Did the Best She Could Do," *Rediff India*, July 25, 2009 (http://news.rediff.com/report/2009/jul/24/hillary-clinton -did-the-best-she-could-do.htm).

31. "Hillary Clinton Did the Best She Could Do," Rediff India; Press Trust of India, "EUM with U.S. Enhances India's Access to Best Tech: Gov," *Economic Times*, August 6, 2009 (http://articles.economictimes.indiatimes.com /2009-08-06/news/28436651_1_defence-policy-end-user-monitoring-india).

32. "Factsheet on U.S.-India Accord on End-Use Monitoring," *Stagecraft and Statecraft* (blog), July 22, 2009 (http://chellaney.net/2009/07/22/factsheet-on-u -s-india-accord-on-end-use-monitoring/).

33. "PM's Statement in the Lok Sabha," July 29, 2009, Prime Minister's Office (http://archivepmo.nic.in/drmanmohansingh/pmsinparliament.php?nodeid=39).

34. U.S. Department of Defense, news transcript, September 20, 2013.

35. In addition to the sources cited in individual footnotes, material in this section draws on the authors' interviews with Commodore Uday Bhaskar, Indian Navy; Capt. (ret) Kenneth Spurlock, USN, former chief, Office of Defense Cooperation, U.S. Embassy New Delhi; A. Peter Burleigh, former U.S. charge d'affaires, New Delhi; Theodore Osius, former political counselor, U.S. Embassy, New Delhi; Leslie Hayden, U.S. Embassy, New Delhi; Col. (ret) Woolf Gross, former Assistant U.S. Army Attaché, New Delhi, and former Northrop Grumman official; Claudio Lilienfeld, Vikram Singh, and Christopher Clary, former Defense Department officials; Cara Abercrombie and S. Amer Latif, Defense Department officials; Peter Lavoy, former Deputy Assistant Secretary of Defense; and unpublished writings by these and other former officials of both countries.

CHAPTER 8

1. Treaty on the Non-Proliferation of Nuclear Weapons (NPT), U.S. Department of State (www.state.gov/t/isn/trty/16281.htm). The cutoff date is in Article IX of the treaty.

2. Interview with authors, February 2013. See also chapter 3.

3. Negotiations for the CTBT in the United Nations Conference on Disarmament were completed in 1996; see chapter 10 for an account of the negotiations leading to India's initial decision not to sign. The United States sought India's signature on the treaty, both for its own sake and in order to strengthen political support for the treaty in the United States.

4. Jaswant Singh, *A Call to Honour: In Service of Emergent India* (New Delhi: Rupa, 2006), pp. 354–80; authors' interview with Jaswant Singh; Strobe Talbott, *Engaging India: Diplomacy, Democracy, and the Bomb* (Brookings Institution Press, 2004), pp. 223–32. See also chapter 3.

5. U.S. Department of State/Bureau of International Information Programs (IIP), "U.S.-India Joint Statement on High Technology Commerce," November 13, 2002 (http://iipdigital.usembassy.gov/st/english/texttrans/2002/11/2002 1114143509pkurata@pd.state.gov0.4453089.html#axzz3eBPauuk6).

6. U.S. Department of Commerce, "Statement of Principles for U.S.-India High Technology Commerce," February 5, 2003 (www.bis.doc.gov/index.php /policy-guidance/india-high-technology-trade/11-policy-guidance/462 -statement-of-principles-for-u-s-india-high-technology-commerce).

7. "Next Steps in Strategic Partnership," quoted at GlobalSecurity.org (www .globalsecurity.org/military/world/india/nssp.htm).

8. The American connections continued. Jaishankar subsequently became Indian ambassador in Washington and then foreign secretary.

9. Interestingly, Indians consider this to be a hallmark of U.S. negotiators. Jaswant Singh wrote that he found Americans excessively fond of checklists and determined not to agree to anything until everything was agreed; see *A Call to Honour*, pp. 298–99.

10. "Announcement on U.S.-India Next Steps in Strategic Partnership, September 2004," U.S. Department of State/IIP (http://iipdigital.usembassy.gov/st /english/texttrans/2004/09/20040917190916ndyblehs0.9136316.html#axzz 3eBPauuk6).

11. Dinshaw Mistry, *The U.S.-India Nuclear Agreement: Diplomacy and Domestic Politics* (Cambridge University Press, 2014), pp. 44–46.

12. Office of the Spokesman, U.S. Department of State, "Background Briefing by Administration Officials on U.S.-South Asian Relations," March 25, 2005.

13. White House Press Release, Office of the Press Secretary, "Joint Statement by President George W. Bush and Prime Minister Manmohan Singh," July 18, 2005 (http://2001-2009.state.gov/p/sca/rls/pr/2005/49763.htm).

14. "PM's Statement on U.S. Visit in Parliament," July 29, 2005, Prime Minister's archives (http://archivepmo.nic.in/drmanmohansingh/pmsinparliament .php?nodeid=12).

15. The composition of the witness roster on the U.S. Senate side was influenced by the committee's anger at being blindsided by the announcement. One of the authors was invited to testify at a subsequent hearing—and was then disinvited because the committee had decided only to allow one nonofficial witness who favored the agreement. Information on the hearings is from the website of the Senate Foreign Relations Committee, Hearing on U.S.-Indian Nuclear Energy Cooperation: Security and Nonproliferation Implications, Wednesday, November 2, 2005 (www.foreign.senate.gov/hearings/us-indian-nuclear-energy -cooperation-security-and-nonproliferation-implications).

16. Reuters, "FACTBOX: U.S.-India Nuclear Deal Business Potential," October 2, 2008 (www.reuters.com/article/2008/10/02/nuclear-india-usa-idUSSP 5726420081002).

17. Mistry, *U.S.-India Nuclear Agreement*, p. 158.

18. International Atomic Energy Agency, Board of Governors, "Resolution on Implementation of the NPT Safeguard Agreement in the Islamic Republic of Iran," September 24, 2005, Board of Governors document GOV 2005/77; "IAEA Votes against Iran," *The Hindu*, September 24, 2005 (www.hindu.com /2005/09/25/stories/2005092516950100.htm).

19. Mistry, *U.S.-India Nuclear Agreement*, provides further detail on the internal debate within the U.S. government; see, for instance, pp. 45–66.

20. White House, "U.S.-India Joint Statement, President's Visit to India and Pakistan," March 2, 2006 (http://georgewbush-whitehouse.archives.gov/news /releases/2006/03/20060302-5.html); "President, Prime Minister Singh Discuss Growing Strategic Partnership," Hyderabad House, New Delhi, press conference transcript, March 2, 2006 (http://georgewbush-whitehouse.archives.gov /news/releases/2006/03/20060302-9.html); U.S. State Department archives, "Press Briefing in India, R. Nicholas Burns, Under Secretary of State for Politi-

cal Affairs, Maurya Sheraton Hotel, March 2, 2006 (http://2001-2009.state.gov
/p/us/rm/2006/62424.htm).

21. "PM's Suo-Motu Statement on Discussions on Civil Nuclear Energy Cooperation with the U.S.: Implementation of India's Separation Plan," March 7,
2006, Prime Minister's archives (http://archivepmo.nic.in/drmanmohansingh
/pmsinparliament.php?nodeid=24). For text of Indian separation plan, see IAEA
Information Circular, INFCIRC 731, "Communication dated 25 July 2008 received from the Permanent Mission of India concerning a document entitled
'Implementation of the India-United States Joint Statement of July 18, 2005:
India's Separation Plan.'"

22. "U.S. Congressmen Attack India's Relations with Iran, Link This to Nuclear Deal," *The Hindu*, May 6, 2007 (www.hindu.com/2007/05/06/stories
/2007050604280800.htm).

23. Mistry, *U.S.-India Nuclear Agreement*, p. 96.

24. H.R. 5682 (109th): Henry J. Hyde United States-India Peaceful Atomic
Energy Cooperation Act of 2006, Public Law 109-401 (www.govtrack.us
/congress/bills/109/hr5682). The key requirements and prohibitions are in Sections 104 and 106 of the legislation.

25. The website of the U.S. Department of Energy, National Nuclear Security
Administration, lists twenty-four agreements. "123 Agreements for Peaceful Nuclear Cooperation" (http://nnsa.energy.gov/aboutus/ourprograms/nonproliferation
/treatiesagreements/123agreementsforpeacefulcooperation).

26. For a summary of the required subjects, see the website of the Arms Control Association, "U.S. Atomic Energy Act Section 123 at a Glance" (www
.armscontrol.org/factsheets/AEASection123).

27. This and other references to the text refer to "Agreement for Cooperation
between the Government of the United States of America and the Government
of India concerning Peaceful Uses of Nuclear Energy (123 Agreement)," in Department of State Media Note 2007/658, August 3, 2007 (http://2001-2009
.state.gov/r/pa/prs/ps/2007/aug/90050.htm).

28. Cole J. Harvey, "The U.S.-India Reprocessing Agreement and Its Implications," Nuclear Threat Initiative, May 5, 2010 (www.nti.org/analysis/articles
/us-india-agreement-implications/).

29. "Indian Team Extends Washington Stay," *The Hindu*, July 21, 2007
(www.hindu.com/2007/07/21/stories/2007072156521600.htm).

30. Some of the best examples included "'Breakthrough' in Nuclear Deal," *The
Hindu*, July 22, 2007 (www.hindu.com/2007/07/22/stories/2007072258300100
.htm); T. S. Subramanian, "India Insisted on Fuel for Reactors' Lifetime," *The
Hindu*, July 23, 2007 (www.hindu.com/2007/07/23/stories/2007072359891200
.htm); Siddharth Varadarajan, "123 Fulfills Prime Minister's Assurances," *The
Hindu*, July 24, 2007 (www.hindu.com/2007/07/24/stories/2007072457750100
.htm).

31. "NDA Briefed on Nuclear Agreement," *The Hindu*, July 27, 2007
(www.hindu.com/2007/07/27/stories/2007072750560100.htm). The NDA refers to the coalition of parties led by the BJP that was in the parliamentary
opposition.

32. Siddharth Varadarajan, "Nuclear Deal Is Satisfactory, Says Kakodkar," *The Hindu*, July 28, 2007 (www.hindu.com/2007/07/28/stories/2007072 859660100.htm); and "Between the Lines of Kakodkar-speak, Support for the Nuclear Deal," *The Hindu*, July 28, 2007 (www.hindu.com/2007/07/28/stories /2007072862431400.htm).

33. "PM's Statement in the Lok Sabha on Civil Nuclear Energy Cooperation with the United States," August 13, 2007, Prime Minister's archives (http:// archivepmo.nic.in/drmanmohansingh/pmsinparliament.php?nodeid=30).

34. "India Begins Talks with IAEA on Nuclear Deal," *The Hindu*, November 22, 2007 (www.hindu.com/2007/11/22/stories/2007112262451400 .htm).

35. IAEA Information Circular 754, "Agreement between the Government of India and the International Atomic Energy Agency for the Application of Safeguards to Civilian Nuclear Facilities," May 29, 2009.

36. Mistry, *U.S.-India Nuclear Agreement*, pp. 166–70.

37. Press Trust of India, "India to Begin Talks with the IAEA Today," *Business Standard*, February 25, 2008 (www.business-standard.com/article/economy -policy/india-to-begin-talks-with-iaea-in-vienna-today-108022501015_1.html).

38. Vinay Kumar, "India will not be a source of proliferation, says Pranab," *The Hindu*, September 6, 2008 (www.thehindu.com/todays-paper/india-will-not -be-a-source-of-proliferation-says-pranab/article1333011.ece); Siddharth Varadarajan, "NSG Lifts Sanctions on India," *The Hindu*, September 7, 2008 (www .thehindu.com/todays-paper/nsg-lifts-sanctions-on-india/article1333454.ece).

39. "H.R. 7081 (110th): United States-India Nuclear Cooperation Approval and Nonproliferation Enhancement Act," Public Law 110-268, text available at www.govtrack.us/congress/bills/110/hr7081.

40. Annie Gowen and Steven Mufson, "Is the India Nuclear Agreement Really the 'Breakthrough Agreement' Obama Promised?" *Washington Post*, February 4, 2015 (www.washingtonpost.com/world/is-the-india-nuclear-agree ment-really-the-breakthrough-obama-promised/2015/02/04/bc0b0dd2-abc1 -11e4-8876-460b1144cbc1_story.html).

41. The negotiating history in this chapter draws on the authors' interviews with Nicholas Burns, Kenneth Juster, Ashley Tellis, Richard Stratford, Geoffrey Pyatt, Leslie Hayden, David Mulford, Shyam Saran, Naresh Chandra, and several other serving and former officials in both governments who were involved in the nuclear negotiations.

CHAPTER 9

1. This principle is enshrined in the original Articles of Agreement of the General Agreement on Tariffs and Trade, Article XVIII, but has been put into practice in a wide variety of international economic agreements.

2. USAID *Green Book*, U.S. Overseas Loans and Grants, 2012 edition (http:// gbk.eads.usaidallnet.gov/data/detailed.html).

3. Dennis Kux, *India and the United States: Estranged Democracies 1941– 1991* (University Press of the Pacific, 2002), p. 79; Rudra Chaudhuri, *Forged in*

Crisis: India and the United States since 1947 (London: Hurst, 2014), pp. 43–46.

4. Kux, *India and the United States*, p. 79–82; Chaudhuri, *Forged in Crisis*, pp. 65–69; Howard B. Schaffer, *Chester Bowles: New Dealer in the Cold War* (Harvard University Press, 1993), pp. 252–53.

5. Schaffer, *Chester Bowles*, pp. 253–34.

6. Kux, *India and the United States*, p. 240–47; Schaffer, *Chester Bowles*, pp. 279–80; Raymond E. Vickery Jr., *The Eagle and the Elephant: Strategic Aspects of U.S.-India Economic Engagement* (Washington, D.C.: Woodrow Wilson Center Press, 2011), pp. 216–17; B. B. Krupadanam, "U.S. Food Aid to India and Its Implications," *Indian Journal of American Studies*, vol. 14, no. 2 (1984), pp. 169–83.

7. Inder Malhotra, *Indira Gandhi: A Personal and Political Biography* (London: Hodder and Stoughton, 1989), p. 95.

8. Kux, *India and the United States*, p. 247–60; Schaffer, *Chester Bowles*, pp. 280–82.

9. Schaffer, *Chester Bowles*, p. 284.

10. Krupadanam, "U.S. Food Aid to India and Its Implications."

11. Kux, *India and the United States*, pp. 257 and 247.

12. Daniel Patrick Moynihan and Steven R. Weisman, *Daniel Patrick Moynihan; A Portrait in Letters of an American Man of Public Affairs* (New York: Public Affairs, 2010), pp. 291–92, 296. Extracts from Moynihan's letters and diaries, edited by Weisman and published posthumously.

13. Moynihan and Weisman, *Daniel Patrick Moynihan*, p. 325.

14. Teresita Schaffer conversation with Gopi Arora, June 1991; "At a Glance—India and the IMF," International Monetary Fund (www.imf.org /external/country/ind/rr/glance.htm).

15. Teresita C. Schaffer, "U.S. Engagement in Indian Health Care: What Is the Impact?" A Report of the CSIS Global Health Policy Center, Washington, D.C., November 2010, p. 8.

16. Schaffer, "U.S. Engagement in Indian Health Care," pp. 11–12.

17. Teresita Schaffer, "Polio Eradication in India: Getting to the Verge of Victory—and Beyond?" Report of the CSIS Global Health Policy Center, Washington, D.C., January 2012.

18. Schaffer, "U.S. Engagement in Indian Health Care"; Schaffer, "Polio Eradication in India"; author's conversations with Dr. Robert Bollinger, Johns Hopkins University; Public Health Foundation of India workshop on U.S. engagement in India's health sector, New Delhi, March 2010; author's experience as health attaché at the U.S. Embassy in New Delhi, 1977–79.

19. "Asian Approaches to Development Cooperation," conference hosted by The Asia Foundation, Washington, D.C. April 23, 2013 (http://asiafoundation .org/media/collection/123/1/asian-perspectives-asian-approaches-to); authors' interview with Shyam Saran, Chairman, RIS, February 2013.

20. Websites of FICCI (http://ficci.com/about-ficci.asp); CII (www.cii.in /about_us_History.aspx?enc=ns9fJzmNKJnsoQCẏKqUmaQ); and NASSCOM (www.nasscom.in/vision-and-mission).

21. The official Indian government website "Indian Image," (http://indiaimage
.nic.in/pmcouncils/tic/noti1.htm), lists the founding members.

22. TNN, "Ratan Tata Softens Stand on Radia Tapes," *Times of India*, August 23, 2014 (http://timesofindia.indiatimes.com/india/Ratan-Tata-softens
-stand-on-Radia-tapes/articleshow/15609905.cms); TNN, "2G Case Accused
Raja Admits He Met Radia, Ratan Tata," *Times of India*, July 8, 2014 (http://
timesofindia.indiatimes.com/india/2G-case-accused-Raja-admits-he-met
-Radia-Ratan-Tata/articleshow/37979998.cms); Dhananjay Mahapatra, "Centre Cites 2G Probe, Radia Links to Oppose Gopal Subramaniam's Appointment
as SC Judge," *Times of India*, June 20, 2014 (http://timesofindia.indiatimes
.com/india/Centre-cites-2G-probe-Radia-links-to-oppose-Gopal
-Subramaniams-appointment-as-SC-judge/articleshow/36852561.cms); "2G
PMLA Case: Former Telecom Minister A Raja, Kanimozhi, and others put on
trial," *DNA India*, October 31, 2014 (www.dnaindia.com/india/report-2g-pmla
-case-former-telecom-minister-a-raja-mp-kanimozhi-and-others-put-on-trial
-2030818).

23. "Federal Advisory Committees Act," P.L. 92-463 as amended, website
of the General Services Administration, U.S. Government (www.gsa.gov/portal
/content/100916).

24. Ambassador Michael B. G. Froman, "The 2014 Special 301 Report," U.S.
Trade Representative, Washington, D.C., April 30, 2014. The title of the report
refers to Section 182 of the Trade Act of 1974, as amended by the Omnibus
Trade and Competitiveness Act of 1988 and the Uruguay Round Agreements Act
(19 U.S.C.§ 2242).

25. Sneha Shankar, "India Says It Will Not Participate in a US Investigation
of Intellectual Property Rights Violations," *India Business Times*, May 2, 2014
(www.ibtimes.com/india-says-it-will-not-participate-us-investigation
-intellectual-property-rights-1579339); Manoj Kumar, "India to Fight U.S.
Trade Probes, Ready for Fight at WTO," Reuters, February 25, 2014 (www
.reuters.com/article/2014/02/25/us-india-trade-usa-idUSBREA1O0MH
20140225); "India not to accept any probe on IPR by the US: Anand Sharma,"
Economic Times, May 2, 2014 (http://economictimes.indiatimes.com/news
/economy/policy/india-not-to-accept-any-probe-on-irp-by-the-us-anand
-sharma/articleshow/34543402.cms); Pramit Pal Chaudhuri, "Modi card helped
India fend off U.S. trade sanctions," *Hindustan Times*, May 1, 2014 (www
.hindustantimes.com/business-news/modi-card-helped-india-fend-off-us-trade
-sanctions/article1-1214505.aspx); Ambassador Michael Froman, "The 2014
Special 301 Report and India," May 1, 2014, USTR (www.ustr.gov/about-us
/press-office/blog/2014/April/The-2014-Special-301-Report-and-India); "USTR
Releases Annual Special 301 Report," April 30, 2015, USTR (https://ustr.gov
/about-us/policy-offices/press-office/press-releases/2015/april/ustr-releases
-annual-special-301).

26. U.S. Department of Agriculture, "Questions and Answers: Importing Indian Mangoes to the United States," APHIS Factsheet, April 2007 (www.aphis
.usda.gov/publications/plant_health/content/printable_version/faq_imp_indian
_mango.pdf).

27. Gavin Rabinowitz, "U.S., India trade mangoes for motorcycles," *Miami Herald*, April 14, 2007 (www.bilaterals.org/?us-india-trade-motorcycles-for).

28. Peyton Ferrier, Everett Petersen, and Maurice Landes, "Specialty Crop Access to U.S. Markets: A Case Study of Indian Mangoes," U.S. Department of Agriculture, Economic Research Report 142, November 2012 (www.ers.usda .gov/media/955332/err142.pdf).

29. Export Import Data Bank, Department of Commerce, Government of India (http://commerce.nic.in/eidb/default.asp).

30. Author's interview with Karan Bhatia, October 22, 2014.

31. U.S. Department of Transportation, "India, U.S. Sign Open Skies Aviation Agreement," press statement, April 14, 2005 (http://2001-2009.state.gov/e /eeb/rls/prsrl/2005/44623.htm); "United States, India Sign Open Skies Aviation Agreement," transcript of Mineta remarks, Arrive Safe, April 14, 2005 (http:// www.arrivesafe.org/united-states-india-sign-open-skies-aviation-agreement/).

32. The discussion of trade negotiations draws on the authors' experience and on interviews with former USTRs Susan Schwab and Carla Hills, former USTR officials Karan Bhatia and Claudio Lilienfeld, former Indian Commerce Secretary Rahul Khullar, and current Indian and U.S. officials (all in 2013).

33. Marie-France Houde, Senior Economist, Investment Division, OECD Directorate for Financial and Enterprise Affairs, "Novel Features in Recent OECD Bilateral Investment Treaties," chap. 6 in *International Investment Perspectives* (Paris: OECD, 2006), pp. 176–78 (www.oecd.org/daf/inv/internationalinvestm entagreements/40072428.pdf); U.S. model BIT text, U.S. Department of State, April 2012 (http://www.state.gov/documents/organization/188371.pdf). This discussion of BIT negotiations also draws on the authors' interviews with current and former U.S. and Indian government officials.

34. Amiti Sen and Deepshika Sikarwar, "Talks with U.S. on for BIPA-like Trade Treaty," *Economic Times*, February 15, 2008 (http://articles.economic times.indiatimes.com/2008-02-15/news/27734232_1_national-treatment -bilateral-investment-foreign-investments).

35. Indira Kannan, "Long Way to Go for India-US Investment Treaty, Says Kirk," *Business Standard*, October 5, 2011 (www.business-standard.com/article /economy-policy/long-way-to-go-for-india-us-investment-treaty-says-kirk -111100500073_1.html); Ministry of Commerce and Industry, Government of India, "India-US Bilateral Investment Treaty Discussions Nearly Complete: Anand Sharma," press release, September 21, 2011 (http://commerce.nic.in /pressrelease/pressrelease_detail.asp?id=2824).

36. With a "most favored nation" clause, the host country promises to give the other country's investors terms as favorable as other treaty partners. With "national treatment," investors receive terms no less favorable than local nationals in its treaties. India normally grants national treatment with restrictions rather than the open-ended undertaking the U.S. sought.

37. U.S. Department of State, "2012 U.S. Model Bilateral Investment Treaty" (www.state.gov/documents/organization/188371.pdf).

38. "U.S. Seeks Strong Investor Protection Rules in Bilateral Pact," *Economic Times*, January 29, 2013 (http://articles.economictimes.indiatimes.com/2013

-01-29/news/36616049_1_investor-protection-bilateral-investment-treaty
-energy-sector); "U.S. in Talks with India on Bilateral Investment Treaty," *Times of India*, March 3, 2012, reproduced at (www.bilaterals.org/?us-in-talks-with
-india-on).

39. Shashank Kumar, "India Loses White Industries Arbitration," *International Law Curry*, February 9, 2012 (http://ilcurry.wordpress.com/2012/02/09
/india-loses-white-industries-bit-arbitration/); Jonathan Choo, "India under the Bilateral Investment Treaty Arbitration Spotlight," *Singapore International Arbitration Blog*, March 3, 2012 (http://singaporeinternationalarbitration.com
/2012/05/03/india-under-the-bilateral-investment-treaty-arbitration-spotlight
/); Ashish Goel, "India-US Investment Treaty Going Nowhere," *East Asia Forum*, August 31, 2013 (www.eastasiaforum.org/2013/08/31/india-us-bilateral
-investment-treaty-going-nowhere/). A senior Finance Ministry official told one of the authors in February 2014 that India would under no circumstances agree to a provision that would allow an arbitration proceeding to supersede the judgment of an Indian court.

40. "India Puts Conditions for Bilateral Investment Treaty with the US," *Economic Times*, July 23, 2013 (http://articles.economictimes.indiatimes.com
/2013-07-23/news/40749425_1_investment-treaty-protection-agreement
-bilateral-investment-promotion).

41. White House, "U.S.-India Joint Statement," September 27, 2013 (www
.whitehouse.gov/the-press-office/2013/09/27/us-india-joint-statement).

42. White House, Office of the Press Secretary, "U.S.-India Joint Statement," September 30, 2014 (www.whitehouse.gov/the-press-office/2014/09/30/us-india
-joint-statement).

43. Government of India, Model Bilateral Investment Treaty, released May 5, 2015 (https://mygov.in/sites/default/files/master_image/Model%20Text%20
for%20the%20Indian%20Bilateral%20Investment%20Treaty.pdf).

44. World Bank Group, "Doing Business: Measuring Business Regulations," 2014 (www.doingbusiness.org/rankings); World Bank "exploring economy" data on India (www.doingbusiness.org/data/exploreeconomies/india/).

45. Briefing for business group by senior Indian tax official, February 12, 2014.

46. Tata press release, October 3, 2008 (www.tata.com/article/inside
/7VqcQt58pCw=/TLYVr3YPkMU=). See also PTI, "Tata Group Leaves Singur Behind," *Economic Times*, October 28, 2014 (http://articles.economictimes
.indiatimes.com/2014-10-28/news/55521431_1_singur-tata-consultancy
-services-tata-ryerson), which describes Tata's efforts to reinvigorate its operations in West Bengal six years after walking out of the plant at Singur.

47. Government of Maharashtra, "Report of the Cabinet Sub-Committee to Review the Dabhol Power Project," reproduced on website of Human Rights Watch (www.hrw.org/reports/1999/enron/enron-b.htm).

48. Raymond Vickery notes that most of the other projects designated for fast-track status ran into problems that either sank the project or led the foreign investor to leave India. The fast-track program itself is not looked on as a success. Vickery, *The Eagle and the Elephant*, pp. 146–52.

49. Unless otherwise indicated, the account of the Dabhol project draws on Vickery, *The Eagle and the Elephant*; Rajesh Kumar and Verner Worm, *International Negotiation in India and China: A Comparison of the Emerging Business Giants* (London: Palgrave MacMillan, 2011), pp. 90–99; Minority Staff, Committee on Government Reform, U.S. House of Representatives, Fact Sheet on Enron's Dabhol Project, February 22, 2002; Thunderbird School of Global Management, "Enron and the Dabhol Power Company," case study released by Harvard Business School, May 21, 2002, TB0159; and the authors' interviews in 2013 with former U.S. Ambassadors Frank Wisner and Richard Celeste and with former Enron official Sanjay Bhatnagar.

50. Cited in Thunderbird, "Enron and the Dabhol Power Company," TB0159, p. 1.

51. Fali Nariman, "India and International Arbitration," *George Washington International Law Review*, vol. 41 (2009–10), pp. 367–78. Exclamation point in original.

52. The discussion of the arbitration process draws on Ronald J. Bettauer, "India and International Arbitration: The Dabhol Experience," *George Washington University International Law Review*, vol. 41 (2009–10), pp. 381–87 (http://docs.law.gwu.edu/stdg/gwilr/PDFs/41-2/4-%20BETTAUER.pdf); Kenneth Hansen et al., "The Dabhol Project Settlement: What Happened? And How?" *Infrastructure Journal*, December 2005 (www.chadbourne.com/files /Publication/a5aa1e52-4285-4bb5-87e6-7201123895a0/Presentation/Publicat ionAttachment/352f8f09-ae96-40fc-a293-720d0b8f0ca8/Dabhol_Infrastruc tureJournal12_2005.pdf).

53. Nariman, "India and International Arbitration," p. 372.

CHAPTER 10

1. Interviews with authors, February 2013.

2. David M. Malone, *Does the Elephant Dance: Contemporary Indian Foreign Policy* (Oxford University Press, 2011), pp. 284–85. As high commissioner, Malone was the equivalent of Canadian ambassador to India.

3. Interviews with authors, February 2013 to April 2015.

4. Interview with authors, February 2013.

5. Amrita Narlikar and Aruna Narlikar, *Bargaining with a Rising India: Lessons from the Mahabarata* (Oxford University Press, 2014) pp. 150–58.

6. Interview with authors, February 2013.

7. The other SAARC members are Afghanistan, Bangladesh, Bhutan, Maldives, Nepal, Pakistan, and Sri Lanka.

8. In addition to the sources specifically cited, this section draws on the authors' interviews with current Indian and U.S. diplomatic and trade officials.

9. Charter of the United Nations, *Our Documents* website (www.ourdocu ments.gov/doc.php?flash=true&doc=79&page=transcript).

10. David L. Bosco, *Five to Rule Them All: The UN Security Council and the Making of the Modern World* (Oxford University Press, 2009), p. 101–3.

11. Paper by the Chairman of the Open-ended Working Group on the Question of Equitable Representation on and Increase in the Membership of the Security Council and Other Matters Related to the Security Council, March 20, 1997, reproduced on the Global Policy Forum website (www.globalpolicy.org /component/content/article/200/41310.html).

12. Edward C. Luck, *UN Security Council: Practice and Promise* (New York: Routledge, 2009), pp. 115–17; Sabine Hassler, *Reforming the UN Security Council Membership* (New York: Routledge, 2013), pp. 80–83.

13. United Nations General Assembly, 59th Session, agenda item 53, Question of equitable representation on and increase in the membership of the Security Council and related matters, Draft Resolution, July 6, 2005, United Nations Document A/59/L.64. The resolution proposed adding ten new seats to the Security Council. The six new permanent ones were to include two Asian countries, one Latin American, and one from the "Western European and Other group," and two unnamed African countries.

14. An illustration of this issue came in a conversation between Teresita Schaffer and Abid Hussain, then Indian ambassador in Washington, shortly after India joined the Security Council in a nonpermanent seat in 1991. India was under intense U.S. pressure to agree to the resolutions ending the first Persian Gulf war. Hussain, in a moment of frustration, asked her, "Do you realize that we will have to go through this for the next two years?"

15. Charter of the United Nations, article 97; "Tharoor Bows Out of Race for UN Secretary General," *Outlook India*, October 3, 2006 (www.outlookindia .com/news/article/Tharoor-bows-out-of-race-for-UN-Secretary-General /420068).

16. This section draws on interviews with Donald Camp, Karl F. Inderfurth, C. Raja Mohan, and a number of former and current officials in the Indian and U.S. governments.

17. See http://zeenews.india.com/business/news/international/us-congress -passes-imf-quota-reform-to-benefit-india-and-china_1836409.html.

18. Interviews with authors, February 2013.

19. This section draws on the authors' experience as U.S. government officials and on interviews with Rakesh Mohan, Margaret Lundsager, Montek Singh Ahluwalia, and with serving Indian officials.

20. "Understanding the WTO: The Organization: Membership, Alliances, and Bureaucracy," World Trade Organization (www.wto.org/english/thewto _e/whatis_e/tif_e/org3_e.htm).

21. This section draws on Teresita Schaffer's experience as a U.S. trade official and on interviews with former and current U.S. and Indian trade negotiators.

22. MEA 2012 annual report, cited in Rohan Mukherjee and David Malone, "India and the UN Security Council: An Ambiguous Tale," *Economic & Political Weekly*, vol. xlviii, no. 29 (July 20, 2013), p. 116.

23. Mukherjee and Malone, "India and the UN Security Council," p. 112.

24. Ibid., p. 115.

25. Michele Kelemen, "U.S. Underwhelmed with Emerging Powers at U.N.," National Public Radio, September 17, 2011 (www.npr.org/2011/09/17/140533339 /u-s-underwhelmed-with-emerging-powers-at-u-n).

26. Except as otherwise indicated, this section draws on the authors' interviews with current and former U.S. and Indian officials with extensive UN experience.

27. Listings of the Like Minded group in climate change negotiations can be found at Digplanet (www.digplanet.com/wiki/Like_Minded_Group) and on the website of Responding to Climate Change (www.rtcc.org/2013/03/03/un -climate-talks-like-minded-group-lay-down-durban-platform-terms/).

28. Nitin Sethi, "After an Ugly Battle G-77-China Developing Countries Win the Day," *Business Standard*, October 19, 2015 (www.business-standard.com /article/current-affairs/after-an-ugly-battle-g77-china-developing-countries -win-the-day-115101900902_1.html).

29. Chandrashekhar Dasgupta, "Climate Change Negotiations: Guarding the 'Overriding Priorities,'" oral history interview in *Indian Foreign Affairs Journal*, vol. 6, no. 2 (April–June 2011), pp. 217–29.

30. See, for example, International Institute for Strategic Studies, "Lima Climate Accord: Positive Steps on the Road to Paris," *Strategic Comments*, December 18, 2014; Michael Levi, "The Lima Climate Agreement Isn't as New as It Seems," Council on Foreign Relations (http://blogs.cfr.org/levi/2014/12/15/the -lima-climate-agreement-isnt-as-new-as-it-seems/?cid=nlc-public-the_world _this_week-highlights_from_cfr-link18-20141219&sp_mid=47666123&sp_rid= dGNzY2hhZmZlckBnbWFpbC5jb20S1); and Nitin Sethi, "India's Gain at Lima: A More United Front of Developing Countries," *Business Standard*, December 15, 2014 (www.business-standard.com/article/current-affairs/india-s-gain-at-lima-a -more-united-front-of-developing-countries-114121400581_1.html).

31. Lalit K. Jha, "India Says It Will Be Deal-Maker at Copenhagen Talks," *Business Standard*, October 2, 2009; Anil Padmanabhan, "India Signals Change in Stance on Climate Deal," *Livemint*, October 12, 2009 (www.livemint.com /Home-Page/NzzmpcgCJ4NOfjiYOsb1nK/India-signals-change-in-stance-on -climate-deal.html); Indo-Asian News Service, "Industrialized Countries Must Cut Emissions: Jairam Ramesh," *India Forums*, October 19, 2009 (www.india -forums.com/news/politics/205148-industrialised-countries-must-cut -emissions-jairam-ramesh.htm).

32. Dasgupta, "Climate Change Negotiations: Guarding the 'Overriding Priorities.'"

33. United Nations Framework Convention on Climate Change, Conference of the Parties, Fifteenth Session, Draft Decision -/CP.15, Copenhagen Accord (http://unfccc.int/resource/docs/2009/cop15/eng/l07.pdf).

34. Prakash Javadekar, Minister of State with independent charge for Environment, Forests, and Climate Change, Speech to High Level Segment of UNFCCC COP-20, December 9, 2014 (www.envfor.nic.in/content/statement-hon%E2%80 %99ble-minister-high-level-segment-unfccc-cop-20-december-9-2014).

35. Nitin Sethi, "Javadekar Warns against Doing Away with Interests of Poor at Lima Climate Talks," *Business Standard*, December 11, 2014 (www.business

-standard.com/article/current-affairs/javadekar-warns-against-doing-away
-with-interests-of-poor-at-lima-climate-talks-114121000140_1.html).

36. Mark Lynas, "How do I know China wrecked the Copenhagen deal? I
was in the room," *The Guardian*, December 22, 2009 (www.theguardian.com
/environment/2009/dec/22/copenhagen-climate-change-mark-lynas).

37. Nitin Sethi, "U.S.-China climate deal lowers expectations of strong
global climate deal in 2015," *Business Standard*, November 13, 2014 (www
.business-standard.com/article/opinion/us-china-climate-deal-lowers
-expectations-of-strong-global-climate-deal-in-2015-114111201412_1.html);
White House, "Factsheet on U.S. and India Climate and Clean Energy Cooperation," January 25, 2015 (www.whitehouse.gov/the-press-office/2015/01/25
/fact-sheet-us-and-india-climate-and-clean-energy-cooperation).

38. Padmanabhan, "India Signals Change in Stance on Climate Deal."

39. Articles of Agreement, General Agreement on Tariffs and Trade, World
Trade Organization (www.wto.org/english/docs_e/legal_e/legal_e.htm and
www.wto.org/english/docs_e/legal_e/gatt47_02_e.htm).

40. Technically, GATT was not an international organization, largely because
the U.S. Congress, which has all responsibility for trade under the U.S. Constitution, refused to authorize the United States to join any more international organizations. GATT handled this by treating itself as a contract, referring to the
members as Contracting Parties, and to the membership as a whole as the CON-
TRACTING PARTIES in all uppercase. GATT obligations applied only to
member countries, but for most members, they became the norm in their trade
dealings with the outside world, regardless of a trading partner's GATT status.

41. Narlikar and Narlikar, *Bargaining with a Rising India: Lessons from the
Mahabarata*, pp. 61–62; Surupa Gupta, "Ideas, Interests, and Institutions: Explaining the politics of India's engagement in the WTO negotiations on agriculture," draft paper prepared for presentation at the 2004 Annual Meeting of the
American Political Science Association, Chicago, September 2–5, 2004.

42. Paul Blustein, *Misadventures of the Most Favored Nations: Clashing
Egos, Inflated Ambitions, and the Great Shambles of the World Trade System*
(New York: Public Affairs, 2009), p. 112.

43. World Trade Organization, Ministerial Declaration, adopted November 14,
2001, Doha (www.wto.org/english/thewto_e/minist_e/min01_e/mindecl_e.htm).

44. Blustein, *Misadventures of the Most Favored Nations*, pp. 112–29.

45. For a list of the most active, see the WTO's "Groups in the Negotiations"
listing (www.wto.org/english/tratop_e/dda_e/negotiating_groups_e.htm#grp017).
India, like many countries, participates in multiple groups.

46. Interview with authors, February 2013.

47. A former U.S. official recalled that this was the vote of confidence to keep
the Indian government in office and in the process rescue the U.S.-India civil
nuclear agreement—see chapter 8.

48. Narlikar and Narlikar, *Bargaining with a Rising India*, p. 63; Blustein,
Misadventures of the Most Favored Nations, p. 263.

49. Audio files on the WTO website: press conference by Pascal Lamy,
July 31, 2008 (www.wto.org/audio/2008_07_31_gc_dgstat.mp3); press confer-

ence by Susan Schwab, July 31, 2008 (www.wto.org/audio/2008_08_30_susan _schwab.mp3); press conference by Kamal Nath, July 31, 2008 (www.wto.org /audio/2008_08_30_kamal_nath.mp3); press conference by Celso Amorim, July 31, 2008 (www.wto.org/audio/2008_07_29_celso_amorim.mp3).

50. Address by Shri Anand Sharma, Union Minister of Commerce and Industry, at the Plenary Session of the Ninth Ministerial Meeting of the WTO, December 4, 2013 (www.wto.org/english/thewto_e/minist_e/mc9_e/stat_e/ind .pdf).

51. Puja Mehra, "India's Stand Prevails in Bali," *The Hindu*, December 7, 2013 (www.thehindu.com/news/national/indias-stand-prevails-in-bali/article 5430252.ece).

52. It also included provisions related to the Doha development agenda that were of particular interest to the African group, with which India had allied itself. These provisions, however, did not become part of the controversy.

53. The *Mahabharata* is replete with take-it-or-leave-it negotiations and stories of heroes single-handedly facing stronger foes, but the one that best fits this situation is the story of Karna's solitary stand on the Kurukshetra battlefield. See Narlikar and Narlikar, *Bargaining with a Rising India*, pp. 39–41. See also Amrita Narlikar, "Peculiar Chauvinism or Strategic Calculation: Explaining the Negotiating Strategies of a Rising India," *International Affairs* (2006), p. 72.

54. Agricultural Negotiations Fact Sheet, WTO, November 27, 2014 (http://wto.org/english/tratop_e/agric_e/factsheet_agng_e.htm); Briefing Note— Agricultural Negotiations, Ninth WTO Ministerial Meeting, December, 2013 (http://wto.org/english/thewto_e/minist_e/mc9_e/brief_agneg_e.htm# stockholding).

55. See, for example, Amrita Narlikar, *New Powers: How to Become One and How to Manage Them* (Columbia University Press, 2010); Gupta, "Ideas, Interests, and Institutions."

56. Except as otherwise indicated, the material in this section draws on Teresita Schaffer's experience and on interviews with former U.S. trade representatives Susan Schwab, Carla Hills, Susan Esserman; former U.S. officials Karan Bhatia, Claudio Lilienfeld; current U.S. officials; and current and former Indian officials from MEA and the Commerce Ministry, all conducted between February 2013 and mid-2015.

57. Former foreign minister Jaswant Singh's article explains India's decision to test; see "Against Nuclear Apartheid," *Foreign Affairs* (September/October 1998), pp. 41–55.

58. Arundhati Ghose, "The Comprehensive Test Ban Treaty: Some Delicate Moments during the Negotiations," oral history, *Indian Foreign Affairs Journal* (April–June 2013), pp. 213–22 (http://associationdiplomats.org/publications /ifaj/Vol8/8.2/ORAL%20HISTORY.pdf). Except where otherwise noted, our description of the negotiations draws extensively on this account and on the authors' interview with Ambassador Ghose.

59. The CTBT Organization's history of the negotiations cites a January 1996 Indian proposal for amending the treaty by requiring all nuclear weapons states to commit to nuclear disarmament within ten years in order for the treaty

to enter into force. See "1994–96 Entry into Force Formula," CTBT Organization (www.ctbto.org/the-treaty/1993-1996-treaty-negotiations/1994-96-entry-into -force-formula/).

60. In an interesting sidelight on the bureaucratics of these negotiations in Delhi, Ghose recalled in her oral history having to clear the text of her speeches with the Ministry of External Affairs in Delhi, a considerable inconvenience at a time when such business had to be done by fax. The ministry initially gagged on the phrase "security interests," which was not normally in MEA's script, but eventually accepted it. Ghose, "The Comprehensive Test Ban Treaty: Some Delicate Moments during the Negotiations," pp. 216–17.

61. Keith A. Hansen, *The Comprehensive Nuclear Test Ban Treaty: An Insider's Perspective* (Stanford University Press, 2006), pp. 38–42.

62. Iran's objection was different from India's: it opposed allowing Israel to join the Middle East/South Asia group in the treaty's organization. Pakistan also announced that it would not sign, but did not join in blocking the consensus. Hansen, *Comprehensive Nuclear Test Ban Treaty*, pp. 41–42.

63. Hansen, *Comprehensive Nuclear Test Ban Treaty*, pp. 41–42; Ghose, "The Comprehensive Test Ban Treaty: Some Delicate Moments during the Negotiations," pp. 213–22.

64. Quoted in Strobe Talbott, *Engaging India: Diplomacy, Democracy, and the Bomb* (Brookings Institution Press, 2006), p. 126.

65. Ministry of External Affairs, "U.S.-India Joint Strategic Vision for the Asia Pacific and Indian Ocean Region," January 26, 2015 (www.mea.gov.in /bilateral-documents.htm?dtl/24728/USIndia_Joint_Strategic_Vision_for_the _AsiaPacific_and_Indian_Ocean_Region).

66. Suhashini Haidar, "India Pushes for NSG Membership," *The Hindu,* November 3, 2015 (www.thehindu.com/news/national/india-pushes-for-nsg -membership/article7834737.ece?mkt_tok=3RkMMJWWfF9wsRohs63AZK XonjHpfsX57%2BwrXqOg38431UFwdcjKPmjr1YQES8R0aPyQAgobGp5I5 FEIQ7XYTLB2t60MWA%3D%3D).

CHAPTER 11

1. Gujral was Indian foreign minister and later prime minister in the late 1980s and mid-1990s. The doctrine ruled out India's use of force in its dealings with its neighbors and called for the settling of all controversial issues by continuous negotiation. In a novel twist, it declared that as the largest and most powerful regional power, India would make unilateral gestures of goodwill to the small states without waiting for them to reciprocate. The doctrine proved more consequential in India's dealings with such weak countries as Bangladesh than in India-Pakistan relations.

2. "India and Pakistan Halt Kashmir Bus in Drugs Row," BBC, February 9, 2015 (www.bbc.com/news/world-asia-india-31296028).

3. Authors' interviews with former and serving officials in both India and Pakistan.

4. Interview with authors, February 2015.

5. For a detailed description of the 2002 crisis from a U.S. perspective, see Polly Nayak and Michael Krepon, "U.S. Crisis Management in South Asia's Twin Peaks Crisis," Stimson Report 57 (Washington: Henry L. Stimson Center, September, 2006). For longer discussions of all three crises, see Howard Schaffer and Teresita Schaffer, *How Pakistan Negotiates with the United States: Riding the Roller Coaster* (Washington: United States Institute of Peace, 2011) and P. R. Chari, Pervaiz Iqbal Cheema, and Stephen P. Cohen, *Four Crises and a Peace Process* (Brookings Institution, 2007).

6. "Fissile Material Cutoff Treaty (FMCT) at a Glance," Arms Control Association, August 2013 (www.armscontrol.org/factsheets/fmct).

7. S. K. Mohanty, "India-China Bilateral Trade Relationship," Reserve Bank of India Study, July 2014 (http://rbidocs.rbi.org.in/rdocs/Publications/PDFs/PRSICBT130613.pdf).

8. Richard H. Solomon, *Chinese Negotiating Behavior: Pursuing Interests through "Old Friends"* (Washington, D.C.: United States Institute of Peace, 2005), pp. 15–21, 76–77, 84–87.

9. Srinath Raghavan, *War and Peace in Modern India* (London: Palgrave MacMillan, 2010), pp. 226–40.

10. Minutes of talk with Zhou, October 20, 1954, cited in Raghavan, *War and Peace in Modern India*, p. 243.

11. Solomon, *Chinese Negotiating Behavior*, pp. 61–65.

12. Raghavan, *War and Peace in Modern India*, p. 245.

13. Ibid., pp. 240–52.

14. Jagat Mehta, *Negotiating for India: Resolving Problems through Diplomacy* (New Delhi: Manohar, 2006), pp. 67–72.

15. Raghavan, *War and Peace in Modern India*, pp. 261–66.

16. Ananth Krishnan, "Crossing the Point of No Return," *The Hindu*, October 25, 2012; Mehta, *Negotiating for India*, pp. 81–82. See longer description of this episode in chapter 6 of this book.

17. Text cited in Claude Arpi, "A statement of Zhou Enlai: sixty-four years ago," *Indian Defense Review*, September 18, 2014.

18. Raghavan, *War and Peace in Modern India*, p. 234.

19. Leo Rose, *Nepal: Strategy for Survival* (University of California Press, 1971), p. 239.

20. The Pakistan-China border settlement also complicated India-Pakistan relations since India challenged Pakistan's right to give away territory the Indians claimed as their own.

21. Ananth Krishnan, "Rajiv Declined China Border Deal in 1988, Hope Now on Modi, Says Chinese Official," *India Today*, April 13, 2015; Sino-Indian Joint Press Communique, Beijing, December 23, 1988, reproduced at www.cctv.com/lm/1064/13/6.html.

22. Text of the September 7, 1993 agreement is reproduced on the Stimson Center website (www.stimson.org/research-pages/agreement-on-the-maintenance-of-peace-along-the-line-of-actual-control-in-the-india-china-border/).

23. Peacemaker.un (http://peacemaker.un.org/sites/peacemaker.un.org/files/CN%20IN_961129_Agreement%20between%20China%20and%20India.pdf).

24. Text reproduced in M. Rama Rao, "Political Parameters, Guiding Principles for Resolving India-China Border Dispute," *Asian Age*, April 12, 2005 (www.asiantribune.com/news/2005/04/12/political-parameters-guiding -principles-resolving-india-china-border-dispute).

25. Interview with authors, April 2015.

26. Ministry of External Affairs, "Agreement between the Government of the Republic of India and the Government of the People's Republic of China on Border Defence Cooperation," October 23, 2013 (www.mea.gov.in/bilateral -documents.htm?dtl/22366/); Ministry of External Affairs, "Memorandum of Understanding between the Ministry of Water Resources, the Republic of India, and the Ministry of Water Resources, the People's Republic of China, on Strengthening Cooperation on Trans-border Rivers" October 23, 2013 (www .mea.gov.in/bilateral-documents.htm?dtl/22368/).

27. Ankit Panda, "India Caves to China on Border Dispute," *The Diplomat*, October 22, 2013 (http://thediplomat.com/2013/10/india-caves-to-china-on -border-dispute/); Sandeep Dikshit, "China Ends Stand-off, Pulls Out Troops from Daulat Beg Oldi Sector," *The Hindu*, May 6, 2013 (www.thehindu.com /news/national/china-ends-standoff-pulls-out-troops-from-daulat-beg-oldi -sector/article4686606.ece); interview with authors.

28. "China Warns India against Oil Exploration in South China Sea," *Maritime Connector*, March 26, 2012 (http://maritime-connector.com/news/offshore -oil-gas-news/china-warns-india-against-oil-exploration-in-south-china-sea/ ?page=4).

29. Ministry of External Affairs, "Joint Statement between India and China during PM's Visit to China," May 15, 2015 (www.mea.gov.in/bilateral -documents.htm?dtl/25240/); Tanvi Madan, "Modi's Trip to China: Six Quick Takeaways" (www.brookings.edu/research/opinions/2015/05/15-modi-china -takeaways-madan).

30. Indrani Bagchi, "India ignores China's frown, offers defence boost to Vietnam," *Times of India*, October 29, 2014 (http://timesofindia.indiatimes .com/india/India-ignores-Chinas-frown-offers-defence-boost-to-Vietnam /articleshow/44965272.cms).

31. White House, "Joint Strategic Vision for the Indian Ocean and Asia-Pacific," January 25, 2015 (www.whitehouse.gov/the-press-office/2015/01/25 /us-india-joint-strategic-vision-asia-pacific-and-indian-ocean-region).

CHAPTER 12

1. The Awami League formed the government in 1972–75 (under Sheikh Mujibur Rahman) and again in 1996–2001 and 2009 to the present (under Sheikh Mujib's daughter, Sheikh Hasina Wazed). Indian Ministry of External Affairs *Annual Report* for 2011 (when the Congress-led government of Manmohan Singh was in office) candidly noted that "since the return of Sheikh Hasina to power in Dhaka, there has been a marked cordiality in the relations between India and Bangladesh" (Introduction, p. xvii).

2. Authors' conversations with retired Bangladeshi diplomats, 2013 and 2015.

3. The Farakka Barrage is located in West Bengal some ten miles west of the international border. Its principal purpose is to make water available to flush the silt out of the port of Kolkata.

4. India adopted a different policy regarding the division with Pakistan of its western rivers, eventually agreeing to the historic 1960 Indus Waters Treaty negotiated under the leadership of the World Bank. But this agreement also provided funding by the World Bank and other international donors for a vast and expensive series of dams and canals. The anticipation of financial assistance no doubt significantly helped to win Indian acceptance of such international participation.

5. Authors' interviews with senior Bangladeshi and Indian officials.

6. Ministry of External Affairs, India-Bangladesh Joint Statement, January 2010 (http://mea.gov.in/bilateral-documents.htm?dtl/19864/).

7. Ministry of External Affairs, "Framework Agreement on Cooperation for Development between India and Bangladesh," September 6, 2011 (http://mea.gov.in/bilateral-documents.htm?dtl/5218/); "India, Bangladesh Roundtable Calls for Restructuring of Joint Commission," *Bangladesh News*, July 3, 2013 (www.bangladeshnews.net/index.php/sid/215591992); interviews with authors. Following the river agreement, India and Bangladesh have also connected their electric grids, a proposal that had languished for years.

8. This is part of what India terms its policy of asymmetric engagement in providing greater market access to its neighbors. Important non-tariff barriers remain, however, and though Bangladesh's exports to India have boomed, they still are only about an eighth of its imports from India.

9. Most of the Bangladeshi enclaves were in the state of West Bengal. The rest were in Assam, Meghalaya, and Tripura. Indian opponents of the agreement charged that India was being shortchanged and that the transfer of this Indian territory to Bangladesh would encourage secessionist elements elsewhere in the country. These contentions may seem strained to outside observers, but they have some resonance among people who revere the "sacred soil" of their Indian homeland.

10. The two sides did reach agreement on an arrangement that permits trucks to cross the "chicken neck" corridor of Indian territory that separates Bhutan and Nepal from Bangladesh. This concession was a bow to the Singh government's policy of providing asymmetric market access to neighboring countries.

11. Press Trust of India, "Bangladesh Government Approves Revised Trade Pact with India," *Economic Times*, April 7, 2015 (http://economictimes.indiatimes.com/news/economy/foreign-trade/bangladesh-cabinet-approves-revised-trade-agreement-with-india/articleshow/46835858.cms).

12. As K. M. De Silva points out: "The Sinhalese, although an overwhelming majority of the population of the island, nevertheless have a minority complex vis-à-vis the Tamils. They feel encircled by the more than 50 million Tamil-speaking people who inhabit the present-day Tamil Nadu and Sri Lanka. Within Sri Lanka, the Sinhalese outnumber the Tamils by more than three to one; but they in turn are outnumbered by nearly six to one by the Tamil-speaking people of South Asia." De Silva, *A History of Sri Lanka* (London: Hurst, 1981), pp. 513–14.

13. This was the 1964 agreement between Shastri and Sri Lankan Prime Minister Sirimavo Bandaranaike that provided for the gradual compulsory repatriation of a small majority of these "Indian Tamils" (and their progeny) to India over a fifteen-year period and that granted them Indian citizenship. Most of the rest were to become Sri Lankan citizens. The future of a smaller number was to be negotiated by the two governments later. De Silva argues in his *History of Sri Lanka* (p. 529) that the agreement marked a "great advance [for Sri Lanka] for the Indian government had been persuaded to recognize its obligations to persons of Indian origin by undertaking to confer Indian citizenship on those who were to be repatriated and by accepting the principle of compulsory repatriation."

14. According to A. Jeyaratnam Wilson, a Sri Lankan Tamil and a serious student of the Sinhalese-Tamil confrontation, Mrs. Gandhi told a gathering of Sri Lankan Tamils during her visit to the United States soon after the massacre that "she would have ordered the Indian army to invade Sri Lanka but had reservations because of the defenselessness of Indian plantation workers" there (Wilson, *The Break-up of Sri Lanka: The Sinhalese-Tamil Conflict* [London: Hurst, 1988], p. 176). Whether or not the prime minister actually said this, fear of Indian military intervention was surely an important element in the way the Sri Lanka government dealt with the crisis then and later. Political leaders in Tamil Nadu insistently called for armed intervention and it is unlikely that Mrs. Gandhi ever ruled it out.

15. Statement of Prime Minister Indira Gandhi in the Lok Sabha on the situation in Sri Lanka, August 12, 1983, quoted in Avtar Singh Bhasin, ed., *India-Sri Lanka Relations and Sri Lanka's Ethnic Conflict, Documents 1947–2000*, vol. 3 (New Delhi: India Research Press, 2001), p. 1539–40. At the same time, India made strenuous efforts to win the sympathy of foreign governments for its position on the Sri Lanka issue.

16. J. N. Dixit, *Assignment Colombo* (Delhi: Konark Publishers, 1998), pp. 3–5. According to Dixit, Rajiv Gandhi told him that although until 1985 India's Sri Lanka policy was influenced by Tamil Nadu politics and ethno-religious considerations, it would henceforth be "responsive to India's security and strategic interests and responsive to the principle of not disrupting the unity and territorial integrity of a small neighbor." Gandhi had added that "within this overall framework, India's endeavor would be to ensure the maximum fulfillment of legitimate Tamil aspirations."

17. These were an All-Party Conference that met intermittently throughout 1984; two rounds of peace talks in Bhutan in July and August that same year; and proximity talks in 1985 (when the Indian representatives shuttled between the contending factions, which did not meet face-to-face). After President Jayewardene's summit-level talks with Gandhi, Indian representatives met with Jayewardene and worked out proposals that were to be "the basis and starting point" for further discussions. But these too failed to win the support of the Tamils and were not well received by Sinhalese political factions either. To Indian dismay, the Sri Lanka government proved reluctant to pursue these proposals, despite its involvement in their formulation.

18. They included the elder statesman G. Parthasarathy, Foreign Secretary Romesh Bhandari, and Ministers of State Natwar Singh and P. Chidambaram. Both Singh and Chidambaram later won senior cabinet positions in Indian National Congress governments. High Commissioner Dixit became foreign secretary and national security adviser.

19. For a good, brief review of this diplomatic activity, see K. Loganathan, *Sri Lanka: Lost Opportunities* (Colombo: Centre for Policy Research and Analysis, 1996), chap. 4.

20. Bhasin, *India-Sri Lanka Relations*, vol. 3, p. 1841.

21. Statement of Indian Minister of External Affairs B. R. Bhagat in the Lok Sabha, February 27, 1986, quoted in Bhasin, *India-Sri Lanka Relations*, vol. 3, p. 1711–22.

22. In *Assignment Colombo*, High Commissioner Dixit argues that "though technically it might have been a violation of international law, in terms of humanitarian necessities the action, in my view, was both politically necessary and morally justified." He found a precedent in the Berlin airlift (p. 333). The Indians had notified the Sri Lankans in advance of the planned flotilla and, subsequently, the air drop, and had asked for their permission. The Sri Lankan government would not agree and subsequently termed the Indian action "a naked violation of our independence . . . and an unwarranted assault on our sovereignty and territorial integrity." (Sri Lankan Ministry of Foreign Affairs, press release, June 4, 1987, quoted in Bhasin, *India-Sri Lanka Relations*, vol. 3, p. 1915.)

23. Other, less consequential Sri Lankan Tamil organizations were willing to endorse it.

24. For the text of the July 29, 1987 agreement and its annexures and accompanying exchange of letters, see Bhasin, *India-Sri Lanka Relations*, vol. 4 (New Delhi: India Research Press, 2001), pp. 1946–52.

25. Some commentators argue that President Jayewardene had asked Prime Minister Gandhi to send in the IPKF so that Sri Lankan forces could be moved south to confront the JVP insurgents. See, for example, P. R. Chari, "India, Sri Lanka and the IPKF Debacle: Remembering 29 July 1987," Institute for Peace and Conflict Studies, New Delhi, August 2, 2013 (www.ipcs.org/article/south-asia/india-sri-lanka-and-the-ipkf-debacle-remembering-29-july-4064.html).

26. Authors' conversation with Dixit, June 1994.

27. Quoted in Sanjay Upadhya, *Nepal and the Geo-Strategic Rivalry between China and India* (London: Routledge, 2012), p.70.

28. The text of the treaty is in the Indian Ministry of External Affairs document, "Treaty of Peace and Friendship between the Government of India and the Government of Nepal, July 31, 1950" (http://mea.gov.in/bilateral-documents.htm?dtl/6295/). During his visit to Nepal in August 2014, newly elected Indian Prime Minister Narendra Modi agreed with Nepalese government officials to "review, adjust, and update the treaty . . . and other bilateral agreements." (*Livemint*, August 4, 2014.)

29. The text of the letter exchanged with the 1950 treaty is in Surya P. Subedi, *Dynamics of Foreign Policy and Law: A Study of Indo-Nepal Relations*

(Oxford University Press, 2005), p. 194. Its most important provision states that "neither Government shall tolerate any threat to the security of the other by a foreign aggressor. To deal with any such threat, the two Governments shall consult with each other and devise effective countermeasures."

30. J. N. Dixit, *India's Foreign Policy and Its Neighbours* (New Delhi: Gyan Publishing House, 2001), p.102.

31. Nepal repeatedly raised the Zone of Peace proposal in the UN General Assembly. It eventually garnered support from over 100 states, including China, before the democratic government installed in 1990 stopped campaigning for it. At a 1983 White House dinner honoring the visiting king of Nepal, President Ronald Reagan announced U.S. endorsement of the concept (www.reagan .utexas.edu/archives/speeches/1983/120783c.htm).

32. For a fascinating account of this epic bureaucratic battle, see Jagat S. Mehta, *Negotiating for India* (New Delhi: Manohar, 2006), pp. 259–73. Mehta was Indian foreign secretary at that time. He strongly supported the concept of separate treaties against the opposition of the Finance and Commerce ministries. Mehta served in the government of Morarji Desai, who tended to be more solicitous of the positions of India's small neighbors than his predecessor Indira Gandhi. According to Mehta, "In Indira Gandhi's mind was embedded the notion that Nepal was not being sensitive to Indian interests. She recalled being embarrassed in the (*sic*) international fora by the demand that India accept Nepal as a Zone of Peace. She felt that Nepal was making a mockery of the Treaty of 1950. The very fact that China endorsed the idea of Nepal being accepted as a 'Zone of Peace' lent credence to the suspicion that it was an anti-Indian conspiracy" (p. 262).

33. The text of the agreement is in Subedi, *Dynamics of Foreign Policy and Law*, pp. 210–12. There is some dispute between India and Nepal about how long the agreement remained valid. The Nepalese claim that they canceled the agreement in 1966. The Indians have not acknowledged this and reportedly circulated the agreement to the Indian media during the 1989 crisis to arouse public support for the embargo.

34. B. K. Tewari and Awadhesh Kumar Singh, *India's Neighbors: Past and Future* (Rohtak: Spellbound Publications, 1997), p. 121; John W. Garver, "China-India Rivalry in Nepal: The Clash over Chinese Arms Sales," *Asian Survey*, vol. 31, no. 10 (October 1991), p. 953.

35. Leo E. Rose, "India's Foreign Relations: Reassessing Basic Policies," *India Briefing* (Boulder, Colo.: Westview Press, 1990).

36. See Tewari and Singh, *India's Neighbors*, chap. 6. In their study, the authors cite D. P. Kumar, "Chinese Anti-Aircraft Guns: Nepal Violated Secret Agreement with India," *The Statesman*, May 26, 1989, and S. D. Muni, "Chinese Arms Pour into Nepal," *Times of India*, September 1, 1988.

37. Garver, "China-India Rivalry in Nepal," p. 958.

38. Indian Ministry of External Affairs, *Annual Report 1989–90*.

39. Indian Ministry of External Affairs, *Annual Report 1990–91*.

40. Ministry of External Affairs, "Statement on the Situation in Nepal," September 21, 2015 (www.mea.gov.in/press-releases.htm?dtl/25825/Statement+on

+the+situation+in+Nepal); Bikash Sangraula, "Nepal Accuses India of an Economic Blockade as Border Trade Freezes Up," *Christian Science Monitor,* September 28, 2015 (www.csmonitor.com/World/Asia-South-Central/2015/0928 /Nepal-accuses-India-of-an-economic-blockade-as-border-trade-freezes-up); Binaj Gurubacharya, "Nepal Turns to India for Fuel after China Restricts Supply," Associated Press, reproduced in *U.S. News and World Report* (www .usnews.com/news/business/articles/2015/10/29/nepal-turns-to-china-for-fuel -after-india-restricts-supply).

41. For a good summary of the incident, see Prashanth Parameshwaran, "The Truth about India's Militant Strike in Myanmar," *The Diplomat,* June 12, 2015 (http://thediplomat.com/2015/06/the-truth-about-indias-militant-strike-in -myanmar/).

CHAPTER 13

1. Planning Commission, Government of India, "Press Note on Poverty Estimates, 2013" (www.planningcommission.nic.i/news/pre_pov2307.pdf). The figures are estimates of the combined rural/urban poverty rate. Both components fell, rural poverty more sharply than urban.

2. Based on People's Republic of China (PRC) Ministry of Commerce trade figures.

3. Shihar Aneez and Ranka Sirilal, "Chinese submarine docks in Sri Lanka despite Indian concerns," Reuters, November 2, 2014 (http://in.reuters.com /article/2014/11/02/sri-lanka-china-submarine-idINKBN0IM0LU20141102); "PLA shows off sub power sending Changzheng 2 to Persian Gulf," *Want China Times,* October 30, 2014 (www.wantchinatimes.com/news-subclass-cnt.aspx?id =20141030000019&cid=1101).

4. Prime Minister Narendra Modi, Speech to SAARC, November 16–17, 2014 (http://pmindia.gov.in/en/news_updates/pms-speech-at-the-saarc-summit/).

5. A good published account of China's calculations and objectives is in Andrew Small, *The China-Pakistan Axis: Asia's New Geopolitics* (London: Hurst, 2015). The same logic was spelled out by numerous Chinese South Asia analysts in interviews in Shanghai and Beijing with the authors in May 2012.

6. John Vidal, "China and India 'Water Grab' Dams Put Ecology of Himalayas in Danger," *The Guardian Global Development,* August 10, 2013 (www .theguardian.com/global-development/2013/aug/10/china-india-water-grab -dams-himalayas-danger); R. N. Bhaskar, "What Chinese Dam on Brahmaputra Means to India," *DNAIndia,* November 27, 2014 (www.dnaindia.com/money /report-what-chinese-dam-on-brahmaputra-means-to-india-2038737); Joydeep Gupta, "Nervous Neighbors," *Chinadialogue,* November 24, 2010 (www.china dialogue.net/article/show/single/en/3959-Nervous-neighbours).

7. The international debate tends to focus on whether India would be a "constructive" leader, which appears to mean one dedicated to preserving and improving the global system from which it is beginning to benefit. For a good discussion of this issue, see Rohan Mukherjee and David Malone, "India and

the UN Security Council: An Ambiguous Tale," *Economic & Political Weekly*, vol. xlviii, no. 29 (July 20, 2013), pp. 112–13.

8. S. Jaishankar, Foreign Secretary of India, IISS Fullerton Lecture, Singapore, July 20, 2015, Ministry of External Affairs (http://mea.gov.in/Speeches -Statements.htm?dtl/25493/IISS_Fullerton_Lecture_by_Foreign_Secretary_in _Singapore).

Index

Abdullah, Sheikh, 30
Acheson, Dean, 19, 113, 185
Acquisition and Cross Servicing
  Agreement (ACSA), 142
Active Electronically Scanned Array
  (AESA), 139
Afghanistan: India's relations with,
  5, 22, 58; Soviet intervention
  in, 40–41, 44, 50, 76; U.S.
  intervention in, 57, 256
Africa: and Bandung Conference,
  23–24; India's economic aid to,
  69, 71; and Non-Aligned
  Movement, 37, 49; Soviet
  interventions in, 40
Agreement on the Maintenance of
  Peace and Tranquility along the
  Line of Actual Control in the
  India-China Border (1993), 265
Agricultural subsidies, 235–36
Agriculture Department (U.S.),
  198–99, 237
Ahluwalia, Montek Singh, 224
Air Force (India), 27, 93, 284
Air India, 200
Aiyar, Mani Shankar, 68
Ambedkar, B. R., 66
Amorim, Celso, 237

Andrus, Jon, 191
Angola, Soviet interventions in, 40
Anticolonialism, 20–21
Antony, A. K., 141
APEC (Asia Pacific Economic
  Cooperation), 244
Arbitration clauses, 202–03
Armitage, Richard, 254
Arms control negotiations, 159,
  242, 258. *See also* Comprehensive
  Test Ban Treaty (CTBT); Non-
  Proliferation Treaty
Arms sales and aid: India-Nepal
  Agreement on Arms Assistance
  (1965), 287–88; and security
  negotiations, 135–42; from
  Sweden, 138; from U.S., 135–49
Army (India), 8, 25, 292
Arora, Gopi, 190
Arunachal Pradesh, 25, 267,
  269
Ashoka (emperor), 5, 6
Asian Development Bank, 267
Asia Pacific Economic Cooperation
  (APEC), 244
Association of Southeast Asian
  Nations (ASEAN), 46, 72, 228,
  244, 296, 301

Atomic Energy Department (India), 83, 143, 158, 163–64, 167, 170, 177, 180
Australia: economic negotiations with, 202; India's strategic partnership with, 138
Awami League, 271, 272–74, 276
Ayub Khan, 30–31

Back-channel talks, 252
Bajpai, Shankar, 114
Bali agreement (WTO, 2013), 239–40
Bandung Conference (1955), 23–25
Banerjee, Kaushik, 191
Banerjee, Mamata, 206, 277
Bangladesh: and China, 58, 298, 304; independence of, 41, 76; India negotiations with, 100, 102, 271–79, 290; and Pakistan, 35, 41; Singh's visit to, 91
Ban Ki-moon, 221
Baru, Sanjaya, 72
Bechtel Corp., 211
Bhai-Bhai, Chini, 25
Bharara, Preet, 123
Bharatiya Janata Party (BJP): and Bangladesh policy, 272, 276; and China policy, 270; and economic negotiations, 208, 210, 300; and foreign policy institutions, 97, 100, 104; and multilateral negotiations, 220, 242; and nuclear cooperation agreement, 152, 161; and post-Cold War foreign policy, 48, 51; and security negotiations, 134; and strategic vision for India, 73, 75–79
Bhatia, Karan, 200
Bhatnagar, Sanjay, 209
Bhutan: and Bangladesh, 277; as buffer state, 19; and China, 58; and multilateral negotiations, 219, 243; treaty with India, 9, 285; and water supply negotiations, 274
Biden, Joseph, 160, 173
Bilateral investment treaties (BITs), 201–04, 206, 211
Bilateral negotiations, 163, 175, 197, 214–15, 235

Birendra (King of Nepal), 286, 289
BJP. *See* Bharatiya Janata Party
Bofors scandal, 138
Bogra, Mohammed Ali, 21
Border Defense Cooperation Agreement (India-China, 2013), 266
Border issues: with Bangladesh, 272, 275–76, 278; with China, 25–26, 113, 259–69; and multilateral negotiations, 237; with Pakistan, 31, 94, 249
Bose, Krishna, 98
Bowles, Chester, 113, 187
Brahmaputra River, 274, 304
Brazil: India's strategic partnership with, 63–64; and multilateral negotiations, 216, 219, 224, 228, 231, 235–36, 245; and nuclear cooperation negotiations, 174
Breakfast Group, 235
Brecher, Michael, 17
Brezhnev, Leonid, 34
BRICS countries: and Indian Foreign Service, 86; India's role in, 64, 68, 72, 302, 304; and multilateral negotiations, 215, 223, 245. *See also specific countries*
BRICS Development Bank, 223
Britain. *See* United Kingdom
British Raj period, 8–11, 82, 109, 249
Broad Power Realism, 60, 69–73, 76–78, 80, 309
Buddhism, 6, 121
Bulganin, Nikolai, 22
Burns, Nicholas, 156, 158–63, 165–66, 170
Bush, George W.: and economic negotiations, 201; HIV/AIDS initiative, 114; and nuclear cooperation agreement, 150, 152, 156, 158, 159, 162, 164–66, 171, 173; and post-Cold War diplomacy, 53

Carter, Ashton, 146–48, 159
Carter, Jimmy, 39
CD. *See* Conference on Disarmament
Centre for Air Power Studies, 103

Centre for Land Warfare Studies (CLAWS), 103
Chandra, Naresh, 93, 114
Chari, P. R., 104, 254
Chellaney, Brahma, 74, 145
China: Broad Power Realists on, 69–72; and economic negotiations, 184, 202; and Gandhi (Indira), 33; Hard Power Hawks on, 74–75, 79–80; and Indian Foreign Service, 87–88; India's economic ties with, 47; India's negotiations with, 17–19, 61, 64, 112, 117, 125, 251–53, 255, 258–68, 296–306; and multilateral negotiations, 216, 218–19, 223–24, 227–28, 231–32, 242–47; and National Security Adviser, 91; and Nepal, 284–86, 288, 290–91; Nonalignment Firsters on, 67–68; and nuclear program negotiations, 162, 174–75; and Pakistan, 35–36; and post-Cold War diplomacy, 55–59; and security negotiations, 112, 129–30, 260, 261, 265, 305; and Sino-Indian War (1962), 15, 25–26, 28, 31; and Sri Lanka, 282–84
CII (Confederation of Indian Industry), 105, 193
Civil Nuclear Agreement (U.S.–India, 2008), 156–76; announcement of, 156–58; commercial dimensions of, 158–62; and Hyde Act, 165–67; and IAEA Safeguards Agreement, 172–73; initial diplomatic efforts, 152–55; negotiations for, 83, 100; and Nuclear Suppliers Group, 173–76; and 123 Agreement, 167–71; political dimensions of, 158–62; post-agreement diplomacy, 177–82; separation plan, 162–65
CLAWS (Centre for Land Warfare Studies), 103
Climate change negotiations, 57, 214–17, 227–30, 232
Clinton, Bill, 52, 53–54, 98, 152, 253

Clinton, Hillary, 143, 144, 160, 177, 230
Coalition building, 215
Cohen, Raymond, 6
Cold War foreign policy: and anticolonialism, 20–21; and Bandung Conference, 23–25; and China, 18–19, 25–28; and Gandhi (Indira), 32–41; and Gandhi (Rajiv), 41–42; and Kashmir, 21–23, 29–30; and Korean War, 19–20; and Nehru, 13–30, 33, 36, 37; and Non-Aligned Movement, 15–18, 36–37; and nuclear program, 38–40; and Pakistan, 21–23, 29–30, 31–32, 35–36; and Soviet invasion of Afghanistan, 40–41; and U.S., 34–35
Colonialism, 15, 20–21, 23, 28, 37, 49, 66. *See also* British Raj period
Communications Interoperability and Security Memorandum of Agreement (CISMOA), 142, 145
Communist Party of India, 18, 171
Comprehensive Test Ban Treaty (CTBT), 51–53, 152, 240–44, 258
Confederation of Indian Industry (CII), 105, 193
Conference on Disarmament (CD), 174, 241, 243, 258
Confidence-building measures, 251, 253, 265
Congressional Black Caucus (U.S.), 160
Congress Party: and Bangladesh, 276; and Cold War diplomacy, 39; and multilateral negotiations, 221; and Non-Alignment Movement, 15; and nuclear cooperation negotiations, 154; and post-Cold War diplomacy, 45, 47; strategic vision for India, 65, 78
Convention on Supplementary Compensation (CSC), 178
Copenhagen Accord (2009), 230, 231
Corruption, 94, 137–38, 195
Costa Rica, 219

CTBT. *See* Comprehensive Test Ban Treaty
Cuba, 37, 129

Dabhol Power Company, 204–12
DAE. *See* Department of Atomic Energy
Dalai Lama, 26, 262, 270
Dasgupta, Chandrashekhar, 229, 231
Declaration on Principles for Relations and Comprehensive Cooperation (China–India), 266
Defense Acquisition Council, 138
Defense Framework Agreement (U.S.–India, 2015), 135, 148
Defense policy, 94–96. *See also* Ministry of Defense; Security negotiations
Defense Policy Group, 134
Defense Procurement Procedures (DPP), 137–39
Defense Technology Initiative, 135
Denmark, 231
Department of Agriculture (U.S.), 198–99, 237
Department of Atomic Energy (DAE, India), 83, 143, 158, 163–64, 167, 170, 177, 180
Desai, Morarji, 39, 129
Developing countries: and Cold War diplomacy, 37; and economic negotiations, 204; and India's strategic vision, 68, 72, 76; and multilateral negotiations, 217, 219, 223, 227–38, 240, 243, 246; and Non-Aligned Movement, 305; and post-Cold War diplomacy, 47, 49; Research and Information System for Developing Countries, 104
Development Assistance Committee (DAC), 192
Disarmament, 51, 88–89, 240–41, 243. *See also* Arms control negotiations; *specific treaties*
Dixit, J. N., 81, 154, 280, 281, 284–85
DPP (Defense Procurement Procedures), 137–39
Dulles, John Foster, 18

Earthquake in Nepal (2015), 307
East Asia: China's influence in, 260, 301–04; and India's strategic vision, 64, 72, 80; and post-Cold War diplomacy, 46. *See also specific countries*
East Asian Summit and Asian Regional Forum, 244
East Pakistan, 263, 273, 275. *See also* Bangladesh
Economic negotiations, 182–212; bilateral trade, 192–204; Dabhol Power Company case study, 204–12; foreign aid, 184–90; and Gandhi (Indira), 36; and Modi, 309; technical cooperation, 190–92. *See also* Bilateral investment treaties (BITs)
Eisenhower, Dwight, 18, 21, 28
End-use monitoring (EUM), 142–45
Europe and European Union: and colonialism, 20; and multilateral negotiations, 217, 222–23, 224, 235–36; and post-Cold War diplomacy, 49. *See also specific countries*
Exceptionalism, 2, 62, 115–16, 308–09
Export Import Bank, 207
Exports: to China, 260; export controls, 137, 142–43, 147, 153–54, 158; and nuclear cooperation negotiations, 152–55; and post-Cold War diplomacy, 45; subsidies, 195. *See also* Bilateral investment treaties (BITs); Economic negotiations

Federation of Indian Chambers of Commerce and Industry (FICCI), 105, 193
Fissile Material Cutoff Treaty (FMCT), 258
Food aid, 183, 184–88, 231, 239
Food Security Act, 109
Foreign Military Sales (FMS), 141
Foreign policy institutions, 82–106; business community, 102–06;

defense forces, 94–96; Indian
Administrative Service, 92–94;
Indian Foreign Service, 84–90;
media, 102–06; National Security
Advisor, 90–92; Parliament,
96–100; political parties, 100–02;
state governments, 100–02; think
tanks, 102–06
Foreign Service Institute (New
Delhi), 88
France: India's strategic partnership
with, 63; and multilateral
negotiations, 218–19; and nuclear
program negotiations, 178
Freeman, Orville, 186, 187
Free trade agreements, 296

G-4, 219–20
G-77, 64, 215–16, 228, 230,
305
Galbraith, John Kenneth, 129
Gandhi, Indira: and Bangladesh, 275;
and Cold War diplomacy, 25, 32,
33–37, 39–41; and economic
negotiations, 187–88; and India's
strategic vision, 11–12, 66; and
Pakistan, 271, 283; and post-Cold
War diplomacy, 47; and Sri Lanka,
280
Gandhi, Mahatma, 6, 77
Gandhi, Rajiv: and China, 264,
265–66; and Cold War diplomacy,
41–42; and Nepal, 289; nuclear
disarmament proposal, 78; and
post-Cold War diplomacy, 44;
and Sri Lanka, 280, 281, 282;
and U.S., 114
Gandhi, Sonia, 221
Ganges River system, 273
Garver, John, 288
Gates, Robert, 253
Gateway House, 104
General Agreement on Tariffs and
Trade (GATT), 233–35
General Assembly (UN): and
Bangladesh water supply dispute,
273; and India-Pakistan border
dispute, 254; Modi's speech to, 7;

and multilateral negotiations, 216,
217–24, 226, 242–43
Generalized System of Preferences
(GSP), 305
Germany: India's strategic
partnership with, 63; and
multilateral negotiations, 219–20
Ghose, Arundhati, 241–42
Globalization, 294, 296–97
Gopal, S., 17, 26–27
Gorbachev, Mikhail, 44
GSP (Generalized System of
Preferences), 305
Gujarat, 93, 118, 206, 269
Gujral, Inder Kumar, 66–67, 250,
268, 271

Hadley, Stephen, 153, 165
Hagel, Chuck, 173
Hard Power Hawks, 61, 73–75,
78–81, 309
Hasina, Sheikh, 274
Henderson, Loy, 184
High Technology Cooperation
Group, 153, 180
Hinduism, 4, 23, 121. *See also*
Bharatiya Janata Party (BJP)
Holum, John, 242
Hormats, Robert, 202
Humanitarian aid, 307
Human rights, 39–40
Hyde, Henry, 161
Hyde Act, 165, 168, 171

IAEA. *See* International Atomic
Energy Agency
IAS. *See* Indian Administrative
Service
ICRIER (Indian Centre for Research
on International Economic
Relations), 105
IDSA (Institute for Defence Studies
and Analyses), 103
IFS. *See* Indian Foreign Service
ILO (International Labor
Organization), 10
IMF. *See* International Monetary
Fund

Imports, 46, 233, 251, 286–87. *See also* Bilateral investment treaties (BITs); Economic negotiations

India: and Bangladesh, 272–78; and British Raj period, 8–10; bureaucracy in, 221, 272; and China, 17, 25, 56, 57, 223, 258–68, 284, 297–305; Cold War foreign policy, 14–42; economic negotiations, 182–212, 294–97; foreign policy institutions, 82–106; and globalization, 294–97; and Kashmir conflict, 251; and Mughal empire, 7; multilateral negotiations, 213–47; negotiation framework, 107–26; and Nepal, 284–90, 291, 299; and Non-Aligned Movement, 15–18, 36–37, 48–49, 303–05; nuclear cooperation negotiations, 150–81; and Pakistan, 21, 29, 32, 52, 74, 186, 243, 248–58, 268, 300; post–Cold War foreign policy, 43–59; pre-independence legacy, 1–13; security negotiations, 127–49; and Sri Lanka, 101, 278–84; strategic visions of, 60–81; and U.S., 302–03

Indian Administrative Service (IAS): and economic negotiations, 12, 118; and Indian Foreign Service, 84–85, 88; and multilateral negotiations, 223–24; and security negotiations, 130; structure and role of, 92–95

Indian Centre for Research on International Economic Relations (ICRIER), 105

Indian Council of Social Science Research, 104

Indian Defence Services College, 141

India-Nepal Agreement on Arms Assistance (1965), 287–88

India-Nepal Treaty of Peace and Friendship (1950), 285, 286

Indian Foreign Service (IFS): and diplomacy, 107, 118, 295; and India's strategic vision, 77, 80; leadership, 88; and multilateral negotiations, 214, 232–33, 240; and

National Security Adviser, 91; and nuclear cooperation negotiations, 154; and security negotiations, 255; structure and role of, 82, 84–90

Indian National Congress: and British Raj period, 8–9; and Cold War diplomacy, 15, 19–20, 26, 30, 33, 38, 42–43; and India's strategic vision, 76; and nuclear cooperation negotiations, 154; and post–Cold War diplomacy, 47; and security negotiations, 272, 286

Indian Ocean Naval Symposium (IONS), 307

Indian Peace Keeping Force (IPKF), 76, 279, 283–84

Indian Red Cross, 282

Industrial development, 89

Indus Waters Treaty (1960), 22, 253, 255–56, 305

Institute for Defence Studies and Analyses (IDSA), 103

Institute for Peace and Conflict Studies (IPCS), 104

Intellectual property, 195–96, 234, 241

International Atomic Energy Agency (IAEA), 151, 155, 158, 162–63, 167, 171–73, 176, 242

International Labor Organization (ILO), 10

International Monetary Fund (IMF): and economic negotiations, 189–90; and Hard Power Hawks, 75; and multilateral negotiations, 222–24

Inter-Services Intelligence (ISI, Pakistan), 56

Investment treaties. *See* Bilateral investment treaties (BITs)

IONS (Indian Ocean Naval Symposium), 307

IPCS (Institute for Peace and Conflict Studies), 104

IPKF. *See* Indian Peace Keeping Force

Iran: and India's strategic vision, 62–63, 67; and multilateral negotiations, 226, 243; and nuclear cooperation negotiations, 161–62, 166

Iraq, U.S. intervention in, 50
ISI (Inter-Services Intelligence, Pakistan), 56
Ismail, Razali, 218, 219
Israel: aid to Sri Lanka, 282–83; and India's strategic vision, 74; and security negotiations, 144

Jaitley, Arun, 239
Jammu, 102, 264
Janata Vimukti Peramuna (JVP), 284
Japan: diplomatic efforts in, 63, 270, 295–97; and India's strategic vision, 74, 79; and multilateral negotiations, 219–20, 224–25, 245; and post-Cold War diplomacy, 46–47; and security negotiations, 145; security negotiations with, 301
Javadekar, Prakash, 231
Jawaharlal Nehru University, 118
Jayewardene, J. R., 280, 281, 282–84
Johnson, Lyndon, 32, 34, 186
Joint Intelligence Committee, 91
Joint Rivers Commission, 274
Joseph, Robert, 159
Juster, Kenneth, 153
JVP (Janata Vimukti Peramuna), 284

Kakodkar, Anil, 158, 170
Kargil, 54, 103, 253, 300
Kargil Review Commission, 103
Karnad, Bharat, 74, 75
Kashmir: and Cold War diplomacy, 21–23, 28–29, 31, 35; and India's strategic vision, 65; and Pakistan, 250–52, 256, 257, 258, 264, 267, 269; and post-Cold War diplomacy, 44, 51, 54–58; and security negotiations, 94, 102, 113, 298, 300; and state governments, 104
Kathmandu, 285–87, 290
Kautilya, 5–6
Kennedy, John F., 26–27, 29, 129, 185
Kerry, John, 123, 173
Khilnani, Sunil, 67
Khobragade, Devyani, 122–25
Khrushchev, Nikita, 22
Kicklighter, Claude, 131–32

Kissinger, Henry, 38
Korea. *See* North Korea; South Korea
Korean War, 19–21
Kumar, Radha, 70, 71
Kumar, Rajiv, 69–72
Kumar, Santosh, 69–72
Kux, Dennis, 38, 187, 188
Kyoto Protocol, 227

Lamy, Pascal, 237
Lantos, Tom, 161, 166
Latvia, 219
Lay, Kenneth, 210
Lehman, Ronald, 159
Liberation Tigers of Tamil Eelam (LTTE), 101, 281–82, 284
Libya, 226, 243
Lutyens, Edwin, 115

Mahabharata (heroic epic), 4
Maharashtra, 183, 206–11
Maharashtra State Electricity Board (MSEB), 206–07, 209–11
Mahindra and Mahindra Ltd., 104
Makers of India's Foreign Policy (Dixit), 81
Malone, David, 214
Mansingh, Lalit, 3, 62
Mansingh, Surjit, 35
Mantri, Raksha, 94
Mao Zedong, 18
Maran, Murasoli, 234
Mark, Rebecca, 207, 209–10
Marshall Plan, 182
Mauritius, 211
Maurya, Chandragupta, 5
McCormack, John, 189
McMahon Line, 261–62
MEA (Ministry of External Affairs): and Indian Administrative Service, 93; and multilateral negotiations, 12, 108, 222, 225, 229; and negotiation protocol, 111–12, 119–20, 123–24; and nuclear cooperation negotiations, 153–54, 163, 167, 180; and post-Cold War diplomacy, 45; and security negotiations, 95, 128–29, 134, 143;

MEA (cont.)
structure and role of, 82–84,
88–89, 98–99, 104
Mehta, Jagat, 107, 112, 113, 125,
263
Menon, Krishna: and Cold War
diplomacy, 16–17, 21, 30; and
India's strategic vision, 71, 72; and
nuclear cooperation negotiations,
170
Menon, Raja, 72
Menon, Shivshankar, 91–92, 162,
170, 174
Mexico: and economic negotiations,
199; and multilateral negotiations,
222, 245
MFN (most favored nation) status,
202, 204, 233
Military: and Cold War diplomacy,
20, 29, 32; Indian Peace Keeping
Force (IPKF), 76, 279, 283–84;
and nuclear cooperation
negotiations, 157; and post-Cold
War diplomacy, 50, 59, 68; and
security negotiations, 130, 133,
140, 143, 257; structure and role
of, 94–96, 102; training programs,
103. *See also* Defense policy;
Security negotiations
Military equipment. *See* Arms sales
and aid
Ministry of Defense (MOD): and
security negotiations, 12, 108,
130–32, 134, 137, 141; structure
and role of, 84, 95–96, 103–04
Ministry of Food and Agriculture, 83
Missile Technology Control Regime
(MTCR), 245–47
Modi, Narendra: and Bangladesh,
275, 276, 277, 290–92; and
China, 268–70, 298–99, 301; and
economic negotiations, 197, 203,
204, 205, 271; election of, 97, 293;
and India's strategic vision, 6, 12,
63, 73, 75, 79; and industrial
development funding, 89; and
multilateral negotiations, 218, 231,
232, 238, 239, 240; and Nepal,

290–92; and nuclear cooperation
negotiations, 179; and Pakistan,
250, 251, 257, 268–70; and
post-Cold War diplomacy, 47, 58;
and security negotiations, 96, 135;
and Sri Lanka, 290–92; and U.S.
relations, 115
Mohan, Raja, 53, 69, 119
Moynihan, Daniel Patrick, 188–89
MSEB. *See* Maharashtra State
Electricity Board
MTCR (Missile Technology Control
Regime), 245–47
Mughal Empire, 7
Mukherjee, Pranab, 100, 134, 141,
246
Mulford, David, 161
Multilateral negotiations, 213–47;
climate change negotiations,
227–32; coalitions, 215–17; and
Comprehensive Test Ban Treaty,
240–44; and multilateral
organizations, 244–47; and UN
General Assembly, 217–24; and
UN Security Council, 225–27;
and World Trade Organization,
232–40
Musharraf, Pervez, 252, 254
Muslims, 7, 22–23, 55, 58, 75, 226,
282
Myanmar: and Bangladesh, 277;
India's military intervention
in, 292; and post-Cold War
diplomacy, 58

NAM. *See* Non-Aligned Movement
Narayanan, M. K., 170
Nariman, Fali, 211
Narlikar, Aruna, 239
NASSCOM (National Association of
Software and Services Companies),
193
Nasser, Gamal Abdel, 24
Nath, Kamal, 199, 237
National Academy of Administration,
92
National AIDS Research Institute,
192

National Association of Software and Services Companies (NASSCOM), 193

National Family Health Survey, 190

National Maritime Foundation, 103

National Polio Surveillance Program, 191

National Security Adviser (NSA): and India's strategic vision, 81; and nuclear cooperation negotiations, 153–54, 163, 165, 170; and security negotiations, 143–44, 146, 253, 266, 285; structure and role of, 83, 90–91

National Security Advisory Board (NSAB), 91, 105–06

National Security Council (NSC, India), 90–91, 130

NATO (North Atlantic Treaty Organization), 145

Navy (India), 127, 301

Nayar, Kuldip, 248

NEFA (North East Frontier Agency), 25

Negotiation framework, 107–26; hot-button issues, 122–25; and national identity, 108–10; personal ties, 120–22; protocol, 119–20; social context, 117–19; strategy, 125–26; tools, 110–17

Nehru, Jawaharlal: on ancient India, 3–4; and China, 261–64; and Cold War diplomacy, 13–30, 33, 36, 37; and economic negotiations, 182, 184–85; and foreign policy institutions, 83, 85, 95, 107; and independence, 1, 8, 10, 293; and India's strategic vision, 60, 63, 66, 73, 75–76; on Kautilya, 6; and multilateral negotiations, 213, 225, 241; and negotiation framework, 112, 113; and Nepal, 284–85; and Non-Aligned Movement, 308; and post-Cold War diplomacy, 44, 47; realist policies, 76; and security negotiations, 129; and Sri Lanka, 279; vision for India, 14, 293

Neocolonialism, 23, 35, 37

Nepal: and Bangladesh diplomacy, 274, 277; and China, 125, 264, 298; and Cold War diplomacy, 19; earthquake (2015), 307; India-Nepal Agreement on Arms Assistance (1965), 287–88; India-Nepal Treaty of Peace and Friendship (1950), 285, 286; and post-Cold War diplomacy, 58; and security negotiations, 284–91

Next Steps in Strategic Partnership (NSSP), 142, 154–56, 158, 180

Nigeria, 222

Nixon, Richard, 35, 121, 188, 299

Non-Aligned Movement (NAM): and Cold War diplomacy, 15, 24–25, 31, 33–34, 36–37; and India's strategic vision, 64, 66, 68, 72; and multilateral negotiations, 215–16, 242; and post-Cold War diplomacy, 49, 305

Non-Aligned Movement Summit, 30, 34

Nonalignment Firsters, 60, 65, 67–69, 71, 76

Non-Proliferation Treaty (NPT), 38, 51, 68, 151, 174, 241, 243, 246, 258–59, 297

North Atlantic Treaty Organization (NATO), 145

North East Frontier Agency (NEFA), 25

North Korea: and economic negotiations, 184; and Korean War, 19–20; and multilateral negotiations, 243

NSA. *See* National Security Adviser

NSAB (National Security Advisory Board), 91, 105–06

NSC (National Security Council, India), 90–91, 130

NSG. *See* Nuclear Suppliers Group

NSSP. *See* Next Steps in Strategic Partnership

Nuclear cooperation, 150–81; announcement of, 156–58; commercial dimensions of, 158–62; and economic negotiations, 196;

Nuclear cooperation (cont.)
  and Hyde Act, 165–67; and IAEA
  Safeguards Agreement, 172–73;
  and India's strategic vision, 78; and
  multilateral negotiations, 246;
  negotiations for, 152–55; Non-
  Proliferation Treaty (NPT), 38, 51,
  68, 151, 174, 241, 243, 246,
  258–59, 297; and Nuclear
  Suppliers Group, 173–76; and 123
  Agreement, 167–71; political
  dimensions of, 158–62; post-
  agreement diplomacy, 177–82; and
  post-Cold War diplomacy, 48; and
  security negotiations, 134, 144,
  148–50; separation plan, 162–65.
  See also Civil Nuclear Agreement
  (U.S.–India, 2008)
Nuclear Suppliers Group (NSG), 155,
  158, 172–76, 181, 218, 245–46
Nuclear weapons: and Cold War
  diplomacy, 38, 40; and India's
  strategic vision, 68, 72, 73, 79; and
  multilateral negotiations, 241; and
  nuclear cooperation negotiations,
  114, 121, 150, 151–52, 164, 168,
  172; and post-Cold War diplomacy,
  51–52; and security negotiations,
  137, 259

Obama, Barack: and economic
  negotiations, 197, 203; and India's
  strategic vision, 64, 80; and Modi,
  47, 115, 270; and multilateral
  negotiations, 218, 231–32, 240,
  244, 246; and nuclear cooperation
  negotiations, 169, 176, 179; and
  security negotiations, 143
Observer Research Foundation, 104
OECD (Organization for Economic
  Cooperation and Development),
  192, 201, 204, 245
O'Leary, Hazel, 207
Open-Ended Working Group, 218, 220
Open skies agreements, 199–200
Overseas Private Investment
  Corporation (OPIC), 207, 211
Oxford, Morris, 109

Pakistan: border dispute with, 23, 54,
  251, 299; and China, 262; and
  Cold War diplomacy, 21–23,
  29–33, 35–36, 38–41; diplomatic
  efforts with, 87, 91, 95, 121, 250,
  252, 258; and economic
  negotiations, 186; and India's
  strategic vision, 71, 74–75, 78–79,
  81; and multilateral negotiations,
  219, 243; and post-Cold War
  diplomacy, 44, 47, 52–58; and
  security negotiations, 5, 7–8, 130,
  248–60, 264, 267–72, 276,
  282–83, 294, 298–300, 303–05
Panchsheel Agreement (1955), 17, 25
Pandit, Vijayalakshmi, 185
Panetta, Leon, 146
Panikkar, K. M., 19, 261
Patel, Praful, 200
Patel, Sardar Vallabhbhai, 73, 285
Paulson, Henry, 161
People's Liberation Army (PLA,
  China), 20, 27
Perry, William, 132
Philippines, 228
PMO. *See* Prime Minister's Office
Post-Cold War foreign policy, 43–59;
  and China, 57–59; and coalition
  governments, 47–48; and economic
  reforms, 45–47; and Non-Aligned
  Movement, 48–49; and Pakistan,
  55–57; and Soviet Union breakup,
  44–45; and unipolar world, 45;
  and U.S., 50–55
Powell, Colin, 156, 253
Powell, Nancy, 120, 124
Power purchase agreement, 207, 210
Prabhakaran, Velupillai, 283
Prasad, Krishna, 289
Prasad, Sharada, 188
Premadasa, Ranasinghe, 284
Prime Minister's Office (PMO):
  and Bangladesh diplomacy, 274;
  and negotiation framework,
  108; and nuclear cooperation
  negotiations, 167, 180; and
  Pakistan diplomacy, 251; structure
  and role of, 82–83, 90

Qatar: and economic negotiations, 209; and multilateral negotiations, 234

Radia, Niira, 194
Raghavan, Srinath, 264
Rahman, Sheikh Mujibur, 275
Rajan, Raghuram, 224
Ramayana (heroic epic), 19
Ramesh, Jairam, 230, 232
Rana, Kishan, 86
Rao, Narasimha, 45, 189
Rao, Nirupama, 120
Reagan, Ronald, 41
Research and Information System for Developing Countries (RIS), 104
Reserve Bank of India (RBI), 224
Rice, Condoleezza, 156, 158, 166, 175
Richardson, Bill, 121
Rodrigues, Francis, 131
Rotary International, 191
Rusk, Dean, 26, 187
Russia: India's strategic partnership with, 63–64; and India's strategic vision, 67–69, 71–72, 74, 77, 79, 304; and multilateral negotiations, 216, 218–19, 242, 245; and nuclear cooperation negotiations, 154, 162, 178; and post-Cold War diplomacy, 49; and security negotiations, 131. *See also* Soviet Union

SAARC. *See* South Asian Association for Regional Cooperation
Sabha, Lok, 96–97, 99, 101, 280
Saran, Shyam, 156, 162, 174
Security Council (UN): China as permanent member of, 297; India's efforts to gain permanent seat on, 258–59; and India's strategic vision, 64, 75; and multilateral negotiations, 213, 215, 217–20, 225–27
Security negotiations, 127–49; and arms sales, 142–49; arms sales and aid, 135–42; and foreign policy institutions, 90, 95–96; framework for, 125, 129–35; and National Security Adviser, 90; and post-

Cold War diplomacy, 57. *See also specific countries*
Senate Foreign Relations Committee (U.S.), 98, 159
Shah, Bahadur, 7
Shahjahan (emperor), 7
Sharif, Nawaz: and China diplomacy, 268, 269; and Pakistan diplomacy, 251, 255, 300; and post-Cold War diplomacy, 54
Sharma, Anand, 202, 203
Sharma, Kamalesh, 221
Shastri, Lal Bahadur, 30–33, 36–38, 279
Shekhar, Chandra, 189
Shiv Sena, 208, 209, 210
Sibal, Kanwal, 153
Sikri, Rajiv, 66–67
Simla Agreement (1972), 55, 253
Singapore, 234–35
Singh, Jaswant, 114, 152, 243
Singh, Manmohan: and Bangladesh diplomacy, 274–75, 277, 278; and China diplomacy, 266, 267; coalition government of, 102; and economic negotiations, 189, 197, 203, 205; and foreign policy institutions, 91, 99, 100–01; and India's strategic vision, 12, 72, 77; and multilateral negotiations, 231; and Nepal diplomacy, 289; and nuclear cooperation negotiations, 150, 152, 154, 156, 158–59, 162, 165, 171–72, 173; and Pakistan diplomacy, 250; and post-Cold War diplomacy, 46, 48, 52, 54, 56; and security negotiations, 134, 145
Singh, Natwar, 158
Sino-Indian War (1962), 29, 32, 38, 44
Solomon, Richard, 261
Somers, Ron, 202
South Africa: and Cold War diplomacy, 37; India's strategic partnership with, 63–64; and multilateral negotiations, 216, 226, 228, 231, 235, 245; and post-Cold War diplomacy, 49

South Asia: and Cold War diplomacy, 21–23, 33, 36, 41–42; and economic negotiations, 204, 297–99; and India's strategic vision, 64; and multilateral negotiations, 219, 222; and negotiation framework, 120; and post-Cold War diplomacy, 44, 47, 50, 55, 59. *See also specific countries*

South Asian Association for Regional Cooperation (SAARC), 217, 254–55, 281, 298

South China Sea, 58, 267, 301

Southeast Asia: and Bangladesh diplomacy, 276; and China diplomacy, 260, 270, 301–04; and Cold War diplomacy, 20, 28, 35, 37; and economic negotiations, 295, 297; and India's strategic vision, 64, 69, 71; and post-Cold War diplomacy, 45, 47, 49, 58; and security negotiations, 127. *See also specific countries*

South Korea: and Cold War diplomacy, 15, 19, 21; and economic negotiations, 184, 295–96, 301; and multilateral negotiations, 221, 245; and post-Cold War diplomacy, 46–47

Sovereignty: and China diplomacy, 263; and Cold War diplomacy, 25; and economic negotiations, 183, 185, 192; and India's strategic vision, 2; and multilateral negotiations, 225; and nuclear cooperation negotiations, 168, 178, 180; and security negotiations, 128, 142, 145, 149; and Sri Lanka diplomacy, 283

Soviet Union: and Cold War diplomacy, 17, 24, 28, 32–34, 37–41, 253, 304; and India's strategic vision, 76; invasion of Afghanistan, 40, 41; military equipment from, 45; and multilateral negotiations, 219; and nuclear cooperation negotiations,

152; and post-Cold War diplomacy, 43–45, 49; and security negotiations, 132. *See also* Russia

SPG (Strategic Policy Group), 91

Sri Lanka: and Cold War diplomacy, 21, 27, 42; independence of, 9; and India's strategic vision, 76, 81; and post-Cold War diplomacy, 48, 58; and security negotiations, 127, 278–79, 281–84, 290–91; and state governments, 100–01

Stalin, Joseph, 18, 19

State Department (U.S.): and Khobragade affair, 123; and negotiation protocol, 119; and nuclear cooperation negotiations, 161, 163; and security negotiations, 144; and U.S.-India relations, 50–55

State governments: and economic negotiations, 191, 194, 205–11; as foreign policy institutions, 84, 89, 100–02; and Kashmir conflict, 55

Stern, Todd, 230

Strategic autonomy: and China diplomacy, 270; and economic negotiations, 185, 188; and India's strategic vision, 2, 62, 69, 73, 77–78, 80–81; and Modi's foreign policy, 293–94, 302–03, 305, 308–09; and multilateral negotiations, 215; and negotiation framework, 125–26; and nuclear cooperation negotiations, 158, 162, 180; and Pakistan diplomacy, 249, 270; and post-Cold War diplomacy, 11–12, 43, 45, 50–51; and security negotiations, 128, 136

Strategic Policy Group (SPG), 91

Strategic visions, 60–81; of Broad Power Realists, 69–73; core ideals, 61–65; of Hard Power Hawks, 73–75; implementation of, 75–80; of Nonalignment Firsters, 65–69; staying power of, 80–81

Stratford, Richard, 163

Subrahmanyam, K., 103–04

Subramaniam, C., 186–88

Subsidies: agricultural, 235–36, 237; export, 195
Sukarno, 37
Supreme Court (India), 203, 211
Sweden: arms sales from, 138; and multilateral negotiations, 247; and nuclear cooperation negotiations, 175
Switzerland, 219, 247
Syria, 226

Taiwan, 268
Talbott, Strobe, 52, 53, 114, 152
Taliban, 57
Tamil Nadu, 100–01, 102, 279–82, 284
Tashkent Declaration (1966), 32, 253, 255
Tata, Ratan, 194
Technology Safeguards Agreement, 144
Technology transfer, 135, 139
Teesta River, 274, 277, 278
Tellis, Ashley, 26, 95
TFA (Trade Facilitation Agreement), 235, 237–39
Thackeray, Bal, 209
Thapar, Karan, 63
Tharoor, Shashi, 221, 222
Tibet: autonomy of, 25; Buddhists in, 261; and China diplomacy, 261–62; and Cold War diplomacy, 18, 19, 25; and Nepal diplomacy, 284, 286, 288; and water supply negotiations, 304
Tito, Josip Broz, 24
Trade agreements, 195, 198–99, 224. *See also* Bilateral investment treaties (BITs); Economic negotiations
Trade Facilitation Agreement (TFA), 235, 237–39
Trade negotiations: free trade agreements, 296; and multilateral negotiations, 216, 224, 232–34, 240, 244; and Pakistan diplomacy, 257. *See also* Bilateral investment treaties (BITs); Economic negotiations

Transit agreements, 274, 276–77, 289
Trans-Pacific Partnership, 296
Tripathy, Amitava, 61
Truman, Harry, 113, 182
Tsunami disaster (2004), 127, 133
Tyagi, S. P., 138

Ukraine, 219
Union Carbide gas plant, 178
United Kingdom: and Cold War diplomacy, 26, 31; colonial legacy of, 9; India's strategic partnership with, 63; and India's strategic vision, 3, 62; and multilateral negotiations, 218, 225; and Pakistan diplomacy, 252–54; and security negotiations, 144; and Sri Lanka diplomacy, 278. *See also* British Raj period
United Nations: and Cold War diplomacy, 19–20, 22, 28, 31, 38; and India's strategic vision, 65, 75; and multilateral negotiations, 221, 225, 241–42; and Nepal diplomacy, 286
United Nations Commission for Trade and Development (UNCTAD), 36, 216, 305
United Nations Economic and Social Council, 214
United Nations Framework Convention on Climate Change (UNFCCC), 227, 229
United Nations Human Rights Commission (UNHRC), 101
United Services Institution, 103
United States: arms sales and aid from, 29, 135–49; and Canada, 201; and China, 67, 71, 74, 232, 301–03, 306; and Cold War diplomacy, 17, 19–20, 22, 26–28, 30, 32–34, 36, 38–41; and diplomatic framework, 110–11, 113–14, 116, 119, 121–25; and economic negotiations, 186–89, 192–202, 204, 211–12, 295–97; foreign policy institutions, 86–88, 91, 93–94; and India's strategic

United States (cont.)
vision, 62–63, 67, 69–71, 74–75, 77–80; and multilateral negotiations, 217–19, 222–24, 227, 230–37, 239, 242, 244–46; and Nepal, 289; and nuclear cooperation negotiations, 150–59, 162–70, 172–84; and Pakistan, 57, 248, 253–54, 256–57; and post-Cold War diplomacy, 44–45, 48–56, 58–59; and security negotiations, 127–32, 135–48; and Sri Lanka, 282–83
Uniting for Consensus group, 219
Upanishads, 4
U.S. Agency for International Development, 190
U.S. Trade Representative (USTR), 195–96, 202, 233, 237–38
Uzbekistan, 32

Vajpayee, Atal Bihari: and China diplomacy, 264; and economic negotiations, 210; and India's strategic vision, 62, 73, 77, 79; and multilateral negotiations, 243; and nuclear cooperation negotiations, 121, 152; and Pakistan diplomacy, 250, 255, 300; and post-Cold War diplomacy, 51, 52, 56, 57

Vivekananda International Foundation, 104, 106
Vodafone, 203

Wassenaar Arrangement, 245
WHO (World Health Organization), 191
WikiLeaks, 63
Wisner, Frank, 53, 132
World Bank: "Doing Business" index, 295; and economic negotiations, 184, 187, 204, 207; and India-Pakistan conflict, 253, 255; and Indus Waters Treaty, 22; and multilateral negotiations, 222–24
World Health Organization (WHO), 191
World Trade Organization (WTO): and economic negotiations, 112, 116, 195, 296; and India's strategic vision, 80; and multilateral negotiations, 215, 224, 232–40
World War I, 10
World War II, 128, 297

Xi Jinping, 267, 269, 298, 300

Yugoslavia, 24

Zhou Enlai, 25, 26, 112, 261–63